WILLIAM BERGER

Verdi with a Vengeance

William Berger was born in California and studied Romance languages and music at the University of California at Santa Cruz. He worked for five years at the San Francisco Opera Company, where he acquired for the company's recorded music collection. He is the author of *Wagner Without Fear: Learning to Love—And Even Enjoy—Opera's Most Demanding Genius*. He contributed to James Skofield's libretto for *The Dracula Diaries*, an opera with music by Robert Moran, and wrote the libretto for *The Wolf of Gubbio* with the composer Patrick Barnes. Mr. Berger has appeared on NPR's *Performance Today* and is a regular commentator on *At the Opera*. He lives in New York and is currently at work on a performance piece, *Karajan's Wake*.

ALSO BY WILLIAM BERGER

Wagner Without Fear

Verdi with a Vengeance

Verdi with a Vengeance

An Energetic Guide to
the Life and Complete Works
of the King of Opera

WILLIAM BERGER

VINTAGE BOOKS

A DIVISION OF RANDOM HOUSE, INC.

NEW YORK

A VINTAGE ORIGINAL
FIRST EDITION, OCTOBER 2000

Library of Congress Cataloging-in-Publication Data
Berger, William 1961–
Verdi with a vengeance : an energetic guide to the life and complete works of the king of opera / William Berger.—1st ed.
p.   cm.
Includes bibliographical references (p.), discography (p.), filmography (p.), and index.
ISBN 0-375-70518-X
1. Verdi, Giuseppe, 1813–1901. 2. Verdi, Giuseppe, 1813–1901. Operas. I. Title.
ML410.V4 B29 2000
782.1'092—dc21
[B]   00-042261

Map © by Cassandra J. Pappas
Author photograph © Lou Rufalo
Book design by Cassandra J. Pappas

www.vintagebooks.com

Printed in the United States of America
10 9 8 7 6 5 4 3 2 1

Contents

viii

THREE | EXPLORING VERDI

PART ONE

(Re) Introducing Verdi

Introduction:
With a . . . Vengeance?

SI! VENDETTA!

I take Verdi's art very personally. It has always been there, constantly emerging in a process that I hope will continue for a long time. The year that Walkmen came out, the first tape I made was all Verdi, selections culled from various recordings I borrowed. Side A was for getting revved up in the morning, going from the mellow (*"Come rugiada al cespite"* from *Ernani*) to the frantic (the love duet from *Ballo*). Side B was the reverse, for calming down in the evenings, starting with the Act I trio from *Trovatore* and winding down to *"Madonna degli angeli"* from *Forza*. And thus I would ride the Van Ness Avenue bus, watching San Francisco roll by like a performance, amazed at the uncanny relationship between Verdi and real life. His music was not so much the soundtrack of life as its actual subtext.

Eventually, the tape became superfluous. All of us carry around a sort of inner jukebox, and mine appears to be set for Verdi. I hear it, or imagine that I hear it, in every situation life presents. I remember going to court to answer for a traffic ticket, imagining that I heard the monks' chant from *Don Carlos* emanating from the chilly Hall of Justice. I remember seeing my late grandmother watching black-and-white TV with all the lights turned out, thinking how much she was like Azucena, the gypsy woman from *Trovatore* who stares at the fire, obsessed with the past. I remember a young woman at a travel agency actually trying to seduce me into buying an island vacation package,

and imagining her singing Aida's evocation of her mountain homeland. I invariably hear the Anvil Chorus at the gym. Any political or
community meeting becomes the Council Chamber scene from *Boccanegra,* but so does any sale at Macy's. I have heard *"O signore, dal
tetto natio"* while driving around the hills of California. And on a few
memorable occasions I have heard *"Va, pensiero"* while making love.

I can't be the only person who has noticed these odd correlations.
On one level, Giuseppe Verdi might well be considered the world's
most popular composer. His music, or at least snippets of it, is
hummed, whistled, and wailed all over the world. His operas are performed more than any other composer's. Opera companies have
been proliferating throughout the world, and especially in the United
States, where new companies are appearing even faster than major
league sports franchises. A recent list of professional opera companies counted seventy-one in the country, and virtually every one of
these has performed Verdi within the last two years. This is in addition to the hundreds of colleges and universities that now offer opera
workshops where Verdi is performed live and, in many instances, on a
par with or exceeding the professional companies. Public television
routinely boasts audiences of three or four million for their opera
broadcasts, a full quarter of which feature the works of Giuseppe
Verdi. We hear bits and pieces of Verdi's music on the radio, on television, and in movies.

Any Verdi fan should be thrilled by all this. Right?

Wrong. These numbers represent tremendous growth and a level
of public consumption that would have been unthinkable years ago,
but they are still paltry compared to the numbers generally bandied
about by American media moguls. Nor should this surprise anyone.
Opera is regarded as a foreign brand of entertainment, a weird and
bastard art form, and something to be apologized for. Recently the
creators of the new musical extravaganza *Aida* felt compelled to say
in an interview that their work was not based on the Verdi opera, but
derived from the original source legend of *Aida.* There was some
amusing subsequent backpedaling when it was pointed out to these
good gentlemen that there is, in fact, no original source legend for

Aida. The creators of the new musical needed to make it clear that they were not decadent Europeans attempting to foist unwanted *haute culture* upon our wholesome American value system.

Am I being extravagant? I wonder. The state of New York is currently running a fascinating, if annoying, television commercial for its lottery. It is filmed during a supposed performance of a Verdi opera. While the prima donna is squawking through a cadenza, a distinctly guy-next-door type pushes a podium onto the stage. Soprano shrieks. The audience of socialites in evening wear (black ties, tiaras, lorgnettes) gasps. The man announces that the "New York State Lotto is now X million dollars!" Socialites run for the exits and the theater is empty in a matter of seconds. "Cool," says Lottoman.

Let's take this apart. The music onstage is *Traviata,* although the costumes look more like *Il trovatore.* The general impression is generic Verdi. The prima donna is not outfitted in a flattering manner, nor does she sing particularly well. The people onstage are meant to look and sound stupid. The audience is every American's nightmare of an opera crowd: all white, all over sixty, and all overdressed. Why a bunch of stiff old millionaires would need to run out to buy lottery tickets is beyond me, but they do. Ironically, this is all filmed at the Brooklyn Academy of Music. The last time I checked, the audience there didn't look like that. Green mohawks and razor blades in the nose are much more *comme il faut* at BAM. No matter. It is necessary to believe that opera audiences look a certain way. It's "where the elite meet to be effete." I have attended hundreds of opera performances all over the world and I can honestly say that I have never once seen anybody using a lorgnette.

If you haven't seen that particular Lotto commercial, it doesn't matter. There are plenty of other examples. It is truly galling that Giuseppe Verdi, of all people, should be used as the touchstone for this symbolism. If you are already an opera fan, then you know that Verdi has been treated with a lot of contempt by musicologists and other experts. The snobbery—yes, snobbery—on the subject of Verdi comes from all sides. I can't think of any artist whose life and work was less tainted by elitism than Verdi. In fact, his reputation has suffered among "serious" music people for this precise reason. At this point, it's worth taking a look at the history of Verdi and the musical establishment to understand where we are today.

VERDI'S MUSIC, even when complicated, has always reached people in a direct manner. Even his later masterpieces, particularly the operas *Otello* and *Falstaff,* have been judged favorably by the public without too much help from the illuminati. Needless to say, this didn't help his reputation in the rarefied realms of music scholarship. At the time of Verdi's death, *Otello* and *Falstaff* were receiving some grudging admiration from the theoreticians, but those who wanted to be perceived as progressive could barely mention Verdi's name without condescension. Melody itself, that rare gift with which Verdi was so ostentatiously endowed, fell out of favor, and for about sixty years we were told that anything hummable was beneath contempt. The music of the future, it was said, would be based on anything but melody as the term was commonly understood.

Amid all this theorizing, the public continued to attend Verdi operas, or at least the half-dozen of them that were offered regularly. The theoreticians deduced the obvious from the public's preferences: Clearly, the people were stupid and vulgar. What else could explain the phenomenon? Some experts rebelled. In the 1920s a German writer named Franz Werfel struggled to balance his love of Verdi with his knowledge of new music. He wrote a novel exploring the supposed "lost years" of Verdi's later career, in which he imagined the composer engaging in long inner dialogues with the theories of Richard Wagner and other music reformers. The novel tells us little about Verdi, but a great deal about the gyrations a man like Werfel thought he needed to undergo to enjoy Verdi. Werfel compiled a good working edition of Verdi's wildest opera, *La forza del destino,* and it was performed with spectacular success in Germany in 1925. There were also successful performances of *Don Carlos* and *Simon Boccanegra,* both basically unknown in that country. When scholars speak of the Verdi Renaissance, they are referring to this movement headed by Werfel and his colleagues in Germany in the 1920s. The fact that Verdi had been performed all along in Italy does not seem to have counted for much in scholastic circles.

Then it was the turn of the English-speaking world to reconsider Verdi. Francis Toye wrote his important study of Verdi's complete works and a good biography in 1930. In his introduction, Toye speaks directly to the need to assess Verdi in spite of what had been said about him over the previous two generations. Toye's influence was great. He even wrote sensibly, if sometimes caustically, about Verdi's most obscure works, which were unknown to him and his reading audience except as dusty music scores in the best-stocked libraries. For the first time, there was an erudite study of Verdi available in English. Not everyone was instantly converted. Ernest Newman, the London *Times* critic whose studies of Wagner remain standards in that field, could never abide Verdi. The mere mention of the name turned Newman, otherwise so sensible and brilliant, into a raving loony. Newman's influence over much of public opinion was greater than Toye's, and the British critic continued to spew forth about the "second-rate musician" (Verdi) well into the 1950s. In general, the music conservatories tended to agree. Few dared to take on Newman.

By the 1950s it became apparent to everyone that Verdi was not going to disappear, like hoop skirts and carriages and so many other artifacts from his era. More scholars began to wonder if they hadn't been wrong about Verdi after all. In art, staying power itself is a sort of validation. In 1958 Frank Walker wrote an excellent study appropriately called *The Man Verdi,* surprising many who had never considered Verdi capable of psychology. The process of "discovering" Verdi continued in subsequent years. In 1971 Charles Osborne published *The Complete Verdi Operas.* Even though Osborne did not reveal anything particularly new about Verdi, his enthusiasm for the corpus of Verdi's work brought the debate to a new level. In 1973 Julian Budden published *The Operas of Verdi,* an erudite three-volume musical analysis of all of Verdi's operas. Budden fought the fossilized academics with their own weapons. His tome is as chock-full of *recherché* tangents and Mesopotamian words as anything published in the field of music. It was becoming almost impossible for the musicologists to dismiss Verdi as easily as they once had.

One might well ask what difference academic debate makes if the public can enjoy Verdi's operas with or without the approval of the nabobs. Actually, the academic debate is extremely important in terms of what gets performed and also in how it affects the public perception of Verdi beyond the opera house. First of all, there is a cultural bias among Anglo-Saxon scholars regarding the Italians. Not even Budden is entirely free of this. There are also plenty of music professors who simply refuse to consider Verdi seriously. Even the Verdi champions of the English-speaking world approach the subject with a great deal of care, often qualifying their love of the music with a certain coyness that would not have disgraced Werfel at his most conflicted. For years I have pondered this curious situation, comparing the scholars' careful (at best) relationship to Verdi to my own deep and personal experience, and I have come to a startling conclusion.

There is something dangerous about the art of Giuseppe Verdi.

By definition, the art form known as opera is uniquely qualified to portray the individual in a communal context. That art form was carried to unsurpassed, and hardly equaled, heights by Verdi's music, possessing as it does a vitality directly comprehensible to any human being. Furthermore, Verdi had a certain sense of humanity in himself, informing his characters with an individual power that is inherently at odds with any overly rigid systematic genre of thought. In other words, Verdi's art confers a magnificent level of dignity upon the individual—on the stage, to be sure, but also, by extension, in the audience. While no one would claim that Verdi's music is inherently erotic in the most common sense of the word, it has the ability to get the hormones flowing. It is life-affirming. Verdi is Viagra for the Spirit.

This is why it must be marginalized from above (so to speak) by the most intransigent academics and from below (so to speak) by the supposed general public as represented by our New York State Lotto spokesman. The two forces are really one, and neither represents the life force. What those two currents of thought fail to recognize is that

Verdi is not a threat to the things they claim to hold dear. Giving Verdi his due does not preclude the development of new and innovative music, nor does it diminish the accomplishments of those who came after. Verdi is a threat to nothing except those who would deny dignity to the individual, those who for one reason or another oppose vitality itself.

This is the vengeance I'm speaking of. Everywhere I look, I see the individual diminished, true creativity reined in and frowned upon, and a certain grayness triumphing. Real emotions are anathema in the home and the office. Fashions in everyday clothing demand that people dress to be unnoticed, while the major clothing chains that dictate such matters seem to be succeeding where even Chairman Mao was only partially successful. The radio (classical and pop alike) plays what it is spoon-fed, and the lack of spontaneity by the music industry has reached such a point that there is even a "top 40" listing for so-called alternative music. As for live lyric theater, I will only say that it has been a very long time since I have seen anybody leave a new show at a Broadway theater in tears or deep thought. But this is only a symptom. All reality is becoming virtual. Love is relegated to greeting cards, while sex is largely a cyberfantasy.

Against all this, I offer Verdi. Not that this is a unique discovery. The numbers I rattled off at the beginning of this Introduction testify that there is a real and growing need for whatever Verdi has to offer, even if these numbers are not in the same league as those of the mass media. But there are good reasons why Verdi is more popular than ever. All music has become more available. Thousands of operas have been recorded and broadcast, including hundreds that were long forgotten. And for all the kvetching, even new operas are probably accepted or commissioned with as much, or as little, regularity as they were a century and a half ago. Once new operas are brought into existence, they are promoted with a support machinery that would have made Verdi or Wagner gag with envy. In this sense, we are living in a sort of golden age. Each of us hears more music, and more diverse kinds of music, than our ancestors could have ever imagined. And the more we hear, the better Verdi—all Verdi—sounds.

This is why we are now seeing the entire corpus (about twenty-seven operas, depending on how you count them) of Verdi's work being performed. Even *Stiffelio,* long missing and presumed dead, was watched by a couple of million people on television, while poor *Alzira,* the supposed ugly duckling of Verdi's "galley years," gets performed by respectable companies. The time when the name Verdi signified the same five operas repeated in an endless cycle is, mercifully, behind us.

The fact that Verdi keeps sounding better and better also explains why his operas, while perhaps old, are not passé. There seems to be a need to believe that we who find great relevance in Verdi must be somewhat retro ourselves (hence the myth of lorgnettes). The trouble is there is no truth to this. A very few artists in history have managed to transcend the confines of their own times. Verdi is one of these few. His work speaks to the human condition on such a level that it will last as long as there are people to hear it. And it improves with each hearing. As they say in *Falstaff,* "*Bocca baciata non perde ventura, anzi rinnova come fa la luna*" (very roughly, "Lips do not grow old through kissing, but rather renew, like the moon").

The purpose of this book is to address the needs of a person exploring Verdi in today's world. The idea is to provide a guide for works that are unfamiliar and, I hope, to provide some new ways of looking at the more familiar works. In other words, I am aiming for the newcomer and the expert alike, which I admit is no simple task. I freely acknowledge my debt to those true Verdi scholars who have worked before me. I do not pretend to scale the heights of Julian Budden's scholarship or erudition. I can only hope the reader will be inspired by attending live performances of Verdi operas to pursue the study of this inexhaustible subject, in which case he or she will naturally come across Budden. One friend of mine suggested, only partially in jest, that I title this book *Bud-den Light.* But Budden had a different mission from my present one. He sought to place Verdi's work in the context of what came before and after each opera. Sources and models for Verdi's operas are studied in great detail. Furthermore, the earlier and less familiar operas are looked at largely with an eye toward how their ideas came to full fruition in the later works. In general, Verdi scholars write as if the entire sixty-year career were nothing but a prelude to *Falstaff.* I call this approach "operatic Darwinism," and I have chosen to avoid it.

One of the great goals of nineteenth-century opera composers was to find a way to transcend the traditional forms of opera. The formal structure of earlier opera was seen as suffocating dramatic vitality. The singer walked on, sang a slow aria, received a message or other interruption causing a change of attitude, sang a fast aria, and swept off the stage amid torrents of applause. Verdi was born into this tradition, and spent most of his career working to find a more organic method of unfolding the drama. This goal was achieved in his final operas, which are consequently the most highly praised by scholars. But great singers have shown us that the earlier style can be as vital as any if performed correctly, while audiences seem to accept that all opera is surreal in any case. This is why Verdi's earlier operas are paradoxically less old-fashioned than they were a hundred years ago. When a major opera company offers *Stiffelio,* for example, it is all very interesting that *Otello* is foreshadowed in some of the orchestral techniques, but not too many people are prepared to shell out the big bucks just because of that.

This book assumes an interest in the opera in question on its own terms, as if the reader will be attending a live performance of it. You will want to know what happens, musically and dramatically, and why. My goal is to open up the opera for the reader, not to micromanage his or her experience of it. Also, I have chosen to share some admittedly subjective ideas on various aspects of the operas. These are in an effort to show the richness of Verdi's work, not to dictate the "true" meaning of a given piece or situation. For this reason, I am confident that even the most knowledgeable of Verdians will find some provocative ideas in these pages.

The Art of Italian Opera

TELLING STORIES through songs predates history and appears to be universal. Get a few people at a campsite away from the television, drop a guitar nearby, and they'll be telling stories and singing songs. Pretty soon a mood will develop, be it happy or melancholy. From this notion to a single story peppered with musical interludes is only a short step. "We met" (happy song), "We were in love" (sweet song), "We split up" (angry song), "I'm devastated" (sad song). The possibilities for variation are endless, and virtually any style of music can be put to service toward this end.

That's the easy part, technically speaking. But how can you make this whole endeavor a single unified work? Instead of telling what happened (talk) and then commenting on it (song), how can you blur the lines between narrative and comment? In other words, what about the parts in between the songs? This question represents one of the reasons why the art form known as Italian opera is simply a different animal from the rest of the world's narrative music traditions. It sprang out of a desire to find, explore, and revel in the music of speech. The beauty of song was something of an afterthought.

The impetus was ancient Greek drama. A group of scholars in Florence in the 1590s were intrigued by the strict metrical forms of the Greeks. The speeches, even the dialogues, could be tapped out in regular rhythms. Furthermore, from paintings and contemporary commentaries on these works, it was apparent that music was used in some degree in these dramas. Tambourines and drums beat out the rhythm, but flutes and other instruments were used as well. Were these lines sung, spoken, or something in between?

The circle of Florentine scholars, called a *camerata,* chose one of their number named Rinuccini to create an appropriate text to be set to music in a way the Greeks might have used in their drama. Rinuccini chose the myth of Daphne for the project, and wrote out a drama in meters based on the Greek forms. However—and this was a key development—Rinuccini rendered this drama not in classical Greek but in contemporary Italian. The point was not to re-create the Greek experience, museum style, but to make it new. Jacopo Peri, a composer of both religious and secular music, was chosen to set the text, with a mandate to bring out rather than overshadow the meaning of the words.

The result was startling. The creators called their little piece an *opera in musica,* a work in music, since it wasn't really drama but it didn't fit into any other known category. Like vulcanized rubber (or, more elegantly, champagne), opera was invented entirely by accident. And the invention, like so many others, would take on a life of its own, far exceeding the goals of its original creators. The complete score for *Dafne* has not survived. Significantly, all that exists is one vocal solo, or what would have been a monologue in a drama. Without realizing it, the *camerati* had created an art form that, at its best, would be able to harness all the narrative, theatrical, and philosophical power of classical Greek drama and combine it with all the primal emotive force of music. Suddenly, opera existed.

While the possibilities of the new art form unfolded slowly, one thing was apparent right away. Opera was expensive to produce. Singers required more rehearsal time than actors, and one needed to hire instrumentalists. Also, design and spectacle played a large part in the proceedings from the start. Since music explored situations more symbolically than words alone, the visual element became an issue. Compare these considerations to the theater of Shakespeare, operating at the same time. Even with virtually no scenery or special effects at all, theater companies in Shakespeare's London had great trouble keeping solvent, and usually required the patronage of the crown or some nobleman in order to stay open. Small wonder, then, that opera very quickly became associated with the courts of the aristocracy.

Early baroque court opera had a high level of "audience participation," with courtiers singing choruses and dancing around some allegory of the local ruler. There would sometimes be fireworks, sometimes an equestrian display, and occasionally even a set piece of music sung by a professional. No one paid much attention to the music as such. Part of the idea was to keep the courtiers busy learning their routines and in sight so they couldn't scheme. The works of this time are great fun to read about, but they have become a footnote in the real story of opera, which was developing along other lines.

Not everyone had forgotten the ideals of the Florentine *camerati*. Perhaps the first to grasp the possibilities was Claudio Monteverdi. He was hired by the Duke of Mantua (a certain Vincenzo Gonzaga, whom we will meet again, in a different incarnation, in *Rigoletto*) to compose music for the court. Monteverdi's *Orfeo*, performed in 1608, is the earliest opera still performed. While it is very different from the blood-and-guts opera of later times, it is still a simple story that uses music to color and emphasize the situation unfolding on stage. No horse ballets for Monteverdi. He had discovered that quality music would suffice to hold an audience's interest, even if that audience had no scholastic interest in Greek drama.

Significantly, Monteverdi thrived most when he left Mantua and went to Venice. Musical tastes in the Republic were sophisticated and Monteverdi could count on people showing up and buying tickets if he continued to write good music and explore the dramatic possibilities of opera. Other Italian cities were following suit, particularly Naples. But the Neapolitans had a certain tradition that was soon to turn the budding opera world on its head. The notion of cutting a small duct in the testicles of prepubescent boys to preserve the high range of their voices began out of a church injunction, enforced only in certain places, against female soloists. Yet soon the castrati, as they were so vividly called, were in demand in the opera houses. They were not generally used to portray female roles, as so many assume, but immediately became popular in the roles of the virile heroes. With their high voices powered with the rest of the machinery of the male body intact, they were apparently exciting and technically proficient singers. The custom was barbaric, but the results were undeniably sublime. In fact, the entire European mentality, from its most refined aspirations to its most depraved nadirs, is represented by the historical experience of the castrati. For the developmental history of opera, they may be regarded as a disaster. As long as a singer can make people pass out in their seats, no one worries too much about subtleties of narrative form. However, audiences learned much about the art of singing from the castrati. People beyond the Venetian lagoon were actually listening to the human voice with more than a passing interest, and were not snoozing during arias while waiting for the fireworks show. The fireworks now occurred in the throats of mutilated men. The ladies were quick to note this, and it is notable that the first sopranos with international careers emerged in the time of the castrati. The star system had arrived, and the great castrati and sopranos caused sensations from Madrid to London to St. Petersburg. A larger style of singing developed than had ever been heard in theaters, churches, or anywhere else, and the opera form consequently began to explore issues in a bigger way. The extravagant became the norm, and the castrati led the way. They were especially cherished in what came to be known as *opera seria* ("serious opera"), which entailed a lot of "noble characters acting nobly." Generally, this meant strutting about in wild outfits, standing perfectly still, and blowing the roof off with vocal histrionics while singing very lofty words that were barely comprehensible but were often read in little books, *libretti,* by audiences.

Some people thought all of this had gone too far, and it was beyond the Alps, significantly, that the discussion turned polemical. In London, which has always prided itself on transcending Continental decadence, half the city went nuts over Italian opera, with its strutting castrati and feuding divas, while the other half clucked in disapproval. John Gay responded with his *Beggar's Opera,* an overt critique of the "unnaturalness" of Italian opera. Gay's work dispensed with recitative, and is basically a play with twenty-two songs interspersed throughout.

The debate over Italian opera was not limited to London. Parisian audiences, unique among Europeans, could never abide the biological realities of the castrati and did not support them. Consequently, the level of singing was probably lower in Paris than in other major European cities. And it was in Paris that the theorizing took flight. A German composer, Christoph Willibald von Gluck, left Vienna for Paris in 1762. In the preface to one of his operas, Gluck wrote that singers and their caprices must be subservient to the overall effect of the drama. He made the recitatives, the "talky" portions in between the great arias, more richly textured and consequently more important and nuanced. Gluck envisioned an audience that paid attention to the entire experience of the opera as a coherent unit. Perhaps German opera's reputation for being somehow more intellectual than Italian opera dates from this time.

When Ludwig van Beethoven decided to turn his attention to writing an opera, he noted Gluck's ideas and decided to go a step further. His only opera, *Leonora* (later revised as *Fidelio*), was written in German. It contained arias and ensembles (including an unforgettable quintet), but much of the rest of the opera contained a sort of amorphous narrative with music written ostensibly to follow the dramatic contours of the words. And the words Beethoven used were very different from anything Gluck would have recognized. In the time of the Napoleonic Wars, it no longer seemed fitting to have "noble characters act nobly." *Fidelio* is wild, illogical, uneven, and a bit crass. Raw emotions were favored over classical restraint. And those wild words were made even more reckless by not being Italian, with its even distribution of consonants and simple vowel sounds. Beethoven pushed the bounds of operatic taste with his one work for the lyric stage. The Romantic era had arrived.

For a long time, the Italians were blissfully undisturbed by the German developments. In Italy, the various genres of the previous century had coalesced into what would be called the bel canto style, typified by the operas of Rossini, Bellini, and Donizetti, among others less well remembered today. The castrati had basically disappeared by this time, but the "big aria" was still the unit around which the opera was built, and beauty of melody became ever more important. The bel canto opera also depended for effect on another holdover from *opera seria,* the grand scena. In the textbook definition of the grand scena, a singer will walk on the stage alone, summarize the current situation (recitative), and comment upon it (slow aria, often called a cavatina.). Then something will happen—a messenger will deliver a piece of alarming news, or something along those lines, and quickly disappear. The singer will then assimilate the news (more recitative), and then explode in a great aria full of vocal fireworks, often called a cabaletta. Exit singer amid thunderous applause.

The reformers, like Richard Wagner and many others, found the commonplaces of the bel canto style to be stifling, mannered, and (here we go again with that word) unnatural. Also, the emphasis on beauty of melody and on vocal excellence ("bel canto" merely means "pretty singing") has led many to believe that it is *merely* pretty singing, and therefore not really capable of any true depth. For many years, bel canto opera lay almost forgotten, with a few exceptions (like Rossini's *Barber of Seville*). The plots and the libretti, moreover, were considered beneath contempt by experts. One of the things that was forgotten was the role a singer might play in bringing this "pretty" music to dramatic life. In the 1950s Maria Callas turned the operatic world upside down with her intense characterizations of bel canto heroines. What Callas achieved, in fact, was to revivify these roles as living, breathing, bleeding humans rather than as music boxes in gowns. With a little of this dedication, audiences rediscovered the inherent drama amid all the loveliness of bel canto opera. It is now again possible to speak seriously of bel canto opera without any sense of embarrassment.

The real problem was the issue of text, and here it becomes necessary to take cultural perceptions into consideration. The French may have had certain difficulties with Italian opera, but they addressed these by slowly developing their own operatic style while simultaneously supporting Italian opera in Paris with a theater of its own that rivaled the Paris Opéra for two centuries. The Austrians were quite satisfied to swallow Italian opera wholesale. Vienna was traditionally a cosmopolis, the capital of a multinational empire that included millions of Italians for centuries. The Spaniards enjoyed their own indigenous *zarzuela* on one night and the Italian opera on the next, with hardly a ripple of argument over which was better. The Russians did whatever the French thought fashionable, and throughout much of the nineteenth century, so did the people of many of the smaller European countries and South America. The nations that had the greatest conflicts with the perceived decadence, frivolity, and silliness of Italian opera were the Protestant "Anglo-Saxon" nations, the Germans and the British.

Music is universal. Much of the difficulty between Anglo-Saxons and Italian opera stems, rather, from cultural perceptions about the meaning and value of words. One of the most significant and influential theories taught by Martin Luther and his colleagues was the literal truth of Scripture. The words of the Bible were to be understood as meaning exactly what they said, no more and no less. This stance is a huge departure from standard Catholic teaching, which depended on the Quadriga, the fourfold level of scriptural interpretation. Luther's ideas caught on in Germany, but no one has ever been able to convince the Italians of the absolute literal truth of anything, least of all poetry.

In the twentieth century, we have learned that words are pointers—sometimes deliberately and even insanely misleading pointers—to deeper realities. Mainstream Lutheran theology has evolved over the years, and no one but the most rigid fundamentalist believes a word is an end in itself, a "term." And yet the Protestant nations continue to adhere more strongly to the cult of words than other nations. Small wonder the repeated phrases, extravagant locutions, and plain old silliness of much of Italian opera strike the people in these countries as ridiculous to the point of being offensive. It is interesting that it was Wagner (a German Protestant) who found the relationship of words and music in Italian opera to be so "wrong" that he determined to redefine their interaction (ostensibly giving primacy to the drama as expressed by the words). He could not even bear to call his creations operas, but preferred the term "music dramas."

Enter Verdi.

Theories and dogma were of no interest to the man from Le Roncole. He was pragmatic in the manner of country people everywhere, and would use what he liked and disregard the rest. As soon as he began to attend operas in Milan, he saw both the strengths and the weaknesses of the bel canto format. Experts debate whether Verdi's early operas were bel canto or the death knell of that form. The key point is that Verdi was able to transform the possibilities of those conventions into a thrilling theatrical genre that even the best bel canto composers, such as Rossini and Bellini, hardly imagined possible. He did this by working with the human situations within a drama rather than by painting the individual words.

The marriage of words and music is a tempestuous relationship. Hearing words sung represents a different sort of truth than reading them on the page or hearing them spoken. Music will accentuate some and lose others in the garble. A few years ago, there was a great cartoon in two panels by Gary Larson. The first panel, titled "What we say to dogs," shows a man berating his dog, saying, "Okay Ginger! I've had it! You stay out of the garbage! Understand, Ginger? Stay out of the garbage or else!" The second panel is titled "What they hear," and the bubble over the man's head reads simply, "blah blah GINGER blah blah blah blah blah blah blah blah GINGER blah blah blah blah blah." In essence, we in the audience of musical theater are so many Gingers, striving to make out the words in between the "punch" words. Verdi strove for the right punch words, or what he called *la parola scenica,* the "theatrical" word. In the hands of a great composer, words are not lost in music so much as they are transformed. The important feelings or issues at stake, *"l'onore, l'amore, vendetta,"* and so forth, are thrust into the audience's consciousness and then the situation is embellished, analyzed, and given meaning by the music. There was no need to destroy the traditions of Italian opera. The ability to look at life with a unique set of tools was there from the first night of *Dafne* in 1597. All that Verdi had to do was probe farther than anyone else had (or has since) with these tools. And in doing so, he left us with a treasure of vital inquiries into the human condition.

What can be done with this art form? First off, the music tells us the context of what the character is saying. A full orchestral doubling of the singer's line implies that the singer really means what he or she is saying (for example, Violetta's outburst in Act II of *La traviata*). Conversely, it can show doubt or ambivalence (as in *Otello,* where the hero's doubts are conveyed by the music). The metamorphosing nature of music, moving more effortlessly than words from one senti-

ment to another, can depict how one emotion can transform into another (as in Act II of *Rigoletto,* where the title character's journey from
rage to desperation is made plausible in three minutes by the music).
The orchestra can show the underlying—even subconscious—issues
behind the words spoken. And all this merely suggests the possibilities for a single singer. The plurality of any given situation can be
explored in opera in a way that eludes spoken drama, even movies. At
one point during Act II of *Aida,* there are twenty vocal parts, each
representing a different experience of the situation at hand. The
ensuing glorious cacophony, however, never loses sight of the unity of
the situation. If a movie were to show the same thing, we would need
cutaway shots giving us a view of each separate reaction. At the opera,
we not only experience them at the same time (as we do in real life)
but explore their relationship to each other. In Act III, Scene I of *Un
ballo in maschera,* a husband plots with two companions to assassinate
his wife's lover. A happy young man enters, unaware of what's going
on, to invite the husband, wife, and two conspirators to a glittering ball.
Amazingly, this unfolds simultaneously to music that unifies the four
very different personal stories. What Verdi found was the point of intersection among these four stories with no compromise to the individuals. In fact, the individual experiences are emphasized by being
examined in relationship to each other. There has never yet been a
playwright, novelist, or movie director who could accomplish the same.

There is no doubt that opera, as an art form, contains more than
its share of absurdities, and no wonder that it has provided source
material for comedians probably since its inception. Its extravagances
require no apologies, but perhaps some explanation. A great movie
director of the caliber of, say, Stanley Kubrick, will use the limitations
of the camera as part of the story being told. A great opera composer
such as Verdi (and there has been none greater) will do the same
thing with opera. No one was more aware of the limits of the theater
than Verdi, and he wrote his works with these in mind. Even the
caprices and shortcomings of singers, the difficulties of creating illusions, and the fickleness of audiences inspired him to summon every
drop of art at his disposal to compensate. In doing so, he wed words
and music in a unique way.

The Life and Times of
Giuseppe Verdi

A Song in Milan

WHILE GIUSEPPE VERDI lay dying in his suite at the Grand Hotel in Milan in January 1901, journalists set up a press office in the lobby and wired bulletins every fifteen minutes to the corners of the world. The streets outside were covered in straw and traffic rerouted in hopes of making the man comfortable in his final hours. Verdi died at 2:30 in the afternoon of the 27th. He had requested extremely simple rites for his funeral, and his wishes were obeyed—partially. A simple, second-class hearse was ordered for the morning of the 30th, with no flowers. Close friends, relatives, and a few officials and musical colleagues made up the actual funeral party. Meanwhile, a gathering of 200,000 people waited in what has been described as absolute silence. This crowd made its way to a church, where a simple rite of blessing was performed, and then to Cimitero Monumentale, where Verdi's body was laid next to that of his wife, Giuseppina Strepponi.

One month later, the Verdis' bodies were transferred to a crypt at the Musicians' Rest Home, which they had founded and endowed, special permission having been obtained from the highest levels of government for this burial. Verdi's wishes for a simple funeral having been fulfilled, there was no reason why the transference of remains could not be a huge official memorial. At the cemetery, Toscanini led a chorus of 820 in *"Va, pensiero"* from *Nabucco,* Verdi's earliest triumph from sixty years before. This time, there was a crowd of 300,000, including major dignitaries and representatives of several governments. According to many reports, the entire crowd spontaneously repeated the chorus *"Va, pensiero."* When the cortege reached the Casa di Riposo, there was more music.

The official response and the spontaneous public outpouring of love and honor were unprecedented phenomena for a man who, although he lived his life in the theater, loathed publicity and avoided demonstrations of affection. Verdi turned down honors and ignored others bestowed upon him. Whenever possible, he declined invitations from nobility, kings, and emperors. He continually referred to himself as a "peasant" (not strictly true) and often listed his occupation as "farmer." The request for an austere funeral had been sincere, but he might have known that the matter would not stop there. Verdi himself had taught the Italians that nothing can silence the voice of a nation.

Roots

Giuseppe Verdi was born on October 10, 1813, in the village of Le Roncole, near Busseto, in the province of Parma. Verdi himself always celebrated his birthday on the 9th, since that is the date his mother once told him and he was a man of habit. At that time, the French under Napoleon occupied all of Italy, so Verdi, speaking in terms of strictest legalities, was born a French citizen. No one would ever mistake him for a Frenchman, however. Throughout his life, he reveled in calling himself a "peasant from Roncole" and bore all the characteristic traits of his native district. Verdi's parents ran a tavern in the village and engaged in any kind of trade they could get their hands on. Although poverty was a trademark of the region, the Verdis were, by local standards, middle-class. Verdi was never a farmer until he became a landowner years later, and such a position is quite different in Italy from that of a peasant.

The province of Parma had been an independent duchy since the sixteenth century, ruled in the eighteenth century by a branch of the same Bourbon family that sat on the thrones of France, Spain, and the Kingdom of Naples (which was all of southern Italy and often Sicily). At various times the arts had flourished in Parma, with music holding particular pride of place. The province itself is flat and featureless and the weather in the region is rarely appealing. But the land is rich and the Parmigiani (as the people are called) have perhaps the best standard of living in Italy today.

This was not the case in 1813. Supporting the French armies took a toll on the agricultural community, and when the Allies beat the French back into France, much of the land and livestock was destroyed. One legend says that Cossacks from the Russian army destroyed whatever they could of the village of Le Roncole as they chased the French. Verdi's mother, Luigia, was said to have hid herself and her infant son in the bell tower of the village church while the rampaging went on. No one has been able to verify the story or prove it false, but the people in the area believe it to this day, and a plaque on the church tower in question mentions the incident as if it were undisputed fact. The wars were real enough in any case, and the land suffered great privations for years to come. As Verdi bluntly said of his childhood on several later occasions, "It was hard."

No doubt it was, even if not quite to the extent that the mythographers (including Verdi himself) would have us believe. Napoleon's conquest of the peninsula had affected every Italian differently, but the idea that there had actually been a place called the Kingdom of Italy would change the status quo forever. Not that this was immediately apparent after Napoleon's downfall in 1815. The Allies met at the Congress of Vienna and tried to restore Europe, Humpty Dumpty–like, to its pre-Napoleonic status, as if the previous twenty-five years had never happened. One thorny problem for the Congress was deciding what to do with Marie Louise, Napoleon's wife and the mother of his son. As the daughter of the Austrian emperor, she could hardly be shoved aside, but the fact that Napoleon had a legitimate heir was a source of potential concern. Marie Louise was given the Duchy of Parma to keep her busy, and her son was held in Austria, closely watched and guarded.

This suited the former empress, who was never much for motherhood, to a tee. In Parma, Marie Louise was free to indulge her favorite addictions, pastries and men. Her appetites for both were legendary. One story goes that the prime minister attempted to curtail Marie Louise's escapades by posting a guard at her bedroom door, only to find the guard in her bed by morning. The duchess's third interest was the opera, and the Teatro Regio was built during her time in Parma. Frivolity, however, was a lesser sin in the eyes of her subjects than the cruelty that marked the other rulers of Italy, and Parma probably experienced less political stress than any other Italian state during Verdi's youth. Music in Parma and in the churches was supported by the government. Beyond this, rich and poor alike enjoyed music at gatherings and any sort of celebration, and wandering musicians were abundant.

The Verdis kept the tavern in Le Roncole and young Giuseppe must have helped with the chores. In 1816, a little sister, Giuseppa, was born. One early biographer informs us that Giuseppa was mentally retarded, but this has not been confirmed. Other early friends of Verdi's attest to a closeness between the siblings before Giuseppa died in 1833, while Verdi was in Milan. In later years Verdi spoke very little about his family, so we can only conjecture. We can safely assume that little Giuseppe must have shown an early aptitude for music, since Carlo Verdi bought his son a spinet (an upright harpsichord) for the boy some time around 1821, an extraordinary gift for the son of a taverner in that time and place. Verdi always maintained a sentimental attachment to the instrument, and it is currently on display in the museum at La Scala. Young Giuseppe began studying the organ at the Church of San Michele directly across the street from the Verdis' tavern, and by the age of twelve had in fact become the organist there. The small village became proud of its pint-sized maestro.

When he was eleven, Verdi was sent to the larger town of Busseto, about three miles from Le Roncole, to study. He continued to play the organ at Roncole, walking back and forth on Sundays and holidays. Busseto was a town of 2,000 people, boasting a few claims to culture. There were good small schools and libraries, and the townspeople even supported a music school and a local Philharmonic Society. Verdi remained in Busseto until 1832, paying as little attention as possible to his standard studies while spending as much time as possible studying with Provesi, director of the music school and Philharmonic Society and organist at the Church of San Bartolomeo. Young Verdi wrote church music, marches for the town band, and the occasional overture for visiting opera troupes, although very little of his juvenilia exists, since he was almost obsessive in destroying it in later years. Antonio Barezzi, a prosperous grocer and enthusiastic supporter of Busseto's musical life, became interested in Verdi's development, and Verdi became a boarder at the Barezzis' comfortable house in 1831. Barezzi became almost a father to Verdi, a relationship that would develop further as Verdi became interested in Barezzi's daughter Margherita, a gifted musician.

We have a clear picture of Verdi in these early years from documents, a few letters, and later reminiscences. He was tall, pockmarked, skinny, awkward, and painfully shy, a trait that many mistook for arrogance. He was a very serious young man who did not seek out social pleasures. Although he could be practical and adapt himself to circumstances when they appeared reasonable to him, he was also stubborn and unforgiving, and could not be budged once he made his mind up. Such was the adolescent Verdi, and he would remain the same into the dawn of the next century.

New Horizons

Barezzi, fervently believing in Verdi's destiny, persuaded Carlo Verdi to petition a local charitable institution, the Monte di Pietà, for a scholarship to send the young man to study at the Milan Conservatory. There was no scholarship available that year, so the impatient Barezzi decided to underwrite Verdi's sojourn in Milan. The country boy arrived in the sophisticated capital of Lombardy in 1832, at first accompanied by his father and Provesi. Provesi made introductions and prepared for Verdi's application to the Milan Conservatory, perhaps the best music school in Italy at that time. Verdi applied in June of that year and was rejected. At nineteen, he was older than the usual age for admittance. Also, the conservatory had filled its quota of foreigners, a category that included Parmigiani. The examination board praised Verdi's talent, but could do no more. He never forgave them.

Years later, when the conservatory asked his permission to name itself after him, he denied the request. "They wouldn't have me young, now they can't have me old," he said.

Verdi stayed on in Milan, supported by Barezzi and eventually also by a scholarship from the Monte di Pietà. While there he studied privately with Vincenzo Lavigna, a composer of modest success. Verdi complained about his training with Lavigna, which entailed formal studies in figures and canons and very little of orchestration and the music he was increasingly drawn to in Milan, dramatic music. After three years of study on an extremely modest budget, Verdi returned to Busseto, where the position of *maestro di musica* had become available.

Verdi would soon learn that politics and music were forever wedded, a truth that would shape his career for decades. Barezzi and his friends supported the choice of Verdi as the town maestro, while opposing them were the conservative elements of the town, headed by the clergy. The local bishop favored Verdi's rival, who was older, more docile, and more respectful of authority than Verdi. Busseto immediately had a scandal, and everyone in the town expressed an opinion. The authorities in Parma temporarily settled the situation with Solomonian wisdom: all music was banned in the churches of Busseto, pending a decision.

Priests and Revolutionaries

Although there were a few priests in the area who backed Verdi's candidacy, the clerical party on the whole opposed him. The contempt was mutual, for Verdi loathed priests throughout his life. He spoke of one incident when he was a youth, serving at Mass as an altar boy. Lost in a reverie induced by the organ, he didn't hear the priest call for him, and the priest, in frustration, kicked young Verdi, who fell down the stairs leading up to the altar. Many have dated his dislike of priests from this point.

This story, however, does not sufficiently explain Verdi's obsessive hatred of the clergy. People in the Italian countryside are quite uninhibited about physical exchanges. If every Italian boy who got kicked by a priest became anticlerical, there would be no church in Italy. I suspect Verdi had other experiences in his youth with the local clergy, matters the intensely private man did not see fit to disclose to history. Whatever his reasons, Verdi maintained his hatred of priests throughout his long life. When he was eighty-six years old and a young relative approached him with a note from a respected scholar and cleric, Verdi tore up the note and told the young man, "Keep away from priests." Incidentally, when the priest kicked Verdi down the stairs, the boy shouted "May God strike you with lightning!" This sign of disrespect caused a little scandal in the town, and even more gossip eight years later, when the unfortunate priest was struck by lightning and killed.

Not that one needed personal reasons for being anticlerical in Italy at that time. We must remember that the pope was a political leader of one of the most important Italian states, and priests in the rest of Italy were, in effect, agents of that state. They held both spiritual and secular duties, and were almost entirely opposed to political innovation. The battle lines were becoming clearer every passing year. On one side were the conservatives—the Bourbons, the Hapsburgs, the pope, and their dependents; on the other, republicans, nationalists, and those who were fired up by the new, largely French ideas. History, of course, has judged in favor of Italian nationalists and against the Hapsburgs and the clerics, but things were not yet so clear in 1832. They city dwellers, the intellectuals, and the lesser nobility saw political advantage in removing the old order. The old aristocracy and the clerics were naturally opposed to this, and so were the peasants, who formed the bulk of the population.

In any case, who had ever heard of an Italian nation, except as another one of Napoleon's crazy ideas? Each district in Italy was fiercely jealous of its neighbors (as they still are), and to most people a government ruling from Milan or Rome would have appeared every bit as foreign as one in Vienna. Venetians had never hidden their contempt for mainlanders, Romans always considered themselves a "people set apart," and the Lombard sense of superiority is the stuff of legend. The Florentine image of their neighbors in Pisa is best represented by the still-current proverb "It's better to have a corpse in the house than a Pisano at the door." It would take a great deal of work before people could realistically conceive of an Italian nation, ruled by Italians. That work was only beginning in the 1830s. A young exiled republican named Giuseppe Mazzini wrote incendiary pamphlets in London that inspired many patriots back home. Secret societies were formed to discuss Mazzini's ideas. One of his central notions was that Italians all needed each other, whether they liked it or not. Without a united Italy, there could be no hope of ridding the peninsula of tyrants. Mazzini's name became hated by conservatives in Italy. The fact that Verdi wore a beard in the "Mazzini style" did not endear him to those elements. Verdi, like so many other young people in Italy at the time, incorporated Mazzini's views into his own. Throughout his life, he would refer to himself as "first and foremost an Italian."

The Maestro of Busseto

A competition for the post of Busseto music director was finally held in Parma in 1836, and again the authorities decided on a policy of appeasement. Verdi was named to head secular music in the town, while his rival was in charge of sacred music. Supposedly one of the examiners at the contest was so impressed by Verdi's musicianship he told him he should be a maestro in London or Paris, not Busseto. In any case, Verdi was probably relieved to keep away from the priests, and he actually had a job and a respectable position in society. In May 1836 he married Margherita Barezzi.

The bond between the two young lovers had developed quietly over the years. Perhaps the wedding took many Bussetani by surprise—Verdi was not the type to parade his feelings. Yet there is no reason to doubt the sympathy between them and the sincerity of their feelings. Margherita must have been bright and lively. We know she was pretty and rather stylish, according to the notions of the time. A daughter, Virginia, was born in March 1837, and a son, Icilio, in July 1838. (The names, derived from Livy's *History of Early Rome,* are a clear statement of identification with republican, as opposed to monarchical or imperial, ideals.)

Verdi continued to write all the expected marches, overtures, and "occasional pieces" for the Busseto Philharmonic Society and the town marching band, but his thoughts were already turning elsewhere. In 1838 his first songs were published in Milan, and somewhere along the line he had begun to compose an opera. He tried to get a work called *Rocester* placed at Parma, but failed. Perhaps parts of *Rocester* found their way into his next project, an opera called *Oberto, conte di San Bonifacio.* He visited Milan in 1838, and must have received encouragement there. Resigning from his post in Busseto, he moved with his reduced family (daughter Virginia having died in August) to the big city in 1839. *Oberto* was announced for production at La Scala in November.

Disaster and Success

La Scala was, then as now, the largest and most important theater in Italy, but this should not lead us to imagine that its history has consisted of two and a quarter centuries of uninterrupted brilliance. Music is always an art in flux, and the tide was ebbing in Milan when Verdi arrived there in 1839. Throughout the previous century, Italians had dominated music, not only in the composition of operas, but in chamber music and, to a lesser extent, sacred music. The Napoleonic upheavals had permanently upset the routine. The castrati vanished as if overnight, becoming a mythical standard of excellence as well as a bizarre musical footnote. Conservatories received less and less funding for less innovative curricula. Italian composers had always wandered Europe to seek their fortunes—Paisiello to St. Petersburg, Boccherini to Madrid, Salieri to Vienna, Lully, Piccini, and many others to Paris—but now it was becoming almost impossible even to make a living in Italy itself. No music paid for itself except opera, and consequently there is very little notable instrumental music from Italy in the nineteenth century. Even the opera was hard hit. Rossini breathed new life into the form in the second decade of the century, but he too went to Paris. After 1829 he inexplicably wrote no more operas, even though he lived another four decades. Bellini and Donizetti had raised hopes, but they too went abroad. Anyway,

Bellini died in 1835 at the tragically young age of thirty-four and Donizetti was already almost paralyzed and mentally ill. Donizetti was yet to write some of his finest operas, but it was clear that his time was limited. Italians could still write operas, but they couldn't write much else, and they couldn't seem to write them for Italy. The time was ripe for a new composer to make his mark at La Scala.

Verdi prepared *Oberto,* barely pausing when his son Icilio died in October of that year. The premiere of *Oberto* was a modest success. Everyone thought the libretto weak, since it had been worked on by several people before Verdi actually set it. Significantly, the singers in the cast were very enthusiastic about the new composer from Busseto. A few other theaters in Italy asked to produce the opera. Giovanni Ricordi, who was busy reinventing the music publishing business, paid Verdi for the rights to the score, and despite the deaths of his children, things were looking up for Verdi. Infant deaths were the norm in that time and place, and he and Margherita were still young. With a career opening up, Verdi and Margherita had every reason to believe they could begin again.

The impresario of La Scala was a man named Bartolomeo Merelli. He was a practical man, a businessman who did wonders to keep the theater afloat and seemed to earn nothing but scorn from the artists and the public for his efforts—a type of person not unknown in operatic circles today. Merelli offered Verdi a contract for three more operas, and Verdi accepted. The next was to be a comic opera. Perhaps there was some confusion about what sort of comic opera was wanted by the management, but Verdi worked on a piece that was more of a pleasant romance with a happy ending than an outright gut-buster. His mood could hardly have allowed otherwise. In June 1840 Margherita died of encephalitis.

Years later, Verdi remembered the three deaths of his family as occurring within a few months of each other. Clearly this was not the case, but the man can be forgiven for having telescoped the accumulated grief into a shorter time span in his memory. The trials were not yet over. The new opera, *Un giorno di regno,* premiered in September 1840 and was a spectacular flop. The audience booed and whistled as only a Scala audience can when they set their minds to it. Verdi, according to the custom of the time, sat in the orchestra pit in full view of the hissing audience throughout the performance. It would have been a living hell for anybody, most of all for a private man like Verdi. The opera was withdrawn after a single performance. Verdi retired into his small apartment and sank into a dismal depression.

"On Golden Wings"

After the loss of his family and the failure of *Un giorno di regno,* Verdi swore he would never write another note of music—an oath he often repeated during the subsequent sixty years. He lingered around Milan for a while, not knowing what to do with himself, until one day Merelli ran into him on the street and handed him a libretto, insisting Verdi read it. Merelli intended to hold Verdi to his contract. In 1840 a flop was only a matter for a few days' gossip in the town where it occurred. It was considered a standard event in any composer's career. Verdi returned to his room and tossed the manuscript on a table. It happened to fall open to a page with the words of a chorus written on it, *"Va, pensiero, sull'ali dorate"* ("Go, thought, on golden wings"). The libretto was for an opera named *Nabucodonosor* ("Nebuchadnezzar") and told the story of the fall of Jerusalem in 587 B.C., including vivid scenes of the Hebrews' exile in Babylon. Verdi tried to forget it and go to sleep, but *"Va, pensiero"* would not let him sleep. He returned to the manuscript and read and reread it through the night until he had it almost memorized by morning. Still firm in his decision never to compose again, however, he sought out Merelli to return it. Merelli stuffed the libretto back into Verdi's coat pocket and ran off into the crowd before any more protest could be voiced. So Verdi kept the libretto, and set a little at a time until he had an opera.

This, at least, was how he chose to remember the event in later years (he was a man of the theater who could dramatize personal history when he wished to). Verdi received the libretto of *Nabucco* (as it was to be called) at a low point in his life and career, and it screamed out at him. The powerful words were written by Temistocle Solera, who was quite a character in his own right. Solera lazed about Milan, hated to work, partied heartily at night, and slept late in the morning.

When Verdi wanted a particular scene changed and Solera took his time about finishing the work, Verdi reportedly would lock him in a room and refuse to release him until the new verses were finished. Not a promising prospect for a collaboration, but the opera was completed and set for production at La Scala. Merelli, always quick to see a bargain, was enthusiastic partially because he already had the sets and costumes available from a ballet on the same subject given in 1837. He also had three new operas to produce during the important Carnival (midwinter) season. He told Verdi it would have to wait until the spring. Verdi refused. It had to be Carnival or never. Not only was it the more important season, but the theater had the services of a notable soprano, Giuseppina Strepponi, during that period only. Merelli decided to get Strepponi's opinion of the new work, and Verdi called on her and played it through. The soprano was enthusiastic, and Merelli begrudingly announced the opera for the end of the Carnival season.

Merelli need not have worried. As rehearsals began for the new opera, La Scala buzzed. The music for *Nabucco* was fresh, brash, and utterly new. Even the stagehands at the theater, notoriously difficult to impress, were said to stop their work and their chattering to sit and listen to the music, and at some points even applauded. Word got out that the new work would be an event, and opening night tickets were at a premium.

The premiere, on March 9, 1842, was one of the great sensations of theatrical history. The opening scene was applauded for ten minutes. The evening built into a frenzy. The chorus *"Va, pensiero,"* which had so impressed Verdi from his first glance at the libretto, struck an enormous chord with the audience, which demanded an encore even though encores were forbidden by the Austrian authorities anxious about political demonstrations in the theater. The Austrians were right to be concerned. Music is often the most powerful expression of thought in a strictly censored society. After the premiere of *Nabucco,* Italians had their own song of freedom, and suddenly the nobody from Busseto was the soul of a movement.

Giuseppina Strepponi

Some of the opening night success also had to do with the prima donna of the evening, Strepponi. This extraordinary woman was already a seasoned veteran of the theater in 1842, although she was still very young. She was born in Lodi in 1815 to a musical family. Her father Feliciano was organist at the Cathedral of Monza and a composer of successful operas. He took his daughter Giuseppina to Milan to enroll her in the conservatory, and she was admitted, although she, like Verdi when he applied, was over the usual age. Feliciano died young, and Giuseppina finished her studies in Milan as a nonpaying student, immediately embarking on a hectic career. For the next five years Giuseppina was almost always engaged in some season or other, not taking time off even for one of her several subsequent pregnancies. She bore a son, Camillino, in 1838, and at least two other children directly after. It is hard to determine the paternity of these children, since she had liaisons with her manager, her leading men, an impecunious count, and, according to one early Verdi biographer, Donizetti. Camillino was left with a family in Florence, the others were either abandoned at orphanages or left with families. (Camillino died as a charity case in Florence in 1862, and no reference to his death has been found in Strepponi's papers.) Strepponi was attractive and smart and must have been a commanding stage presence. But the constant singing and childbearing were taking their toll. By the time of the rehearsals for *Nabucco,* there was concern whether she could still be relied on to sing well, a problem exacerbated by the extreme difficulty of the role Verdi had written. Strepponi acquitted herself well, however, and her voice did not crumble until the following seasons.

Solidifying Success

Merelli quickly offered Verdi a bonus for another opera, leaving the payment space blank for the composer to fill in any amount he wished. Strepponi advised him to ask for the same amount Bellini had received for his opera *Norma,* and Verdi agreed, adding a little to that sum to make a point. For a source, Solera suggested an epic poem popular with the Milanese called *I lombardi alla prima crociata,* "The Lombards at the First Crusade." The tale begins in Milan itself and moves to Jerusalem. It had patriotism, war, religion, and a love story, and was sure to make an effect. Verdi set to work, once again locking Solera in a room to get him to complete the verses. This time, that scheme failed, as Solera discovered he was imprisoned with Verdi's wine cabinet and helped himself freely, toasting his own genius at every completed line of verse. Somehow, this "odd couple" of Milan finished their opera, and rehearsals began. The police asked for the libretto, as was customary, and thus began Verdi's problems with censorship, which would plague him for the next twenty years. The cardinal of Milan (an Austrian) objected to the presentation of religious images on an operatic stage. *Lombardi* had crosses, Jerusalem, an Ave Maria, and even a baptism! What next, holy communion served as refreshment in the lobby? The police chief summoned Verdi, Solera, and Merelli to a meeting to discuss necessary changes. Verdi refused even to attend, showing more indications of his soon-legendary stubbornness. "It will be performed as it is or it will not be performed at all," he went on record as saying. Merelli sheepishly pleaded as a businessman: The production was paid for, and so on. He also added a barely veiled threat. There was already much buzz about this new opera. What would the Milanese do if the Austrian authorities prohibited its performance? The police chief got the message, and so did the cardinal. Only the Ave Maria was changed to *"Salve Maria,"* and the opera was presented as written. Verdi had won the first round of the battle. *Lombardi* premiered in February 1843 to a deliriously enthusiastic audience, the patriotic chorus *"O signore, dal tetto natio"* becoming for a while as famous as *"Va, pensiero."* The audience cried, shouted, and clamored for war. The police did nothing to interfere with the performance, but from that moment on Verdi was harassed by censors, and in the future they did not relent as easily as the cardinal had.

Verdi had proven that *Nabucco* was no fluke, and he was now the center of attention in Milan. He always maintained the gruff manners of his youth and made neither friends nor casual conversation easily. He did, however, meet several people who would influence his life for decades. Among these were the Count and Countess Maffei, who would separate amicably within a few years but would both remain in Verdi's life. Count Andrea Maffei was a talented literary amateur who occasionally collaborated with Verdi. Countess Clarina Maffei established a fashionable salon where artistic ideas were discussed; she also had a keen interest in politics, and, like Verdi, supported Mazzini's ideas for a united, independent republic of Italy. Nowhere were art and politics more firmly entwined than in the countess's own home.

As interesting as life in Milan became for Verdi, the world beyond was beckoning. Merelli, who was also the impresario for the Vienna Opera, took Verdi to the Austrian capital to unveil *Nabucco*. Verdi was unimpressed by his first trip to a truly foreign country. Indeed, throughout his life, Verdi showed little interest in travel for its own sake. In addition, he was quite underwhelmed by Merelli's presentation of *Nabucco* in Vienna. It was time to move outside of the Scala machine. Venice's Teatro la Fenice made a handsome proposition for a new opera, and connected Verdi with Francesco Maria Piave, a neophyte jack-of-all-trades in the theater and a budding librettist. Verdi accepted enthusiastically.

Piave was a native of the island of Murano in the Venetian lagoon. He also functioned as the stage director of La Fenice, and had a good instinct for theatrical situation. He lived more riotously than Verdi, but most important, knew how to defer to the composer's wishes. He and Verdi developed a solid working relationship that would span the next two decades. Verdi let his hair down, so to speak, with Piave, and they may have even accompanied each other in some of the carousing for which Venice has always been famous. Over the next few years, Verdi's letters to Piave make reference to a certain "angel" in Venice, a woman who apparently caught Verdi's attention and with whom the librettist acted as a go-between.

Ernani was produced at La Fenice in March 1844, after many troubles with the censors, the management of La Fenice, and the singers. It was a success, and, after the first few performances, a rave. Verdi did not stick around Venice to accept the blandishments of fans. He already had other plans.

The Galley Years

Thus began what Verdi later called his "years in the galley," which saw the output of eleven operas in five years. In the two years after the success of *Ernani* in Venice, he produced *I due Foscari* for Rome (a success), *Giovanna d'Arco* for La Scala (another success, but Verdi was so disgusted with Merelli's management and conditions at La Scala in general that he refused to have anything to do with the theater for the following twenty-four years), *Alzira* for the Teatro San Carlo of Naples (a great flop), and *Attila* for Venice (a great success). Verdi griped about the pressure to produce, in the manner of workaholics everywhere, even while campaigning for more work. To keep up this pace he needed a loyal and devoted assistant, which he found in the person of Emanuele Muzio. Although only twelve years younger than Verdi, Muzio treated Verdi with biblical respect for the next forty-five years. He assisted in the musical preparation, correspondence, packing, and every mundane detail of his idol's life. A recent poster to an Internet newsgroup said you can tell the die-hard Verdi fans in the world—they're the ones who have lapdogs named Muzio. Even with Muzio's help, however, Verdi was feeling as if he had become something of an opera factory, and ached to do something different. In 1847 Piave prepared a libretto out of *Macbeth*, Shakespeare being Verdi's particular favorite even though the Bard was only just beginning to be read and performed in Italy. The opera was given for the self-consciously sophisticated audiences of Florence, where it was cheered, but the work was too radical to make the same splash in the other houses. Also in 1847 Verdi accepted a large offer to compose for Her Majesty's Theatre in London, and he and Muzio went there to produce *I masnadieri*. On the way, Verdi stopped in Paris for a few days, sending Muzio on ahead to London. Interestingly, Giuseppina Strepponi was living there at the time, giving music lessons to ladies now that her voice was gone. There are many theories about when Verdi and Strepponi became lovers, but there is much to be said for dating their liaison from the time of this visit to Paris. Verdi never discussed it, and in any case was off to London within a few days. Verdi was never a great sightseer, and in London he complained mostly about the air pollution and high prices in the world's largest city. He also complained that the food was "too spicy" for his tastes, surely the only time in history an Italian has had that particular issue with English food. He did admire English manners and dress, but thought it a great mistake for Italians to ape the English. *I masnadieri* was a success in London, with Queen Victoria and the Duke of Wellington in the opening night audience applauding Jenny Lind, the Swedish Nightingale, in the prima donna role. Verdi visited Mazzini and hurried back to Paris.

Back in Paris, he appears to have spent a good amount of time with Strepponi, although evidence is scanty. He also received an offer from the Paris Opéra, the most important theater in Europe. Although he knew he was running a great risk, he dressed up *I lombardi* in French garb and the French language, added some rather good music, and even included a ballet, which was *de rigueur* at the Opéra. The "new" opera, presented as *Jérusalem,* was not enthusiastically received. But Verdi was amusing himself in Paris anyway. He invited Barezzi for a visit, and Barezzi met Strepponi and spoke enthusiastically about her in his subsequent letters. Verdi had committed to write an opera for the publisher Lucca, whom Verdi found obnoxious. He diddled with the Byron poem *The Corsair* and eventually began setting it to music.

We tend to think of the galley years as Verdi's most overtly patriotic period, composing operas that were primarily propaganda pieces for the Risorgimento (the name eventually given to the great awakening of Italian national consciousness in the mid–nineteenth century), but Verdi's operas always worked on a human level first and foremost. For Verdi, patriotism was a simple and universal human emotion. By 1848 people were responding to Verdi's operas well beyond the hotbeds of Italian nationalism. Besides conquering all the major Italian cities, he had had reasonably successful premieres in London and Paris, and his works had been performed and cheered from Constantinople to New York to Buenos Aires and beyond. Verdi already belonged to the world, and that world was about to explode.

The Explosions of 1848

It doesn't seem to have occurred to Verdi, Countess Maffei, or any other Italian patriots that the Austrians and the French might be having troubles of their own. In Vienna, riots began when students demanded governmental reforms including, of all things, a constitution. Unrest spread rapidly throughout Europe, although there was no international committee overseeing events. In Paris, republicans and socialists clamored for change. Verdi managed to finish off *Il corsaro* and send it to the publisher Lucca, promptly forgetting about it. Perhaps events in Paris, besides Barezzi's visit and Strepponi's increasingly interesting company, were distracting him. In February, King Louis-Philippe of France surprised the revolutionaries by basically agreeing with them, abdicating, and retiring to a comfortable life in England. For lack of a better plan, a republic was declared. Verdi was thrilled, thinking a strong French republic would be most advantageous to his hopes for Italy.

Back in Milan, a boycott had been organized against the state-controlled tobacco monopoly. Patriots refrained from public smoking as a sign of protest. The Austrian officials ordered their soldiers to smoke as much as they could wherever they could be seen by the most people. The soldiers were jeered, fights began, and the soldiers fired on the people. Barricades appeared instantly throughout the then-narrow streets, the people rose up in a display of unity that surprised everybody, and the famous *cinque giornate* of Milan had begun. The five days of insurrection were successful, and the Austrians withdrew, to the delirious joy of the Milanese. Verdi heard the news and rushed to Milan, arriving in early April. Meanwhile, the Venetians, led by patriot Daniele Manin, had also succeeded in expelling the Austrians and declared a republic on March 24. Verdi was impressed to hear that Piave had taken up arms as a common soldier in Venice's defense, and wrote letters gently gibing him for being a dilettante-turned-militiaman. Milan was in turmoil, and Verdi and his friends were at the vortex of the excitement. Countess Maffei was one of fifty-two ladies who nursed the wounded. Strepponi's friend Princess Cristina Belgioioso, long active in political circles, collected 160 volunteers in Naples, sailed them north, and marched into Milan at their vanguard dressed, it is said, as Joan of Arc. In early May Verdi visited Busseto, quite incidentally buying a farm at the village of Sant'Agata, then returning to Milan.

The initial headiness of the *cinque giornate* having passed, there remained the thorny question of what to do. Some, including Verdi and Countess Maffei, favored the declaration of a republic, but would the republic include other Italian states or only Lombardy? Should it unite with Venice to form a northern Italian republic? Another party still favored the plan of a united Italy with Pope Pius IX as president, and in fact Pius was known to have sounded out the Austrian emperor on this idea. (The emperor laughed at it.) When Pius finally made a statement of intent, it was not what many had expected, let alone hoped for. In the Allocution of April 29, the pope in effect renounced any involvement with the movement for Italian independence and unity.

However strongly Verdi felt about the republic, it wasn't enough to keep him in Milan. Pleading urgent business, he returned to Paris at the end of May. Much of the urgency of his business seems to have involved Strepponi. They rented a house in the suburb of Passy and lived together throughout the summer of 1848. The revolutionary movements, without any common aim or coordination, exploded chaotically all over Europe. In June, the workers of Paris, feeling marginalized by the new republic, revolted. Meanwhile, Lombardy voted for annexation with the neighboring Kingdom of Piedmont, hoping to get some troops out of their King Carlo Alberto. Carlo Alberto had granted his country a constitution and was theoretically interested in the idea of ruling over rich Lombardy, but the Austrians had other plans. Marshal Radetsky regrouped the Austrians and defeated the Piedmontese-Lombard troops in several engagements throughout July. In August, Carlo Alberto withdrew from the battlefield and back into his own territory, booed by the Milanese who had hailed him as a savior. Now Milan lay open to reoccupation. Muzio and Countess Maffei, among many others, fled to Switzerland. Throughout the summer, Verdi worked on a flagrantly patriotic opera with the talented Neapolitan librettist Salvatore Cammarano, who had written the libretto for *Alzira*. Ricordi knew there would be no chance of producing the new work in the Austrian-occupied north nor in Bourbon Naples, which had somehow survived the storm.

Meanwhile, the nearly forgotten *Il corsaro* premiered that year in Trieste, the most securely Austrian city in Italy and the one northern city where Verdi's name did not carry revolutionary magic. It flopped, and was withdrawn after three performances. Verdi did not care. The revolution was flaring up again. In November, Pope Pius quietly escaped from Rome, according to one colorful (but alas, apocryphal) account dressed as a chambermaid. Elections were announced for Rome—on the one hand an unthinkable turn of events, but to romantics with a sense of history the most natural thing in the world. Countless republicans, including Mazzini and a firebrand named Garibaldi, flooded Rome like air rushing into a vacuum. Verdi himself arrived to produce the new opera at the Teatro Argentina, and found the city in a fervor. Verdi's opera had arrived at the perfect moment. The people had long been accustomed to hearing their aspirations proclaimed through music, so much harder to censor than speech or prose. But the new opera promised to proclaim those sentiments flagrantly and with a minimum of metaphor. *La battaglia di Legnano* premiered on January 27, 1849, to a delirious audience. The opening words, *"Viva Italia!,"* set the tone. The entire final act was encored. The opera, direct and powerful, genuinely stirred the Romans. At the end of one act, the hero, who is locked away in a tower and would rather risk death than the dishonor of missing the fateful battle, dons his sash, repeats *"Viva Italia!,"* and leaps out the window. The audience went crazy. One young patriot, in a supreme moment of audience identification, emulated the opera's hero, jumping out of a fourth-tier box and landing, unhurt, in the orchestra pit. Or so the story goes.

All of which might flatter lesser souls like you and me, but Verdi found the attention uncomfortable. He left for Paris in early February, claiming sadness at having to abandon Italy in her hour of need. He moved into either Strepponi's apartment or an apartment in her building, we are not sure which. Thus he missed the declaration of the Roman Republic of February 9. In Paris, elections had been held in December and Prince Louis Napoleon Bonaparte was elected president. Nobody was certain what the election would mean for Italy, which needed more help than ever. Marshal Radetsky decisively defeated the Piedmontese forces in March at Novara, and King Carlo Alberto abdicated. His son, Vittorio Emanuele II, assumed the throne and sparked a bit of hope by insisting on retaining his country's constitution, despite Austrian pressure to relinquish it and assume absolute authority. Meanwhile, the republicans at Rome fought on against great odds, Garibaldi so distinguishing himself by his bravery that he was made chief of high command. The teetering republic was finished once and for all when Prince-President Louis Napoleon sent French troops to occupy Rome in July in the name of Pope Pius IX. Verdi, in Paris, was disconsolate, and avoided meeting the prince (soon to be emperor) whenever he could weasel out of it. He worked on another opera with Cammarano, a distinctly apolitical work to be called *Luisa Miller.*

As Italy settled into a semblance of order, Verdi decided it was time to go home. It is hard to know why he had spent so little time in Italy during the First War of Italian Independence, as it came to be called. One can't level accusations of cowardice at him—his subsequent actions preclude that. Perhaps he felt unequal to the political role his presence would have conferred on him, or perhaps he felt, as did many other Italians, that one could be of just as much use in Paris. In any case, Verdi would remain in Italy during her hardest times, which were yet to come.

The Return of the Very Prodigal Son

In September 1849, Strepponi visited Verdi in Busseto, and went on to visit Florence, perhaps arranging for the education of her son Camillino. Verdi went with Barezzi to Naples for the reasonably successful premiere of *Luisa Miller* at the Teatro San Carlo. They returned to Busseto for Christmas, Strepponi joined Verdi there, and this time she stayed for the next half-century. There doesn't seem to have been any momentous decision made immediately. Indeed, Verdi wrote a quick note to Piave telling him to persuade the mysterious Venetian "angel" to postpone a planned visit. Nevertheless, Strepponi stayed in Busseto as Verdi's wife in all but name. Busseto is a small town, and everybody knew she was living at the Palazzo Cavalli, the most prominent private residence in the town. What they didn't know was whether she had married Verdi, and Verdi refused to explain his private life to anybody. Even Barezzi received nothing but a terse letter. Strepponi lived in absolute seclusion at the palazzo, with nobody but Muzio and the servants to talk to. She could not walk about the town or even attend Mass there. The Bussetani were annoyed by what they perceived as a snub, but they could only revile Verdi up to a point. He had, after all, put their town on the map. Instead, they vented their contempt toward the supposedly conniving, "foreign" woman who had stolen their famous native son from their affections. In effect, Strepponi became the Yoko Ono of Busseto.

Barezzi, after a brief cooling period, maintained his bond with Verdi, but Verdi's biological father Carlo was having none of it. We can only measure the rancor of their quarrels by the fact that Verdi settled his parents on a small plot of land in the district, provided modestly for their well-being, and drew up a bill of separation. Basically, he divorced his parents. It seems impossible that the quarrel was based exclusively on *l'affaire* Strepponi. Verdi could hardly have expected his parents to approve of the setup. In perhaps her most interesting detective work, Mary Jane Phillips-Matz has found a great deal of circumstantial evidence suggesting that Strepponi abandoned an infant at a nearby charitable institution during this period. An illegitimate child at this point would explain the increase in tensions with family and neighbors, and we know Strepponi was remarkably fertile. (Since Phillips-Matz's theory was published, commentators have twisted themselves into pretzels to prove that the level of pathos Verdi achieved in his subsequent father-daughter scenes was a direct result of the guilt he felt over this abandonment.) Whatever the underlying tensions, the split with his parents was all but complete.

Verdi wrote to an agent who was handling financial and legal details, "as far as the world is concerned, Carlo Verdi has to be one thing, and Giuseppe Verdi something else." The rancor and gossip only increased when Verdi's mother, Luigia, died in June 1851. Verdi grieved and withdrew into seclusion for a while, yet we don't find him as devastated at this period as he would be in other dark periods in his life. No artist ever explored filial love as well as Verdi, but he seemed remarkably unencumbered with the sentiment himself. He never lost sight of his responsibilities as a landowner, and in fact bought himself another small farm at the village of Sant'Agata, in the same district but outside of Busseto and at a reasonable distance from his father. There he devoted himself to farming, adding to his land and constantly improving it for the rest of his life.

Hunchbacks, Gypsies, and Whores

If Strepponi had no life to speak of at Sant'Agata, it suited Verdi perfectly. While still in Busseto, he had written *Stiffelio* with Piave, a very unusual story set in contemporary times about a Protestant minister who publicly forgives his wife's adultery. It was given at Trieste in 1850, after horrific mutilations from the censor, and was an utter flop. Verdi and Ricordi tried to retrieve all the copies of the score they could find pending a revision, and the result is that one of Verdi's operas was basically lost until pasted back together in the 1960s. But Verdi was not derailed. He also wrote *Rigoletto* at this time, again with Piave for La Fenice. It was a stunning success despite the endless wrangling with the Austrian censors, more reactionary than ever after the late upheavals. Working again with Cammarano, Verdi wrote *Il trovatore* for the Teatro Apollo in Rome. Poor Cammarano died before completing the libretto, and Verdi sent money to his widow and their six daughters. The premiere on January 19, 1853, was a great success despite floods that kept the riverside theater almost underwater throughout the run. Audiences went into frenzies over the work and it was soon played around the world, but Verdi heard complaints about the grimness of the opera and about its high body count. He wrote Countess Maffei, "But after all, in life isn't everything death?

What else exists?" Meanwhile, Verdi had also been working on a project with Piave for La Fenice, an operatic treatment of the play *La Dame aux camélias,* which was causing such a stir in Paris. *La traviata,* as the new opera was called, was not a success at its premiere in Venice a mere six weeks after the *Trovatore* premiere in Rome. But it triumphed in another theater in Venice the following year, beginning the opera's unending reign of popularity.

Verdi found a poet in Venice named Antonio Somma, whose ideas interested him greatly. Somma proposed an outline for an opera on Shakespeare's *King Lear,* which Verdi had already discussed with Cammarano, and they corresponded about the project in great detail. The ghost of this unwritten opera hangs over much of Verdi's career; though he shelved the project, he never officially pronounced *Re Lear* dead. While theorizing about *Lear,* Verdi received a tangible commission from the Paris Opéra. He signed a contract for an unspecified libretto, to be provided by Eugène Scribe. Verdi and Strepponi returned to Paris in October 1853.

Transformations in Paris

Although the revolutions were over, Paris was still astir in those years. Prince-President Bonaparte had made himself Emperor Napoleon III and essentially dictator of France in 1852. However much this may have disturbed Verdi the republican, Verdi the pragmatic landowner was clearly impressed with the public works program transforming Paris with an awesome blend of modernism and élan. Napoleon III had the Bonaparte talent for showmanship. His marriage to Eugenia Montijo at Notre Dame Cathedral was an imperial circus. Baron Haussmann was already busy planning the boulevards, monuments, and sewer systems of the glorious city we know today. Industry and commerce were active. The Paris Exhibition of 1855 was to celebrate the dynamism of France, and the musical centerpiece would be Verdi's new opera.

This was not as paradoxical as it appears to us. Paris, then as now, was eager to be perceived as the center of world, not merely French, culture. For his part, Verdi needed a major success at the Opéra to move up a notch on the international scale, the previous *Jérusalem* having been a rehash and only a moderate success. But working at the Opéra presented challenges of its own. A work given at the Opéra had to follow a certain formula—five acts, with grand costumes and colossal choruses, a major ballet somewhere in the middle, and, of course, the whole affair in French. Then there were the Byzantine intricacies of the state-run facility, with hundreds of rehearsal hours and every decision overseen and debated. Scribe did not consider it part of his job to change lines for Verdi, and in fact took very little active part in creating the new piece. Verdi asked to be released from his contract. The Opéra refused. Finally, *Les Vêpres siciliennes* went into rehearsal. At a late date in the rehearsal process, the prima donna simply disappeared. She eventually returned to Paris, refreshed from a long vacation with her lover. The premiere in June was a success, especially among the many Italians who were in Paris. Verdi didn't accept another commission from the Opéra for over a decade. After a summer of business dealings and inspection of the city's new works, he and Strepponi returned to his farm at Sant'Agata.

Sant'Agata and Two Misfires

Verdi was adding to his holdings and becoming one of the largest landowners in the district. Full of the latest agricultural innovations from the Paris Exhibition and elsewhere, Verdi set about bringing his farms up to date. But Verdi was not yet quite ready to become a full-time farmer. He went to Venice to see a revival of *Traviata*, now reveling in the applause. In Venice, he and the management of La Fenice got so chummy that he accepted another commission for the following season. He then made a quick trip to London and Paris to pursue various lawsuits under the developing copyright laws. Returning to Sant'Agata, he worked with Piave on a sprawling romantic Spanish drama about a fourteenth-century doge of Genoa named Simone Boccanegra. Verdi was more eager than ever to do something truly innovative in opera, but the premiere of *Boccanegra* was not a success with the Fenice audiences. "I thought I'd done something passable, but it seems I was mistaken," he wrote Countess Maffei. Critics raved about the subtle use of the orchestra and the avoidance of many traditional operatic devices, but the audiences were frankly bored. *Boccanegra* scored a few successes outside of Venice, but more than a few failures, and Verdi put it aside for more than two decades. If there was one thing Verdi found unacceptable, it was a bored audience. He also revamped *Stiffelio* for the opening of a small new opera house in Rimini, throwing the action back to the Middle Ages. This was more conventional but made even less dramatic sense. *Aroldo,* as it was called, had a good deal of new and excellent music, however, and it was played around the peninsula for a few years before being categorized as a curiosity piece. After *Aroldo,* he corresponded with Somma about finishing *Re Lear* for Naples. Whenever possible, he retreated to Sant'Agata and tried to keep abreast of political developments through newspapers and letters. Italy was stirring again, and this time Verdi would not be in Paris for most of the excitement.

Viva V-E-R-D-I!

The Hapsburgs, the Bourbons, and the pope, who, between them, still ruled all of Italy except Piedmont, had failed to ingratiate themselves with their subjects after regaining their lands in 1849. If anything, they had become more repressive and intolerant. The idea of ejecting them all was becoming more viable to the average person than it had been a decade before. The rulers themselves thought otherwise. The only ruler on the Italian peninsula who stood to gain from ejecting the Austrians and the Bourbons was Vittorio Emanuele II, the king of Piedmont. His family, the House of Savoy, was one of the oldest in Europe, which gave him a certain legitimacy to those made nervous by republics and Bonapartes. In 1852 the remarkable Count Camillo Cavour became prime minister of Piedmont. Cavour had every intention of uniting Italy as a kingdom under the House of Savoy, a farsighted plan that would not have been popular with anybody except him and possibly Vittorio Emanuele at that time.

Cavour set about on his plan incrementally. In 1855 he persuaded his country to send an expeditionary force to join the British, French, and, of all people, the Austrians in their war against Russia in the

Crimea. He didn't care a whit about the Crimea; what he wanted was a seat at the postwar conference table, and he got it. Meanwhile, the Piedmontese force fought bravely in a small but fierce battle and won the admiration of the French. Verdi was in Paris working on *Vêpres* when news of the victory was announced and crowds spilled onto the streets waving French and Piedmontese flags. French public sentiment grew in favor of Piedmont and, by implication, in favor of the Italian nation. Despite the thorny issue of the French army in Rome bolstering the pope's waning temporal power, Cavour felt that France was Italy's natural ally, and Verdi entirely agreed. When Cavour sat at the conference table, he forced the "Italian question" onto the agenda, and managed to get a military commitment out of Napoleon III, who was eager to reduce Austrian power. Then he continued warming Italians to the idea. Back in Italy, fervent republicans slowly accepted the inevitability of the House of Savoy scheme. One of these was Countess Maffei; probably through her, Verdi was at last convinced. Only Garibaldi refused to budge, swearing up and down that he would march through Italy, conquer Rome, and establish a republic.

Odd that as soon as he became at least a pragmatic monarchist, Verdi chose to write an opera about the assassination of a king. Verdi and Somma realized they could never complete *Re Lear* in time for the contracted Naples premiere, and they scurried to find another subject. Verdi was instantly fired up over *Gustave III, ou le bal masqué,* a play about the Swedish king's assassination at a masked ball. The opera was accepted by the San Carlo in Naples, provided Verdi and Somma agreed to a hundred absurd changes in the libretto insisted on by the censors. He withdrew the opera from the San Carlo. After a few compromises and some clever changes of setting, all arranged by Somma with no damage to the music, the new opera was produced at the Teatro Apollo in Rome on February 17, 1859. Verdi and Strepponi arrived in the Eternal City amid another frenzy. Rumors of war and alliances were circulating. In January, Vittorio Emanuele had addressed the opening of the Piedmontese parliament with a stirring speech in which he stated he could no longer be insensitive to the cry of pain that was reaching his ears from the whole of Italy. It was the first solid rallying cry and political vision Italian patriots really had. Suddenly somebody figured out that Verdi's name was an acronym for "Vittorio Emanuele, Re d'Italia," and walls everywhere proclaimed *"Viva VERDI!"* The people shouted the cry when passing each other on the streets. In this environment, it was surprising that anybody bothered to listen to the music of the new opera, now called *Un ballo in maschera.* The press reviews, however, were calm, apolitical, and very favorable. Verdi had scored a great musical success as well as an accidental political one.

There was as yet no *Italia* for Vittorio Emanuele to be *re* of, but Cavour was putting that country together by bits and pieces. He did back flips to instigate a war with Austria, and finally weaseled a challenge over the town of Piacenza, near Busseto. The Austrians fell for it and crossed the Ticino River into Piedmont. One eyewitness recorded that the prime minister was so overcome by the declaration of war that Cavour, in a rare moment of incontinence, ran to his window and sang the first lines of *"Di quella pira"* from *Trovatore* to the startled people in the piazza below. Napoleon III arrived in Italy in mid-May with a large army, and Verdi was so impressed by this apparently altruistic gesture that he was momentarily ready to forgive the French their *"blague* and their insolent *politesse."* Throughout May and June of that year, Verdi and Strepponi expected the Austrian army to pass through their fields at any time. But although the Austrians carried out brutal attacks and destroyed as much of Piacenza as they could as a parting gesture, the bloodbath took place farther north and Sant'Agata was spared. Vittorio Emanuele II led the Franco-Piedmontese troops to victories at the end of May and the beginning of June, surprising everybody with his battlefield courage. On June 24, the carnage peaked at the battle of Solferino, with 240,000 men deployed and 30,000 casualties. The Austrians sued for peace, and suddenly, before anybody quite realized what had happened, the nation of Italy existed.

Marriage

In the midst of all this excitement, it is astounding that Verdi and Strepponi chose to legalize their relationship at last. On August 29,

1859, they traveled to the small village of Collange-sous-Salève, near Geneva. They had brought along the pastor of a church in Geneva, and were quietly married with only the coachman and the bell ringer of the church as witnesses. Returning to Busseto, they made no announcement of the marriage. The only mention of the event is a letter Verdi wrote many years later. The Verdi scholar George Martin relates a local legend that the composer, as was customary, had sworn to his dying first wife that he would not remarry, and for many years had felt bound by this promise. Phillips-Matz has suggested that the marriage may have occurred in that year because Strepponi's son Camillino turned twenty-one, and Verdi would therefore no longer become financially responsible for him by marrying his mother.

Forging a Nation

The new Kingdom of Italy survived and even grew, despite its shaki ness. Parma voted to unite with the Kingdom of Italy, and Verdi was one of the Parmigian delegates who presented the results of the plebescite to Vittorio Emanuele. Garibaldi landed in Sicily and began his volunteer march up the peninsula. The Bourbon monarchy of Naples fell. Soon all of Italy except the Veneto, still in Austrian hands, and the reduced area of the Papal State were part of the new kingdom. Cavour, however, understood the many problems facing Italy. Truly unifying the disjointed country would require a masterful manipulation of symbols as well as brilliant statesmanship. He personally asked Verdi to stand for Parliament. The composer allowed himself to be enrolled in the election (although refusing to campaign) and was elected as the representative of his district over someone he freely admitted was the better candidate. Verdi, however, was needed in Parliament not for Italian opinion but for world opinion. The northern countries tended to view Italians as an undeniably talented race who cooked well and sang pretty but who could hardly be expected to govern themselves.

It was an uphill battle. At Turin the new Parliament convened amid near-anarchy. Strepponi attended and was given a prominent seat in the visitors' gallery. In one measure of her isolation at Sant'-

Agata, the other representatives from Parma did not recognize her and in fact reported that she was not there. During deliberations, Verdi kept his eye firmly on Cavour when voting time came, following the prime minister's lead in every roll call. Garibaldi entered the chamber dressed in field uniform, kicking over tables, ranting at Cavour, and even snarling at the king. Verdi and many other Italians decided Garibaldi was a hero best worshiped from a distance. For all his admirable qualities, Garibaldi's talents did not include the state-craft needed by the new nation. The national moment of hope at the formation of the new kingdom quickly passed, and was doomed for-ever when disaster struck. Cavour died on June 6, 1861.

After Cavour's death, Verdi became even less interested in Parlia-ment than he had been. When a lucrative offer to compose a new opera for St. Petersburg came, he accepted it and prepared to go to Russia. He had long been considering Hugo's *Ruy Blas* as a subject for an opera, but the czarist government rejected the story of evil noblemen and virtuous servants flat out. Instead, Verdi settled on another wild Spanish play, *La Fuerza del Sino,* by the Duke of Rivas, translated for him by his wife. After finishing this literary task, Strep-poni set about having fur sewn into their overcoats and packing the supplies of pasta, rice, wine, and salami that Verdi would need to keep him happy in Russia.

Escapades Abroad

The Verdis arrived in St. Petersburg by rail in December, and the fabled city did not fail to impress them in both its positive and nega-tive aspects. They allowed themselves to be entertained by the rich in a way they avoided in Paris and Italy, but Strepponi's letters are full of references to the wretchedness of the poor. There were problems at the opera as well. The prima donna fell ill, and Verdi suggested post-poning the premiere of the new opera, *La forza del destino,* until the following autumn. He and Strepponi did some sightseeing, and then returned to Paris the following February.

Once back in Paris, Verdi had a new project of a type that was not to his liking. The London Exhibition had managed to get famous composers from several countries to write new music celebrating Europe's cosmopolitanism. Verdi was persuaded to write a *Hymn of the Nations* for the event, lest Italy, of all countries, go unrepresented at the music festival. The text was by a young protégé of Countess Maffei's, an intense twenty-year-old student from the Milan Conservatory named Arrigo Boito. Verdi and Boito met in Paris and worked out the cantata, which was written for heroic tenor and huge chorus, praising the new age of the brotherhood of man, and climaxing in a great blaze of English, French, and Italian patriotic songs. (The Prussian, Russian, and Austrian anthems were pointedly left out.) Verdi went on to London to produce the *Hymn* successfully during a time when the new Italian nation seemed on the brink of civil war. Garibaldi's volunteers were threatening to march on Rome and take it by force, but they were dissuaded by the continued presence of French troops in the Eternal City. Eventually, Italian government troops fired upon Garibaldi's men at Aspromonte, and the country was in deep disillusionment.

In the fall the Verdis returned to Russia. With rehearsals for *Forza* well under way, they went to Moscow to catch a performance of *Il trovatore,* where they were recognized, cheered, and banqueted. The glittering premiere of *Forza* was held on November 10, 1862, in St. Petersburg. Reviews were enthusiastic. The czar and czarina came to the fourth performance and bestowed honors on the composer. He and Strepponi crowed over the sold-out houses and praised the Russians and their hospitality.

New Currents and Changing Times

Only in hindsight can we see that something was amiss. Apparently not all the audience had been thrilled with *Forza,* although Strepponi chalked up the few hisses and boos to a German faction, presumably partial to Richard Wagner and his theories about "the music of the future." But there was genuine cause for concern. *Forza* was a great sprawling opera in the grandest Romantic tradition, with unlikely plot devices against violent shifts of tone. It featured monks, gypsies, soldiers, pilgrimages, battles, and a lot of windy posturing about honor.

It also demanded the sort of singers who could stand at the footlights and blow wigs off in the balcony. *Forza* did not pretend to philosophical debate. In a word, it seemed old-fashioned. This realization must have shocked Verdi. Just three years before, he was still known as the rabid republican who wrought havoc on the rules of good musical taste and who lived in sin with his woman. Suddenly he was the legally married symbol of the old guard. Was he to become obsolete, a grand figure of the Risorgimento, honored with bronze statues but marginalized by the nation he helped to create? Cavour was dead, and the people were as annoyed by Garibaldi as they were bored by Vittorio Emanuele. Perhaps Verdi's day had passed as well. He returned to Sant'Agata after his *Forza* travels, concentrated on farming and improving the land, and swore that he was done with music.

A new generation was making noise in Italy. They looked to Germany as the center of everything that was modern and forward-looking in Europe. Among these was Arrigo Boito, the gray-eyed poet of the *Hymn of the Nations*. Boito was the son of an artist from Padua and a Polish countess, who separated when the boy was still young. A prolix writer as well as a promising music student, Boito began a series of articles and essays about the "new generation" ready to redefine Italian art. His friend Franco Faccio completed an opera that promised to turn musical Europe on its head. It premiered at La Scala amid a torrent of essays and journalistic analyses, many of them by Boito. The opera created a much greater stir in the newspapers than in the theater, where it played for a mere five nights. Boito, at least, was impressed, and at a banquet he recited a toast in the form of an ode to the revolutionary new art, which would cleanse the altar of Italian art, now befouled like the wall of a whorehouse. The ode was published, Verdi read it, and (not without reason) understood it as an insult to himself. He wrote furious letters to his friends, saying that he would be the first to come and worship at any new altar of art if anyone proved good enough to erect one. Boito perhaps had no idea Verdi was steaming over this ode, and blithely continued to express his contempt for the status quo. He set forth his artistic creed that the sublime was superior to the beautiful. The horizon, the sea, and the sun were sublime because they were spherical, and Dante, Shakespeare,

and Beethoven should likewise be considered spherical. Verdi jumped
on Boito's confused aesthetics. Pumpkins, of course, are spherical,
but, coarse peasant that he was, he didn't see what this had to do with
making music. "To make music you need one simple thing: music."

Fortunately, Verdi kept his thoughts to his personal correspon-
dences, and refused to be drawn into any public debate. He apparently saw something he liked in Boito. When Tito Ricordi began to
suggest that Verdi revise the ending of *La forza del destino* in 1865 for
a hoped-for Italian production, Verdi said he was bored with Piave
and wanted somebody more "creative." Piave, in any case, would not
be able to work with Verdi again. He suffered a stroke in 1867 and
was an invalid until his death in 1876. Instead of Piave, Verdi and Tito
Ricordi, son of Giovanni, discussed the possibility of Boito doing the
revision of *Forza*. This plan came to nothing, but it shows that Verdi
remembered Boito, and not just as the author of the offensive ode.
When Boito's opera *Mefistofele* flopped spectacularly at La Scala in
1867, impresarios wrote Verdi and told him the "time was right" for
the long-awaited Scala production of *La forza del destino*. Verdi wisely
postponed the *Forza* production to avoid the appearance of capitaliz-
ing on Boito's failure. His reticence would pay off. Within a few years,
Faccio, Boito, and Verdi came to realize they shared the same vision,
and the apotheosis of Italian art that the younger men had sought in
spheres would in fact materialize in collaboration with, of all people,
Verdi. In the meantime, Boito began work on his next opera, *Nerone*.
He would continue to work on it (or at least say he was doing so) for
the next fifty years, and it was still uncompleted at the time of his
death in 1918.

Disillusionment

All that lay in the future. For the moment, there were other considerations. The Italian nation, without Cavour to guide it, seemed lost
and hopelessly divided. In 1864 Pius IX issued the "Syllabus of
Errors," which condemned democracy, freedom of the press, liberalism, and practically everything invented since the Middle Ages as fundamentally un-Catholic. Good Catholics were admonished to avoid

participation in the new Italian state, whose government, therefore, was deprived of many able administrators. The king inspired nobody after his moment at Solferino. Verdi did not stand for reelection to Parliament. In 1865 he revised *Macbeth,* perhaps his most experimental opera to date, for a production in Paris. It was not a raging success. In 1866, Prussia, led by their brilliant and stern prime minister Otto von Bismarck, provoked a war with Austria. Italians saw this war as a chance to drive the Hapsburgs out of the peninsula forever. Volunteers rushed to form an army of the Veneto, including Faccio and Boito, who saw action at the front and earned genuine admiration from Verdi. The Austrians were quickly routed by the Prussians. At the peace conference, the Austrians ceded the Veneto to France, which then handed it over to Italy. Verdi was thoroughly disgusted, feeling that Italy had allowed its own honor to be compromised by this transaction. His next commission reflected his disappointment. Schiller's play *Don Carlos,* which Verdi had long been considering as an opera, became the basis for his next lucrative commission from the Paris Opéra. The story, with its vacillating king, young hothead revolutionaries, and evil reactionary churchmen, moved Verdi in new directions, and he poured his experience, emotions, and, above all, his disillusionment into it.

Don Carlos was a success of sorts in Paris. The audience loved the great arias but were mystified by many of the innovations in the score. The opera's anticlericalism did not go unnoticed either. When the character of King Philip II tells the Grand Inquisitor, "Be quiet, priest!" the Empress Eugénie turned her back on the stage. Verdi, it seemed, could not win for losing. He was either a dangerous radical or hopelessly retro. In 1869 Verdi finally ended his twenty-four-year divorce from La Scala and produced a revised version of *La forza del destino* there. It was a smash success. He noted bitterly that everybody complained of old-fashioned operas based around big arias, but those were the only operas they ever paid to see. When *Don Carlo* (as the Italians call it) was produced in Bologna in October 1867, some people were stumped by the massive work, but many were impressed, and none more impressed than the "spherical ones." Verdi was no longer seen by the best musical minds as a voice from the past. This was small consolation, however. Even though Verdi's relations with his father had long been cool at best, and perhaps because of their differences, Verdi was quite depressed by his father's death during the time of the Paris *Don Carlos* rehearsals. One bit of light shined through the gloom. A seven-year-old cousin named Filomena, who had been living with Carlo Verdi, came to live at Sant'Agata. The Verdis adopted her and called her Maria, arranging for her education. Little Maria would later marry a local man named Carrara and settle in the area, becoming a great consolation to the Verdis. But the Verdis could not know this at the time, and the dark mood persisted, exacerbated by the death of Antonio Barezzi in July 1867. Verdi and Strepponi were at his bedside when the great benefactor died, crying the words *"Mio Verdi!"* as he breathed his last.

A Conductor, a Soprano, and a Winter Home

Much of the success of the Bologna *Don Carlo* was due to the conducting of Angelo Mariani. The art of conducting was only just emerging as a major force in European music at the time, and many thought it more important for symphonic (i.e., German) music than for Italian opera. For years, Mariani had been raising the level of orchestral playing in Italian opera houses and demonstrating its importance. Verdi wholeheartedly approved of Mariani's work. They had been friends since the early 1850s, and Mariani visited frequently at Sant'Agata. By the mid 1860s the conductor was quite famous in his own right. His mistress was an excellent Czech soprano named Teresa Stolz, who was making a name for herself as an interpreter of Verdi's music. At this time, the Verdis took an apartment in the Palazzo Sauli-Pallavicino in Genoa, beginning what would become their lifelong habit of spending winters in that city's mild climate. Mariani's apartment was on the floor above.

Strepponi must have been thrilled to have a winter home away from Busseto. Matters had not improved between her and the Bussetani, and in fact Verdi's relations with his *paesani* were also deteriorating at this time. The townspeople decided they needed an opera house, to be named, of course, after Verdi. The practical Verdi thought this was a needless extravagance for a farm town that could not even maintain its own roads and bridges. What galled Verdi, besides the inappropriate expense, was the town gossip that suggested Verdi owed a contribution to Busseto, since the town had, in a sense, made him. He flew into a rage. "They made me?" he asked. "Then why haven't they made any others?" Eventually, the theater was built, but he and his wife were conspicuously absent from the opening, and stayed away. For Strepponi, there was less chance than ever of making friends in or around the town.

When the Genoa apartment was chosen, she made a trip to Milan to buy furniture and supplies. She decided to hatch a plot to call on the Countess Maffei, whom she had never met. Of course, such behavior must be kept a secret from Verdi, so it was all handled quietly. When they finally met, the two women liked each other immediately and fell into each other's arms. La Maffei suggested they call on the legendary Alessandro Manzoni, whom she was in the habit of visiting after Mass on Sundays. Verdi worshiped Manzoni, whose novel *I promessi sposi* had played no small part in the forging of an Italian national consciousness, but the adulation was always from afar. The two had never yet met. Don Alessandro, like Verdi, lived very quietly despite his fame, and received the ladies without ostentation. He gave Strepponi a signed photograph as a gift for Verdi. Upon returning to Sant'Agata, Strepponi let the photograph slip out and land on Verdi's lap. When he asked about it, she casually said that the great man had given it to her when she and Countess Maffei dropped in on him. After catching his breath, Verdi smiled, and Strepponi, relieved he was not angry, joyfully told him all about her secret meeting with La Maffei and how they became instant friends. That Strepponi, who was quite at ease in the greatest salons of Paris and St. Petersburg, was reduced to girlish excitement by a simple little act of self-assertion demonstrates what her life had become.

An Aborted Salute to a Great Artist

Rossini died in Paris in 1868, leaving Verdi the undisputed master of the Italian music scene. While he and Verdi were never intimate, they had met and corresponded jovially every now and again. Verdi decided the great man should be memorialized, as much as an impetus to current Italian music as a salute to past greatness. He suggested that he and several other prominent Italian composers should collaborate on a Requiem Mass, to be given at Bologna (under Mariani) a year from the date of Rossini's death. But the project never came to fruition. Verdi composed at least some of the section allotted to him, but others dithered and finally it appeared impossible to get a good chorus together for the actual performance. Verdi and Strepponi blamed Mariani. This was not strictly fair, since there was only so much the conductor could do, but the friendship was damaged and would never recover.

Desert Breezes and Northern Storms

The next offer came from a rather unusual source. A French Egyptologist named August Mariette wrote a story he published privately and circulated among friends. He showed the story to the viceroy of Egypt, which was technically a part of the Turkish Empire, suggesting that it would make a great opera to celebrate the opening of the Suez Canal. The viceroy gave the go-ahead, and money was to be no object. The favored choices for the commission were Gounod, Wagner, and, lastly, Verdi. (Fortunately, Verdi did not know of this.) Verdi read a sketch outline for the opera and immediately saw possibilities in it. He detected the hand of a veteran of the theater in the sketch, and in fact was amused to hear that the old rascal Temistocle Solera had been seen in Cairo.

Whether Solera had a hand in what became *Aida* or not, we will probably never know, but Verdi at least was interested in the project. The Suez Canal opened in 1869, before any opera had been commissioned. A great celebration was held, with the foreign dignitaries led by the Empress Eugénie herself. The viceroy decided he enjoyed being a stop on the international glamour circuit, and pressed for the honor of a Verdi premiere. Arrangements were handled through Paris. Du Locle, the librettist of *Don Carlos,* was to write the libretto in French, Verdi was to choose a translator and set the music directly to the Italian text. He also had carte blanche in choosing the singers and conductor and in mounting the production, which was all to be built by the finest designers in Paris. The libretto was actually created by Antonio Ghislanzoni, who was entirely docile to Verdi's wishes. In fact, Verdi came closer to writing his own libretto for *Aida* than for any other of his operas. Work progressed smoothly under this setup, and soon Verdi was ready to deliver his score. The premiere, however, would have to wait for more momentous events to work themselves out.

France had been nervously watching Prussia's increasing domination of German affairs. Bismarck noted this concern and decided the time was ripe to use it toward his ultimate goal of uniting Germany under Prussia. He egged on Napoleon III until the less savvy French emperor declared war on Prussia. Italy announced its neutrality. In July, Pope Pius IX called a rare Vatican Council, where, with much arm-twisting, the College of Cardinals decided it was a propitious moment to "reveal" the doctrine of papal infallibility. This effectively ended any chance of dialogue between Rome and the other nations. The Germans routed the French army at Sedan on September 2, capturing Napoleon. The Third Republic was declared in Paris on September 4. The French troops withdrew from Rome, and Vittorio Emanuele calmly occupied the city, simultaneously making it the capital of Italy. Pius went kicking and screaming into self-imposed exile inside the Vatican. Verdi was left strangely cold by this long-awaited moment, and in any case was too depressed by the French defeat to celebrate the incorporation of Rome. He wrote to Countess Maffei, saying that the younger generation was wrong to idolize everything German—at heart they remained a cold, half-civilized race who would bring about the ruin of Italy. "It will not come tomorrow, but it will come," he wrote. When the Germans laid siege to Paris, Verdi was affected more directly. The entire production of *Aida,* slated for its Cairo premiere in January 1871, was stuck inside the city. After some wrangling, the Cairo premiere was delayed until the following winter, along with the subsequent Scala premiere.

A Different German Invasion

Mariani arranged to conduct the premiere of *Lohengrin* at Bologna in November 1871. In other words, the first production of a Wagner opera in Italy would therefore occur just a few months before the Italian premiere of *Aida,* now slated for La Scala in February 1872. Journalists had a field day comparing Verdi to Wagner and imagining a great rivalry. They still do. Verdi was interested in hearing *Lohengrin* but tried to sneak into the theater quietly and avoid a ruckus. Not a chance. First of all, he ran into Mariani, of all people, at the train station, and gruffly walked away. Even though Verdi took care to sit quietly in the back of a box in the Bologna opera house, word got out that he was present, and he was given a fifteen-minute ovation—the very thing he never quite knew how to handle. The singers were nonplussed, and apparently the performance was not very good. Verdi made notes in the margins of the score, sometimes excited, sometimes bored. In the future, he would study Wagner's music at the piano rather than in the opera house. He and Mariani never saw each other again.

The Kingdom of Italy was trying to find an official position for Verdi, who wanted nothing of the sort. He did send along some advice for the new directors of the Naples Conservatory, however. Verdi was not a theorizer; he was, however, quite concerned that Italian composers remain true to their tradition, especially the vocal tradition. He urged the government to institute free choral societies open to all who might be inclined to attend in any town of stature. The true course forward for Italian composers was an immersion in the roots of Italian polyphony of the Renaissance and such composers as Marcello and Palestrina. Verdi was urging new directions in music using the ancestral models as a departure point so that the new music would have a foundation in the music of the people. It was the very same thing Wagner was advocating for his new German nation.

The premiere of *Aida* took place in the Khedive's shiny new opera house in Cairo on Christmas Eve, 1871. Verdi was not there, since he was much more concerned with the Scala premiere in February 1872.

Both were huge successes, and Verdi made a lot of money on the opera. *Aida,* grand and marvelous and very easy to appreciate, was soon playing around the world. It was, actually, full of musical and operatic innovations, but they were subtle and the opera didn't appear to break much new musical ground. It seemed as though Verdi had consolidated everything he had learned over the years. This, however, was a debate for the experts. The public adored *Aida* and immediately took it to their hearts.

The Home Front

Meanwhile, Mariani was dying, but the Verdis did not reach out to him. Strepponi, even more than Verdi, seemed bent on causing the man misery. He wrote her to tell her that his doctors were unable to help with the agonizing pain of his bladder cancer, and in desperation he had decided to go to the holy shrine of Loreto to seek consolation. She wrote him back a cruel letter, chastising him for now adding hypocrisy to his many other sins. This is all so unlike Strepponi that we must wonder if she had some other reason for hating Mariani so. Like Verdi and his priests, something is missing from the puzzle. In general, Strepponi could deal with all sorts of difficult personalities, and none more touchy than her husband.

She would need all the tact she could muster in the next few years, for her husband had reached that point in a man's life when he is most apt to act foolishly out of male vanity. The focus of Verdi's blandishments was none other than Teresa Stolz, on whom the composer was doting. La Stolz had an open invitation to visit Sant'Agata, and may have even quietly bought some land in Verdi's district. Gossip had begun even before, when Stolz was still Mariani's mistress and, briefly, his fiancée. In fact, the Verdis had bad-mouthed the conductor so frequently to Stolz that it can't have helped her opinion of him, but malicious tongues said bluntly that she had left Mariani for Verdi and his greater fortune. After Mariani's death in 1873, the Verdi-Strepponi-Stolz triangle became ever more entwined. At one point, a newspaper carried a scurrilous story of how Verdi's wallet had been found in the sofa of La Stolz's hotel room, where he had made himself "quite comfortable." Throughout all this silliness, Strepponi acted as if nothing were wrong and continued to correspond with Stolz, only occasionally dropping a hint that some discretion was called for. Once, Stolz responded to yet another invitation to Sant'-Agata with a letter to Strepponi, wondering if she wasn't wearing out her welcome. "You are never too much in the way," Strepponi wrote back, "as long as you and we remain the honest, loyal hearts we are." Strepponi must have felt a certain sympathy for Stolz as a fellow artist doing whatever she must to further her career in a hypocritical world.

Lux Perpetua

Alessandro Manzoni died in May 1873. Verdi, typically, did not attend the huge funeral, but went alone to Manzoni's grave a week later to commune with the man's spirit. The spirit must have communed back, because Verdi then submitted a plan to the city of Milan that he write a Requiem Mass honoring Manzoni, to be performed on the first anniversary of Manzoni's death. The city was to assume the costs of the first performance, to be held in a church, and Verdi would retain the rights to the piece after Ricordi published it. Some objected to civic money going toward the work, but the offer was too tempting to resist, and it was clear that Verdi would write the Requiem in any case. Milan might as well be a part of the process, since Manzoni was such a feature of the city.

Verdi must have been itching to write a Requiem ever since the *Libera me* for the projected Rossini Requiem started to collect dust on his shelf. Manzoni's death sparked a mood of reflection in the composer, and questions about the value of fame, worldly endeavors, and ultimately life itself. Verdi had not found satisfactory answers in the Christian religion, but he was thoroughly imbued with that tradition. It was natural that he would want to express his own answers, or lack of them, in a Christian vocabulary.

The *Requiem* was given as a concert, rather than as part of a liturgical service, in the Church of San Marco in Milan on May 22, 1874. Stolz sang the soprano part and Maria Waldmann, Verdi's favorite mezzo, sang the important mezzo part. The audience was amazed, but could only gasp in admiration since they were, after all, in church. Three performances at La Scala followed, the first conducted by Verdi, and the audiences cheered and demanded encores. Many assumed this would be Verdi's last major composition, and thought this was the perfect cap to a brilliant career. All the shortcomings of Verdi's earlier work seemed transcended, and the whole nation rejoiced in what appeared to be a national success. Not all Europe shared that joy. Hans von Bülow, the great pianist and conductor and, not incidentally, first husband of Wagner's second wife Cosima, happened to be in Milan at the time and saw fit to take an ad out in a newspaper to announce that he was not there to attend the *Requiem*. He continued, in his usual less-than-endearing style, to say that he disapproved of all Verdi's music. Bülow's new idol, Brahms, stated bluntly that Bülow had made a great mistake. Anyone could see that Verdi's *Requiem* was a work of genius.

Crisis and Truce

Verdi apparently liked what was said about the *Requiem,* particularly by fractious and theoretical-minded Germans other than von Bülow. A few very successful performances at the Opéra Comique in Paris convinced Verdi that the *Requiem* needed maximum exposure north of the Alps. He arranged a tour for the work, which, with any luck, would become a sort of triumphal march through musical Europe. He even agreed to conduct the performances. He took great care with the singers, and spent what Strepponi began to think was an unwarranted amount of time with Stolz. A great amount of biographical detective work has gone into the investigation of whether Stolz was, in biological fact, Verdi's mistress. Such an issue was probably regarded by Strepponi as incidental. What mattered was that she was feeling neglected.

In the spring of 1876 Verdi was coaching Stolz for the Paris production of *Aida.* Although Strepponi might have been happy to be in the glittering city, which was nicely recovering from the severe wounds of the 1870–71 war, she must have wondered why they only spent time in Paris when Stolz was singing there. And, really, how much coaching does any singer need? Strepponi finally mentioned to Verdi that his frequent calls on a woman who was "neither his wife, nor his sister, nor his daughter" must be easily "misconstrued" by the outside world. Verdi, in the manner of exposed husbands everywhere, became furious. Strepponi was devastated, and continued the discussion in letters written to her own husband in the same house.

Besides the blow to her pride, Strepponi wondered how Verdi's attentions to Stolz might affect her material well-being. If Verdi abandoned her (even though there was no divorce possible), her own resources would be very meager and she would basically be a social outcast. She pleaded with Verdi to do whatever he wanted so long as she were not cast aside. Strepponi even went so far as to write Verdi a letter suggesting they move to Milan, where they could be close to Stolz and where Strepponi could at least take an occasional walk and do some shopping. This pathetic measure did not prove necessary. There was a gradual change in Stolz's letters to the Verdis. If there were love letters from this time, they have not survived. Nor are there any major gaps in the correspondence suggesting times when love letters might have been written. She began to write even more warmly to Strepponi while keeping her comments to Verdi strictly about theater news and business. Strepponi's tact and patience were paying off, as she and La Stolz further developed their sisterly friendship. A crisis was averted, and Verdi and Strepponi did not part. In fact, Strepponi's mood perceptibly improved in the late 1870s, and Stolz became a valuable friend to both Verdis for the balance of their lives.

Convoluted Plots

To all appearances Verdi was retired by the late 1870s. The manor house at Sant'Agata had become the comfortable villa we see today, and winters were spent at Genoa. The Verdis had moved from their winter apartment in the Palazzo Sauli-Pallavicino to the much more comfortable and elaborate Palazzo Doria-Pamphili, then at the edge of town. There were trips to the spa at Montecatini and occasionally to Paris. In Busseto, there was Maria Carrara, the Verdi's adopted daughter, and her new baby to fuss over. And there was money. The farms were turning profits and the improved contracts with the House of Ricordi were bearing fruit even as international copyrights were becoming more effective. No one could have blamed Verdi if he had retired at that point.

There were those in Milan, however, who thought Verdi had yet to compose his ultimate masterpieces. First among these was the remarkable Countess Maffei, who, with her long and comfortable friendship with Verdi, knew him better than anybody except Strepponi. La Maffei saw that the composer was in excellent health, both physically and mentally. Like many people from the countryside, Verdi appeared to get stronger every year. For her, there could be no thought of retirement.

Countess Maffei was still entertaining Faccio and Boito in her salon, and now had made a conquest of Giulio Ricordi as well. Giulio was the third generation of his family to head the House of Ricordi. His grandfather Giovanni had always been a bit distant and very businesslike with Verdi, while his father Tito had run afoul of the composer by mismanaging his accounts. Giulio and his family would become part of the Verdis' very small circle in future years. For the moment, he was making it his special project to appeal to Verdi on a personal as well as professional level. He joined with Faccio, Boito, and La Maffei in hatching a plan. Verdi agreed to conduct a performance of the *Requiem* in Milan in July 1879 as a benefit for victims of a recent flood. It was, in fact, Stolz's last public appearance. The Verdis, undoubtedly at Strepponi's instigation, invited Faccio and Ricordi to dinner at their suite in the Grand Hotel. The conversation appears to have been well rehearsed, and the subject of Shakespeare was broached. Faccio just happened to know that Boito was very interested in *Othello,* and Verdi was persuaded to meet with Boito the next day. The two had not seen each other since the *Hymn of the Nations* almost twenty years before, but they had clearly thought a great deal about each other.

Boito had kept busy since his "spherical" days. Even though *Mefistofele* had been a grand fiasco at La Scala in 1868, it was revised and performed again at Bologna in 1875 with success. It has remained in the repertory of Italian theaters ever since, and every ten years or so American companies "rediscover" *Mefistofele* with great fanfare. Boito also wrote librettos for Catalani and, most famously, *La gioconda* for Ponchielli, which premiered with success in 1876. *La gioconda* has remained in the world's repertory ever since, despite its reputation as the most absurd potboiler in all of Italian opera—no small distinction. Yet Boito's words for *Gioconda* are powerful and singable, jumping out at the audience with a sharpness and clarity quite rare in nineteenth-century Italian opera. In him, God created the perfect collaborator for Verdi.

Nor was the match only perfect on an intellectual level. Boito's father disappeared when he was very young, and perhaps even the young radical's contempt for the old order can be understood in Oedipal terms. Verdi became, in many ways, the father he always wanted. The two men respected each other's great love of privacy and a bit of distance in personal relationships. They continued to use formal terms of address in most of their letters, and Boito always addressed Verdi as *"Maestro."*

But first a collaboration had to be forged. Boito called on Verdi the day after the dinner party, and pitched *Othello*. Verdi pronounced the idea good, and Boito reappeared a mere three days later with a sketched outline. Verdi gave him another go-ahead, although hedging a bit. "It will be good, for you, for me, for someone," he said breezily. Boito worked and Verdi returned to Sant'Agata.

This is when Strepponi's enormous influence became most apparent. If Verdi felt any pressure to compose, he would toss the whole project aside, even if only to prove that he could. Strepponi corresponded secretly with Boito, Ricordi, and the others, telling them when it was a good idea to mention the project, when not to, when to be optimistic, and when to discuss problems. When Strepponi informed Ricordi that the "chocolate project" (their code word for the opera) must be set aside for the moment, he acquiesced. The publisher had a second plan. He suggested Verdi take another look at *Simon Boccanegra,* long collecting dust on the shelves. Verdi was enthusiastic about revising the failed opera, insisting that only Boito would suffice as a collaborator. Verdi pressed him and soon the two had created a new and excellent opera, successfully premiered at La

Scala in 1881, out of the wreckage of what had been the mature Verdi's biggest failure.

Work resumed, intermittently, on the "chocolate project." Ricordi sent a *panettone,* the traditional Lombard Christmas cake, to Sant'-Agata every year, with the partial figure of a Moor carved in chocolate atop the cake. One year it would perhaps have legs, he would hint. Verdi tinkered with revisions of *Don Carlo,* and avoided all talk of the new opera. As singers were sounded out, however, word spread over Italy and beyond. Speculation in the salons and the newspapers centered on what sort of an opera the new work would be. Was there any way a man of Verdi's age could keep up with the enormous developments in music? And if he could, what direction would he take? More than Verdi's reputation was at stake. It seemed that the entire relevance of Italian opera to the modern world would be decided by Verdi and Boito's new opera.

"La Gloria d'Otello"

Although the newspapers speculated on the progress of "Boito's *Iago,"* Verdi never spoke of it publicly and blithely pretended the new work was a secret. If anyone pressed him about it, he insisted he was not writing the opera, and would sulk for a few days. Whenever he was actually working, however, his spirits soared. He apparently sensed the import of the new opera, not only for his own reputation, but for Italian art as well. The Countess Maffei died in July 1886, and Verdi was of course grieved by this enormous loss, but *Otello* was too far along to be derailed. Finally, the great night approached.

It has often been said that *Otello* would have been a triumph at its première no matter what appeared on the stage. This is no doubt true. Even if it had been a flop, the public's affection for the composer of *Trovatore, Traviata, Aida,* and so many of their favorite works would have assured a success. Even so, *Otello* surpassed all expectations. The musicians in the audience were astounded by the brilliant use of the orchestra and the uniqueness of the vocal lines, the poets were amazed by the supple adaptation of the drama, and even the "laity" were deeply moved. Most interestingly, *Otello* was definitively

Italian art, without the slightest hint of imitation of Wagner or any-body else, and was even instantly recognizable as Verdi. Yet it was Verdi transformed, and the transformation mystically justified the art of the whole nation. Critics would still sneer at typical Italian music, using many references to its appropriateness to barrel organs, but they would always have to make an exception for *Otello*. Even the mercurial Hans von Bülow was moved to write Verdi, begging for-giveness for his earlier snotty comments and pronouncing his "con-version" complete. Verdi wrote back a kind letter, and presciently confided to friends that he was concerned for von Bülow's sanity.

A Brief Hangover

Predictably, a period of melancholy followed the excitement of the *Otello* premiere. The death of the Countess Maffei was swiftly fol-lowed by Muzio's, and Verdi's letters of the period are gloomy and maudlin. He retreated to his Sant'Agata/Genoa/Montecatini circuit and insisted he was done composing. He also worked on some phil-anthropic projects, including the establishment of a small hospital in his district that is still operational today. He pointed with pride to the low emigration from his district, while other Italian districts were los-ing their populations wholesale to the attractions of the New World. Finally, he made a casual statement: "If I were thirty years younger, I would begin working on another opera tomorrow—provided Boito wrote the libretto." Streppomi had spent most of her adult life learn-ing to decode Verdi's hints, such as this one. The Bear might be approached for another project.

Falstaff

Boito, as always, had been keeping busy since *Otello*. During the exciting days of the Milan premiere, he began to see rather a lot of Eleanora Duse, the actress who was making herself the undisputed star of the Italian stage. It became a very grand sort of affair, with coded love letters and a few weeks each summer spent together in such romantic spots as abandoned convents in the Alpine foothills. In fact, Boito and Duse seem to have expended more energy in staging their affair than in actually having it, and Boito jumped at the chance to work with Verdi again. He suggested a reworking of Shakespeare's *Merry Wives of Windsor,* making judicious cuts and adding several scenes from *Henry IV, Parts I* and *II* in order to focus on the fascinating character of Sir John Falstaff. Verdi was excited. *Otello* could only be followed by a comedy. And now he had reached a vertiginous level of fame and popularity wherein he could write whatever he pleased and have complete control over every aspect of a production. It would be a sweet revenge for the humiliations of *Un giorno di regno,* his only other comedy. That, of course, had been fifty years before, but half a century was nothing to Verdi, and he keenly remembered insults from even earlier days. He made a few halfhearted protests to Boito—he was too old, Boito needed to finish *Nerone,* and so on, but Boito nimbly countered every argument. Finally, Verdi admitted he was eager to compose *Falstaff,* as they would call the work. Of course, total secrecy had to be maintained, and if anybody asked Verdi what he was doing, he insisted he was working on a little trifle for his own amusement rather than for the public.

Odd, but people still tend to take Verdi at face value on this point, and the cliché that *Falstaff* was never meant for the public is repeated in every opera house foyer as if undisputed fact. It simply is not true, however. From very early in the creative process, he and Boito discussed possible singers, set designs, and so on. Verdi not only wanted a chance to prove that *Otello* was no fluke. He also wanted a box-office success, and hoped that *Falstaff,* with its ideal marriage of text and music, would spur Italian opera on to ever greater heights.

In some ways, *Falstaff* surpassed even Verdi's expectations. He and Boito worked largely by correspondence along with frequent visits to Sant'Agata and meetings in Genoa and Milan, but the harmony of their collaboration was such that the text and music of the new opera appeared to come from the same source. *Falstaff* dispensed with arias and set numbers and presented a seamless tapestry of musical and theatrical ideas so skillfully arranged that even today musicians marvel at it. The general republic responded as well at first. The premiere at La Scala in 1893 was another *furore,* followed by a triumphant premiere in Rome the same year (with Verdi and Boito in attendance).

Newspapers reported that Verdi was to be honored with the title "Marquis of Busseto." Verdi, always true to his roots and genuinely appalled at the idea, wrote a cabinet minister begging King Umberto of Italy to spare him the embarrassment. The minister answered that it was only a rumor. Verdi was informed that "the King of Art in the world today could never be the Marquis of Busseto in Italy."

For a few seasons, *Falstaff* remained great box office, while people jostled to see and hear this revolutionary new work whose music was written by an eighty-year-old composer considered old-fashioned a generation before. There were some doubters. George Bernard Shaw, for one, said that Verdi had turned to this new style of composing through the text without arias and set numbers because he had run out of good tunes like *"La donna è mobile,"* the ubiquitous hit tune from *Rigoletto.* Other experts assumed Shaw was merely being contrary and dyspeptic, but in the end the public tended to agree with him. *Falstaff* received great honors and genuine admiration (especially from Germans such as Richard Strauss), but after a few seasons the public let it be known that they preferred the warhorses like *Il trovatore* and *La traviata.* Verdi was a little bitter when he realized *Falstaff* would never replace his earlier hits, but it hardly mattered now. He had written as he had wanted, and posterity is grateful. In any case, his operatic career was coming to a close.

There was still a new version of *Otello* to mount for the Paris Opéra, which required a French translation and, of all things, a ballet. We see both the gruff and the pragmatic sides of Verdi in his negotiations with the Opéra at this point. Of course inserting a ballet into *Otello* was an anomaly, but Verdi yielded to tradition and wrote the ballet music for the Paris *Othello,* which was presented amid great fanfare in 1894. It was the last music Verdi composed for the stage, and the last time he and Strepponi visited Paris, the city that had been so important to their relationship and their lives.

A Superb Monument

By the mid 1890s Verdi was very wealthy. He and Strepponi still regarded Maria Carrara as their daughter, and could well provide for her growing family. Yet the Verdi estate, in land, cash, and investments, was huge, and Verdi sought a sensible plan for it after his death. With typical secrecy, he approached Boito, whose brother, Camillo, was an architect. Contacting as few extraneous people as possible, Verdi worked with Camillo Boito on plans for a retirement home for musicians. Great efforts were made to make the home as uninstitutional as possible, and Verdi participated in the plans down to the smallest detail. Ground was broken in 1895 for the Casa di Riposo per Musicisti. Verdi arranged for his posthumous royalties to support the home for seventy-five years after his death.

The Verdis now varied their Sant'Agata/Genoa/Montecatini circuit with more and more trips to Milan. Their friends were Boito, his brother Camillo and his wife, La Stolz, Strepponi's sister Barberina, Giulio Ricordi and his family, and a very few others. Verdi worked on composing music for some sacred texts, including a "Te Deum" and a "Stabat Mater Dolorosa." He met with musicians and even the occasional journalist. Everybody commented on his healthful appearance, his energy, and even a certain visual beauty the man had achieved in his old age. Nobody except Strepponi, Ricordi, and Boito knew that Verdi had suffered a mild stroke in January 1897.

Strepponi's Death

Now it was Strepponi's turn to be ill. Throughout the summer of 1897, she ate little and could barely move. Verdi put the finishing touches on an "Ave Maria" and a "Laudi alla Vergine Maria" and sent them off to Ricordi in October to be published with the "Te Deum" and the "Stabat Mater" as the *Quattro pezzi sacri*. With the scores, he sent a note that Strepponi was not getting better. Boito came for a visit and left to arrange for the premiere of the *Quattro pezzi sacri* in Paris. Verdi stayed with Strepponi, supported in vigils by Maria Carrara and her family. On the afternoon of November 14, Giuseppina Strepponi died.

Strepponi asked that her funeral be extremely simple, at dawn, without flowers or speeches. A service was held at the village church of Sant'Agata, with local families present along with dignitaries from the district and beyond. After the service, the coffin was sent to Milan, where it was received by Boito (only just returned from Paris), the Ricordis and their employees, and various friends and dignitaries. She was buried in the Cimitero Monumentale of Milan.

So passed what was, on balance, a remarkable life. Verdi's grief was, predictably, private, but we may safely assume it was genuine and profound. Strepponi's knowledgeable advocacy had helped to create Verdi in the time of *Nabucco,* when he might have quit composing altogether. Throughout their long life together, Verdi does not appear to have asked her forthright advice on his music—he didn't ask for advice from anyone directly and only hinted for direction from Boito. But it is safe to conjecture, from the way she handled his relations with the outside world and the thousand small and large ways she coerced him to compose, that her influence was enormous. During their long life together in Italy, from the days of *Stiffelio* to the time of *Falstaff,* Verdi always challenged himself in new directions and each work of art has an individual identity. We may imagine, though we can never know, how much having Strepponi at his side facilitated this huge growth. And if her life at Sant'Agata was a quiet purgatory, any life for a woman in her position at that time would have involved severe compromises. She sacrificed much of herself to music early in life, but the sacrifices of the balance of her life significantly helped that art achieve its greatest heights ever. She well earned the heartfelt affection her name enjoys among music lovers today.

The Grand Old Man

Verdi continued his routine as best he could after Strepponi's death. He continued to make improvements on his farms. He went to Milan and supervised construction and details for the Casa di Riposo. He went to Montecatini every summer. Verdi had created a family about

him, and was usually accompanied by Barberina Strepponi and Maria
Carrara and her family at Sant'Agata, and the Ricordis, Stolz, and the
frères Boito in Milan and at Montecatini. He complained that the
cook at Sant'Agata was an assassin, and enjoyed nothing more than a
game of cards. He insisted life was ebbing from him, and wondered
aloud why he was still alive, while at the same time amazing
everybody with his health and vigor. Stolz visited frequently. Their
letters from that time are clearly love letters, despite the fact that
Verdi was pushing ninety and Stolz herself was in her late sixties.
There are even hints of physical intimacy in the letters. Verdi seemed
younger than ever. Yet there could be no more operas to write. His
eyesight and memory were failing, and, moreover, there was little left
to compose. The *Quattro pezzi sacri* were applauded, but they lacked a
context, being perfectly appropriate for neither the theater nor the
church. Boito arranged their premiere at La Scala during a concert
that included a Schubert piece and a Schumann symphony. The audience was sparse. Verdi told Boito not to discuss it with him. A sparse
audience is a failure—plain and simple. When King Umberto of Italy
was shot by an assassin in 1900, Queen Margherita wrote a simple
and heartfelt prayer, published in the newspapers. Verdi considered
setting the prayer, and jotted down some notes, but was never able to
apply himself to the task.

Death

Verdi was in Milan for Christmas and New Year's Day, 1901. He
intended to move on to Genoa in February and continue his routine.
It was not to be. On January 21 he suffered a stroke. His doctor was
called, but could do nothing. The hotel and the city of Milan immediately went on a death vigil. Receiving last rites on the 26th, he lapsed
into a coma and died on the afternoon of January 27. Boito, Stolz, the
Ricordis, the Carraras, and a few other close friends were present. As
soon as the news of the death was announced, crowds gathered in
front of the hotel, maintaining silence. Shops, businesses, and government offices were closed for "National Mourning."
    Shortly after Verdi's death, the rising poet and playwright Gabriele

D'Annunzio (who became Eleanora Duse's lover since—in fact, before—her relationship with Boito cooled down around 1898) wrote of Verdi, "He sang and wept for all," encapsulating the composer's ultimate achievement. Lately there has been a desire to see Verdi as something of a saint. This is partly in response to his life-affirming art and also partly due to a barely conscious comparison of Verdi to the man people persist in seeing as his rival, the other colossus of opera, Richard Wagner. Wagner was in some ways despicable and has been called to account for his influence on many of the horrors of the twentieth century. If Wagner is the Archfiend, many find balance by casting Verdi as the all-good Anti-Wagner. But Verdi's art has withstood all deprecations and his life was important enough to be considered on its own merits without comparison to anyone. Verdi was no saint. His human flaws are apparent in his relationship with his wife, his parents, and in every aspect of his life. To canonize him is to do the one thing his art should teach us never to do—that is, to deprive him of his humanity. The man who "sang and wept for all" was always entirely himself, whether he was speaking to kings or to his farmhands. And by remaining true to himself, the peasant from Roncole found a voice to speak for the entire world. It resounds today, louder, more gloriously, and more urgently than ever.

Map of Verdi's Italy

PART TWO

The Operas

Oberto, conte di San Bonifacio

PREMIERE: La Scala, Milan, 1839. Libretto by Antonio Piazza with some verses by Temistocle Solera.

THE NAME

Pronounce it just as it reads, with the last word being "Bo-nee-FATCH-o." Usually one just calls it *Oberto*, unless striving to ridicule the extravagance of early Romantic opera.

IT IS ALMOST impossible to speak of *Oberto* outside of its historical context as Verdi's first completed and produced opera. Even in its own day, audiences were struck by the possibilities in the then new opera, and Verdi was given a contract to write three more operas for La Scala on the power of this. In other words, even when it was new it was most remarkable as a pointer toward great things to come. In retrospect, all this is apparent. It doesn't take a scholar to hear harbingers of *Nabucco, Attila,* and especially *Il trovatore* in *Oberto*. It does, however, take a scholar to sit through an opera solely to judge how it affected a composer's subsequent career. If you are lucky enough to attend a performance of *Oberto*, you may dismiss your fears. *Oberto* is a very good opera, and in the hands of exciting singers it presents some lovely music, a great quartet, and a sophisticated final scena.

CAST OF CHARACTERS

OBERTO, COUNT OF SAN BONIFACIO *(bass)* An imperious role requiring a bass with presence.

LEONORA *(soprano)* His daughter. "Leonora" is the diva name *par excellence,* and our heroine in this opera may well be considered an *in vitro* analog of her more famous namesakes in *Forza* and *Trovatore.* The name seems to imply a woman with an almost leonine quality.

RICCARDO, COUNT OF SALINGUERRA *(tenor)* The chief cad. A real loser, with, however, some excellent music to sing.

CUNIZA *(mezzo)* The sister of Ezzolino of Romano (whom we never see in the opera).

IMELDA *(mezzo)* Cuniza's companion.

THE OPERA

Act I

Scene 1: A delicious countryside [*sic*] near Bassano.

The ladies and gentlemen of the court of Ezzolino pass to the castle to greet Riccardo, who has come to marry Ezzolino's sister Cuniza. Leonora appears, alone and sad. Riccardo had sworn love to her, seduced her, and abandoned her. Now she is rejected by her lover and, because of the disgrace, by her father Oberto as well. Oberto appears, still denouncing his daughter. She insists she wants revenge on Riccardo, and will expose and denounce him publicly. Oberto blesses Leonora, and they leave together in pursuit of revenge.

Comment: The Overture (which Verdi called a sinfonia*) is in the standard form of pretty tunes arranged in increasing order of frenzy. Those familiar with the other operas of the time will notice a certain difference* between this and those of Donizetti. Oberto's is very forthright, almost a bit coarse. Clearly, a new composer was arriving. Riccardo sings an aria most notable for its stratospheric range. Much more interesting is Leonora's scena alone, where her recitative includes a double octave descent. The subsequent aria is graceful with hints of an impending explosion—the Verdi soprano about to be born. After this comes the first of Verdi's magnificent scenes for father and daughter.

Scene 2: A grand apartment in Ezzolino's castle.

Imelda and the guests greet Cuniza and Riccardo on their wedding day. All depart except the lovers. Cuniza expresses foreboding, but Riccardo comforts her with a vision of their future happiness. They leave. Leonora enters, while Oberto conceals himself. Cuniza enters, and Leonora tells her of her seduction and abandonment by Riccardo. Oberto reveals himself and confirms the story, to Cuniza's horror. Oberto hides again, and Cuniza calls for Riccardo and the guests. When all are gathered, Cuniza confronts Riccardo with his conduct, confirmed by Leonora and eventually Oberto, who again comes out of hiding. The guests express dismay.

Comment: The Riccardo/Cuniza duet and the following trio with Oberto do not quite scale the heights, but both sadness and urgency are conveyed well. In the hands of a good singer, Oberto's aria is gorgeous. The final quartet is probably the opera's biggest "hit," and Strepponi was often amused to find Verdi whistling it in later years. Solera wrote this part of the libretto, and the stylistic bluntness that would make Nabucco such a phenomenon is apparent.

Act II

Scene 1: Cuniza's room in the castle.

Cuniza confides to her attendants that Riccardo must marry Leonora. Her own brief happiness is over.

Comment: *This is the mezzo's big scene, but no one, least of all mezzos, thinks very highly of it.*

Scene 2: A remote spot on the castle grounds.

A band of knights ponder the unpleasant situation. They disperse. Oberto appears, having challenged Riccardo to a duel and awaiting a reply. Oberto has risked much in coming to this castle, from which he had been banished. The knights appear and tell Oberto that Cuniza has interceded with Ezzolino, and the banishment is lifted. He thanks the knights courteously, and determines to call upon Cuniza to thank her. They depart. Alone, Oberto declares that the pardon is of no interest to him. All he wants now is vengeance.

Riccardo arrives, declining to duel with such an old man as Oberto. Oberto taunts Riccardo until he draws his sword, but Leonora and Cuniza appear and stop the fight. All four reflect on their various positions: Riccardo ponders his shame, Leonora admits to herself that she still loves him, Cuniza steels her determination that Riccardo do the right thing, while Oberto can only think of vengeance. Cuniza commands Riccardo to marry Leonora. Oberto quietly tells Riccardo to pretend to accept so they can leave and continue their duel. Riccardo offers his hand to Leonora. Oberto goes into the woods to await Riccardo and the ladies depart. The knights reappear, still debating the curious developments. A cry is heard from the woods. Riccardo runs forth, having killed Oberto and now filled with remorse. He begs forgiveness and slips away.

Cuniza enters, telling Imelda she knows something has gone wrong. The courtiers find Oberto's body. Leonora appears, and is informed of her father's death. A messenger appears with a letter for Cuniza. Riccardo has fled, leaving all his possessions to Leonora. Leonora, again deprived of lover and father, despairs, asking heaven for death, while the others pray she be comforted.

Comment: *The final scene of the opera shows us Verdi coming into his own, with a distraught soprano running a gamut of emotions and concluding in a remarkably mature sad aria. Throughout the scene, the chorus* *interjects, sometimes soaring, often merely emphasizing the soprano's state. It is imbued with a kind of breathing quality, a raw human vitality that would become Verdi's trademark. He had the ability to depict this from the beginning, and would refine and expand it through the remainder of his long career.*

Un giorno di regno

PREMIERE: La Scala, Milan, 1840. Libretto by Felice Romani.

THE NAME

Unfortunately, since this is one of Verdi's "obscure" operas, you will generally have to use the complete title for people to know what you're talking about. Furthermore, it doesn't translate well, so saying "A King's Day," or, more colloquially, "King for a Day," will get you nowhere. It is pronounced "oon JOR-no dee Ray-nyo."

IN THE RATHER UNLIKELY event that people hear this opera, they inevitably ask one question: Why was it *such* a flop at its premiere? Nobody, as far as I know, is claiming this work is a great masterpiece, and yet it is certainly as good as many other bel canto comedies that pop up periodically. The music is extremely genial and at times strikingly lovely. Critics say that its initial failure was due to the fact that *Un giorno di regno* is more of a pleasant romance than a gutbusting comedy in the manner of Rossini's *Barber of Seville*. This is hard to credit, since it is very rare that audiences actually guffaw even at the best comic operas (especially outside of Italy). I think that Verdi's music must have genuinely offended the Milan audience on some level we wouldn't understand even if it were spelled out for us. The opera has not been able to escape its opening night reputation, and Verdi did not seek to rehabilitate it as he did with some of his other operas that were failures at first. Instead, Verdi waited a mere fifty years and wrote another comedy for La Scala, *Falstaff,* a masterpiece of the highest order. His revenge was all the sweeter for having taken a half-century.

CAST OF CHARACTERS

THE CAVALIERE BELFIORE, DISGUISED AS KING STANISLAO OF POLAND *(baritone)* This role calls for comic ability as well as a typically Verdian long legato line.

BARON KELBAR *(bass)* A comic, or *buffo,* role. The Baron is the bumbling father notable for his all-too-human foibles, such as a bit of greed, rather than a truly evil character.

THE MARCHESA DEL POGGIO *(soprano)* A young widow, Baron Kelbar's niece. The role calls for light coloratura as well as some heft and some surprising low notes interspersed throughout.

GIULIETTA *(mezzo-soprano or soprano)* The Baron's daughter.

LA ROCCA *(bass)* The Treasurer of Brittany. Another *basso buffo.*

EDOARDO *(tenor)* La Rocca's nephew. This is a lovely tenor role of the *leggero* variety, perhaps the only true *leggero* role Verdi wrote.

THE COUNT IVREA *(tenor)* The Commander of Brest. Purely a plot function. This poor schlemiel is expected to stand about and smile while his betrothed says things like "I'll marry you if my lover doesn't show up within an hour."

DELMONTE *(tenor)* Belfiore's steward.

THE OPERA

Act I

Scene 1: The gallery of Baron Kelbar's castle near Brest.

The servants prepare for a double wedding in the castle. Giulietta is to marry La Rocca, whom she does not love, at the urging of her father the Baron, while the Baron's niece the Marchesa del Poggio will marry the Count Ivrea because she thinks her true love, the Cavaliere Belfiore, has deserted her. The Baron and La Rocca enter, gloating over the wedding as the culmination of their plans. Delmonte announces the arrival of King Stanislao of Poland, and Belfiore enters disguised as the King (who is actually on his way to assume his throne). Asking who is to be married, Belfiore is shocked to hear the name of del Poggio, his love. He dismisses the others and dashes off a note to the court of Poland, asking permission to give up the charade and "abdicate." Edoardo appears, asking to accompany the "King" to Poland since he has been jilted by his lover Giulietta. Belfiore accepts Edoardo, and they leave, but not before they are seen by the Marchesa del Poggio, who recognizes Belfiore and swears to renounce love if Belfiore is false to her.

Comment: Confused yet? We're supposed to be. The conventions of comic opera in the bel canto period dictate that confusion must be established immediately to set the proper tone. The comic duet between the two basses is another stock-in-trade of the genre, so much so that by the time Verdi wrote La forza del destino *he would be able to imply a certain amount of comic relief just by having one bass interrupt another with a few interjections. The rest of the first scene of this opera is attractive, the baritone Belfiore even getting a beautiful slow aria in what would become the great Verdi tradition. After he is alone, the baritone has some unaccompanied recitative. It is quite dull. Verdi did not have Rossini's (not to mention Mozart's) ability to make this form come alive, and he solved the problem by dispensing with* recitativo secco *altogether after this opera.*

The duet with the lyric tenor Edoardo and Belfiore is delightful, if a bit fluffy. The Marchesa's final scena calls for coloratura and trills galore.

Scene 2: The castle garden.

Giulietta bemoans her unwanted marriage. Peasants offer her flowers, comment on her sadness, and depart. Edoardo, La Rocca, the Baron, and Belfiore (as the King) approach. Belfiore announces that Edoardo has been made First Lieutenant, and he permits Edoardo to chat with Giulietta, since they will shortly be related by marriage. Meanwhile, he orders the other men to discuss military issues at some distance away so that the lovers may be able to converse privately. The Marchesa enters, and now wonders if the King really is Belfiore. The Baron and La Rocca wonder what gifts they might expect from the King, who summons them to leave with him. The two lovers ask the Marchesa for help, but she is preoccupied with her own love problems. Eventually, the three consider that the situation is not so sad, since they are all young and in love. Life looks promising after all.

Comment: *Giulietta's role lies rather high for a standard modern mezzo-soprano, as did Rossini's heroines. The scene develops into what is probably the high point of opera, the fascinating quintet. Edoardo and Giulietta sing of love, while the men with their lower voices chatter away comically. It lacks the white-hot dramatic brilliance of the analogous scene in* Un ballo in maschera, *but the important point is that Verdi was already able to explore the internecine relationships of plural emotions in a sophisticated manner. The following sextet brings all the divergence together, while the trio for the Marchesa, Giulietta, and Edoardo is a marvelous ending to the scene.*

Scene 3: The gallery, as in Scene 1.

Belfiore, attempting to help the young lovers, offers La Rocca the hand of a wealthy Polish princess in lieu of Giulietta's, and La Rocca agrees. The Baron enters with the wedding certificate, and La Rocca blithely informs him he has changed his mind. The Baron erupts in a fury, and the Marchesa, Giulietta, Edoardo, and a swarm of servants rush in, all in a state of great excitement. When Belfiore reappears, all are embarrassed to have the King see them acting so badly.

Comment: The finale of this scene is constructed so that the Marchesa's high voice forms the trunk that all the voices twine around. Although the situation is standard comic opera goofiness, we can see Verdi's talent for spotlighting the plight of the individual amid a hostile social environment.

Act II

Scene 1: In the gallery, as before.

Servants clean and fuss about whatever is going on in the castle. "Gentry are like that," they conclude. Edoardo enters and unburdens himself to the servants, still thinking Giulietta is to marry La Rocca. The servants leave and Belfiore enters with Giulietta and La Rocca. Belfiore orders La Rocca to settle a handsome estate on Edoardo so he can marry Giulietta, and La Rocca agrees. All depart except La Rocca, who now faces the Baron's fury. They rush off to fight a duel.

Comment: Critics are divided about the servants' chorus, but I find it charming. Edoardo's address to them is elegant and lovely, despite the pesky high C written into it. The scene ends with another rather silly faux-heroic duet for the basses.

Scene 2: A hall of the castle, off the garden.

The Marchesa is still unsure whether the King of Poland is actually Belfiore. He appears, and the two question each other but say little. Belfiore asks about the Marchesa's true love, and she hints that she would return to him if she could. Belfiore cannot say more, so the Marchesa assumes indifference on his part and affirms her intentions to marry the Count Ivrea. Servants announce the Count's arrival, the

Marchesa leaves to meet him, and Belfiore, furious, slinks off else-where. Giulietta and Edoardo enter. He is miserable because, although he now has permission and means to marry Giulietta, he believes he is enlisted in the King's service. Giulietta promises to beg the King for Edoardo's release. The Baron enters with the Count Ivrea and the Marchesa, who says that her marriage to the Count will proceed if Belfiore does not show up within an hour. Belfiore, still disguised, enters and orders the Count to accompany him on a mission of state. All are perplexed by this development, but just then a courier arrives with news from the court of Poland. The real King has arrived and assumed his throne, and the fake King is to be promoted to Marshal for his service. The Baron asks who the impostor is, and Belfiore reveals his true identity, claiming to have remained faithful to his first love, the Marchesa. All rejoice, not least the servants, who note that the double wedding will take place after all, with happier brides and grooms.

Comment: The scene between Belfiore and the Marchesa is really quite extraordinary. The orchestra plays tricks and the singers feign lighthearted-ness while concealing their true emotion. Intelligent singers can make much of it, since this is precisely the sort of situation for which opera is the best vehicle. The Marchesa has some real singing to do after the duet scene. First is a cavatina with double octave jumps followed by a spry cabaletta. In theory, this should bring the house down. The balance of the opera is strictly pro forma, although quite pleasant. One of the other problems with Un giorno de regno *is that it is just a bit too long for its own scope. Pity, because there is much to recommend it.*

Nabucco

PREMIERE: La Scala, Milan, 1842. Libretto by Temistocle Solera.

THE ROLE OF *Nabucco* in history is well known; the opera itself, less so. Numerous important productions since the Second World War have demonstrated, however, that *Nabucco* is much more than a period piece of historical curiosity. Even the stiffest scholars agree that the opera has a commendable structural coherence to frame its undeniably muscular score. It may be crude and even vulgar, but it is disarmingly honest in its aims and achievements. The choruses are generally impressive, often splendid, sometimes inspiring. Of the individual roles, the prima donna is unforgettable, the baritone lead a great star turn with ample opportunity to display Verdian elegance as well as sheer power, and the bass sonorous and magnificent. The association of *Nabucco* with Italian history is famous, but should not prejudice people into thinking this work has nothing to say to us today. It is a walloping night of lyric theater, and as such it stands in the repertory today.

It would be naive, however, to pretend that *Nabucco* doesn't also provide critics with plenty of opportunity for condescension. There are silly moments, both musically and dramatically. But a bemused smile does not disqualify a whole work. In fact, a little giddiness helps to open one up for the full emotional impact of the work. Laugh, if you will, at some of the prima donna's antics or the convenient thunderbolts and collapsing idols on the stage. All the same, you'll be registering an increased heart rate and probably muttering "Bravo, Verdi!" by the end of the night if you remain in your seat. If we love Verdi for anything, it is because he discovered the musical analog to the essential biorhythms of human life. Although he would explore and refine that discovery throughout his long career, it can already be found in full blossom in *Nabucco.*

CAST OF CHARACTERS

NABUCCO *(baritone)* The Babylonian king, known in Scripture and history as Nebuchadnezzar. An excellent lead role for a baritone who can, despite the fireworks going on around him, deliver a long, rich, and, yes, sweet vocal line.

FENENA *(soprano or mezzo-soprano)* His daughter. Fenena is invariably upstaged by Abigaille. If she isn't, something is seriously wrong.

ABIGAILLE *(soprano)* His presumed other daughter, actually the child of slaves and adopted by Nabucco. Abigaille is one of opera's most outstanding bitches, not so much in what she says as in the number of octaves she takes to say it.

ISMAELE *(tenor)* A Hebrew, and nephew of the King of Jerusalem. A rather small role by lead tenor standards.

ZACCARIA *(bass)* The High Priest of the Hebrews. A very impressive bass role, with important lines in choral ensembles. Ideally, he should sound as if he is speaking for God.

ANNA *(mezzo-soprano)* Zaccaria's sister.

THE HIGH PRIEST OF BAAL *(bass)* Yet another deep-voiced clergyman at the opera house.

ABDALLO *(tenor)* An elderly minister in court of Nabucco.

The action takes place in Jerusalem in 587 B.C. and in Babylon shortly afterward.

HISTORICAL NOTE: The united Kingdom of Israel was divided after the death of King Solomon into a northern kingdom, known as Israel, and a southern kingdom, known as Judah. Israel fell to the Assyrians in 712 B.C. Judah, including Jerusalem, held out until 587 B.C., when Jerusalem was captured by Nebuchadrezzar (as he is now usually known) of Babylon. Solomon's Temple was desecrated and destroyed in this conflict, and the most important people of Judah were taken to Babylon. Solera was sloppy with these facts, sometimes referring to the Babylonians as Assyrians. He also has them worshiping Baal, who was the chief god of the Philistines, not the Babylonians.

THE OPERA

Part I: "Jerusalem"

Setting: The interior of the Temple of Solomon.

The people are huddled in the Temple, fearing God's wrath in the form of the Assyrian soldiers who are storming Jerusalem and the Temple itself. The Levites exhort the maidens to prayer, and they beg mercy from God. Zaccaria, the High Priest of the Hebrews, enters, leading Fenena by the hand. He tells the people to have hope yet, since God has granted them a hostage—Nabucco's own daughter! The people are elated at this news, and Zaccaria reminds them how God helped their ancestors. How can they perish if they have faith in this same God?

Ismaele enters, announcing Nabucco's advance. The people are terrified, but Zaccaria prays that the God of Abraham scatter the false Baal as the rising sun scatters the night. All withdraw except Ismaele and Fenena.

Comment: The opening scene of Nabucco *is an ambitious and extravagant choral collage. It begins with a full chorus singing of terror at the invasion of their homeland, followed by a men's chorus and a women's chorus, respectively. (The comedian Anna Russell, usually more famous for her riffs on Wagner, did an equally excellent analysis of this opera, and pointed out that the women's chorus here was "rather jolly" music for a bunch of virgins who were about to be raped.) Zaccaria's entrance is made with fierce declamatory recitatives, followed by a sonorous, slow, and lyrical passage appropriate to his soothing message. This is all too rare in opera, and we discover that basses, given half a chance, can sing as beautifully as anybody else. The scene concludes with a rousing aria from Zaccaria, which is interrupted by exclamations from the chorus, first in parts and finally in unison. The ensemble after Ismaele's entrance is a more elaborate dialogue between the High Priest and the people. The overall structure, then, goes from full chorus, to parts, to solo, back to parts, solo/choral antiphon, and concludes in full chorus. The individual voice is defined within the group politic. The scene is monumental and extremely effective.*

Ismaele runs to Fenena, his secret love, but she wonders who could speak of love on this day. He finds her even more beautiful now than when they met. He had been sent to Babylon as Judah's ambassador, but was put in prison, and Fenena had rescued him despite the jealous wrath of her sister, Abigaille. Fenena does not want to hear these memories while she is a slave in Jerusalem, but Ismaele promises to deliver her. Abigaille, Fenena's supposed sister, rushes in, sword in hand, followed by Babylonians disguised as Hebrews. They have taken the Temple. She is furious to find Ismaele with Fenena, and swears vengeance. Softening, she offers Ismaele his life in return for his love, but he refuses. Fenena calls upon the God of Israel, whom she now recognizes as true, to save her.

The Hebrews rush in, panicking. Nothing can stand before the Babylonian king and his troops. Hebrew soldiers follow, telling that Nabucco is entering the very precincts of the Temple. Zaccaria is repulsed by such blasphemy. Abigaille announces Nabucco, who enters in his chariot. Zaccaria calls the king a madman, to trespass on the House of God. "What are you saying about God?" asks Nabucco blithely. Zaccaria grabs Fenena and threatens to slit her throat unless Nabucco leaves immediately. Nabucco orders the Hebrews to their knees. Where was their God in battle? Zaccaria attempts to kill Fenena, but Ismaele saves her. Nabucco orders the Temple burned and plundered. The Hebrews curse Ismaele, and Abigaille gloats that the loathsome race will be eradicated.

Comment: Ismaele apparently made quite an impression in Babylon, probably more than his unimpressive role will make on us. Abigaille, conversely, takes the stage the way Sherman took Georgia, with a vocal line plunging to B below the staff and rising to high B. Even in the trio, which is a bit more restrained, she has two high C's to hit to make sure you keep noticing her. Vocal drops and leaps will characterize her throughout the opera. Small wonder the role has been forcing sopranos into early retirement ever since Strepponi's day. The trio she sings with Fenena and Ismaele is noisy and brief, and the chorus enters quickly. Individual concerns like love are suppressed by the command situation throughout the opera. Nabucco's entrance, which marks the beginning of the finale, is to a jaunty little march of an almost Mozartean feel. Clearly, Abigaille is meant to scare us more than Nabucco. The subsequent ensemble is built, uncharacteristically for Verdi, around the vocal line of the bass Zaccaria. It ends in a great presto of general anxiety, or what my grandfather used to call "music to scratch fleas by."

Part II: "The Unbeliever"

Scene 1: A room in the royal palace in Babylon.

Abigaille is reading a parchment she has discovered among Nabucco's belongings, stating that she is actually the daughter of slaves, adopted by Nabucco. Well, she is little better than a slave anyway, since Fenena has been appointed regent while the King is on campaign. Her jealousy of Fenena is boundless, but let them all beware! Once, she was capable of sympathy, but no more. The High Priest of Baal enters with soothsayers. Fenena is setting the captured Hebrews free. The priests of Baal have spread the rumor that Nabucco is fallen in battle, and the people are calling for Abigaille to take the throne and massacre the Hebrews. Abigaille agrees, and gloats that a slave will topple the throne in blood and avenge Baal.

Comment: *This scene is basically all Abigaille, and is in standard bel canto grand scena form of recitative, graceful cavatina, a "messenger" who changes the mood, and an explosive cabaletta. Even the recitative is demanding, including another drop from high C to C two octaves below. Nor does she just hit the lower note and take a breath; she actually has a phrase to complete while wallowing down there in the lower reaches. Do not try this at home. The cavatina is surprisingly lovely for this witch, but the following cabaletta is war fury all over again (two more high C's). The aria ends on a curiously normal note, but most sopranos opt for another high C anyway at this point.*

Scene 2: A great hall in the palace.

Zaccaria is walking, accompanied by a Levite carrying the tablets of the Law. God has chosen him to accomplish a miracle—the conversion of Fenena. He enters Fenena's rooms. Levites assemble in the hall. Who has called them? Ismaele appears, but they recoil at the sight of the cursed traitor. Anna, Fenena, and Zaccaria enter the hall, and Anna asks mercy for Ismaele, since he has saved a Hebrew maid. Fenena has accepted the God of Israel. Abdallo rushes in, announcing the death of Nabucco and the revolt of the people, led by Abigaille. The High Priest of Baal enters with Abigaille, demanding the crown from Fenena. In the confusion, Nabucco enters, takes the crown, and places it on his own head, daring anyone to seize it. All are amazed. Nabucco addresses the crowd. The Babylonian god Baal has proven worthless, since he rendered them all traitors. The god of the Hebrews is no better. Therefore, there will be only one god worshiped in Babylon—Nabucco himself! The soldiers cheer, but the High Priest of Baal is stunned and the Hebrews appalled. Zaccaria warns against blasphemy, but Nabucco orders the old man first to be sacrificed at his altar, followed by all his race. Fenena demands to die as well, since she is now a Hebrew. Nabucco orders her to her knees to worship him as a god. At that moment, a thunderbolt strikes Nabucco to the ground, the crown falling from his head. Nabucco cries, tormented by unseen forces. Zaccaria announces that heaven has punished the blasphemer, but Abigaille takes the crown and places it on her own head, swearing that the greatness of the people of Baal shall not diminish.

Comment: The scene opens with a marvelous aria for the bass as Zaccaria prepares to accomplish the conversion of Fenena. Verdi is never inspired to write great music by religious sentiment alone. In this broad cantabile, we sense an old man regaining, after sore trial, his life's purpose. The following filling up of the stage is accomplished swiftly, a buildup for the startling finale. All is silence as Nabucco puts the crown on his head, then each soloist enters to a similar theme, and finally the chorus exclaims in unison. We have been prepared since the first scene for unison choral exclamations, so the effect is perfectly convincing. The thunder and lightning is, of course, pure kitsch, but what follows is superb. Nabucco begins his mad scene by blithering anxiously, then expands into a plea for mercy that is full of pathos. This must be unique in opera, where madness is almost always indicated the other way around. Zaccaria and Abigaille each make their points in single lines—no aria, no further ensemble. This is the beginning of Verdi's long process of encapsulating a whole cabaletta in a single phrase, a process he continued to refine with great effect to the end of his career.

Part III: "The Prophecy"

Scene 1: The Hanging Gardens of Babylon, with Abigaille enthroned near an image of Baal.

The Babylonians are praising Abigaille, as powerful as Baal. The High Priest hands her a death warrant for the Hebrews, and she feigns reluctance to sign. Nabucco enters, his mind distracted. Abigaille dismisses the courtiers. Nabucco must sign the Hebrews' death warrant—the people demand it. A vague thought troubles Nabucco and he refuses. In that case, says Abigaille, the god of the Hebrews triumphs. Nabucco sets the royal seal on the document, and then remembers Fenena. She will die with the others, says Abigaille. Nabucco searches for the document proving Abigaille's real origins. She produces the document and tears it up. Nabucco begins to realize the hopelessness of his position, and begs for mercy, but Abigaille thinks only of the massacre to come. Trumpets announce the execution of the Hebrews. Nabucco orders guards to him, but none appear, and Abigaille informs him that he is her prisoner. He begs for mercy as she gloats over her rule.

Comment: *Verdi became famous for his touching portrayals of fathers and daughters, but this scene is just shrill cruelty. As such, it is not without a certain novel charm.*

Scene 2: The banks of the Euphrates River.

The Hebrews sit by the banks of the river and think of their homeland, so beautiful and so fallen. What bitter memory! Why does the golden harp of the prophets hang mute on the willow? Let it speak to them of the time that was! May the Lord inspire it with a harmony that pours virtue into suffering.

Comment: *The chorus "Va, pensiero" is the famous excerpt from* Nabucco, *the piece that alone assured the immortality of Verdi's name in the popular conscience. Structurally speaking, it is a musical phrase stated twice, a quiet bridge, a restatement of the original idea, a forte then piano break, and a final restatement of the original idea. It is as simple and unforgettable as the finest anthem or folk song. Rossini first pointed out that it isn't so much a chorus as an aria for multiple voices. Indeed, there is no harmonization until the break, when the voices first hit a high volume level. The parting of the voices adds to the intensity, making it seem as if the higher voices are chewing up the scenery, even though the actual note is merely F (and therefore sung with no loss of confidence or control). Even with this economical harmony, however, the overall effect is of an entire nation singing with a single voice. The orchestration also remains unobtrusive. Repeating woodwind figures accompany the final restatement of the main theme with attention-grabbing rhythm. The effect reminds us of the small eddies and whirlpools of a stream becoming the inexorable flood of a raging river, a beautiful subliminal effect and absolutely appropriate to the setting, the situation, and the lyric.*

There could not have been a better statement of national aspiration than "Va, pensiero." It still gets Italians teary eyed, even die-hard leftists. The chorus is a powerful depiction of all human aspiration amid disappointment, and therefore has particular claims on our beginning-of-the-millennium sensibilities.

Zaccaria rallies the spirit of the people. Why should they weep? Already the Lord has decreed the destruction of proud Babylon. Soon people will search the sands in vain to find a stone that marked the spot of the once-proud city.

Comment: *Zaccaria's "rally-the-troops" prophecy is a fitting muscular ending to the scene introduced by the melancholy of "Va, pensiero." It covers a two-octave range, which may be Romantic opera's shorthand for letting us know that the focus of power is shifting from the Babylonians (represented by Abigaille) to Zaccaria and the Hebrews. This, incidentally, was the passage that Verdi coerced out of Solera by locking him in the room. The longing for freedom, then, is clearly patent in the lyrics.*

Part IV: "The Broken Idol"

Scene 1: A room in the palace.

Nabucco wakes up from a deep sleep, disoriented. He calls for his sword and for the sack of Zion. Voices outside call for Fenena, and from the balcony Nabucco sees her being dragged to her execution. A flash of lightning and thunder clear his mind, and he realizes he is a prisoner. In profound repentance, he calls on the Hebrew god to forgive his pride. Abdallo enters with soldiers. Seeing Nabucco restored to sanity, they rush out with him to save Fenena and restore him to his throne.

Comment: *The aria "Dio di Giuda" is based on a very symmetrical poetic structure, disarming in its simplicity. It is not melodically extravagant or inventive, yet it can make a powerful impression. We will see that Verdi is at his best when he allows the baritone to pour out a beautiful* *tone over a long legato line. The contrast between this aria and all the intensity that has preceded it is also striking. It is, in effect, the eleven o'clock ballad. Italian opera is full of mad scenes, but a "sane" scene— that is, "I was bonkers but I feel fine now, thank you"—is all too rare. In the hands of an artist, "Dio di Giuda" can make the entire audience feel that all is right with the world, or soon will be.*

Scene 2: The altar of Baal in the Hanging Gardens of Babylon.

Fenena and the Hebrews are led to the sacrificial altar. Shouts of praise for Nabucco are heard in the distance, and the High Priest of Baal calls for a quick sacrifice of the captives. Nabucco enters with soldiers and orders the altar torn down. The statue of Baal falls by itself and shatters on the ground. Nabucco orders the Hebrews to return to their native land, where they may rebuild their temple to the one true God. The Hebrews praise this multiple miracle. Abigaille is brought in by two soldiers, bedraggled and repentant. How can she atone for her many sins? The Hebrews exhort her to trust in God, who raises up the afflicted. Asking that she not be damned, Abigaille collapses and dies. Zaccaria tells Nabucco that in serving Jehovah, he will truly become the king of kings.

Comment: The scene opens with a protracted "Dead March." Budden bluntly calls it a "lame" piece of music. Indeed, it is not the score's best moment. Fenena's prayer is much more interesting, lying rather low in the voice and extending the famous "virility" of this opera even into the place where one would have expected tinkly harps and a tweety vocal line. Nabucco arrives on stage with the subtlety of the Marines, and the crashing idol is great fun. More significant is the explosive unaccompanied chorus of the Hebrews, as great a test of the chorus's abilities as "Va, pensiero." Abigaille's death requires a whole different vocal tone than she has yet demonstrated if we are to believe her repentance is genuine. No one knows why she expires at the end—she just does. The final tableau is very brief, and could be interpreted to imply that the fate of individuals— even such a harpy as this one—always merits the last word in the epics of history.

I lombardi alla prima crociata

PREMIERE: La Scala, Milan, 1843. Libretto by Temistocle Solera.

THE NAME

This opera is generally known among Verdi people simply as *Lombardi* ("loam-BAR-dee"). If for some arcane reason you need to use the full title, it's "ee loam-BAR-dee AH-la PREE-ma cro-CHAH-tah." It means "The Lombards at the First Crusade."

VERDI'S FOURTH OPERA followed quick on the heels of the mania for *Nabucco,* and created almost as much excitement as its predecessor. Solera turned to an epic poem by Tommaso Grossi, a popular writer of the era and friend of Manzoni. Grossi's poem was a historical epic written in a self-consciously retro style that used both form and content to awaken patriotic pride in the people of northern Italy. The resulting opera is an intensely virile work of great musical and theatrical vibrancy but also with a certain air of wildness about it.

Lombardi is blatant propaganda intended to flatter the Milanese (Lombard) audiences of the time. Whereas *Nabucco* disguised its patriotism with a veneer of biblical metaphor, *Lombardi*'s opening night audiences in Milan were amazed and delighted to see the curtain rise on the facade of Sant'Ambrogio Church, as familiar a part of their city's landscape then as now. If the libretto were taken as history, one would believe that the Lombards conquered the medieval

Kingdom of Jerusalem all by themselves, although there are a few scattered hints that the French might have helped a little. This sort of audience flattery has earned the opera a bit of scorn from critics, but *Lombardi* proved popular beyond its initial run in Milan. It played the rounds of Italian opera houses and was produced outside of Italy, in fact becoming the first Verdi opera given in New York (1847). The same year it was first produced in New York, Verdi decided to rework it (as *Jérusalem*) to be his debut at the Paris Opéra.

After its first enthusiastic run of the theaters, *Lombardi* fell into a state of disfavor for many years. Solera's incoherent libretto is usually blamed for this. Verdi's music was thought to be powerful in places but weak in others. *Lombardi* was given only on rare occasions in Italy until the end of the Second World War. After the war, several important productions were given in Italy, but the opera only really became popular again within the last generation or so. Judging by the score alone, much of the work appears primitive to the point of absurdity, but in an emotionally committed performance *Lombardi* can come alive.

Verdi has provided material for an exciting evening. It's true that *Lombardi* contains an unlikely and cloying plot, much out-of-fashion poetry, several irksome marches, and a good deal of vocal anarchy, but on the other hand it possesses one thing that justifies its popularity today—an abundance of sheer vitality. That vitality, so marked a feature of *Nabucco,* is present here in a greater variety of forms: a remarkable prayer for the soprano, an interesting and varied bass role, two great choruses among several lesser ones, two exciting chew-'em-up soprano moments, an amazing trio, and much lyric opportunity for the tenor. Our era has found much truth in unevenness, and *Lombardi* can pack a wallop.

CAST OF CHARACTERS

PAGANO *(bass)* Son of Lord Folco. The bad guy, until he becomes a good guy. (This doesn't happen very often in opera.)

ARVINO *(tenor)* His brother. Supposedly a good guy, but hard to love. While he forgives his brother anything, he finds it very easy to want his daughter dead just for speaking out of turn. In any case, Arvino is the second tenor of the opera, the lead being Oronte. Even though the role is designated "comprimario" (ranking just below the primary singers), he must compete in several important ensembles and even gets a very difficult solo scena.

VICLINDA *(soprano)* Arvino's wife. Another comprimario role who must pull some weight in an ensemble. Viclinda, however, is sadly dispatched toward the beginning of the opera, and it is not uncommon to hear a less than marvelous singer in the role.

GISELDA *(soprano)* The daughter of Arvino and Viclinda. A true spinto role, demanding powerful vocal fireworks and the ability to sing very sweetly at times. Because of this, Giselda is even more of a minefield in many respects than Abigaille in *Nabucco*.

PIRRO *(bass)* Pagano's squire. The role is brief but at times quite important in the ensembles. Verdi specifically asked for a very deep bass.

ACCIANO *(bass)* The Muslim Tyrant (Sultan) of Antioch.

SOFIA *(soprano)* His wife, secretly a Christian. She also gets dispatched after providing some important plot information, without even getting any important ensemble lines like her Italian counterpart Viclinda.

ORONTE *(tenor)* The son of Acciano and Sofia. This is the lead tenor role, though more lyric than the heftier, if shorter, Arvino. Oronte is, quaintly, the name of the river of Antioch.

The action takes place in Milan in A.D. 1095, and in Antioch and the environs of Jerusalem in 1098–99.

THE OPERA

Act I: "The Revenge"

Setting: The piazza in front of the Church of Sant'Ambrogio in Milan.

Citizens gather in front of the church, exchanging news of an interesting event. Years before, the two brothers Arvino and Pagano both longed for the maiden Viclinda. She chose Arvino, and Pagano attacked Arvino as he walked with his bride to the wedding. Condemned to exile, Pagano wandered for many years, praying at the holy shrines and repenting of his crime. Now he has returned, prostrate, to Milan, and inside the church a celebration of thanksgiving is taking place. The citizens remark that Pagano still has the same terror in his eyes. Can a wolf really become a lamb? Pagano, Pirro, and the priors of the city arrive in the piazza with Arvino, Viclinda, and their daughter Giselda. Pagano kneels and formally declares contrition. Arvino embraces him, to the cheers of the crowd, yet Arvino is seized by doubt. The people doubt the sincerity of the embrace—Judas betrayed the Lord with a similar gesture! Meanwhile, Pirro lets Pagano know that a hundred men are waiting to serve him. Only Viclinda and Giselda seem happy. A prior announces Peter the Hermit's call to arms against the infidels, and names Arvino commander of the Lombard crusaders. Arvino and Pagano swear to bury their ancient enmity in the war, and the people cheer. All depart except Pirro and Pagano. From afar, a chorus of nuns is heard praying for peace. Pagano mocks their prayers. How could he forget his love for Viclinda? Pirro assembles the gang of cutthroats for Pagano to command, and he swears to shed blood.

Comment: Instead of an Overture, Verdi begins with a short Prelude, contrasting the crusaders' fervor with repentance and salvation. The curtain rises on the men's chorus, accompanied by stage musicians, called a banda. The women enter, accompanied by the orchestra, and the men and women join for a very fast and confusing chorus. The banda resumes as Arvino, Pagano, Viclinda, and Giselda do their business. When the priors enter and praise the reconciliation, there is an excellent and rousing ensemble. The various players are depicted with contrasting music, Pagano's line distinctly out of kilter with the others'. The announcement of the crusade elicits a huge unison chorus, which becomes a snappy march played by the banda.

The people depart and we hear the offstage nuns' chorus, a piece of remarkably sensuous music, considering the circumstances. Pagano sings of his love (for such it is called in Romantic opera) for Viclinda to a marvelously demented andante, full of whacky leaps and drops not unlike Abigaille in Nabucco. *He finishes with an aggressive cabaletta of distinct "I'm so evil" flavor, and the scene closes with Pirro and the chorus of cutthroats (quick change here for the gentlemen of the chorus—expect black cloaks) repeating his theme. The whole scene, then, is wild, anarchic, and somewhat messy, but distinctly rousing.*

Scene 2: A gallery in the palace of Folco, father of Pagano and Arvino.

Viclinda asks Giselda to pray with her. If God should protect Arvino, then they will walk barefoot to the Holy Sepulchre. Arvino enters, concerned about a more immediate danger than the crusade. He orders the women to their rooms. Viclinda kneels, and Giselda says a prayer to the Virgin. They withdraw.

Comment: Giselda's prayer, "Salve Maria," *is in utter contrast to the previous scene. It is preceded by Viclinda's recitative, which the orchestra decorates with shivers passed among the strings to depict her uneasiness. Giselda then prays, to splendidly diaphanous accompaniment, in a melody that begins in formlessness but finds its way by the end. It is a superb study of the process of prayer, beginning with memorized words but finally imparting a sense of completeness to the individual. This is one of the undisputed "hits" of the opera.*

Pirro and Pagano enter, extinguishing the lamps. Pagano goes to Arvino's room, bent on murder, and sets the room on fire. He returns dragging Viclinda, who cries for her husband. As the fire is extinguished, Arvino and his men appear. Pagano cannot believe Arvino is still alive. Whose blood, then, is on his sword? "Your father's!" exclaim the women. Arvino attempts to murder his parricidal brother, but Giselda stops him, telling him not to add crime to crime. In horror, Pagano tries to kill himself, but is stopped by Arvino's men. All agree to let Pagano's life continue and torment him with remorse.

Pagano joins in the curse on his head, calling for the mark of Cain to brand him forever as he wanders in exile, pursued by vengeful demons for the rest of his life.

Comment: This action scene is particularly notable for the swiftness with which everything occurs. Pagano's music is slimy throughout, until at the very end he and the others indulge in another rousing chorus.

Act II: "The Man of the Cave"

Scene 1: A room in the palace of Acciano, Tyrant of Antioch.

Ambassadors ask Acciano, seated on his throne, if the rumor is true. Acciano assures them he saw the gleam of the crusaders' evil swords. They invoke the wrath of Allah on the invaders. All depart. Acciano's wife enters with their son, Oronte, who asks news of the captured Giselda, whom he loves. Sofia assures him Giselda longs for him. Oronte confesses his love for Giselda and is willing to convert to her faith for her. Sofia, a secret Christian, tells Oronte love has sent an angel for his salvation. They leave.

Comment: For exotic Saracen music in this scene, Verdi wrote fast and disjointed rhythms. Apparently, the Muslims are no more serene than the Christians in this work. Oronte's love andante is marked by odd rhythms, yet it is strangely convincing and the first real moment of lyric beauty for solo male in the score.

Scene 2: The mouth of a cave in the mountains.

A hermit comes from the cave, noting the silence in the valley and looking forward to the day when he hears the crusaders' approach with the cry "God wills it!" It is Pagano, who has truly repented of his many sins and now seeks atonement by delivering the Holy Land into the crusaders' hands. He sees a Muslim approaching, and begins to withdraw into the cave, but the Muslim begs for guidance. It is Pirro,

Pagano's former aide, who fled his homeland after the murder of Folco and relinquished his faith. Pagano does not reveal his identity, but tells the penitent to have hope. Pirro admits he is entrusted with the walls of Antioch. They hear the crusaders' approach in the distance. The hermit tells Pirro to atone for his sins by delivering Antioch to the crusaders. The crusaders draw closer; Pagano hears that they are Lombards. Pirro hides in the cave and Pagano dons his helmet and sword. Arvino approaches Pagano and asks the holy man's prayers—his daughter Giselda is held prisoner in Antioch. Pagano, unrecognized, swears that the daughter will be saved, and Anitoch will fall that very night. The Lombards cheer the fall of the infidels and their foolish god.

Comment: The scene opens with some beautiful orchestral scene painting, an overall dreary texture in the lower instruments punctuated by a few flutes. The desert may be harsh, but man has always found spiritual renewal there. The stately cadences of Pagano's romanza tell us immediately that he really has changed this time, his sincerity culminating in the repetition of the crusaders' motto "God wills it!" ("Dio lo vuole"). This will become an important phrase in subsequent scenes. Almost immediately, we hear the crusaders approaching, signaled by the banda playing a remarkably jaunty little tune. The rather rude chorus of "Foolish Allah" ("Stolto Alla") descends to the level of its words, and the curtain descends amid a lot of noise.

Scene 3: In the harem of Acciano's palace.

The women taunt Giselda and her foolish pride. They hurry off. Giselda prays to her mother in heaven, asking to be relieved of her insane love for Oronte. The women of the harem are heard crying for help, followed immediately by crusaders calling for blood. Sofia and the other women run in, with Turkish soldiers, pursued by crusaders. Sofia tells Giselda the city fell from treachery, and both Acciano and her son Oronte have been slain. Arvino and the hermit enter, and Arvino joyfully calls Giselda to his arms. Giselda recoils in horror and almost madness. What blood! she cries. No! No! This is not God's just cause! Insanity and lust for the Muslim wealth rule the crusaders, not piety. No, God does not will it! The fallen will rise and wreak vengeance for the bloodshed, all will die far from their homeland. She prophesies the death of the crusaders and centuries of oppression for the people of Europe, since it was never the word of God for men to shed blood. Arvino is furious at Giselda's words and draws his dagger, but is prevented from acting by the hermit. All assume Giselda has lost her reason.

Comment: *The opening women's chorus is nerve-wracking, but it is intended to be. A very fast 6/8 rhythm is decorated with triangles, long associated with oriental music by Europeans. The rest of the scene is dominated by Giselda. She begins with a brief and lovely prayer to her mother (who has died, poor thing, without ever getting a solo). Sofia, the harem women, Arvino, Pagano, and the crusaders all tumble in within a few bars of music, and the spotlight, so to speak, reverts to Giselda. Giselda basically flips out after she cries "Dio non lo vuole!" and the balance of the scene uses all the devices of a mad scene. The superb irony, of course, is that her words and her sentiments are perhaps the only sanity we see in the whole evening. Perhaps it is the mad women of opera who are the true voices of reason.*

Act III: "The Conversion"

Setting: The Valley of Jehoshaphat, with the Mount of Olives. Jerusalem can be seen in the distance.

Crusaders, women, and pilgrims enter the valley bareheaded, greeting the holy city. Here the Nazarene wept for the fatal city, and mankind was saved. Behold, the living God comes in terrible war! They pass through the valley. Giselda appears, disheveled. She can find no peace. Oronte appears, dressed as a Lombard. He had only been wounded, and in cowardice thought only of his love for Giselda. He fled the battlefield and has lost everything. Giselda swears to follow him. He advises her to consider well. He can offer her nothing but wandering, exile, and loneliness, with the cry of the hyena for their song of love. Not dissuaded, she bids farewell to her countrymen and her native skies, asking her mother's forgiveness from heaven. Crusaders are heard calling for arms in the distance. Oronte and Giselda flee.

Comment: The pilgrims' chorus, "Gerusalem!," reaches a beautiful crescendo and fadeout as the chorus passes over the stage. The broad theme perfectly depicts the sheer amount of miles traveled by these people, while the solo cello figures convince us of the sincere emotion they feel as they see their goal at last. The invocation to the "terrible God of war" is primarily carried, appropriately enough, by the basses. Oronte and Giselda are reunited in nervous recitative and extravagant phrases. (Later, Solera blamed Verdi for the dreadful line about the hyena.) Their subsequent duet is moving, however, picking up the tempo as they determine to flee. The fast section is very brief and free of hyperbolic ornamentation. It is a genuine rush of emotion rather than a posturing.

Scene 2: Arvino's tent.

Arvino regrets he ever had such a base, sacrilegious girl, who has disgraced his name. Knights enter with news. Pagano has been seen among the crusaders' camp. What villainy can the criminal be planning now? Arvino swears to kill Pagano.

Comment: This scene is one of the real reasons why Lombardi *is not given very often, since the tenor singing Arvino must rise to the heights of a star tenor. Managers are lucky enough to find one lead tenor these days. The soliloquy is not short, and the tenor must work to make it interesting. The subsequent chorus is scored for basses and tenors, which means that Arvino must really give voice to be heard.*

Scene 3: The interior of a cave. There is an opening in the rear, with the River Jordan in the background.

Giselda helps the wounded Oronte, who is dying. Giselda prays to cruel heaven. The hermit appears and tells her it is blasphemy to blame God for misfortunes. He offers Oronte new life if he will embrace the Christian faith, and Giselda urges Oronte to live for their now-sacred love. Oronte is fading. The hermit urges acceptance of God at this supreme hour, and Oronte accepts. He is baptized as he dies, and tells Giselda they will meet in heaven.

Comment: The scene opens with a long prelude and extended violin solo. In effect, it is a miniature violin concerto, and as such is a worthy rarity among Verdi's works. Like a concerto, it is composed of three movements: fast, slow, and fast. Musicians don't find much to admire in it, but it has a great effect on the audience. It focuses the ear (so to speak) to a fine point after all the great comings and goings of the opera. The final trio is a famous and popular excerpt, and, done well, a fine example of Italian lyricism. It begins as recitative, with the solo violin reappearing to comment as Giselda lays Oronte down. The violin plays yet again as the hermit promises Oronte redemption, and we realize that the violin has been the signifier of salvation all along. The baptism (which could not be shown on stage at the premiere, but is now invariably shown with great ostentation) is depicted by shimmering cellos and basses in the orchestra—an unexpected and striking effect. Pagano blesses Oronte while the lower strings continue their support and the solo violin weaves up and down the scale. Giselda's line provides the joy, as she declares their love is no longer a sin, and Oronte dies gorgeously. The trio is basically the stylistic key to the opera as a whole, and reading it from a score is not impressive. Nor will it make an effect if sung according to current notions of proper vocal production. Another ineffable something is needed, particularly in Oronte's vocal line—every bit of style and expression the tenor can muster.

Act IV: "The Holy Sepulchre."

Scene 1: A cave near Jerusalem.

The sleeping Giselda sees a vision of celestial spirits, who tell her that the fountain of Siloam will gush forth with sweet water for the crusaders, dying of thirst. She asks for Oronte to speak to her from heaven, and he tells her to go to her people and lead them to the fountain. The vision vanishes. Giselda awakes, agitated. The voice still resonates in the depths of her soul. She leaves to tell the warriors of the Cross about the spring.

Comment: Giselda's vision of heaven is quite conventional, with an abundance of harps and an offstage celestial chorus. Budden thinks Verdi's vision of heaven is "likely to reconcile most of us to the prospect of eternal perdition." Oronte is supposed to appear on a cloud with a harp, not an easy picture to pull off in the theater these days. (A production at La Scala in the early 1980s decided to play it at face value, and sent poor José Carreras out onstage in a white robe and even a pair of white wings, looking for all the world like a rather tall kindergartener in a Christmas pageant.) His stately solo does not impress musicians, but is probably the most plainly lyrical music in the tenor's role, an opportunity to sing pretty and nothing more. For a complete change of tone, Verdi provides Giselda with her most notable cabaletta of the evening, "Non fu sogno," which is as fleshy a piece of music as he ever wrote for soprano.

Scene 2: The Lombards' camp near Rachel's tomb.

The crusaders and pilgrims ask God, who called them forth from their native homes, not to let them perish in the desert. They remember the streams, lakes, and vineyards of Lombardy. How painful is that memory!

Comment: The chorus "O Signore, dal tetto natio" was as famous and as popular in its day as "Va, pensiero." Its popularity rested on its long, shamelessly lovely melodic line and soft undercurrents of rhythm, as well as on its sentiment. Basically, you can gripe about this chorus's frank emotionalism (and its tweety flute figures that annoy a lot of people), or you can surrender to its pleasures, since the broad melody has timeless appeal.

In the distance, voices are heard calling "To Siloam!" Giselda, Arvino, and the hermit enter, announcing that the fountain is flowing.

All must slake their thirst and prepare for war. Trumpets announce the battle, which follows immediately in the near distance.

Comment: The original production included a note in the libretto explaining that Arvino has found Giselda and the two have reconciled. This family forgives almost as easily as they draw daggers on each other. You will also notice that at no point do the crusaders actually drink the miraculous water. The final chorus is very noisy, leading directly into the battle music. The "battle" takes place while the curtain comes down and the scenery is changed, the Lombards represented by the same jolly march to which they had walked to Pagano's cave in Act II, Scene 2, and the Muslims represented by the tune of their chorus at the beginning of Act II, Scene I. A great chord thunders out like the clash of arms, and the Muslims' theme is heard as a wail in the banda, marked "lamenting" in the score. Apparently they have lost. The music dies away. It's all a bit convenient, and far from the highlight of the evening.

Scene 3: Arvino's tent.

Sounds of battle are heard. The hermit, wounded, is brought into the tent by Arvino and Giselda. The hermit reveals he is Pagano, and begs for Arvino's pardon before he must answer for his crimes. Urged by Giselda, Arvino embraces Pagano. Relieved, he asks to see the holy city once again. The tent is opened to reveal Jerusalem in the background, with the Cross flying from its parapets. The people praise God, Pagano thanks God for the last sight, and Giselda recommends his soul to Oronte and Viclinda.

Comment: Pagano's initial phrases are beautiful and light, the sort of sincerity that has eluded his public pronouncements throughout the opera. The grand finale is a hymn of praise for soloists and chorus as the captured city of Jerusalem is revealed. The ensemble is a steady crescendo with a final key change in the last bars.

Ernani

PREMIERE: La Fenice, Venice, 1844. Libretto by Francesco Maria Piave.

THE NAME

The accent is on the second syllable, "air-NAH-nee." Ernani is the name of a small town in northern Spain, which is used as an alias for the hero of the story.

Ernani is a wild gem of Romantic opera, graced with more melody in its few hours than most composers managed in a lifetime. It boasts three solos that rank as "greatest hits," plus superb trios, a rousing martial chorus, and perhaps the most irresistible concertato in the Verdi canon. The story, as such, is a trial to modern patience. The Victor Hugo play on which the opera is based revels in trashing the Aristotelian principles of dramatic unity. Chances for low comedy are abundant; indeed, Hugo wrote some of these scenes as comic relief. The comedy, however, seems to have escaped Piave and Verdi. There are two scenes of multiple lovers hidden in cupboards, for example, making us wonder if the "pure" heroine is not actually a tramp of the first order.

While Ernani is not as blatantly political as its two predecessors, it was considered fairly radical in its time. Anything written by Hugo was automatically a defiance of the authorities. The hero of the play is a bandit who acts with a greater sense of honor than the surrounding nobility. The characters rave at great length about their honor, and generally act without any except when they are grandstanding. The whole aristocratic domain of honor itself is implicitly critiqued. The heroine's disdain for the "despised embrace" *("l'aborrito amplesso")* of her older suitors was understood to signify Italy held in a disgraceful embrace by Austria. The swelling pride induced by the line "Glory and honor to Charles V!" (in the great ensemble finale of Act III) was too much for the audiences of 1845 to resist, and they were soon singing along. One production in Bologna substituted the name Pio Nono (Pope Pius IX) for Carlo Quinto. This was in 1846, during the brief moment after the elevation of Pius IX when the best hope for Italy was a pope-president elected by an international college of cardinals. Accustomed to reading subtexts in a censored society, the first audiences saw what we can only sense—that *Ernani* is intensely political.

The censors raised their eyebrows over the Hugo-inspired opera, insisting on a few minor changes in the libretto. They objected to the overall crudeness of the drama, the drawing of swords in the conspiracy scene, and the manner in which the King was addressed. Verdi mostly stood his ground and even fought to preserve the integrity of the original drama—a novel concept in Italian theaters at that time. Fortunately for him, the Austrian censors in Venice were too caught up in details to notice that the whole feel of *Ernani* was incendiary.

CAST OF CHARACTERS

ERNANI *(tenor)* A bandit in the hills of Aragon (northeastern Spain). Actually, our hero is Don Juan of Aragon, a nobleman bent on vengeance against Don Carlo, King of Spain, who killed Ernani's father. The original details of the story are lost in the present drama.

DON CARLO *(baritone)* King Charles I of Spain, and, after Act III, Holy Roman Emperor Charles V.

DON RUY GOMEZ DE SILVA *(bass)* A grandee of Spain.

ELVIRA *(soprano)* Silva's niece and betrothed.

GIOVANNA (*soprano*), Elvira's confidante; DON RICCARDO (*tenor*), the King's steward; JAGO (*bass*), Silva's steward.

THE OPERA

Act I

Scene 1: Dusk in the mountains of Aragon.

Brigands are drinking. Their leader Ernani enters, sad. They ask him to tell them his troubles. He thanks them heartily and tells them his sorrow. He has heard the voice of an Aragonese maiden, and it has landed on his jaded heart like morning dew on faded flowers. Old Silva, however, intends to marry her. If Ernani loses this maiden, the first who has ever aroused love in his heart, he will surely die. The brigands ask if she is brave enough to follow them, and agree to help take her away. Excited, he looks forward to winning Elvira, the consoling angel of his hard life of exile.

Comment: The opening chorus moves through four separate melodies. This is an early example of Verdi's obsession to keep a forward pace in his operas. Ernani's romanza describing his maiden love, "Come rugiada al cespite," *is as refined and pretty as anything in bel canto, calling for several sustained trills. Right away, we know this is not your average bandit. His cabaletta,* "O tu che l'anima adora" *is rousing good fun and galloping ardor. The two solos combined are often performed as a scena in recitals and on "greatest hits" albums, with the orchestra taking over the few intermediary chorus lines with no musical loss. The problem is that tenors have been decorating the cabaletta with interpolated high C's for the last century and a half, and audiences have come to expect the added squawks. When performed as written and with taste, it is an excellent aria.*

Scene 2: Elvira's rooms in Silva's castle.

Elvira is alone and unhappy. Silva's attentions make her crave Ernani more. If only Ernani would take her away from the hateful embrace of the old man, she would follow him anywhere. Maids enter carrying gifts from Silva, who intends to marry Elvira the next day, but she scorns them, since no gem can transform hate into love. Don Carlo enters calling for Elvira. She asks what brings His Majesty to her at this hour. Love, he replies. She calls him a liar, but he assures her that kings do not lie. And her honor? Carlo promises her the honor of his court, but she scoffs. Carlo asks if she can really prefer the love of a brigand to that of the King. Every heart carries a secret, she tells him. Carlo seizes her, but she grabs a dagger from his side and threatens to kill them both. Suddenly Ernani enters. Carlo recognizes the bandit and magnanimously offers to let him go. Ernani declares his hatred for the King, who killed Ernani's father. Elvira threatens to stab herself if the two men do not stop arguing. Just then Silva enters, offended at finding two men in Elvira's rooms. The King's retinue enters and Silva, at last recognizing the King, kneels. Carlo claims he was visiting the castle incognito to consult Silva on a matter of state, and, unwilling to take unfair advantage of Ernani's situation, claims the bandit is part of the royal retinue. He dismisses Ernani, who leaves swearing to pursue Carlo at a later date until his honor is avenged.

Comment: *The scene opens with melancholy cellos. Elvira picks up a bit when thinking about her clandestine lover. Her aria "Ernani involami" (which means "Take me away, Ernani," and not, as some would have it, "Ernani, fly into me!") is famous for its huge range and its scary exposure of the soprano's voice. A good soprano, however, makes us unaware of the difficulty of the aria. After a brief "pretty ladies" chorus, Elvira sings her cabaletta, which is usually paired with "Ernani involami." Trills galore, but also plenty of the low chesty notes that characterize Elvira throughout the opera. Carlo sings a beautiful baritone arching tune, typically high and fluid. He sounds genuinely in love with Elvira, but shortly attempts to rape her. From a slow and remarkably tender (considering the circumstances) scene, we move toward a brisk galloping trio with Ernani's entrance. Silva stops the action, literally and musically, when he enters. The old man sings a beautifully expansive and self-pitying aria, which culminates in a martial challenge. Each of the four lead characters now has*

*sung a solo roughly depicting his or her nature and situation. From here to
the end, most of the character development will be in ensembles of various
configurations. The chorus enters and an ensemble builds, while all carry
on about their honor.*

Act II

Setting: A magnificent hall in Silva's palace, festooned for the forthcoming wedding of Silva and Elvira.

Guests announce the wedding day. Silva enters, summoning a pilgrim who has asked for hospitality into the hall. Elvira enters in her
bridal attire, and Silva praises the beauty of his bride to the pilgrim.
The pilgrim offers a wedding gift to Silva—his own head! Throwing
off his cape, he reveals himself as Ernani, pursued by the King. Let
Silva hand him over to the King and claim the reward. But Silva has
offered hospitality and cannot compromise his honor. He steps out,
followed by his men. Ernani rebukes Elvira for faithlessness, but she
insists she intended to stab herself on the altar. They embrace. Silva
returns and swears vengeance on the couple. The King's approach is
announced, and Ernani begs Silva to hand him over for execution.
This Silva will not do. He will exact his own revenge rather than
depend on the King to avenge his honor for him. Elvira is sent off to
her rooms, and Ernani is hidden in an alcove. The King enters,
demanding to know why the castle is armed. Silva protests his loyalty
to the crown, but Carlo asks why Ernani was allowed into the castle.
He must be surrendered, but Silva answers that he has extended hospitality to the bandit and cannot reverse his offer without losing
honor. If the King must have a head, then let him have Silva's. Carlo
orders the castle searched, but Ernani is not found. Elvira bursts in
and throws herself at the King's feet. Carlo decides to take Elvira as
hostage to ensure Silva's loyalty. Silva begs him not to, since he loves
her. Then, says Carlo, hand over Ernani. Silva tells him to take Elvira,
since he cannot hand over Ernani. Carlo leaves with Elvira and his
entourage. Silva then lets Ernani out of the hiding place behind the
portrait, demanding he come outside and face Silva's wrath. Ernani

refuses to fight the old man. He will let Silva kill him, but asks to see Elvira one more time. When he finds out that Silva let her be taken by the King, he explodes. Carlo is in love with Elvira also! Silva, shocked, calls his soldiers. He orders Ernani outside to be killed before he attempts to recapture Elvira, but Ernani begs to be allowed to help save Elvira. Silva can kill him after they rescue her. Ernani gives Silva the hunting horn at his side. Let the old man blow the horn when their mission is done, and, wherever he is, Ernani will kill himself. He and Silva embrace in an oath. The soldiers appear, ready to do battle for Elvira.

Comment: If the four lead characters all seem absolutely ridiculous in this scene, we can assume Victor Hugo meant them to be. Silva's obsessive loyalty to the code of hospitality is rendered absurd when he blithely hands over his bride to Carlo. Hugo was trashing the aristocrats' hypocrisy in their selective evocations of honor. Whether or not Verdi grasped this is quite debatable, however. There's not a note of irony in the score in this act—just fast and furious high drama. Verdi, it seems, wished to gloss over with speed and ferocity what he didn't want to explore with irony. The opening chorus is one of a long tradition of bridal choruses in opera whose excessive happiness is at odds with the bride's true feelings. The subsequent extended trio between Ernani, Elvira, and Silva is all action. The middle section, when Silva departs momentarily, is the only love duet in the opera for Ernani and Elvira. Silva protests his love for Elvira to Carlo in a very touching solo, slow and dignified, as befits his years. After Carlo leaves with Elvira, and after the utter goofiness of the "kill me now / kill me later" dialogue, Silva and Ernani join in an oath duet that just misses being truly exciting, despite the choral accompaniment.

Act III

Setting: The crypt containing Charlemagne's tomb in the cathedral at Aachen, Germany.

Carlo enters with Riccardo. Is this the place? Yes, answers Riccardo. The conspirators who plan to assassinate him will meet in this crypt, while the electors of the Empire try to deprive Carlo of the imperial crown. Carlo will wait in the tomb. He advises Riccardo to signal him with three cannon shots if he is elected emperor. Riccardo leaves. Amid the tombs, Carlo muses on the illusions of youth and swears to be worthy of the imperial throne if he is elected to it.

The conspirators enter, with Silva and Ernani among them. They draw lots to choose an assassin. Ernani's name is chosen. Silva offers him his life if he will let Silva kill Carlo, but Ernani refuses. The conspirators clamor for a sacred oath at this moment. They call for the lion of Castile to awaken, and let every corner of Iberia answer the roar.

Three cannon shots are heard. Carlo appears from Charlemagne's tomb. The conspirators cry that it is the ghost of the old Emperor, but Carlo answers that he is the Emperor Charles V, and they are traitors. He strikes the bronze door three times with the hilt of his dagger. Six electors enter, announced by trumpets and followed by soldiers and a dazzling contingent of Spanish and German nobility. Elvira and Giovanna are led in by Riccardo, who proclaims Carlo Holy Roman Emperor. Carlo orders the commoners to prison, and the nobles to the block for beheading. Ernani demands to be beheaded, since he is Don Juan of Aragon, a count and a duke of Segorbia and Cardona. He sought vengeance for his father and his country, but did not kill Carlo. Let Carlo now take his head. Let it be so, answers Carlo. But Elvira begs for clemency. The supreme crown has fallen to Carlo—let him be worthy of it! Better to treat the conspirators with contempt, since remorse will follow.

Carlo gazes at Charlemagne's tomb and addresses the "supreme Carlo." He had coveted Charlemagne's reputation; now he wants his virtues. He swears that he will follow his predecessor's great example. All are pardoned. Let Ernani and Elvira be married and love each other always. All glory and honor to Charlemagne, he cries. All glory and honor to Carlo V, replies the crowd. Silva alone grumbles that his honor is yet unavenged.

Comment: *This single act, for all its supposed crudeness and youthful shamelessness, is absolutely perfect. The opening prelude, played by bass* clarinet, clarinets, and bassoons, is spooky and evocative. Carlo's recitative is full of subtleties and character directives. His aria "O de' miei verd'anni" is vintage Verdi—the baritone voice accompanied by cello. After diaphanous orchestral accompaniment, the big line "E vincitor de' secoli il nome mio farò" is doubled by the full orchestra. This was considered crude, but note how elegantly the cello echoes this explosion at the end of the aria. What begins as a sentiment (baritone voice and cello) becomes something of a public proclamation (full orchestra), to return within the character as an honest conviction (cello). The cello, as so often in Verdi, signifies sincerity. Understanding the shape of this aria will help to inform the glorious finale to the act.

When the conspirators show up, their chorus "Si ridesti il Leon di Castiglia" is one of the most convincing marches ever penned. The first time it is sung, it is sung lightly with a mere tapping in the orchestra. The second time it is a full forte with the orchestra whipping time like flags in the wind. In the hands of a good conductor and a disciplined chorus, this can be inspiring and even thrilling. In the hands of hacks, it can become background music for tossing pizza dough.

The cannon shots, the pounding on the bronze door, and the stumbling in of the entire imperial court can be clunky, but the repartee quickly takes over. Elvira voices her objections in a solo that is all but an aria, with a line that hits the lowest registers before soaring to the highest. Her descent and ascent, however, is achieved incrementally rather than with the sudden drops and whoops that marked Abigaille in Nabucco. It makes Elvira sound like a woman with some valid gripes, rather than a hysterical harpy.

The great concertato finale begins with Carlo's haunting and extremely simple solo, "O sommo Carlo." As we will see often in Verdi, the point of departure is the simple, exposed baritone voice. He then addresses the conspirators and the lovers in broken phrases, forgiving all and wishing the lovers luck. He recovers his regal voice at the stentorian line "A Carlo Magno sia gloria e l'onor," mostly sung on a single note and full of import. At the last word, the orchestra swells to a giant crescendo while all on stage answer "A Carlo Quinto sia gloria e l'onor" in fortissimo unison. After a few lines in this vein, all fade away (and a good choral diminuendo is no easy accomplishment), and Carlo sings an infectious melody in 3/4 time. Ernani, Elvira, and Silva decorate the melody with interjec-

tions, the full chorus explodes again, and the structure is repeated. The melody is unabashed sweeping lyricism of an unmistakably Italian nature. The effect is of giant waves forming, crashing, and receding, while the individual (Carlo) remains always discernible. The whole ensemble emanates from his raw, genuine inner feelings, and, as such, is probably opera's most forthright depiction of a prolonged orgasm. If this scene fails to impress you, go no further. Italian opera isn't for you after all.

Act IV

Setting: A terrace of the castle of Don Juan of Aragon in Saragossa.

Dancers are celebrating the wedding of Elvira and Ernani. They notice one masked guest in a black domino who appears to be intent on destroying their happiness. All leave. Ernani and Elvira come out onto the terrace. From a distance, the sound of a horn is heard. Ernani instantly pales. The horn blares twice more. Elvira asks Ernani why he shudders, and he feigns illness, sending her inside to find him some medicine. Silva appears. He presents Ernani with the horn and reminds him of his promise to die. Ernani knows happiness for the first time in his life. How can he leave it now? Silva scoffs, offering Ernani the choice of poison or a dagger. Where is Spanish honor? Elvira reappears, begging Silva to stop. She loves Ernani. All the more reason for him to die, replies Silva coldly. Despite her pleadings, Ernani must fulfill his oath and stabs himself in the chest. With his dying breath, he asks her to live and remember him. She faints, as Silva gloats over his final vengeance.

Comment: Before we burst our sides over Ernani's utterly avoidable suicide, we must take a look at suicide in the context of Romanticism. The Sorrows of Young Werther, *with its morbid and suicidal hero, was still the influential novel of romantic Europe. Venetian audiences in particular would have understood the political implications of a young hero committing suicide. The first Italian novel,* The Last Letters of Jacopo Ortis, *an analog of* Werther *written by the Venetian Ugo Foscolo, posits suicide as a sensible and idealistic response to blighted love and hopeless politics. The impossibility of real love reflects the futility of seeking freedom, political or spiritual. Suicide, then, is the ultimate defiance, and is—symbolically, at least—sexy as hell. The mystique surrounding the deaths of James Dean and Kurt Cobain suggests that this notion is not limited to the early nineteenth century. Be all this as it may, Verdi wrote a very short act constructed mainly as a trio finale. The dominant rhythm is an insistent 9/8 beat, implying forces out of control driving all toward destruction.*

I due Foscari

PREMIERE: Teatro Argentina, Rome, 1844. Libretto by Francesco Maria Piave.

THE NAME

It means "The Two Foscari," which is the title of the source, a verse play by Lord Byron. "Foscari" is the family name of the two leads. The accent is on the first syllable. *"Due"* is two syllables, "doo-ay." Don't call the opera *The Two Foscari* unless you're an eighty-year-old literature professor at Oxford.

IN THE SPRING of 1844, Verdi was riding a great wave of success. He and Piave were contracted to write an opera for the Teatro Argentina in Rome, and as a source they eventually settled on *The Two Foscari,* a verse play by Lord Byron. The great English poet had settled in Venice after many years of wandering, and immersed himself in the city's history and its many beauties and pleasures. *The Two Foscari* is based on incidents in the 1450s. The Doge Francesco Foscari must uphold the stringent Venetian law even when it condemns his only surviving son Jacopo to exile. Jacopo dies in transport to exile, and the aged Doge dies of grief. History is not well served by Byron's play. In reality, Jacopo was an intractable rotter, and the Venetian government showed great clemency and respect for the Doge in not executing Jacopo at the earliest convenient opportunity. No matter. Byron rhapsodizes on Venice and also explores the severity and secretiveness of the Venetian state.

When setting this strange piece, Verdi captured Byron almost too well. The many moods of Venice are there, beautifully depicted, as are deft attempts at the operatic portrayal of statecraft. But, as in Byron, there is more poetry than drama in the work. Nothing actually happens. There is no moment of decision, no moral dilemma, none of the great devices of tragedy. When we first see the main characters, they are sad. Then they are sadder. Then they're dead. Slow curtain, the end.

Verdi himself sensed this problem. Nine years later, corresponding with the librettist Antonio Somma about creating an opera on *King Lear,* he wrote, "I should refuse to write on such subjects as *Nabucco, Foscari,* etc. They offer extremely dramatic situations, but they lack variety. They have but one burden to their song; elevated, if you like, but always the same." Perhaps because of this invariability of tone, *I due Foscari* has not claimed the same place in the modern repertory as *Ernani* or other early works of Verdi. Yet it has glories. The music, if not the drama, is of a consistently high level. The role of Doge Francesco Foscari is a tour de force for a great baritone who can find drama in his voice. The tenor role of Jacopo is easily one of the most lyrical and least strident Verdi ever wrote, and the prima donna role of Lucrezia gets to express much righteous indignation without (one hopes) turning into one of the viragos who populate many Romantic operas. A good director can find inherent tension in the fabled secret workings of the Venetian government. Most impressively, the opera preserves a superb economy, never wearing out the singers or the audience.

CAST OF CHARACTERS

Francesco Foscari, Doge of Venice *(baritone)* A very sympathetic role, prized by star baritones for its lyricism. The challenge is to portray the inherent nobility of this Doge of Venice while offering glimpses of the tragedy of a very old man losing his son and facing disgrace after a lifetime of selfless service.

JACOPO FOSCARI *(tenor)* Francesco's only surviving son. A tenor role requiring lyricism above all else.

LUCREZIA CONTARINI *(soprano)* Jacopo's wife. Lucrezia is a difficult role, since she must sing with all the fire of a bel canto diva in a mad scene while convincing us that she is a sympathetic character.

JACOPO LOREDANO *(bass)* Member of the Council of Ten and an implacable bad guy, ruled by vengeance and family honor. He is also called Loredan.

BARBARIGO *(tenor)*, a Venetian nobleman; PISANA *(soprano)*, Lucrezia's companion.

NOTE: Piave included a long *antefatto,* or "introductory note," in the libretto for the first performances. You will need to know the following: Francesco Foscari was elected Doge (ruler) of Venice over Pietro Loredano, who never forgave him. Pietro and his brother died shortly afterward, and of course poison was suspected. Pietro's son Jacopo Loredano publicly blamed the Foscari. Meanwhile, the Doge's son Jacopo Foscari was accused of receiving gifts from foreign princes, a major crime in Venice, and was banished to a small town. Jacopo Foscari wrote letters to Francesco Sforza, the Duke of Milan, asking him to intercede with the Venetian government for him, and these letters became public in Venice, provoking a scandal. Meanwhile, Donato, the head of the Council of Ten, which had condemned Jacopo, was assassinated, and suspicion fell on Jacopo Foscari, who was brought back to Venice, tortured (while his father, as head of state, watched), and condemned to exile in Crete. This, at least, is how Piave understood the story, and the opera begins as the state council prepares to inform Jacopo of his sentence.

THE OPERA

Act I

Scene 1: A hall in the Doge's Palace, outside of the Chamber of the Council of Ten.

Members of the Giunta, or assembly, are gathering. Silence and mystery, they repeat to each other, made Venice great. Barbarigo asks if all are assembled. Loredano, clearly eager for the proceedings, urges all to move into the chamber. Chanting their devotion to justice, they withdraw.

Comment: The Prelude begins with excellent "spooky" music, with bassoon and clarinet over pizzicato strings. This is the Venice of horrible secrets. The members of the Giunta enter from opposite ends of the stage, repeating their phrases so we primarily hear the words silenzio *and* mistero. *They are like a ghastly parody of a liturgy. Byron, in his eagerness to convey his sense of dread regarding the Venetian government, imagined a semipermanent state body called a Giunta, one that is less scary than the truly intimidating Council of Ten, whose existence is a historical fact.*

Jacopo Foscari is led in by the Fante, the officer of the Council, who tells him to await the verdict there. The Fante withdraws. Jacopo goes to a window and looks out at Venice, recounting his lonely exile. The Fante returns to bring Jacopo into the Council and receive his sentence. Jacopo hesitates—how can he face his father the Doge as a criminal? He feels only hate. He knows he is innocent. He enters the Chamber.

Comment: Jacopo's musings out the window are exquisite, appropriate to a view of Venice. The strings, marked pianissimo legerissimo, play rapidly alternating notes while a solo flute trills above them. If you can't see moonlight on the lagoon with this music, you probably shouldn't ever go to Venice. This moves into a formal cavatina, slow and plaintive and likewise scored very lightly, allowing the tenor to sing sweetly without pushing. After the Fante returns, Jacopo sings a flashy and defiant brief solo. Verdi and Piave have telescoped all the ingredients of a grand scena into an economical and refined short scene for the tenor.

Scene 2: A great hall in the House of the Foscari.

Lucrezia runs in, followed by ladies. She will not calm down, she tells them. She must go see the Doge. How can a father watch his own son be condemned? And she must speak to the Council, since she is the daughter of a Doge and the daughter-in-law of the present one. Her companion Pisana enters in tears. Is it death, then? No, answers Pisana. In their mercy the Council has voted for exile. Lucrezia explodes. Mercy? What mockery! Now let the patricians (the governing nobility) tremble. God's justice will pay them back. Lucrezia's attendants advise her to trust in God.

Comment: The curtain goes up in a frenzy, and Lucrezia appears like a battleship with all guns blasting. In fact, this is pretty much her mode throughout the opera. When she boasts of her lineage and status, she does so with a two-octave vocal drop. It takes a very refined prima donna (and how many of those do you find?) to make this role win our sympathy. She does get a lovely prayer to sing, to a tune we heard in the Prelude. But she rages again at her cabaletta, when she warns the patricians to tremble. This aria, though brief, is as wild as anything in Nabucco.

Scene 3: A hall in the Doge's Palace, as in Scene 1.

The members of the Council and the Giunta gather and address each other. Jacopo was silent, but the letter from Sforza of Milan condemned him. Let him return to Crete, alone. Let all the world know the impartiality of Venetian justice, which falls equally on commoners and the son of the Doge.

Comment: The chorus opens antiphonally again, as it did in Scene 1, but unites for a classic early Verdi "idiot chorus." Verdi and Piave are almost going out of their way not to show us the Chamber in action by having the news of the sentence put into the scene at the Foscari palazzo, and returning to the Council only after they have left the Chamber.

Scene 4: The Doge's private apartments in the Palace.

Francesco enters. Alone at last, he can vent his true feelings. He is nothing but a crowned slave! His old father's heart must weep, since the father's eyes have no more tears to shed. Lucrezia enters, weeping. What else can she do, she asks Francesco, since she has no thunderbolts to cast at the old white tigers who call themselves a Council? Francesco bids her remember to show respect for the laws of her country. The laws are only vengeance and hatred, she replies, and Francesco knows this, too. Let him, the cruel father, give Jacopo back to her. Francesco, stunned by the insult, protests that he would do anything to free Jacopo. But he is innocent, she replies. Jacopo only wrote the condemning letter out of desperation to see Venice again. But that was a crime, and now he will receive the punishment. If Francesco has no legal right to grant a pardon, suggests Lucrezia, let him at least come with her and beg for mercy in front of the Council. Perhaps some respect will be paid to his age and fatherly pain, if not his title. The tears in Francesco's eyes give Lucrezia a ray of hope.

Comment: *The scene opens in sadness, a cello introduction ornamented only by violas. Francesco's romanza "O vecchio cor chi batte" is dignified and restrained, as befits the situation. It takes a baritone of great taste to give it inner meaning. Lucrezia, however, enters in an obvious rage. Francesco addresses her as "daughter," and the subsequent scene is one of Verdi's many stunning father-daughter encounters. This scene, like its analogs in later operas, is characterized by many different interjections, brief solos, and asides by the singers while the orchestra keeps the unity. The result, somehow, is a single structure with a clear shape, yet much more information has been revealed than in a standard duet where two people sing roughly the same music. This format would become one of Verdi's great accomplishments.*

Where does the emotional power of these scenes come from? Psychoan-

alysts now agree that we ourselves play every role in our dreams. If we allow that opera, in its insistent unreality, is like a dream, then we can imagine that every character on stage represents a different aspect of ourselves. In a sad and difficult situation, one inner voice might advise calm and submission to the order of things, while another would be screaming for action. The "passive" voice might "sound" old and tired, while the "active" voice would be high and strident. The father-daughter dialectics represent the divided self in conflict. Yet this divided situation has a single overall feeling to it. Nobody nailed this moment like Verdi.

Act II

Scene 1: The state prisons.

Jacopo is languishing in the *pozzi*, the dank prisons at the water line. He imagines an old man carrying a severed head and flinging it in his face. It is Carmagnola, the fierce mercenary general who was beheaded by order of the Council of Ten. Jacopo pleads his innocence with the ghost.

Lucrezia enters, consoling Jacopo, but he does not recognize her at first. When he does, she tells him of the sentence of exile, crueler than execution. Sounds of singing and dancing are heard from outside. A gondolier passes. There, all is laughter; in the prison, all is death. Jacopo and Lucrezia promise that their love will unite them though they be separated.

Francesco enters. He may cry now, though in the Council Chamber he had to feign severity. Jacopo is happy to hear his father still loves him. The three embrace.

Loredano now appears at the cell, coldly announcing that the ship for Crete is ready. Jacopo and Lucrezia warn Loredano that his implacable hatred of them will come back to him, Francesco resumes his official stature and advises Jacopo to obey the laws, and Loredano muses on his hatred of all the Foscari.

Comment: *The prison scene is superbly murky. The introduction, solo cello and solo viola, is weird, haunting, and ravishing. Jacopo's hallucina-*

tion of Carmagnola is a chance for the tenor to chew a little scenery. It's also a deft psychological stroke. Every Italian of 1844 would have recognized the image of a man walking with his own severed head in his hand from Dante (Inferno, XXVIII). Jacopo is feeling guilt about the rift his crime has caused with his father, the head of the government.

Lucrezia and Jacopo begin a very disjointed love duet, which is interrupted by the gondolier's barcarole — another ironic juxtaposition of the tourist city with the tortures of the pozzi. The couple resume their duet now accompanied by harp, sadly reminding them of the lapping waters of Venice beyond the walls. Francesco arrives as a private citizen rather than enrobed as the Doge. It may be significant that when he had an opportunity for a father-son reunion, Verdi needed the presence of a daughter figure as well. Indeed, the three-way embrace is very clumsy to manage on stage. Loredano's appearance signals a quartet, wherein Jacopo and Lucrezia fulminate against the mean old man. Loredan and Francesco, though each full of emotion, sing in restrained and measured tones, stifling the emotion of the younger couple with the severity of Venetian law.

Scene 2: The Chamber of the Council of Ten.

The Council and the Giunta gather for the formal sentencing of Jacopo. Loredano enters with Doge Francesco, who takes his seat of honor. He has come because the Council wished it; he will respect the law, wearing the Doge's face, though he also wears a father's heart. He prays for strength as Jacopo is brought in. Jacopo begs his father for a word to the Council, but Francesco does not speak. Will they never meet again, then? In heaven perhaps, replies Francesco. Loredano orders Jacopo to the ship, but Lucrezia enters with her two sons and several other ladies. Jacopo takes his sons in his arms and carries them to the Doge's throne, making them kneel there in supplication. Lucrezia asks mercy and even Babarigo is moved to ask Loredano to relent, but Loredano is deaf to their pleas. The Councilors consider that clemency would set a bad example, implying the law can be circumvented for the Doge's family. Loredano orders Jacopo to the ship, forbidding his wife and children to join him. The Doge, Loredano, and the Councilors repeat the order. The law has spoken.

Comment: This scene begins with static phrases depicting the intransigence, if not the fossilization, of the Venetian government. A certain rhythmic regularity persists throughout the scene, even though Jacopo's plea develops into a stunning sextet with choral accompaniment. The orchestration remains simple, but it is one of the most effective moments in the opera, a study of emotional outpouring within formal restraints.

Act III

Setting: The (old) Piazzetta of San Marco, with the lagoon and the Isle of Cypresses (San Giorgio Maggiore) in the background. Dusk.

Masquers appear, preparing for a regatta. Soon there is a festive crowd. The bank becomes thronged with gondolas. Loredano and Barbarigo enter, Barbarigo noting how happy the people seem and Loredano commenting that the people don't care who is Doge as long as they have such festivities. The people sing a barcarole to the brave gondolier who will row through the waves into the arms of his sweetheart. Suddenly, trumpets announce the presence of Messer Grande, the Chief Justice of Venice. The people disperse in fear before the representative of Venetian justice, and even the gondolas disappear while a galley flying the Lion of Saint Mark approaches. Messer Grande hands the captain of the galley a paper, and Jacopo is led out of the palace, under heavy guard and followed by Lucrezia and the ladies. Jacopo says farewell to Lucrezia. Loredano removes his mask and orders Jacopo aboard. The people and Barbarigo are saddened, Lucrezia nearly beside herself, and only Loredano expresses joy at this revenge on the Foscari. Jacopo tells Lucrezia that they will meet again in heaven, and boards the galley.

Comment: The chorus and barcarole are, of course, an attempt to lighten the atmosphere. The problem is that this device has come a little too late in the evening for it to be effective. The sudden shift in tone from gaiety to severity is a startling setup for yet another sad ensemble. Jacopo and Lucrezia can give more vent to their feelings here than in the Council Chamber. The ensemble is lovely and very simple but quite expressive.

Scene 2: The Doge's private apartment.

Francesco laments Jacopo's exile. Death took three sons from him, now a living death takes the fourth and last. He removes the *corno,* the Doge's crown. Better to be dead than carry around that useless weight. And now he must die alone. Barbarigo enters in haste. He bears a letter from the criminal Erizzo, who on his deathbed confessed to the murder of Donato. Francesco is joyous. Now his innocent son can be restored to him! But Lucrezia enters, almost crazed. Jacopo died of grief as the ship left the lagoon. She calls for grief to yield to vengeance, and leaves.

A servant announces the Council of Ten, who demand to speak to the Doge. Francesco wonders what further humiliation awaits him. He replaces the *corno* on his head while the Council and the Giunta gather around. Loredano says the Council and the Senate agree that the aged Doge must retire. They are there to remove the ducal ring. Francesco refuses to comply. Twice he has asked to abdicate, and twice been refused. Now no mortal will remove him. The men demand it. He asks for Lucrezia, and removes the ducal ring from his finger. Loredano attempts to remove the *corno,* but Francesco tells him his hands are unworthy to touch it. He removes it himself. Lucrezia appears, and Francesco takes her arm to leave. A bell tolls, signaling the election of a new Doge. Loredano joyously breaks the news to Francesco, but Barbarigo and the others tell him the old man has suffered enough. Let his pain be respected. Francesco hears his own death foretold in the tolling of the bell; with a cry of "My son!" he dies. Loredano looks upon Foscari's body, and says, "Now I am repaid!"

Comment: *The final scene of the opera is as gloomy and sad as the synopsis suggests, and is primarily a tour de force for the baritone. His opening andante would, in standard bel canto procedure, require a cabaletta for* *emotional closure, but Francesco is no longer emotionally capable of a cabaletta. Lucrezia's entrance with bad news fills this need. From then on, the scene is a steady decline, beginning with an exhausted aria for Francesco and a painfully sad ensemble. If the baritone can portray pathos without chewing up the scenery, Francesco's death scene is devastating. If not, it is rather dull. Loredano's final line is a reference to an entry he supposedly made in his account book after the death of Doge Foscari, where he wrote, "The Foscari have repaid me."*

Giovanna d'Arco

PREMIERE: La Scala, Milan, 1845. Libretto by Temistocle Solera.

THE NAME

The title refers to Joan of Arc, and is pronounced "joe-VAHN-nah DAR-ko." The first name alone usually suffices among Verdi fans.

THIS WAS Verdi's fifth opera written for La Scala, and his last for many years. It was wildly successful at its premiere, made the rounds of important Italian theaters, and then basically disappeared.

Commentators often credit the initial success of *Giovanna* to the general giddiness of Italian audiences of the time, fueled by a rush of nationalist fervor finding its expression in their new idol, Verdi. There is truth in this, but only oblique truth. Patriotism and war are not the keys to this opera, although they are present. The opera is best when it focuses on its title character. Giovanna lives on an entirely separate level from the world around her—musically, dramatically, and, of course, spiritually. Her music is dignified and occasionally transcendent. This can be appreciated on the macro level, as the voice of an oppressed nation, or on the individual level. The nexus of the individual and the communal voice represented by Giovanna is the source of the emotion-based patriotism of the opera. Budden felt the opera was, in the final analysis, a vehicle for a star prima donna, albeit one lacking in vocal fireworks. Giovanna is actually the first of Verdi's many prima donna roles that encapsulate an archetype. We will see this come to full flower in *Traviata.*

Giovanna has not achieved great popularity outside of Italy. There is an unevenness to it, a lack of a single vision of what the work should be when it moves beyond the lead characters. However, it is well worth hearing. The very simple father-daughter-lover (read baritone-soprano-tenor) conflict at the center of the story is forthright and involving. Like *I due Foscari, Giovanna* manages to tell its story in about two hours, soaring to a few superb heights along the way.

CAST OF CHARACTERS

CARLO VII *(tenor)* King of France. This is our tenor hero, who of course must fall in love with our prima donna heroine. Carlo is something of a wimp who must let his sweetheart win battles for him, a scandalous idea. While he is sympathetic, his music tends to be somewhat too introspective for the average tenor to make interesting.

GIACOMO *(baritone)* A shepherd. Verdi rarely erred when he had a baritone father figure to work with. If Giacomo's words make him sound like a cruel and hateful man, some of his music wins our sympathy through sheer lyricism.

GIOVANNA *(soprano)* His daughter. History's Joan of Arc, sort of. Giovanna is the definitive "woman outside of society," who defies societal expectations in a spectacular way. Abigaille in *Nabucco* is outside of society because she is such a strident, power-craving virago. Giovanna, on the other hand, is either following divine revelation or at least sincerely believes she is. Her role dominates the opera, largely through a certain sustained dignity.

DELIL *(tenor)*, an officer of the King; TALBOT *(bass)*, the English commander.

NOTE: The source of the story is *Die Jungfrau von Orleans,* by Friedrich Schiller. The great German Romantic dramatist paid even less attention to history in this story than in his sprawling work *Don*

Carlos. The love affair between Carlo and Giovanna is pure theatrical license.

THE OPERA

Overture

Comment: *The Overture is a perfectly constructed little summary of the work. It begins fast, moves to a pastoral andante section, and ends fast and loud. We get the picture of the simple shepherdess surrounded by great and noisy events.*

Prologue

Scene 1: A field outside of Rheims, after battle.

The French people question officials about the recent defeats at the hands of the English. The situation is grave. King Carlo VII enters, sad but still dignified. He absolves the people from their oaths of loyalty, and tells them he will abdicate in favor of the English King. If God must punish France, let Him punish Carlo alone. In a vision, the Virgin had commanded him to lay his crown and arms at the feet of her statue. The people tell Carlo there is a statue of the Virgin in the forest nearby, but it is in a dreadful spot where demons congregate. Carlo says he will go there and do as his vision commanded. He will set aside his painful crown there, and seek the peace that is the right of even the poorest beggar. The people pray for the King to recover his fighting spirit. Until then, they will follow him, though he forbids it.

Comment: *The opening chorus is sung against insistent rock-and-roll-like string beats, creating a mood that would be fully explored later in* Trovatore. *Carlo is not our typical tenor. He makes his official pronouncements against full orchestral punctuations, then becomes more graceful when describing his dream and addressing the Virgin. This portrays the gulf between official and genuine feelings. The chorus interrupts with some goofy witch-and-devil music, repeating "Guai!" ("Woe!") nine times. Carlo's closing exit is surprisingly languid, depicting both his capac-*

*ity for reflection and his present defeated state. The quiet ending is very
daring.*

Scene 2: A clearing in the woods, with a shrine to the Virgin.

A storm is dying down. Giacomo approaches the shrine of the Virgin. His daughter has been coming to this oak tree cherished by
witches. Could she be in the snares of the Devil? He will wait and see.
Giovanna arrives. Her soul is unsettled, yearning to fight in battle.
She prays to the Virgin for a sword and helmet, then, shocked at her
own audacity, asks pardon for her bold request. Charles enters and
sets his arms at the base of the Virgin's statue. Meanwhile, Giovanna
hears a chorus of demons telling her she's a beautiful girl, but she's
crazy if she wastes her youth in piety. A chorus of angels bids her rise
and accept her destiny as the savior of France, warning her to beware
if her heart should succumb to worldly love. Giovanna leaps to her
feet and approaches Carlo, whom she recognizes as the King. God
has heard his prayers, and she will deliver him to glory. Giacomo
appears, unseen. He suspects that Giovanna has given herself to the
Devil out of a mad love for the King. He swears a father's wrath on
her, while Giovanna and Carlo praise God and the Virgin for the
granting of their highest dreams.

Comment: *The opening storm music is over very quickly. Verdi may not
have intended a bell to be rung during this, but you can expect to hear one
if you're lucky enough to attend a performance of this opera. Why err on
the side of understatement? Giovanna's prayer is broad and noble, growing bolder (read "higher") as it continues. As she asks the Virgin for forgiveness, there is an elegant quote of the previous "march" theme in the
strings. In other words, Giovanna says she repents of her pride, but she still
yearns for martial glory.*

  *It's worth taking a close look at the jaunty offstage Devils' Chorus,
since it's Verdi's first assay into this realm. "Tu sei bella" is a waltz of the
most unpretentious kind, accompanied by harmonium and triangle.
Within days of Giovanna's premiere, this chorus was heard on barrel
organs throughout Milan, and the tune was repeated by street singers*

throughout Italy in no time. Musicologists feel this popularity proves the banality of the tune. Conversely, one could look back with a sigh on the days when pushcart vendors sang music premiered at La Scala the previous evening. Budden was genuinely offended by it, saying it had an "innocent vulgarity which reeks of the Neapolitan café." Program notes apologize for it and audiences tend to titter.

Act I

Scene 1: The English camp near Rheims.

The English commander Talbot commiserates with his soldiers and their followers. How can all of their victories have been erased in a single day? The soldiers tell Talbot human valor is no match for the powers of hell. Giacomo bursts on the scene promising that the wicked woman who strikes them shall be delivered to them. How can a Frenchman speak such rash words? There is more, explains Giacomo. There are also the words of a father who has been betrayed by his daughter. The English swear revenge on the vile seducer Carlo.

Comment: *The scene opens with unmistakable panic music. The English are not only defeated, they are astounded by events. Giacomo's solo* "Franco son io" *and his cabaletta* "So che per via dei triboli" *are superbly restrained, appropriate for a father trying to subdue his feelings. But it takes a baritone of the highest quality to make subdued into interesting, and the best baritones are not often available for this role.*

Scene 2: A garden of the royal residence at Rheims.

Giovanna seeks refuge from the palace festivities in the quiet garden. She decides to return at once to her woods, her father, and her simple life. Carlo approaches, asking why she has left the palace. She tells him it is time for her to leave. The Virgin's work is done. Stung, Carlo tells her his love for her is pure and honorable, and he intends to marry her immediately. She begs him to stop, feeling herself succumbing to his sweet words. When she confesses her love for Carlo, she hears the angelic chorus telling her to beware of human love. Giovanna is amazed that he doesn't hear the voices. She must be accursed to hear such things; her father must have cursed her. The members of the court appear. All is ready for the great wedding of Carlo and Giovanna. Carlo hopes that the cheers of the crowd will restore her good spirits. Giovanna hears the demons again, singing victory to Satan. This stupid peasant girl thought she was pure. Hah! Giovanna desperately cries that she is accursed, deaf to Carlo's pleas. He seizes her by the hand and leads her away, while the demons revel in their victory.

Comment: As with "Tu sei bella" in the Prologue, the Devils' Chorus here tends to send commentators into fits. Budden laments Verdi's inability to portray the underworld, saying about this chorus "of genuine horror there is none." This is correct, but is this necessarily a failure on Verdi's part? Horror is a genre particular to the northern European cultures. The Devil, like any tourist, behaves differently in Italy than he does in Germany. In Italian folklore, devils are everywhere and are quite comfortable mixing with people. In Dante's Inferno, *the true terrors are represented not by devils but by the souls (i.e., the people) in Hell. That is Verdi's point as well. Any genuine horror must be conveyed by Giovanna, not by the demons. Nor do we need a Freud to inform us that the innocent girl is experiencing a hysterical reaction to the sex act, since only she hears the voices. As an Italian, Verdi was primarily interested in this issue. Muzio praised "Tu sei bella" as distinctly Italian, and he was talking about more than the melody. He was referring to the Italian understanding of the Devil and his works.*

The Calvinist doctrine of predestination never caught on in Italy, where Catholic theologians argued the supremacy of free will. In other words, for all the evocative power and "genuine horror" in northern portrayals of the Devil, it is the individual human who chooses salvation or perdition. The drama takes place not in the cosmos but in the human. Failure to grasp this point of view will result in a misunderstanding of this opera and the later Requiem.

Act II

Setting: The square of Rheims, in front of the Cathedral of St. Denis.

The people are gathered for the long-delayed coronation of King Carlo. A long procession of soldiers, heralds, lords, and ladies enters the cathedral, followed by Giovanna and Carlo. Then Giacomo appears, alone. He must denounce his daughter, his only hope and consolation in his old age, but may God at least save her soul from eternal damnation. Trumpets and a hymn are heard from inside the cathedral. Giovanna runs out of the cathedral, very agitated, followed by some of the crowd and Carlo. He begs her to stay—she is the savior of France, the patron saint of the nation! Giacomo steps forward and denounces such blasphemy. Carlo must know that Giovanna sold her soul to the Devil to win his love. All are amazed by this news, and ask God for help in discerning the truth. Giacomo challenges Giovanna to deny the accusation, but she remains silent. Carlo begs her to say one word, that the people may be reassured, but she refuses. The people denounce Giovanna, Carlo calls them cruel and ungrateful, swearing he will always love her, and Giacomo tells his daughter her disgrace will be her redemption. Giovanna welcomes this ordeal as a purgation of her guilty soul. The people wonder what history will say about this moment.

Comment: The bell-ringing procession that opens the act is very noisy, but rather pro forma. Giacomo's solo, "Speme al vecchio ora una figlia," is an expansive baritone melody that must be made interesting by the sheer beauty of the singer's voice. The act doesn't really take off until the general confrontation, which is basically in the form of a trio with choral backing. At one point, Carlo, Giovanna, and Giacomo sing a fuguelike a capella trio, which is a very blunt yet effective "close-up" technique. When the chorus and orchestra resume, Giacomo's melody is again very broad and graceful, suggesting sympathy for this rather obnoxious old man, while

Carlo and Giovanna sing in unison, implying genuine love. While one's patience is tried by Giovanna's refusal to answer the witchcraft accusation, we must remember the guilt that she is carrying inside her for succumbing to human love. She is an extreme example of a woman at odds with society, a type that Verdi would depict more convincingly in his subsequent operas.

Act III

Setting: A fortress in the English camp.

Giovanna is lying in chains. From outside, sentries announce the French attack. Giovanna realizes where she is, anxious to break her chains and join the battle. Giacomo enters unseen. She prays for strength. For a brief moment she had abandoned her mission and succumbed to love, but now she rededicates her soul to her sacred mission. Giacomo realizes his daughter has been pure and steps forward and sets her free, asking her forgiveness. She is strengthened by her suffering and her father's blessing. He urges her back to the battlefield, realizing her mission comes from God. She draws her father's sword and rushes into battle. Giacomo goes to the window and sees his daughter rush into the fray on a white charger, rescuing Carlo. The French take the fortress.

Carlo enters with soldiers. How grateful he is, again, to Giovanna! He forgives Giacomo the accusations, as Giovanna had. Delil enters, and Carlo asks news. Are the English still fighting? Yes, replies Delil, but Giovanna has fallen. Carlo, disconsolate, begs his soldiers to stab him. Mournfully, the French bring in the senseless body of Giovanna. A celestial glow seems to surround her body. She opens her eyes, which the people hail as a miracle. Carlo begs her not to die, while Giacomo begs forgiveness. Giovanna praises the French troops, asking for her own battle standard, that she may bear it to heaven and present it to the Virgin. Angels welcome her return to the celestial sphere, while demons grumble that heaven's triumph is a torment for them.

Comment: *One would imagine a long scena for the soprano at the beginning of this act, but we rush directly into the rather "tinny" battle music, which Giovanna comments on as if hallucinating. The duet between her and her father is exquisite—they sing similar music in remote keys. Even when reconciling, these two seem to inhabit different worlds. The subsequent battle music is very brief, and the stage fills up again for the finale. Carlo's romanza mourning Giovanna's fall, "Quale al più fido amico," is touching and haunting in the best early Verdi style. The following funeral march is strange and vague, only becoming clear in the subsequent ensemble. The demons at the end are delightfully depicted by a brass band. They stop just short of crying out, "Rats! Foiled again!"*

Alzira

PREMIERE: Teatro San Carlo, Naples, 1845. Libretto by Salvatore Cammarano.

THE NAME

Pretty simple, if you remember that voiced *z* sound in Italian: "al-DZEE-ra."

Alzira is *generally* cited as Verdi's worst opera, a distinction occasionally shared with *Il corsaro*. It was not a success at its premiere, and Verdi never showed any interest in revising it. In fact, later he famously said, *"Quella è proprio brutta"* ("That one's really ugly"). *Brutta* is also the word Italians use for bad weather, as the British will say "nasty."

I wonder what people would say about this opera if Verdi hadn't been moved to condemn it so bluntly. These days, we are seeing *Alzira* pop up in various productions. Much is wrong with it, but attending a performance of it is hardly a waste of time. It isn't a problem of melody or vitality—this is Verdi, after all. But it is interesting to see how melody and vitality alone require a certain something else to send us over the edge. *Rigoletto* is a string of good tunes, but it is also white-hot lyrical-dramatic inspiration from the first notes to the last. *Alzira* just has the string of good tunes. Listening to it will help clarify what Verdi was accomplishing when he was "on," which was almost all the rest of the time.

The difference between *Alzira* and *Rigoletto,* besides a span of six busy and highly informative years, lies in the story. When Verdi is fired up over a story, it shows in the music and the handling of the dramatic situation. The story concerns a moment of conflict between native Peruvians and Spanish conquistadors, with all the attendant philosophical issues of Christianity, "noble savages," and so forth. It is always fascinating to study cultures in conflict, but this aspect of Voltaire's play, on which the libretto is based, seems to have eluded Cammarano and Verdi entirely. In the opera, there is very little difference between Spaniards and Peruvians, either musically or dramatically. Seeing all people as fundamentally the same is good ethics, but not always good opera. Much of the philosophy of Voltaire's play was lost at Verdi's insistence, who kept nagging Cammarano to make the story faster and terser. The result is a very brief opera, despite all its outrageous action and exotic locales. Verdi never wrote a more frenetic score than *Alzira.*

CAST OF CHARACTERS

ALVARO, SPANISH GOVERNOR OF PERU *(bass)* The father figure. Alvaro causes even more trouble than the average colonial governor. His name, like his more famous namesake in *La forza del destino,* is pronounced with the accent on the second syllable in Italian.

GUSMANO *(baritone)* His son. Gusmano is the classic callous European in confrontation with the "noble savages" of America.

DUKE OVANDO *(tenor)* The sententious voice of Spanish authority, almost a herald figure.

ZAMORO *(tenor)* The chief of a Peruvian tribe. Zamoro is as noble, statuesque, and unreal as any European fantasy of an Indian. We never quite get a direct line on this guy, which is one of the opera's shortcomings. That said, he has some, well, noble music to sing.

ATALIBA *(bass)* The chief of another Peruvian tribe.

ALZIRA *(soprano)* Ataliba's daughter. Our heroine, truly in love with Zamoro, to whom she remains loyal.

ZUMA *(mezzo)* Alzira's sister.

OTUMBO *(tenor)* A Peruvian warrior.

THE OPERA

Prologue: "The Prisoner"

Setting: A vast plain in Peru. Sunrise.

A band of Peruvians, led by Otumbo, dance around Alvaro, the Spanish Governor, whom they have captured and now threaten with death. Their chief Zamoro arrives by canoe. He frees Alvaro, telling him to return and tell his people about the clemency of a savage. Tribesmen escort Alvaro away. Otumbo explains that Zamoro's betrothed Alzira and her father Ataliba have been captured by the Spaniards. Zamoro calls his men to arms.

Comment: *The Prologue is a rush of strings and voices, a sort of operatic equivalent of a cattle stampede. Even Zamoro's first solo after Alvaro leaves, technically an andante, is rather bombastic for the melancholy of the moment. The finale is, predictably, very loud and fast.*

Act I

Scene 1: A plaza in Lima.

Alvaro is formally resigning his position of governor in favor of his son Gusmano. Gusmano first declares peace with the Incas, and asks their chief Ataliba for Alzira's hand to seal the peace. Despite himself, Gusmano is in love with the Inca princess. Alzira will not accept, despite her father's urgings, since she still loves Zamoro. Gusmano insists he will have Alzira.

Comment: *The plaza scene is entirely pro forma. Only Gusmano's solo, as he wonders how a conqueror conquers a human heart, achieves any lyricism, if the baritone is up to it. The finale is pure thunder.*

Scene 2: Ataliba's (guest) room in the Governor's Palace.

Zuma and her attendants gaze upon the sleeping Alzira, wondering if the princess has found peace in death. Suddenly Alzira awakes, calling for Zamoro. Did she just see him? Was it a ghost? She relates her dream of floating away in a canoe, rescued by Zamoro. Perhaps he is alive after all! Ataliba enters, ordering his daughter to marry Gusmano. How can he ask such a thing? Zuma says a Peruvian prisoner asks to speak alone with Alzira. The others leave, and Zamoro enters, relieved that she has not in fact betrayed him. They fall into each other's arms just as Gusmano, Ataliba, and the others return to the scene. Zamoro recognizes Gusmano as the Spaniard who had treated him so badly in prison, bending him on revenge against the invader race. Gusmano orders Zamoro's execution despite the signed pact and the pleas of his father Alvaro. Suddenly, the battle alarm is sounded, and Gusmano tells Zamoro to meet him on the field of battle.

Comment: *The opening of the scene is remarkably delicate, with Zuma and the ladies floating interjections above a diaphanous string accompaniment. It is a moment of relief, and not a moment too soon. Alzira's narrative aria is descriptive of the canoeing action, and a little silly. The father-daughter duet, while not of the same caliber as Verdi's more famous efforts in the genre, contains a lovely and moody central section, with oboes and bassoon denoting melancholy. The love duet, if we can call it that, between Zamoro and Alzira, is over before it starts. When everyone is gathered in the room, the state is set for a very lush concertato. Every Verdi opera, no matter how low on the scale, will have at least a moment of utter lyric gorgeousness. This is the moment in* Alzira.

Act II

Scene 1: The fortifications of Lima.

The Spaniards are celebrating their victory over the Peruvians. Zamoro is led in among the prisoners. He is sentenced to be burned at the stake at dawn. Alzira pleads with Gusmano, who tells her she has the power to save Zamoro's life. Despite her revulsion, Alzira consents to marry Gusmano.

Comment: The opening soldiers' chorus is extremely typical, but scholars admire the way it magically morphs into a funeral dirge when Zamoro is dragged on, without actually missing a beat.

Scene 2: A cave.

Zamoro, in a cave with his followers, is told of Alzira's impending marriage. Cursing her betrayal, he swears vengeance.

Comment: The orchestral prelude to this scene is superbly moody, created by shimmering strings and sad woodwinds. You almost wish Verdi had slowed down the pace even more and expanded this scene. Zamoro's solo is accompanied by clarinet, which Verdi always uses to excellent effect. One can almost start to care for Zamoro in this scene.

Scene 3: The great hall of the Governor's Palace in Lima.

Guests celebrate the new Governor's wedding. Just as Gusmano is about to take Alzira's hand, Zamoro, disguised, stabs him. To everyone's surprise, Gusmano pardons Zamoro, urging him to take care of Alzira. Bidding his father farewell, he dies.

Comment: The finale is even better than the first act concertato, an excellent ensemble of various points of view converging into one frozen moment of communal experience. In fact, it is infuriating. If Verdi had found some time to involve us more with these characters, particularly Zamoro, the finale to the opera would be devastating. As it stands, it is moving, propelled by Verdi's two most characteristic instruments, cello and clarinet.

Attila

PREMIERE: La Fenice, Venice, 1846. Libretto by Temistocle Solera.

THE NAME

The accent is on the first syllable, AH-teel-la. Yes, it refers to the Hun.

Attila is basically a patriotic opera depicting the moment in history when the Roman Empire was collapsing before invading barbarians and Italy lay exposed to the full fury of the Huns. It also focuses on the founding of the city of Venice by mainland refugees seeking shelter in the lagoon. The rise of Venice out of the destruction of the barbarian invasions was an irresistible metaphor for the Risorgimento, as a debased Italy looked for hope under Austrian domination.

The Rio Alto (Venice) scene won over the audience, and is still probably the best crowd-pleaser in the opera. The prima donna has a beautiful moonlight romanza in addition to her usual rousing cabalettas. There are some excellent ensembles. The tenor role is congenial and easy to cast, compared to Ernani. The baritone role has some opportunities for Verdian legato singing. Also, he gets to toss off the famous patriotic sound bite of the evening, "You will have the Universe; leave Italy for me!," sung in an arching phrase of sterling Verdi. More than anything else, the opera provided the bass with a rare and heroic title role. But the opening night critics gave *Attila* a beating, and they were not just being contrary. The plot, as such, tries your patience even more than your credulity. The characters, with the exception of Attila, are impossible to trust, and all are impossible to love. And the music and situations become generally less interesting with each successive act.

For a while, none of this mattered. *Attila* made the rounds of the Italian houses and was very popular. After the Risorgimento it faded. Recently we have seen more of it, in Italy and abroad, when a bass has had the clout to force a revival. While Verdi offers a few great bass roles, Attila is his only lead role for that voice.

CAST OF CHARACTERS

ATTILA *(bass)* The King of the Huns. A magnificent role for a star bass. At the time of the opera, Attila is ravaging northern Italy and preparing to sack Rome itself.

EZIO *(baritone)* A Roman general. A mercurial and hard-to-love character, who does, however, get some stunning music to sing.

ODABELLA *(soprano)* A young lady of Aquileia. Odabella's father, the King of Aquileia (an ancient town in northeast Italy), has been killed by Attila, and she is bent on revenge. Odabella is a demanding role, vocally and dramatically.

FORESTO *(tenor)* A knight of Aquileia. Foresto is in love with Odabella. This is a remarkably lyric, rather than heroic, tenor role.

ULDINO *(tenor)* Attila's Breton slave.

LEONE *(bass)* An old Roman. As we will discover, this "old Roman" is history's Pope Leo, who averted the sack of Rome by parleying with Attila. He appears in only one scene in this opera, but must make a spectacular impression with his authoritative voice.

THE OPERA
Prologue

Scene 1: Night, amid the burning ruins of Aquileia.

Barbarians are praising the delights of war and their god-leader Attila. Attila enters and the crowds prostrate before him, praising him and his wars.

Uldino, Attila's Breton slave, enters with Odabella and other maidens of Aquileia. Attila is displeased—had he not ordered all the inhabitants of the city slaughtered? Who dared to spare the women? Uldino answers that these women fought as brave soldiers, and seemed to be a worthy living tribute to the King. Attila is surprised. What could have inspired valor in women? Sacred love of the homeland, replies Odabella vigorously. Yes, while the barbarians maraud, their women stay weeping in the carts, but he will always see the Italian women, breasts girt in iron, fighting in battle! Attila, who always respects courage, is impressed with Odabella, and grants her any wish. Immediately, she asks for her sword. Attila presents her with his own. Odabella grasps it joyously. The holy hour of vengeance is at hand. Attila questions this new feeling in his soul, which had only ever loved destruction. The barbarians praise Attila. Odabella and the women leave.

Comment: The opening chorus is crude and basic—these are barbarians, after all. Their opening words, "groans, pillages, shouts, blood, rapes, ruins, massacres, and fires are Attila's game . . .," get the point across, in case the music is too subtle. Attila's entrance is impressive, with long and very low stentorian phrases for the basses. He should communicate authority and severity right away. A little sex appeal helps, too. Odabella likewise must impress as soon as she opens her mouth, with a forte line and an immediate two-octave drop. Her subsequent aria is broad and lovely. After Attila gives her his sword, she breaks into her cabaletta, "Da te questo or m'è concesso," which is surprisingly refined and pretty.

Ezio, the Roman emissary, enters with some officers. Attila salutes the famous soldier as a worthy adversary. Ezio asks to speak to Attila alone. The others leave. Ezio confides that the Roman Emperor is a weak boy. If Attila and Ezio join forces, nothing could stop them. Attila will have the Universe, but let him leave Italy for Ezio. Attila scorns the proposition. If the bravest Roman hero can be a traitor, the people are lost, the King is a coward, and their God must be impotent. Attila will carry the faith of Odin with him. Ezio recovers himself. Then let Attila hear his official message, but Attila will not listen. He will destroy proud Rome with his armies. Ezio reminds him that the Romans had defeated those armies once before, at Chalons-sur-Marne, and would do so again. They part.

Comment: Ezio sings his proposal in a combination of recitative and aria, culminating in the great arching line "Avrai tu l'universo, Resti l'Italia a me." When Attila rejects the proposal, Ezio does a complete 180, and vaunts his martial capabilities. This about-face is typical of the characters in this opera. It makes it hard to believe anything they're saying, and lends weight to the charge of "hollowness" often raised against the patriotic operas of this period. The scene ends with a duettino that demands a lot of testosterone from the bass and baritone.

Scene 2: The Rio Alto in the Adriatic lagoons. A few huts are raised on piles connected by planks. A stone altar is half-built. Night.

A storm is raging over the lagoon, where hermits have taken refuge from the Huns among the swampy mudflats. The storm subsides and dawn appears. A bell tolls, signaling the morning. Hermits come out of the huts and gather around the stone altar. The storm has passed, but the waves still rage in the lagoon. The hermits praise the Creator and hear their prayer echoed by voices from the water. Small boats approach, carrying Aquileian refugees, led by Foresto. He directs the Aquileans to build huts among this enchantment of sea and sky. The refugees hail him, who alone saved them. He thinks of his love Odabella, now fallen to the Huns. The people tell him to have hope. Perhaps she has escaped the fate he fears for her. Foresto addresses the swamps as a homeland. Now it is a desolate ruin, but it will live again, rising from the algae of the swamp like a Phoenix, to be the wonder of land and sea. The people repeat this acclamation.

Comment: This celebrated scene begins with a storm, which passes quickly. The bell tolls, and the chorus of hermits, all basse, begin chanting rather than singing. The sunrise is depicted in the orchestra by flutes and sweet strings playing antiphonally and climbing, step by step, up the scale. A horn joins in when the hermits resume their prayer, building to a great crescendo and even a cymbal crash at the line "Lode al Creator." *Instead of being followed by a silence, however, the climax is "echoed" by higher voices offstage as the monks look out onto the "lagoon." It is a superb effect. In a good production this is a powerfully evocative moment and an excellent manipulation of imagery. In the Bible, creation happens when the "Spirit of God was moving over the face of the waters"* (Genesis 1:2). *Spirit equals breath, and in a sense, breath equals song. The result of the miracle here is Venice. Conquering the sea is a victory of life over death, which makes Venice an architectural analog of resurrection. God's wrath (the storm) gives way to God's bounty (the sunrise), which unites the people and founds a new nation (Venice–Italy). The image of the Phoenix was a direct appeal to the Venetians who were watching the premiere, and who were in fact sitting in the Fenice ("Phoenix") theater amid the very swamps in question.*

Contemporary audiences are only peripherally interested in Risorgimento politics, if at all, yet they have recently gone to see Attila *for the star bass, and left the theaters talking at least as much about the beautiful Rio Alto scene. The scene convincingly dramatizes the idea that human aspirations and ideals have a source and an echo in the divine order. In doing so, it also suggests that daring to hope for a better future is in itself both a political act and a spiritual exercise.*

Act I

Scene 1: A moonlit wood.

Odabella cannot sleep. Even at this hour, when tigers rest, she roams. She imagines seeing her father's face in the clouds. Then she imagines seeing her lover Foresto, and begs the stream to stop murmuring so she can better hear the voice of her beloved ghosts.

Foresto enters, dressed as a barbarian. He repulses Odabella's embraces, accusing her of betraying her country and her murdered father at Attila's feasts. She reminds him of the story of Judith, who slew the invader general and saved Israel. Odabella shows Foresto Attila's sword, the very instrument by which she will slay the monster. Foresto throws himself at her feet, but she directs him to her breast instead, and they unite in rapture and vengeance against the invader.

Comment: Solera's words are often great to sing, but he also gives into jarringly inappropriate allusions on occasion. What tigers? The fabled tigers of Aquileia? Moreover, the words suggest that Odabella is nervous and anxious for battle, but the music suggests otherwise. Her romanza "Oh! nel fuggente nuvolo" is sung pianissimo to a marvelously errant melody, doubled in the orchestra by clarinet and flute decorations, and then by harp. It suggests sadness and confusion rather than resolution.

When Foresto enters, their confrontation is mostly in angry recitative broken by bits of arioso. They unite for the ending duet, which is more of an oath duet than a love duet. Actually, in Verdi it's often hard to tell the difference. Maybe that's the point.

Scene 2: Just outside Attila's tent. Uldino is asleep on tiger skins at the foot of Attila's bed.

Attila wakes up in terror, calling for Uldino. He tells Uldino his dream. He was about to enter Rome, swollen with pride, when an old man seized him by the hair. The old man smiled and commanded, "You are chosen only as the scourge of mortals. Withdraw now! This is the soil of the gods!" Attila recovers himself and orders Uldino to summon the captains. They will descend on Rome faster than ever! Uldino leaves. Attila addresses the ghost of his vision. He will battle Rome.

Comment: Attila quotes the ghost, whom we will meet shortly, in threatening stentorian lines that begin thunderously and die down toward

their end. Attila then does a surprising 180 with no new outside informa-
tion: "I feel better, let's go sack Rome!" The subsequent cabaletta is rous-
ing good fun.

Uldino returns with the barbarian armies. Attila tells them Odin calls
them to glory. Trumpets sound, but these are immediately followed by
distant voices of women and children. Attila marvels at this sound. This
is not the echo of trumpets! Leone and six elders enter the camp, followed by maidens and children, clad in white and carrying palms. Attila
recognizes the old man from his dream. Leone approaches and repeats,
"You are chosen only as the scourge of mortals. Withdraw now! This is
the soil of the gods!" Attila imagines he is being harassed by giants in the
sky bearing flaming swords. He prostrates himself at Leone's feet. The
barbarians are amazed at their own emotion before these weak voices
and at Attila prostrate for the first time. The Italians marvel at the might
of God. As Goliath was defeated by a shepherd, as a humble Virgin
saved mankind, and as the faith was spread by simple people, so now
the king of heathens retreats before a devout crowd.

Comment: The barbarian trumpets and male voices give way to the
ethereal angelic chorus at the beginning of this scene. It's a reworking of
the hermit-refugee contrast that worked so effectively in the Rio Alto
scene. That scene was about unity and creation, this is confrontation.
Leone is of course history's Pope Leo. The Imperial censors of the time
would not let the 1846 libretto say that, but everybody knew who was
meant, and productions today do not resist the spectacle of a pope in full
white vestments making a grand entrance. His lines, of course, are an exact
repeat of Attila's quote from the previous dream sequence, each line again
hitting with an initial "punch" before fading. Attila's breathy, broken
recitative, as he falls before Leone, leads into a sumptuous concertato. The
unified ensemble suggests that all on the stage are equally amazed by the
surprising events and the apparent intervention of God in human affairs.

Act II

Scene 1: The Roman camp, with Rome in the background.

Ezio enters, reading a letter. There is truce with the Huns. He must return to Rome, by order of the Emperor Valentinian. If only the spirits of the Roman ancestors could arise around them for a moment, for who now can recognize Rome in this vile cadaver? Some of Attila's slaves arrive with Roman soldiers. Attila wishes to speak to Ezio and his captains. Ezio says they will come, and the soldiers and slaves depart. One slave remains. It is Foresto, disguised. He confides that he is a Roman, though he does not reveal his name. There is a plan. Attila will be killed. Let Ezio and his troops await the fire that will signal a general assault. Ezio prepares for heroic warfare. If he dies, then it will be a hero's death, and all Italy will mourn the last of the Romans.

Comment: The baritone's big scene is in standard format: recitative, romanza, new information, and cabaletta. It's all good musically, but it's not possible to get a handle on Ezio from it. In an opera where everybody changes position on a dime, this guy sets the pace. This has the effect of making all the patriotic vaunting sound rather hollow.

Scene 2: Attila's camp, as in Act I, set for a banquet. Odabella, dressed as an Amazon, is sitting in a place of honor.

The barbarians sing the pleasures of drinking and feasting on severed limbs and heads. Ezio enters with his followers, now including Foresto dressed as a warrior again. Ezio and Attila greet each other. The Druid priests warn Attila that it is fatal to sit at table with Ezio— omens of blood-red clouds, howling mountain spirits, and shrieking birds have already appeared. Attila dismisses the priests, directing the priestesses to lighten the air with their harps. Suddenly, a gust of wind extinguishes the torches, and all are amazed. The barbarians are terrified of the dark spirit of the mountain wind. Foresto tells Odabella their vengeance is at hand, for Uldino has poisoned Attila's cup, but she insists that she is appointed by God to strike the invader down. Attila must not die by the treacherous hand of his own people. Ezio reminds Attila that there is still time to join forces. Attila dismisses Ezio's offer, but notices to himself that his own courage is fading. Uldino remembers that he is a Breton, a slave, and he must not falter now to perform the deed.

The sky clears. Attila rallies himself, and calls for a toast to Odin. As he is about to drink, Odabella, who has been avoiding Foresto, pulls the cup from his lips. It is poisoned! she tells him. Attila furiously demands who did it, and Foresto bravely steps forward. Attila draws his sword, but Odabella demands that she alone should be allowed to dispose of Foresto, since she revealed the plot. Attila grants her Foresto, and declares she will be made Queen of the Huns in the morning. Odabella tells Foresto to flee for his life, Foresto accuses her of betrayal, Ezio looks ahead to battle the next day, Uldino considers that he will remain loyal to the "warrior," while the barbarians call for death.

Comment: The scene opens with another coarse barbarian chorus. The priestesses' chorus is rather tinselly, as befits their derided religion. The moment of darkness (and silence) is followed by not one but two ensembles. Here is Verdi in an early, rather confusing, attempt to keep the action flowing through the ensemble. Ezio is waffling again, Odabella stalling, and we learn that Uldino too is a schemer. The final ensemble, after Attila announces his marriage, is more of the same. The libretto doesn't even specify to whom Uldino is now swearing eternal loyalty (it's Ezio).

Act III

Setting: The wood, as in Act I.

Foresto, alone, tries to calm his fury. Uldino enters and tells him the procession bearing Odabella to Attila's tent will pass this way. Foresto orders him to Ezio's camp, where he and his soldiers are preparing to fall upon the barbarians. Foresto then muses on his upcoming revenge. Faithless Odabella, how can angels have such wicked hearts?

Odabella enters in terror, still dressed in armor. She begs the ghost of her father to leave her—she has fled the disgrace and will take revenge on Attila yet. Ezio calls for the torch signal, before it's too late. Seeing Foresto, Odabella drops to her knees and begs mercy. She was always true to him. Foresto scorns her words as false. Ezio suggests they argue later.

Attila enters, asking why his beloved has fled. Is this a new plot? Odabella was his slave, now she is his bride. He spared Foresto's life. He saved Rome for Ezio. Now he will punish them all. Odabella tells Attila he murdered her father, and casts the crown from her head. Foresto tells Attila his clemency was a mockery, since the barbarian stole his country and his love. Ezio tells Attila the fury of the whole world and divine vengeance spared Rome. Soldiers approach crying for death and vengeance. Attila calls them traitors. Foresto tries to stab Attila, but Odabella rushes in and kills Attila first, offering his death as a sacrifice to her father. Attila, dying, says "You too, Odabella?" Soldiers run in. God, the people, and the King of Aquileia are avenged.

Comment: *This act opens with Foresto alone. He sings a very pretty cavatina, "Che non avrebbe il misero." Odabella, on the other hand, enters shrieking to a harp accompaniment (odd combination), swearing that she's been true but not giving any more information. Foresto rebukes her, and we are left to wonder why these women in Romantic opera don't just stick up for themselves, give the whole story, and tell the tenors to shut up. At least Odabella protests her innocence, which is more than poor Giovanna d'Arco got to do.*

When Attila arrives, the final confrontation is quick, furious, and interesting. Prophetically, the Italians are united in purpose only when the enemy is present. The Italians each denounce Attila with their own particular gripes, and of course it is Odabella who takes the final action. She seems determined to emasculate Foresto at every opportunity, although one must admit he seems to be loving every minute of it. Attila's quotation of Julius Caesar as he falls only confirms that Attila is the true hero of this opera.

Macbeth

PREMIERE: Teatro alla Pergola, Florence, 1847. Revised version: Théâtre Lyrique, Paris, 1865. Libretto by Francesco Maria Piave.

THE NAME

For our purposes, the opera is called *Macbeth*. In Italy, it has always been called *Macbetto,* and still is occasionally announced as such on placards, although the English title is now becoming standard. The character in the opera, however, is referred to in the Italian, since neither God nor anyone else can get Italians to pronounce the English *th* sound. But that's no excuse for an English speaker to call the opera *Macbetto*.

VERDI WAS DETERMINED to do something very different at this point in his career, and the result is an opera not quite like any other. In lieu of the standard operatic love interest, we explore one of the most superbly twisted married couples of all literature. The psychological possibilities of opera itself took a great leap forward with this work. Macbeth is one of the most challenging and rewarding roles in the baritone repertory, perhaps second only to Rigoletto. Lady Macbeth may well be Verdi's most challenging female role, both vocally and dramatically. The only other major "characters" in the opera are the witches (a chorus), who, according to Verdi's understanding of the story, are the motivators of the plot. The Macbeths, then, share a huge burden, and the opera basically succeeds or fails on their merits.

Macbeth was a great success at its premiere, but it did not embark on a triumphal tour of the world's opera houses as *Ernani* or *Nabucco* had. It was a bit too *sui generis* for such wide appeal, and Verdi himself was not sure he had got it quite right. He decided to revise the opera for a production in Paris in 1865. As we have seen, the Paris production was not a success, and Verdi was bitter about it. Yet this is the version invariably given today. The revision amounted to the loss of two rip-snorting cabalettas (which are very good in themselves and make appearances on recordings and in concerts), a new and extraordinary aria for Lady Macbeth, a superb new chorus, and some more refined orchestration. Some complain of the "grafted" nature of the revision, and there is always somebody to defend the "purity" of the 1847 edition. Yet the Paris revision makes a better opera. The few places where the styles clash are a small price to pay for the significantly more profound music.

CAST OF CHARACTERS

MACBETH *(baritone)* A general in King Duncan's army. A great and challenging lead role.

LADY MACBETH *(soprano or mezzo-soprano with a really wide range)* His wife. A sort of Abigaille with brains.

BANCO *(bass)* Another general in Duncan's army. Banco is a comprimario with some important music to sing before he is killed off. Fortunately, Verdi does not require an aria from his ghost.

MACDUFF *(tenor)* A Scottish nobleman. Macduff is also a listed as a comprimario role, although he has an excellent aria to sing.

MALCOLM *(tenor)* Son of Duncan. Malcolm sings primarily in ensembles.

Mime roles

DUNCAN, King of Scotland; FLEANCE, Banco's son; HECATE, the goddess of night (when the Act III ballet is given, which is rare).

Other roles

WITCHES (here a chorus, rather than Shakespeare's three); WOMAN IN ATTENDANCE ON LADY MACBETH *(mezzo-soprano)*; DOCTOR *(bass)*; MACBETH'S SERVANT *(bass)*; MURDERER *(bass)*; HERALD *(bass)*; FIRST APPARITION *(baritone)*; SECOND APPARITION *(soprano)*; THIRD APPARITION *(soprano)*.

THE OPERA

Act I

Scene 1: In the woods.

While a storm rages, three groups of witches gather and compare tales of their powers. Macbeth and Banco arrive, see the witches, and ask who and what they are. They hail Macbeth as Thane of Glamis, Thane of Cawdor, and King of Scotland, to his astonishment, since he is only Thane (Lord) of Glamis. Banco asks for news of his own future, and they greet him as less and greater than Macbeth, never king, but father of kings. The witches vanish.

Macbeth and Banco ponder the witches' words. Messengers from King Duncan arrive and inform Macbeth that the Thane of Cawdor has been beheaded, and the King grants the title to Macbeth. Macbeth notes that the witches' words are now two-thirds true, but he will not lift a grasping hand for the crown itself. Banco considers that devils often speak truth only to cause greater harm. The messengers wonder why Macbeth is not more joyful at the news. All leave. The witches reappear, preparing for their wild ride. Macbeth will soon return to them to hear more. They vanish.

Comment: *Everyone has a great time trashing the witches' music in* Macbeth. *Toye says it "must be dismissed as another of Verdi's failures in* *the realm of the fantastic." George Martin is reminded of girls trick-or-treating, and Budden says, "Verdi's witches, like Shakespeare's, are of St. Trinian's." Budden hits the nail on the head when he cites Shakespeare as the source of the problem. The words are silly—why shouldn't the music be? As in* Giovanna d'Arco *the true horror is in the human protagonists. Yet this time Verdi has confused the situation by insisting in his letters and instruction on the dramatic importance of the witches. Most directors opt for shock effect, and you can expect a lot of tits and leather in this scene. The important point is not the witches themselves but how Macbeth reacts to them, and smart directors will focus on this issue. His music after their apparition is as serious as any in opera.*

Scene 2: A hall in Macbeth's castle.

Lady Macbeth reads a letter from her husband, telling of the witches' prophecy and how it has already become true in part. Macbeth aspires to greatness, but is he willing to be wicked enough to take it? The road to power is full of misdeeds. Once embarked upon it, one must not falter. She bids her husband hurry to her, she will give him the courage to carry out the bold enterprise. The throne awaits! A servant announces the imminent arrival of the King, followed by Macbeth. The servant withdraws. Alone, Lady Macbeth calls on all the powers of hell who inspire mortals to bloody deeds to wrap her in darkness.

Comment: In this, the Letter Scene, the orchestra blasts its introduction to Lady Macbeth, who then startlingly enters speaking the letter without music. (Some productions opt for a voice-over of Macbeth speaking the letter instead. Yuck.) Lady Macbeth commences singing soon enough though, and then hang on to your hats. Like Abigaille in Nabucco, *she must sing leaps, drops, piercing high notes, and scary low notes. If Lady Macbeth can convince you that she is obeying an inner logic, the music comes alive as drama. Otherwise, it's athletic vocalizing, the sort in which the lady might as well be singing about a great sale at Macy's.*

Macbeth enters and greets his Lady, who greets him as Cawdor. The King comes tonight, he says. And leaves? Tomorrow. Then? Macbeth understands, but what if the blow should fail? It will not fail, she says, if Macbeth does not falter. They withdraw to greet the King. A cortege passes by, with King Duncan, Macbeth and his Lady, Macduff, Malcolm, Banco, and other thanes and courtiers. When the royal cortege has passed, Macbeth reenters and tells a servant to bid his wife ring a bell when his nightly drink is ready. The servant withdraws.

Alone, Macbeth looks at a dagger. Is it real? A vision? It bids him commit the crime. But a dagger cannot speak or act. Only his mind gives it the power to seem so. A bell is struck. Duncan's death knell, Macbeth says. He steps into the King's apartment. Lady Macbeth appears. Was it the cry of the owl she heard? What if Duncan should awake before the dagger falls? Macbeth returns. It is done. He stares at the blood on his hands. She tells him not to look at it. Macbeth tells her that he heard courtiers pray for God's help as he passed them, and tried to say "Amen," but the word froze upon his lips. Why could he not say the word? Foolishness, she chides, which dawn will dispel. A voice within him told him he had murdered sleep forever. But, she asks, didn't another voice urge him on, warning against half measures? She tells him to return to the room and smear the sleeping guards with the bloody dagger so they might be accused, but he refuses to reenter the room. She snatches the dagger from him and goes in herself. A knocking at the door is heard. Macbeth stares at his hands. The ocean would not be able to wash them of their blood! Lady Macbeth comes back, saying she too has blood on her hands, but a splash of water will clean them. The knocking becomes louder. She pulls him away, while he regrets the crime.

Macduff enters with Banco. It is time to wake the King. Macduff goes into the King's chamber. Banco thinks over the strange night, with screams, ill-omened birds, and earth tremors. Macduff comes back, too horrified to speak. Banco runs into the King's chamber, and soon the whole household gathers, crying treason and murder. Banco announces the assassination of King Duncan. All, including Macbeth and his Lady, ask hell and heaven to help them find and punish the murderers.

Comment: *In lieu of a duet between the Macbeths as they determine to commit the murder, there is an intense but brief recitative. Lady Macbeth* *gets to toss off a ringing flourish and a two-octave drop to emphasize her motivational abilities. Duncan and his retinue cross the stage without singing (presumably to spare the expense of hiring another singer just so he can be murdered), to two minutes of a very pro forma march. At this point a good director focuses on the Macbeths hiding their real emotions and donning their public persona, a shift they will be unable to manage later, in the banquet scene. Macbeth's dagger narrative is choked and formless, a series of gasps punctuated by a few full exclamations, rising up the scale only to fall again. The accompaniment is almost entirely winds and soft horns, shifting keys and implying the hallucinations of a fevered mind.*

The murder itself is not depicted in the orchestra—only the screeching owl, eerily signified by an English horn and bassoon. The subsequent duet was unlike anything ever heard on the operatic stage, and is still marvelously disturbing. It is considered a seminal moment in the growth of opera, being a formal duet yet containing dramatic momentum. Lady Macbeth's music implies nagging, nervousness, and action, while Macbeth seems to be withdrawing into a detached world of fantasy refuge. The concluding chorus is convincingly menacing and melancholy.

Act II

Scene 1: A room in the castle.

Lady Macbeth consoles her husband. What's done is done. Duncan's son fled to England, and all have assumed him guilty. Macbeth is King. Yet Macbeth worries about the witches' prophecy. Why should Banco's sons reign? Of course, Banco and his son are not immortal. Other blood must flow. She asks if he will be firm. He declares that eternity is opening its gate for Banco, and leaves. Alone, she greets the night, which will veil new crime. She revels that throne and scepter are hers at last.

Comment: The aria "La luce langue," the second of Lady Macbeth's three big solos, was written for the Paris revision of the opera, replacing a blasting but rather conventional cabaletta. "La luce langue" is hard to categorize; it has the feel of recitative, cavatina, and cabaletta all at the same

*time. The orchestra provides superbly sinuous accompaniment but we get
no rhythmic signals to tell us what sort of aria this is. Listen for the subtleties of harmony in the orchestra and the places where Lady Macbeth's
vocal line seems to be almost out of tune with the orchestration. Her imagination is beginning to torture her—a process that will be her undoing.
There are also remarkably sweet and lyric passages in her vocal line,
revealing her sense of guilt. Despite her brave words, Lady Macbeth
knows perfectly well that she is committing evil. Both the bloodlust and
the guilt-before-the-fact are present in this extraordinary aria.*

Scene 2: A wooded park on the castle grounds.

Two gangs of murderers gather, ordered by Macbeth to kill Banco.
Banco appears nervously with his son Fleance. It was on a night like
this that Duncan was killed. The assassins fall on Banco and kill him,
but Fleance escapes.

Comment: *The conspirators' chorus is standard tip-toe music, interrupted
by exclamations of "Trema, Banco!" as the good gentlemen of the chorus
brandish their daggers and strike threatening poses. Banco begins his excellent solo almost as a funeral dirge, the antithesis of what the chorus was
singing. It evolves into a very broad and lovely cantabile.*

Scene 3: The banquet hall in Macbeth's castle.

The court cheers King Macbeth, who welcomes the guests and
bids his Lady propose a toast. She sings a drinking song, asking all to
lose their cares in music and wine. One of the murderers appears at a
side door. Macbeth goes to him, and is told that Banco was killed but
Fleance escaped. Macbeth dismisses the murderer and returns to the
table. Calmly he notes that Banco, the noblest of the lords, is absent.
He himself will fill the vacant seat. As he approaches the table,
Banco's ghost appears to Macbeth alone. Horrified, Macbeth cries,
"Never shake your gory locks at me!" The guests assume Macbeth is
unwell, but Lady Macbeth bids them stay, whispering to her husband
to pull himself together. But does she not see the sight? Can the dead

return to earth? The ghost vanishes. Macbeth asks the guests to pay no mind to his outburst, and Lady Macbeth resumes her drinking song. Banco's ghost rises again, and Macbeth fumes at it. The guests are shocked at the proceedings, and Macduff determines to leave the accursed country. Macbeth resolves to see the witches again, while Lady Macbeth considers his own fear has created the ghost, since the dead do not return to the earth.

Comment: Lady Macbeth's drinking song, or brindisi, *is a masterful manipulation of a very traditional form. Her solo is, at first glance, a four-square melody, easily repeated by the "guests," but the melody is punctuated with leaps and drops suggestive of one barely holding on to sanity. Ideally, one can almost see her grasping her drinking cup with white knuckles like a life raft. Macbeth's hallucination is usually indicated by lights or other techniques, although some directors will actually traipse Banco across the stage. The concertato finale is less satisfying to most people than Verdi's usual ensembles, such as in* Ernani.

Act III

Setting: The witches' cave.

The witches stir their hellish brew in a large cauldron.

Comment: This, of course, is the "double, double toil and trouble" moment. Verdi obliged the Parisians with a "mime" of Hecate and the infernal powers at this point. For many years, productions dispensed with the ballet, even though the music is quite enjoyable. The ballet has been creeping up again lately in productions. Big mistake. This opera has a magnificent sweep of unified drama, and the ballet interrupts it. Buy the ballet music on a recording instead and play it while you house-clean.

Macbeth enters alone, asking the witches to tell him his future. They ask if he would hear it from them or from the powers they obey. He asks for the powers, and the witches call forth the spirits. A helmeted head rises from the cauldron and tells him to beware Macduff, and vanishes. Thunder, and a bloody child appears, telling Macbeth that no man of woman born will harm him. It vanishes. Macbeth is heartened at the news. Macduff may live then; but no, he reconsiders. Macduff must die after all. Thunder and lightning, and a child appears, saying Macbeth shall be invincible until Birnam Wood moves against him. It vanishes. Macbeth is relieved, for never, not even by magic, did a forest move. He asks the witches if Banco's descendants will rise to his throne. The cauldron vanishes, and the specter of eight kings arises, passing by one by one. Last is Banco, with a mirror in his hand. Macbeth draws his sword and attacks the phantoms, but stops, realizing they have no life. And they shall live? They shall live, answer the witches. Macbeth faints and the witches dance around him.

Macbeth revives. The Queen enters; he tells her of the prophecies. They agree that Banco's son must be found and put to death. The enterprise must end in blood, since in blood it was begun.

Comment: *The apparitions are, respectively, a baritone and two sopranos. Expect to hear them from offstage and amplified to the rafters. The apparitions and the parade of Banco's unborn royal children were greatly revised for the Paris production, a truly hair-raising combination of brass instruments providing the orchestral color. Then Macbeth has a powerful vocal solo that amounts to his big aria. One of the lost cabalettas of the original version appeared at the end of the scene, which made more dramatic sense than a duet with Lady Macbeth, but proved almost impossible to sing after this long scene. As it stands, the concluding duet is a breathy bit of competitive singing, and the effect is of two people pushing each other inexorably toward destruction.*

Act IV

Scene 1: A barren spot on the English border.

Refugees stream across the border, mourning the tomb that was their country. Their cries ascend to heaven, yet heaven seems to propagate the sufferings. The knell rings always, but no tears are shed for the suffering or the dead.

Comment: *The chorus "Patria oppressa!" may well be Verdi's greatest ever. It is often compared to "Va, pensiero," but God knows why. That chorus was the moment of hope amid adversity, but this chorus is pure misery and barrenness. You won't be able to whistle this one on your way out of the theater—Verdi wrote an almost amorphous melody, relying on disturbing dissonant harmonies and chromatics. Listen to this chorus a few times and you'll be privy to the well-kept secret that Verdi could be as revolutionary as Wagner and Liszt.*

Macduff cries out for his murdered wife and children. Alas, his paternal hand was not there to shield them from the murderers, since he was a fugitive. He asks God to bring him face to face with the tyrant, that he may kill him or consign him to God's justice.

Comment: *In Macduff's only aria, "Ah, la paterna mano," the surgical scars of revision are evident. It is a beautiful romanza, often featured on "greatest hits" albums, yet its bel canto beauty is a striking contrast with the near-formlessness of the preceding chorus.*

Malcolm enters at the head of English troops. He tells Macduff that retribution is at hand, and tells all who love their country to cut branches from nearby Birnam Wood to hide behind, and follow him to battle.

Comment: *Malcolm and Macduff rally the people with a standard unison duet repeated by the chorus.*

Scene 2: A hall in Macbeth's castle.

A doctor and a lady of the court wait in the darkness for Lady Macbeth, who, it is said, has been sleepwalking of late. Lady Macbeth appears. The doctor notes that her eyes are open, but she sees nothing. Why does she rub her hands? She imagines she is washing them, answers the lady. Lady Macbeth sees a spot on her hand, commanding it out. A soldier, afraid to go into the King's room? Shame! Who would have thought the old man had so much blood in him?

Will these hands never be clean? The smell of blood . . . All the perfumes of Arabia cannot sweeten the smell. Come, wash yourself! Banco is dead, he cannot come out of his grave. To bed, to bed, what's done cannot be undone. There's a knocking at the gate! Come, Macbeth, let not your pallor accuse you. The doctor and the lady are horrified, asking God for mercy on Lady Macbeth.

Comment: The celebrated Sleepwalking Scene is unique in opera. Verdi instructed that it be sung in an ugly voice, giving weird pointers like "suffocated voice" and "without music." The counting of the spots, "uno, due," is often barked or croaked. Yet at other points in the passage Verdi instructed that the voice be "spiegata," which means "open" but can also mean "outstretched." The last note of the scene is a high D flat, marked to be sung as a "thread of voice." Verdi was asking an almost impossible versatility of the singer, since she must apparently be able to inhabit two conflicting realms at the same time. Indeed, we find out later that this is her death aria, and the score would indicate that part of her is already disembodied while another part is all too encumbered with humanity. Both aspects must be portrayed convincingly. Several major careers have been made on the ability to mine the divergent treasures of this scene.

Scene 3: A room in the castle.

Alone, Macbeth rails at the traitors. He does not fear them, remembering that no "man of woman born" can harm him, yet he feels his life draining away. There will be no comfort in his old age, and no pleasant words on his monument, but only curses as his funeral dirge. Women's voices are heard crying, "She's dead!" A lady of the court enters to tell Macbeth the Queen is dead. "Life . . . 'tis no matter," he mutters. "It is a tale of an idiot, sound and fury, signifying nothing." The lady withdraws. Soldiers enter hurriedly, telling Macbeth that Birnam Wood is moving toward them. Crying deceit at the hellish prophecy of the witches, he calls for arms, and the soldiers follow him out to death or victory.

Comment: Shakespeare's famous soliloquies do not get matching arias in this scene. Macbeth's phrases are short and broken. The orchestra, however, revels in deep, rich sonorities, with the cellos in evidence. Verdi found what only the very greatest actors can portray in drama—an underlying humanity in the character of Macbeth that, despite his heinous actions, earns sympathy.

Scene 4: A broad plain.

English soldiers advance behind branches of trees. Macduff orders them to throw the branches down and take up their arms. They pass on. Macbeth appears, pursued by Macduff, who calls him the butcher of his children. Macbeth sneers that no man born of woman can harm him, but Macduff tells him he was not born, but ripped from the womb. They fight. Women pass by, bemoaning the sad day and praying for their children. Macbeth falls. Such is his due, he considers, for trusting in the prophecy of hell. He dies. In the distance, soldiers cry victory. Malcolm enters with soldiers and others. Macduff hails him as King, and the people rejoice.

Comment: Opera is superbly capable of depicting all the issues leading up to, surrounding, and following both sex and battle, but depictions of the great moments themselves are usually a trial on our credulity. The battle in Macbeth *is unconvincing but brief, and we can move on to the final victory chorus, which is excellent. It is not a tune you will whistle as you leave the theater; indeed, the people of Scotland are depicted as too exhausted to rejoice. The finale is an adroit mixture of relief and pensiveness perfectly appropriate to the situation.*

I masnadieri

PREMIERE: Her Majesty's Theatre, London, 1847. Libretto by Count Andrea Maffei.

THE NAME

It is pronounced "ee MAH-znah-DYAIR-ee." The *s* before the *n* is voiced; for full effect and great Italian sound, let it buzz in your nostrils while you say it.

WHEN VERDI ACCEPTED the lucrative offer from London to compose a new opera, he chose *Die Räuber* by Schiller as his source. Schiller's play is Romantic wildness at its most extreme, surpassing even Hugo's *Hernani* in its violent extremes and outrageous situations. The hero of *Die Räuber* is rejected by his family (for a crime unspecified in the opera) and feels equally separated from his fellow outlaws. He pours his heart out in soliloquies to nature, his only real companion. The young outcast hero who communes better with nature than with people has often appeared in our own time, in our cowboys, sailors, bikers, hippies, and more recently, the yuppie who "gives it all up" to go hug trees in the forest.

The problem with *I masnadieri* is that Verdi's rather proper music is fundamentally at odds with the revolutionary story. Perhaps Verdi was trying to have it both ways at once. He only succeeded in creating a very disjointed work that is difficult to digest whole. That said, there is no shortage of excellent music or dramatic situation in *I masnadieri*. Much of the choral music is ambitious and impressive. Since no director has ever, to my knowledge, found a way to make the chorus look convincing as they tippy-toe on and off stage in search of jolly rape and plunder, *Masnadieri* is most frequently given in concert (unstaged) performances, where the full beauty of the music can be appreciated with the least distraction.

CAST OF CHARACTERS

CARLO MOOR *(tenor)* The moody, disaffected hero, son of the old Count Moor, a German lord. Moor is merely the family name, without allegorical meaning.

FRANCESCO MOOR *(baritone)* Carlo's amazingly evil and sadistic younger brother.

THE COUNT MASSIMILIANO MOOR *(bass)* The old Count, frail and nearly dead from starvation by the final act. This is another reason *Masnadieri* works better in concert, since few operatic basses have the dramatic ability to convince us that they are starving to death.

AMALIA *(soprano)* Massimiliano's orphaned niece, in love with the banished Carlo. Amalia, written for Jenny Lind, is quite an unusual role in the Verdi canon, close in spirit to earlier, bel canto roles.

ARMINIO *(tenor)* A member of the Moor household.

ROLLA *(tenor)* One of Carlo's lawless companions.

MOSER *(bass)* The local pastor. Moser's role is brief but potentially extremely powerful.

The action takes place in rural Germany at the beginning of the eighteenth century.

THE OPERA
Prelude

Comment: *The Prelude is an all too brief, beautiful, and moody mini-concerto for cello.*

Part I

Scene 1: Outside a tavern.

Carlo Moor is immersed in a volume of Plutarch, disgusted with his own era of cowards and longing for the great days when German hordes captured Roman eagles. From inside the tavern he hears the drunken, rowdy song of his fellow discontents, and dreams of receiving a pardon from his father so he can return to his home and quit this dissolute life. Then he will be able to see his love Amalia again. Rolla and several young men enter hastily with a letter for Carlo. Carlo is sure this will be the long-awaited pardon from his father, but drops the letter and runs out when he realizes it's from his brother instead. Rolla reads the letter to the others. It says that, according to their father's wishes, Carlo must never think of returning home unless he wants to live as a prisoner on bread and water in a dungeon. Carlo returns, incredulous that his endless pleas for mercy could be rejected by his father. Rolla and the others suggest they form a gang of brigands. When they suggest Carlo lead them, he readily accepts.

Comment: *Carlo is clearly at odds with his peers, who appear to be students. When Carlo calls on the spirit of Arminius, he is not referring to his father's old servant, whom we will shortly meet, but to the German leader who defeated the Roman legions in the time of Augustus. The rest of the scene is laid out in conventional bel canto form. Carlo sings a pretty romanza when he remembers Amalia, which includes a woodwind accompaniment that foreshadows Amalia's own music shortly. The "messenger" of grand scena tradition is the letter, and Carlo (in recitative)* *determines to become an outlaw on the spot. His companions transform with similar rapidity, and accompany Carlo's cabaletta with pages and pages of noisy repeated oaths. This instant change from malcontent students to outlaws would have seemed much less jarring to audiences of 1847, who were quite familiar with revolutionary youth groups on the brink of explosion.*

Scene 2: A room in the Moors' castle.

Francesco gloats that his father has cut off Carlo, since Francesco tore up Carlo's letter and substituted another. At last he has his revenge against nature for making him the younger brother—now he must punish his father for the same crime! The worn-out old carcass is barely alive anyway, but he takes too long to die! Now, to find a dagger that will not betray the hand that wields it . . . Ah hah! He calls his servant Arminio, and asks him if he is loyal. Of course, replies Arminio. He tells Arminio to go in disguise to the old man and tell him that Carlo died on the battlefield at Prague. Francesco will supply more "proof" later. Arminio leaves. Alone, Francesco rejoices that he will soon be master of the castle, and the benign rule of his father will give way to his own rule of tears, fear, suspicion, and suffering.

Comment: *Francesco, you may have deduced, is the bad guy. You wouldn't know it from his beautifully expressive andante. His cabaletta, however, is quite unusual and a good opportunity for the baritone to project some character. The orchestral scoring is deliberately harsh and the vocal line is high, mostly written above the staff. It is marked pianissimo and creates a certain gaspy quality, appropriate for the outrageous lyrics he's singing.*

Scene 3: A bedroom in the castle.

Amalia contemplates Massimiliano Moor in his sleep. She cannot hate the old man, even though he banished her love, Carlo. She remembers Carlo and his embraces like a divine dream. But it has vanished, and will never return.

Comment: *Structurally, this cavatina, "Lo sguardo avea degli angeli," is interesting in its length without any discernible repetitions, something very daring at the time and an early attempt at a dramatic narrative. The vocal line itself, however, is filled with trills and decorations obviously written to showcase Jenny Lind, sweet almost to the point of gooeyness. It ends with a cadenza a piacere—that is, sing anything you want as long as it's difficult and gets attention.*

Massimiliano mutters Carlo's name in his sleep. How unhappy the boy must be! Amalia wakes him. He asks the girl whose happiness he has destroyed not to curse him, and she assures him she will not. He says he is dying, but, without Carlo, who will mourn him? Amalia wishes she too could die, so she could at least be with Carlo in heaven.

Francesco enters with Arminio, disguised, who says that he has just returned from the battlefield, where Carlo died bravely. Before he died, Carlo gave him a sword, on which he wrote with his own blood, "Amalia, death releases you from your oath. Francesco, be Amalia's husband." Massimiliano, remorseful, regrets the curse he placed on Carlo. Amalia loses herself in grief, Francesco thanks Satan for his help and asks the additional favor of letting his father die on the spot, while Arminio regrets his role in this deception. Massimiliano faints and is presumed dead, while Francesco exults in his new status as master of the castle.

Comment: *Massimiliano's and Amalia's duet is simple and pretty, a father-daughter interaction with remarkably little conflict. The subsequent quartet is an excellent ensemble of opposition. Each voice is introduced individually and according to character (she gets flute accompaniments to remind us that she's pure and pretty) and then blended together. She sings two high C's at full voice in the course of the ensemble, and ends with a cadenza to a high C sung piano. It is a stunning depiction of a passing moment. Francesco brings down the curtain with some characteristic growls.*

Part II

Scene 1: A graveyard next to the castle's chapel. Above one of the tombs can be read the name Massimiliano Moor.

Amalia prays at Massimiliano's neglected tomb. Revelers inside the castle call for drink to celebrate, while Amalia is appalled by this rejoicing over a father's bones. Yet Massimiliano has now found the peace of which he deprived Carlo. Only she is alive to mourn them both. Arminio enters, asking forgiveness. She tries to be rid of him, but he tells her that Carlo is alive, as is Massimiliano! Arminio leaves. She rejoices that the universe is once again filled with love.

Francesco approaches. He is tired of Amalia's mourning, and tells her of his love for her. She rejects him as the monster who forced her love to his death. Infuriated, he threatens her with a convent to tame her pride. Calling him a vile tyrant, she rejoices that at least she would be separated from him. In that case, he threatens, she must remain with him as his mistress. Francesco drags her by the hair until she pleads for mercy. Pretending to embrace him, she draws his dagger and threatens to kill him. He withdraws, wondering what whips, chains, and strange new tortures he shall have to invent for her.

Comment: Amalia enters to very somber, even spooky music. The off-stage chorus sings a capella at first, then breaking into a very jarring beat. The people of the castle are more than evil—their very nature is menacing to Amalia. Her cavatina here is more elaborate than her previous one, but still with plenty of room for decorations. After Arminio's news that the two men are still alive, she breaks into a cabaletta that again reminds us of the original presence of Jenny Lind, the Swedish Nightingale. That nickname must have been truly appropriate, because this aria is best described as "tweety." The following duet with Francesco is surprisingly slow, though written in a forward-moving ¾ time. The vocal singing can get very competitive here. When Francesco threatens Amalia with the convent, he snarls, "The four walls will know how to humble your neck!" The word he uses for neck, however, is "cervice," referring to the cervical vertebra at

*the base of the neck. Threatening to put her in a convent to tame her cervix
is easily misunderstood, at least by modern audiences.*

Scene 2: In the forest, with Prague in the background.

Some highwaymen are lazing in the forest. Others enter, saying
that Rolla has been taken prisoner and will be hanged. Excitedly
exchanging news, some tell others that their captain, Carlo, has sworn
to burn Prague down. In the distance, a fire can be seen. Women are
heard screaming. Rolla runs in, out of breath and demanding a drink.
Rolla tells the men Carlo set a fire, started a riot, and in the confusion
nabbed Rolla before he could be hanged. Carlo comes in, looking
sad. The men cheer him. He orders them to prepare to leave at dawn.

Alone, Carlo contemplates the sunset, comparing his own degraded
state with nature's perfection. Bound to a life of crime, rejected by
earth and heaven, still he thinks of his maiden. Rolla and the highwaymen intrude, telling Carlo they are surrounded by a thousand
armed men. Carlo urges the men to battle.

*Comment: The opening of this scene is the most startling and dramatic
chorus in the opera. It begins with a split of tenors and basses as the news
passes back and forth. Sopranos are added to give the shrill note needed to
signify a general panic. After Rolla's news, the male chorus sings in rollicking fashion. The whole offstage riot and recapture of Rolla are accomplished in a few minutes with no loss of momentum in the drama. The
whole mood subsides quickly and skillfully (and literally, since the whole
chorus "falls asleep" onstage). Carlo begins his meditation on nature with
a very lightly accompanied recitative. His romanza is superbly expressive.
The closing chorus is extremely noisy, complete with crashing cymbals.*

Part III

Scene 1: The edge of the forest near the Moors' castle.

Amalia, running from Francesco, is lost in the forest. In the distance, she hears the highwaymen singing of their life of rape, plunder,

arson, and death. Carlo enters, and she, not recognizing him, begs for mercy. When he reveals himself, they rush into each other's arms, swearing never to be parted again. She tells him of his brother's treachery. Together, they look forward to a life together on earth and an eternity in heaven.

Comment: Amalia, alone onstage while we hear snippets of the menacing chorus, should be a great dramatic moment, but it is handled rather quickly. Even the subsequent duet with Carlo is rather guarded emotionally, with oom-pah-pah accompaniment that sounds more like a call to arms than a love duet (a frequent situation in Verdi).

Scene 2: In the forest, by the ruins of an old castle.

The highwaymen are drinking and praising their life of crime. Some day, they'll all mount the scaffold and go to the punishment they have earned, but till then, there's wine, la ra, la ra . . .

Comment: Here we hear the full chorus whose snippets we had heard in the previous scene. Verdi, presumably, was trying to show the highwaymen's utter indifference to everything sacred, a contrast to Francesco's more genuine evil. To do this, he gives the highwaymen here a long chorus of "we love to rape, la ra, la ra." It is truly idiotic.

Carlo enters, and the highwaymen cheer. Carlo tells them to sleep as he keeps watch. Amalia deludes herself if she thinks they are united. He looks at the sleeping bandits. Even the evil find rest, but he cannot. He draws a pistol from his belt and loads it. But can he do it from fear of a life of suffering? No! Pride must triumph over pain! He throws the pistol aside.

Arminio enters. He speaks toward the tower of the old ruined castle, saying he has brought food. A voice from within says starvation is near. Carlo leaps out and orders Arminio to stop. Begging for mercy, Arminio tries to stop Carlo from entering the tower, but is overpowered. He flees. Carlo enters the tower and brings out a starving old man. Carlo recognizes the voice of his father, who tells him Francesco has locked him in the tower. Three months before, a stranger had brought news that his son Carlo was dead. Massimiliano had fainted and was presumed dead, only to revive inside a coffin. Francesco lifted the lid, sneered, and shut it again, ordering the coffin to be thrown into the ground. Later, the faithful Arminio hid him in the tower, where he has been ever since. Massimiliano faints again. Carlo fires his pistol to revive him, then tells the awakened highwaymen the frail old man's story. Carlo orders the highwaymen to their knees. They swear to avenge the wronged old man.

Comment: Massimiliano's narrative retelling his story is something of a hybrid, being neither a unified melodic aria nor a morphing dramatic narrative. It does, however, boast a fabulously spooky string accompaniment as well as giving a great bass scope to make something dramatic of the vocal line. The antiphonal, faux-liturgical finale, as Carlo demands an oath of vengeance from the highwaymen, is a striking dialogue, quite effective on stage.

Part IV

Scene 1: In the castle.

Francesco runs about the castle, agitated and certain he is being pursued by shadows. He orders a servant to bring the pastor to him, and confides his nightmares to Arminio. He had a vision of the Last Day, when, confronted at the foot of Sinai by three shining figures, he watched as his many sins were piled onto a scale, balanced by the Redeemer's blood. A single hair plucked from the whitened head of a frail old man made the scale crash on the side of sin, and a voice thundered from heaven, "For you, cursed one, the Son of God did not suffer." Arminio leaves in contempt, and Moser the pastor enters. Did Francesco summon him to mock religion again? Francesco feigns indifference, but asks which are the sins most offensive to God. Patricide and fratricide, responds the pastor. Francesco commands him to be silent. Arminio rushes in, warning of the attack by the highway-men. Francesco demands absolution from Moser. The pastor tells him only God can absolve him, and warns him of the lightning and thunder of God's vengeance. Francesco kneels for the first time, and calls on God, adding that it will be the last time he ever prays. Moser says God is denying forgiveness to such arrogant prayers. Francesco rises angrily, declaring that hell will not make a fool of him. He rushes out as the people cry that the fortress is crumbling.

Comment: *The baritone's big scene is marvelously dramatic, with trum-pets and the bass voice of the pastor signifying all the wrath of hell. The Verdi of the* Requiem *and the Philip/Inquisitor scene in* Don Carlos *is already present here.*

Scene 2: In the forest, by the ruined old castle. Dawn.

Massimiliano is seated on a rock, dejected. He still does not recog-nize Carlo, who is amazed that the old man does not seek vengeance on Francesco. Carlo manages to get Massimiliano's blessing. The highwaymen enter without Francesco, who has escaped. They drag in Amalia, however, who rejoices to find Carlo. He is appalled that she should find him among his men, and confesses to her and his father that he is their leader. Amalia decides to share Carlo's fate, whatever it be, and Massimiliano regrets the suffering he has caused. The high-waymen remind Carlo of his oaths to lead them. Realizing he cannot leave them, he pulls a dagger out and stabs Amalia. Carlo goes in search of the hangman as Amalia dies.

Comment: *The opening of the scene is beautiful and melancholy, with shimmering strings introducing a lovely duet for bass and tenor, a rarity in Verdi. When they sing together, they are doubled by the cellos, often a sig-nifier of truly warm feelings for Verdi. The finale of the act is all sound and fury. It is basically a quartet, with the chorus as a somewhat louder soloist. Carlo's final, desperate act of murder is a trial on our patience. All the more reason to enjoy this opera in the concert hall rather than the theater.*

Il corsaro

PREMIERE: Teatro Grande, Trieste, 1848. Libretto by Francesco Maria Piave.

Il corsaro shares, with *Alzira,* the distinction of being regarded as the absolute nadir of Verdi's output. As such, it holds a certain morbid fascination for opera fans. Merely having seen it confers status. *Corsaro* has its rewards. The problem lies not in a lack of ideas, but in a lack of cohesion. Conventional wisdom says that Verdi was simply not interested in this work when he wrote it, in Paris, with the revolutions of 1848 raging around him. Also, the opera was contracted for Ricordi's rival Lucca, whom Verdi never liked. In addition, there is the story itself, a wild narrative poem of Byron's that tends toward the moody and introverted rather than the sorts of dramatic situations that really inspired the composer. Finally, the opera was produced at Trieste without Verdi's participation. Yet there are subtleties and excellent moments in it, particularly in the orchestral writing, that show great development on Verdi's part. The vocal writing is challenging and occasionally quite exciting. In fact, this is one of the real reasons why *Corsaro* is so rarely performed. The tenor role is written for a heroic voice, and there are two lead soprano roles. If one could assemble the proper cast to perform *Corsaro* adequately, one wouldn't. One would produce *Trovatore* instead. At least with that opera the audience would be guaranteed a payoff at the end of the night. In *Corsaro,* much effort is expended for relatively little catharsis. Still, I maintain that second-rate Verdi is better than most other options, and this opera has superb moments.

CAST OF CHARACTERS

CORRADO *(tenor)* A corsair (pirate). Corrado can lament the cussedness of the human race and his own isolation with the best Romantic heroes.

MEDORA *(soprano)* His true love. Medora's repertory of actions range in scope from passing out to dying.

SEID, PASHA OF CORONE *(baritone)* The evil baritone who actually is not particularly evil.

GULNARA *(soprano)* A harem girl, the Pasha's favorite. This is the actual prima donna role, with some devilishly difficult music.

GIOVANNI *(bass),* one of Corrado's corsairs; SELIMO *(tenor),* a soldier of the Pasha's; EUNUCH *(tenor, naturally);* SLAVE *(tenor).*

THE OPERA

Prelude

Comment: *Without a doubt, this is the noisiest prelude in the Verdi canon. A brief and lovely middle section only accentuates the sound and fury. The themes derive from the prison scene in Act III, where they are effective. Here they are rather annoying.*

Act I

Scene 1: The corsairs' isle in the Aegean Sea.

While the corsairs in the distance reflect on their exciting life, Corrado wanders along the shore. Mankind is hateful to him. His own life is an endless disappointment, and he refers to an unnamed incident that caused him to live at odds with the human race. Giovanni enters and hands Corrado a letter from a Greek sympathizer. Corrado summons his men, telling them they will sail that evening to attack the Pasha Seid's city of Corone.

Comment: The opening scene is instantly recognizable as a Romantic locus, peopled with Romantic types: outlaws, a tenor who is their leader yet distinctly above them in some sense, and a hero's loneliness so profound it becomes violent and hostile. The opening chorus is strictly framework, but Corrado's andante solo is lovely. The orchestral writing receives great praise from scholars, as it generally does throughout the opera. The concluding cabaletta of this scene is remarkably crude but rather fun.

Scene 2: Medora's rooms in an old tower.

Medora is pining for Corrado, who suddenly rushes in, telling her he must leave for a while. She declares she will die of grief during his absence. A cannon shot summons Corrado to battle, and Medora faints.

Comment: Medora's "pining aria" is beautiful and haunting, lying a little low in the soprano voice and accompanied by a diaphanous arrangement of harp, solo cello, and solo bass. The duet builds craftily into a climax—we are told in musical terms what we are not permitted to see onstage. It is a rare, purely sexual moment in Verdi, and only partially convincing, if pretty to listen to. Medora, like a good Romantic heroine, can faint at will.

Act II

Scene 1: Gulnara's rooms in Pasha Seid's palace.

Harem girls attend to Gulnara, the Pasha's favorite. Gulnara, however, detests the Pasha and longs for freedom and true love. A eunuch enters to summon Gulnara to a banquet the Pasha is giving to celebrate his sure victory over the pirates. Alone again, she prays that heaven will grant her heart's desire.

Comment: *No "Turkish" chorus would be complete without cymbals and triangles, and Verdi has obliged here with a fun chorus of no great weight. Gulnara's scena, however, is really top-rate. The andante is quite lush. Budden finds the concluding cabaletta of "no distinction whatsoever," while Osborne calls it "absolutely glorious." The difference, of course, lies in performance. A blood-and-guts soprano can have a field day with it.*

Scene 2: Pasha Seid's banquet hall.

Seid, attended by soldiers, enters the hall and orders a hymn of praise to Allah be sung. A slave admits a holy dervish, who tells his story and begs protection from the Pasha. The Pasha sees his fleet burning in the distance. The dervish tosses back his hood to reveal that he is—Corrado! The corsairs rush into the banquet hall and a battle ensues. Corrado gallantly orders the rescue of the women, giving the Pasha's men time to rally. The corsairs are defeated and Corrado taken prisoner. Gulnara and the harem girls beg for his life, but the Pasha orders him tortured to death.

Comment: *The Allah chorus, if we may call it that, does not soar. The interchanges between Seid and the disguised Corrado almost rise to the level of a good Verdian duet scena. The battle scene is a pain but brief. The finale is gorgeous: The thread of melody around which the ensemble builds undergoes a slight variation each time it is sung by a different character. It is rather unique in the Verdi canon, and worthy to be heard more.*

Act III

Scene 1: Seid's rooms in the palace.

Seid, alone, is happy for his victory but saddened by his failure to win the one woman he loves. Gulnara, he fears, loves Corrado. He sends for her and tells her of Corrado's impending tortures to test her reaction. When Gulnara is visibly upset, Seid falls into a jealous rage. He rushes out, and Gulnara determines to take action herself.

Comment: The baritone solo scene runs the gamut of emotions in a very little amount of time. One needs a good singing actor here, as in Foscari, *to make something of it. The subsequent duet scene begins in an almost courtly atmosphere, slowly becoming wilder as the two cast off formalities and reveal their true feelings. Finally, they each hit high notes and storm off. It is a study in formal disintegration toward anarchy.*

Scene 2: Corrado's prison cell.

Corrado languishes in chains. His thoughts turn to Medora, whom he will never see again. He falls asleep. Gulnara enters quietly and gazes at the sleeping pirate. He awakes. She tells him she will help him escape. Corrado finds such treachery beneath him, but Gulnara is determined, even when she discovers that Corrado is already sworn in love. A storm rises. Gulnara withdraws. She returns, having killed the Pasha. Now Corrado rouses himself. He must, in fairness, rescue Gulnara, even if he cannot love her. They escape.

Comment: Corrado's prison scene is the one "hit" of the opera, its poignancy achieved by solo cello and solo viola. The duet with Gulnara is praised by scholars as an early effort by Verdi to set an interaction between characters sentence by sentence. The storm must be the briefest in opera— barely long enough to kill the Pasha.

Scene 3: A cliff overlooking the sea on the corsairs' island.

Having heard of Corrado's capture, Medora is dying on the cliff while pirates and their women comment in sympathy. A ship is sighted, and Corrado and Gulnara appear. Medora admits she poisoned herself when she heard of Corrado's capture. Gulnara graciously refuses Medora's thanks for saving Corrado's life. She acted out of love, yet she knows her love is in vain. Medora asks Corrado to hold her, and she dies in his arms. Corrado, overcome by grief, leaps off the cliff into the sea. Gulnara and the others are horrified.

Comment: *The final scene opens with another scene of languishing desolation as Medora's life ebbs, but no work needs two "eleven o'clock ballads." The rest of the scene is built around a lovely trio for tenor and both sopranos, and a little "competitive singing" can be expected from the ladies at this point, translating into diva-antics the love rivalry of the story. Corrado's leap off the cliff is another Romantic cliché, later used more effectively in* La battaglia di Legnano.

La battaglia di Legnano

PREMIERE: Teatro Argentino, Rome, 1849. Libretto by Salvatore Cammarano.

THE NAME

The title refers to the battle of Legnano (a town in Lombardy) in 1176. The *gl* and *gn* sounds tend to confuse Americans, not least because of deliberate mispronunciations by Italian-Americans who wish to seem more assimilated. (Witness New York Yankees announcer Phil Rizzuto's trashing of the name "Pagliarulo" for years on the radio.) *Battaglia* is pronounced "bah-TAH-lya," and *Legnano* is "le-NYAH-no." It is no harder to pronounce than *lasagna*.

WHEN CAMMARANO AND Verdi decided to write a shamelessly patriotic opera to respond to the First War of Italian Independence (as it is now called), the librettist found a French play that laid out the issues of a love triangle against a background of war with great simplicity. By changing the setting to Milan in 1176, Cammarano magnificently paralleled current events. In the twelfth century, the Holy Roman Emperor Frederick, known to history as Barbarossa because of his red beard, was trying to subjugate the various cities in northern Italy. The cities formed the Lombard League to frustrate Barbarossa's plan. The decisive battle was fought at Legnano, where the Emperor was knocked from his horse and presumed dead. Lombard independence from imperial domination was assured for centuries.

This was too perfect for an Italian to resist in 1849. At that very moment, the soldiers of the Austrian emperor (political heir to the Holy Roman Emperor) were preparing to subjugate the Italian peninsula yet again. Verdi urged Cammarano to write a brief and sharp libretto stressing unity among the Italians. Cammarano did so, beautifully. While there are obvious anachronisms in a bunch of twelfth-century Lombards crying for Italian unity and screaming *"Viva Italia,"* the point was made that without unity there would never be an end to Italian troubles. Verdi put a great deal of feeling into the score. The result is a great opera, if it is judged on its own terms.

The events around the premiere of *La battaglia di Legnano* are considerably better known than the opera itself. The opening night was probably the most raucous evening in Verdi's life, a hysteria Verdi did not find congenial. After the temporary collapse of the Italian independence movement, *Legnano* didn't stand a chance of getting performed under the reactionary censors. It was tricked up as *The Siege of Haarlem* at one later point, but was not successful in that guise. *Legnano* must be entirely what it is or it is nothing at all. By the time Italian unification and independence were achieved, the opera seemed like a reminder of the naive political mistakes of 1849, and it was not revived. In the twentieth century it has had fitful reappearances in Italy and England, with a few concert performances in America and elsewhere.

Common wisdom says that *Legnano* cannot win audiences today because it is too much of a cut-and-dried "us-against-them" propaganda piece written for a now-remote historical moment, despite its excellent music and swift action. But the problem with this opera is not that it's a propaganda piece but rather the nature of Verdi's propaganda. Barbarossa, the villain, is not particularly evil. He is brutal, but this is the Middle Ages, you know. He is cold, remote, and foreign—but also rather grand, certainly noble, and no coward. Herein lies the problem. The code of chivalry tended to exalt the enemy to underscore the bravery of combating them. We, on the other hand, feel the need to belittle, humiliate, and, ideally, dehumanize (cf. the aliens in alien invasion movies) the enemy before we can destroy them. Thus President Bush called the president of Iraq by his first name during the Persian Gulf War, deliberately mispronouncing it "SAH-dum," and thus the *New York Post* headlines currently refer to Slobodan Milosevic of Serbia as "Slobbo." In other words, the propaganda of *La battaglia di Legnano* is alienating to modern audiences not because it is too simplistic but because it is not simplistic enough.

Which is really a shame, because it is a splendid work, even with its difficult and clumsy moments (the tenor donning a patriotic sash and leaping out the window being the most obvious example). Verdi was clearly touched by the story, and responded with an excellent score. The communal canvas is masterly, the economy of expression is impressive, and the whole opera is barely two hours long.

CAST OF CHARACTERS

ARRIGO *(tenor)* A soldier from Verona, wounded in a previous battle and presumed dead, in love with Lida.

ROLANDO *(baritone)* A knight from Milan, and friend of Arrigo.

LIDA *(soprano)* A lady of Milan, once in love with Arrigo. Lida has lost both her parents and all her brothers in the war, and marries Rolando when she hears reports of Arrigo's death.

IMELDA *(mezzo-soprano)* Lida's maid.

MARCOVALDO *(baritone)* A German prisoner in Rolando's castle.

FREDERICK BARBAROSSA *(bass)* The Holy Roman (that is, German) Emperor, in battle with the cities of northern Italy.

FIRST CONSUL OF MILAN *(bass);* SECOND CONSUL OF MILAN *(bass);* MAYOR OR PODESTÀ OF THE CITY OF COMO *(bass);* ARRIGO'S SQUIRE *(tenor);* HERALD *(tenor).*

THE OPERA

Overture

Comment: *The excellent Overture combines personal and patriotic sentiments somewhat more successfully than the opera itself. It begins and ends with patriotic marches. The middle, slow part is the background music of the scene where Arrigo writes his mother. Critics praise it, and this Overture currently appears on a compilation recording of music recommended for figure skaters!*

Act I: "He lives!"

Scene 1: On the streets of Milan, near the walls, in 1176.

Soldiers from various northern Italian cities are gathering, cheered by the people. They cry *"Viva Italia!"* and anticipate the Lombard League's victory over the German Emperor Barbarossa. Arrigo, arriving with the soldiers from Verona, salutes Milan, greatest of Lombard cities. Rolando enters and is thrilled to see his friend Arrigo, wounded in battle and presumed dead, among the throng. Trumpets blare, announcing the Consuls, who thank the soldiers for resurrecting Milan after the Imperial soldiers had destroyed her once already. Rolando leads all present in an oath to defend Milan. All depart.

Comment: *The opening words of the chorus, "Viva Italia!" signal the main theme of the opera, yet the chorus is restrained and thoughtful rather than bombastic. Arrigo's narrative, likewise, is the most thoughtful music he sings all evening. Rolando's solo is tender baritonal lyricism. The final oath is led, a capella, by the Consuls (basses), the orchestra joins in to swell the emotion, and finally decrescendos again as all depart to remarkably subtle music.*

Scene 2: A shady spot by the moats outside the walls of Milan.

Lida's attendants wonder why she alone should be so gloomy, leaving the general celebration. Lida tells them she cannot forget her slain brothers and parents. She has often begged God for death, but He saw fit to give her a son, and now she is a mother. Marcovaldo enters, and Lida asks what he, a prisoner, is doing there. Marcovaldo says Rolando gave him freedom of the grounds up to the tower. "So you come to stare at his wife?" she asks, and he humbly admits a secret love for her. Lida commands his silence. Imelda enters with astounding news. Rolando is coming . . . with Arrigo! "He lives!" cries Lida, her agitation noted by Marcovaldo. Lida says nothing to the others, but thinks that soon she will see her love again.

Rolando and Arrigo enter. Rolando bids Lida welcome their hero, and notices Arrigo trembling. Arrigo claims his wounds pain him, but Marcovaldo is now certain of his suspicion. Rolando invites Arrigo to stay with him and Lida again. Trumpets sound, and Rolando dismisses Marcovaldo and the women. A herald announces an emergency meeting called by the Consuls. Imperial troops are advancing again. Rolando leaves quickly to prepare for war. Immediately, Arrigo accuses Lida of faithlessness. She tries to explain that he had been reported killed, she was orphaned and alone, so . . . She pleads for kindness, but he orders her away. She asks him to kill her, but he pushes her away and runs out.

Comment: The requisite "pretty maidens all in a row" chorus that opens the scene is gentle and scored with nice subleties and decorations. Lida's oddly introspective recitative is all over the place—up, down, and in between. Her slow aria is extremely moody, but when she blurts out "Egli vive!" it is in a full diva explosion above the staff. Her subsequent cabaletta, an "aside," is packed with difficult and significant coloratura. Marcovaldo admits his love in a single line of recitative, typical of the opera's economy of expression. He's insincere and he's the bad guy—that's all we need to know. Arrigo bursts in with typical "I'm a tenor and you've cheated on me!" blather, and we immediately lose any real sympathy for him. What was the poor girl supposed to have done, enter a convent? And how would that have simplified the situation? Although we dislike him, the duet that ends the scene is exciting, each line overlapping but never unifying until the end.

Act II: "Barbarossa!"

Setting: The Council Chamber in the Town Hall of Como.

Leaders and magistrates assemble in the hall. The Podestà announces representatives from the Lombard League, and Rolando and Arrigo enter. Rolando tells them the Imperial forces are split. Now is the time to strike. Let Como and Milan bury their ancient rivalry to unite for their common country. The magistrates remind Rolando that they have a treaty with Barbarossa, but Arrigo calls that shameful and asks them plainly if they are Italians or not. Rolando says he hears the poetry of the Italian language in their speech, but sees only barbarians in their thoughts and deeds. What reply should Arrigo give the League? Suddenly, Barbarossa enters, saying he will give the answer himself. A tragic fate awaits the Lombards. Rolando and Arrigo tell the Emperor to save threats for the battlefield. Barbarossa orders the shutters of the windows opened, revealing masses of German troops and terrifying the magistrates. "Here is my reply to your League," he says. The two friends tell him mercenaries cannot long conquer a people who struggle for liberty, nor change their destiny. "I am the destiny of Italy!" cries Barbarossa. All cry for war, merciless and final.

Comment: This male-only scene makes for an interesting deployment of voices. Arrigo and Rolando address the room in a melodic and graceful duet. If Arrigo had one note of the same lyricism in his confrontation with Lida, this opera would have a superb human element. Frederick's sudden entrance is startling, dark, and very sarcastic. The conflict is expressed in an ensemble—the bass and the bass chorus over which the baritone and the tenor seem to soar. They are, in fact, taking the vocal part usually reserved for women in ensembles, and the effect is excellent. The finale is a noisy chorus, and we realize that the whole scene has been constructed as a crescendo, exploding into the call for war.

Act III: "Disgrace"

Scene 1: The vaults of the Church of Sant'Ambrogio.

The Knights of Death, each wearing a black sash with the figure of a skull on it, enter the dark chamber to take their sacred oath. Arrigo appears asking to take the vow. Tomorrow there will be a battle at Legnano. He will die or triumph with the Knights. Arrigo kneels and an old Knight silently places his own sash on him while the others cross their swords over his head. All swear to avenge Italy's injuries or die in the attempt.

Comment: The music for this static ritual scene is appropriately dark and murky, but misses being truly harrowing. The final oath chorus is not a rouser, as one might expect, but a spooky curse on the cowards. While Verdi and Cammarano were undoubtedly making reference to many of the secret revolutionary societies prevalent in Italy in their own time, it is hard for us today not to see the rituals of fascists and even the Ku Klux Klan in all the death imagery and hocus-pocus. Still, the secrecy is well represented by the subdued music, which makes for a necessary relief from the ceaseless action of the rest of the opera.

Scene 2: A room in Rolando's castle. Night.

Lida is distraught. Imelda asks her what the problem is. Lida confesses she has written a painful letter. Yet this letter could avert tragedy. Arrigo? asks Imelda. Yes, admits Lida, giving her the letter to pass to Arrigo. Rolando enters, telling Imelda to bring in his son. He wonders at Lida's tears. The boy is brought in, and he, Rolando, and Lida embrace. Rolando instructs his wife to care for their son if anything should happen to him in battle. The boy must be taught to remember that he is an Italian, and love God and his country. Lida, weeping, leaves with the boy. Arrigo enters. Rolando confides that he has the most terrible suspicions. He asks Arrigo to care for Lida and his son if he should die. They embrace, and Arrigo leaves, crying.

Marcovaldo enters, and immediately tells Rolando that Arrigo and Lida have disgraced him. He gives Rolando the letter, which he has snatched from Imelda. Rolando reads Lida's words, begging to see Arrigo once before the battle. Rolando swears vengeance.

Comment: *Lida's scene has been described as a mad scene without an aria, something that's very hard to pull off in the theater. The heart-tugger between Rolando, Lida, and the boy (who does not sing, thank God) is exquisite, separate phrases overlapping then uniting in a gorgeous cantabile. Arrigo's farewell is likewise tender. Rolando's final jealousy aria bursts out of nowhere without the typical orchestral introduction, and is quite convincing. Why Lida would prefer Arrigo to Rolando is a question not answered by the music.*

Scene 3: A room in the castle tower, with a balcony beyond the window. Arrigo's black sash is on a chair by the window. Night.

Arrigo notes the quiet of the night, with only the rippling of the moat below to be heard. He sits down to write a letter to his mother. Lida enters, accusing him of cowardice in wanting to die. He asks why he should live, since she doesn't love him any more. She admits that she loves him still, but they must part forever—she for her son, Arrigo for his mother. Since Arrigo was deaf to her letter, she had to come here and say this to him in person. He is telling her that he never received the letter when knocking is heard at the door, followed by Rolando's voice calling Arrigo. Arrigo sends Lida out on the balcony and closes the shutters.

Rolando enters and looks around. He has come to hasten Arrigo to battle. It is still night, says Arrigo, but Rolando moves to show him day is breaking. Opening the shutters of the balcony, he sees Lida standing there. She stammers an explanation, as does Arrigo. There is silence. Suddenly, Lida and Arrigo fall at Rolando's feet, and Rolando thunders revenge. Arrigo swears to Lida's innocence. Rolando draws a knife and Arrigo demands to be killed, but suddenly Rolando is struck with an idea. He knows a worse vengeance than mere death . . . dishonor! Rolando quickly exits the room, locking Arrigo and Lida in it as the trumpets summoning the soldiers sound. Arrigo is distraught. The soldiers will say he has hidden on the fateful day, and curse his name. He hears the Knights of Death pass, and swears he will accompany them. Brandishing the sash of the order, he runs to the window, cries out *"Viva Italia!"* and leaps off the balcony. Lida collapses.

Comment: Yes, well, that little curtain closer with the tenor flying out the window might be another reason we don't see this opera staged very often. The scene differs from other examples of airborne singers mostly in that Arrigo lives through the experience. Cammarano is quite careful to make reference to the moat below the balcony.

The moody introduction to the act, one of Verdi's more interesting bits of orchestral music, seems most directly to refer to Arrigo's nervousness and sadness. In the following trio, interesting harmonies and many staccato phrases convey the situation. Arrigo's final cry, however, is as long, loud, and heroic as the tenor can possibly make it.

Act IV: "To Die for the Country"

Setting: A square in Milan, with a church in the background.

A crowd of women, old men, and children are kneeling in the square, asking God to protect the sons of the nation. Lida prays that God spare both Rolando and Arrigo, the greatest heroes of Italy. The Consul enters with senators and a throng, announcing victory. The enemy is defeated, the Emperor knocked from his horse by Arrigo the Veronese! The Consul and his suite enter the church to give thanks to God, the citizens fall into each other's arms weeping with joy, trumpets blare and bells ring. A sad trumpet call is heard, and the Knights of Death carry on Arrigo, wounded, followed by Rolando, silent. Arrigo calls for Rolando's hand. He swears to Lida's innocence. Lida and Rolando both draw near, Rolando's compassion causing him to weep. Truly, he who dies for his country cannot have an evil soul. A trumphal cart approaches, draped with banners. Arrigo calls for a banner, and the people hand it to him, praising and thanking God, asking Him to open the gates of heaven to the noble hero. Kissing the banner, Arrigo dies.

Comment: This act, all of which was encored during the initial run, is several different minioperas all in about fifteen minutes. Verdi was justly proud of the opening tableau, with the various whispering choral divisions, single organ notes, and Lida's prayer soaring (lightly) over all and providing a focal point. The victory chorus is a mere four lines of deliberately naive melody. It is a picture of popular sentiment, nothing more, nothing less. Everything quiets down for Arrigo's entrance, and the subsequent trio is a melodic weaving of voices arriving at a point of acceptance. The trio resolves and transforms with Arrigo's line about the goodness of one who dies for his country. It is one of those simple, arching phrases Verdi could always create at the right moment. Cammarano deliberately left the meaning open in the Italian, "Chi muore per la patria Alma si rea non ha." Is the sense that such a man could not lie, or that he must in general be a good man? It seems to start as the specific reference to Arrigo's oath, and become generalized when restated by the chorus. When the people hand him the banner to kiss, they repeat the phrase (once only), and Arrigo dies. The opera ends on a touching note as the people, rather than cheering their victory, consider the cost of freedom and the need for faith in their cause. If people today knew this opera more than they knew about it, it could not be dismissed as a rabble-rousing potboiler.

Luisa Miller

PREMIERE: Teatro San Carlo, Naples, 1849. Libretto by Salvatore Cammarano.

Luisa Miller is an opera the world forgets periodically, but always rediscovers with a sense of affection. It has all the fire and vigor of Romantic opera at its wildest framed within a manageable story about characters who are, by operatic standards, remarkably normal and familiar. The source was Schiller's *Kabale und Liebe,* a play about romantic love, intrigue, poison, simple villagers, and evil aristocrats. Verdi was immediately drawn to the intimacy of the work. Focusing on the young girl of the story, a girl who is both typical and extraordinary, Cammarano fashioned a coherent libretto which suggested that heroism and nobility of spirit can reside even, and especially, in the girl next door.

If there is a problem with *Luisa Miller,* it lies in the very simplicity of the title character. She has none of the extreme qualities that make archetypes out of other operatic heroines. A soprano who relies solely on the music to create a personality and a subtext for her will not thrill people in this role. Throughout Verdi's lifetime, he rarely supported revivals of the opera, and it languished for a long time. It had to wait until the general Verdi revival of recent years before being considered standard repertory.

That said, *Luisa Miller* remains a gem. The opera gets more interesting with each passing page of music. The ensembles, quartet, and final trio are first-rate, and the big tenor aria is one of the loveliest in opera. In fact, the tenor role is exciting throughout, if not especially subtle; Budden was moved to call it "a tenor's opera." But Luisa can win our affection as well, especially when portrayed by a soprano with stage presence. The baritone role can also be moving.

CAST OF CHARACTERS

LUISA MILLER *(soprano)* A village girl.

RODOLFO *(tenor)* The son of the new Count, in love with Luisa. At first, he keeps his identity a secret, calling himself Carlo.

MILLER *(baritone)* Luisa's father, a widowed, retired soldier.

COUNT WALTER *(bass)* Rodolfo's father, recent inheritor of the local title and castle, and therefore the ruler of the area.

WURM *(bass)* The Count's steward. With a name like that, he's obviously the bad guy.

DUCHESS FEDERICA *(mezzo)* A relation of Rodolfo's, in love with him since childhood. She was forced to marry an aged duke at the imperial court, who has rather conveniently died and left her his fortune. She returns to her homeland to marry Rodolfo.

LAURA *(mezzo-soprano)* Another village girl, and Luisa's friend.

THE OPERA

Overture

Comment: *The Overture is one of Verdi's best and most interesting. Instead of combining contrasting themes, it uses the theme of Luisa's sadness in Act III as its basis, changing the emotional emphasis with varying orchestration and accents.*

Act I

Scene 1: A pleasant village in the Tyrol.

Miller and his daughter Luisa are greeted by villagers, who have gathered to celebrate Luisa's birthday. Laura says they will all go to church to celebrate but Luisa is nervously looking for someone. Miller asks her to be careful, since this Carlo she obviously loves is a stranger and only just arrived in the village with the new Count. Luisa allays her father's fears. This young man is good and pure and she knows her love comes from God. A young man jumps out of the crowd to greet Luisa. Luisa rejoices to see "Carlo," and they sing of their love, but Miller worries that "Carlo" may be a seducer and a heartbreaker. Bells ring, and all except Miller go into the church. Wurm enters. His heart is raging with jealousy. Didn't Miller promise Luisa to him? No, answers Miller, and he denies influencing his daughter in any way. Marriage is sacred, and fathers should imitate God by ruling with kindness, not cruelty. In spite, Wurm tells Miller that this "Carlo" is really Rodolfo, the son of Count Walter. Does Miller suppose a nobleman would be proposing an honorable arrangement to a village girl? Miller is distraught; he had feared this very thing! He begs heaven to torture him in any way, but to protect his daughter, his one treasure.

Comment: The opening, with its chorus of happy, well-scrubbed peasants, might make you think you came to the theater on the wrong night and will see a genial comic opera. Luisa's song is pretty, the scoring as simple as the girl who sings it. The expected cabaletta is actually a brief love duet, which develops into a pleasant choral ensemble, with only Miller's voice singing a fascinatingly discordant descant. This "sour note" develops further in the duet between Miller and Wurm. What looks like it will be a standard baritone-bass "call-to-arms" duet actually becomes a broad scena for Miller, with the bass adding decoration. Miller's almost-solo at the end is prime baritone time. If he has the vocal goods, he will milk it for all it's worth.

Scene 2: A room in Count Walter's castle.

Count Walter asks Wurm if Rodolfo has lost his reason in falling for a village girl. Wurm says the boy is a hothead, then leaves to bring Rodolfo in. Alone, Walter considers that he is only trying to advance his ungrateful son's position in the world. Rodolfo enters, and Walter tells his son he will soon marry his cousin Federica. She always loved the boy and was forced to marry the Duke, but the Duke died, leaving her with his title and court connections. Rodolfo protests that he does not seek advancement at court, but his father orders him to obey. The Duchess enters, followed by many attendants, greeting her cousins. Walter and the others withdraw, leaving Rodolfo so he may propose to the Duchess. The young man decides to be honest and straightforward, telling Federica that he loves another. She is furious. If Rodolfo were to stab her, she would forgive him, but a rival she will never forgive. They depart.

Comment: Count Walter's aria, "Il mio sangue," is a broad and difficult solo with cadenzas and jumps into the higher registers. The music is filled with pathos even though he is one of the bad guys. The Duchess enters to classic Verdian ditzy music; obviously, we are not meant to be favorably impressed by this lady. The hollowness of her frilly music will be in direct contrast with Luisa's often deceptively simple music. The Duchess's confrontation with Rodolfo just misses being truly interesting, as the two explore various moods, each briefly, before resolving and storming off.

Scene 3: A room in Miller's house.

Luisa is waiting nervously for her love, and hears nothing but the distant calls of a hunting party. Miller enters and collapses into a chair. His fears were right! he tells his daughter. Not only is Carlo really Rodolfo, but he is about to be married to a great lady of the court. Rodolfo bursts into the room, having heard Miller's denunciation, and begs Luisa to trust him. His name has changed but his heart has remained true. Taking her hand, he kneels before Luisa and declares he is her husband. Miller believes him, but worries about the Count. Mysteriously, Rodolfo explains he knows a secret that would make the Count grovel at his feet. Just then Count Walter appears. He accuses Luisa of seducing his son. Insulted, Miller challenges the Count to fight, whereupon the Count calls in archers from outside the house to arrest both Miller and Luisa. Laura and the villagers run in to see what is happening. Luisa throws herself at the Count's feet, pleading mercy, but Miller orders her to stand. She is innocent and need kneel only to heaven, not to this "beast." Luisa prays to God, asking why she must be trampled so if she was created in His image, Rodolfo pleads with his father, and Walter maintains his fury at his son. Laura and the villagers express pity for Luisa, while the archers complain that they must obey their lord. Rodolfo threatens to kill Luisa rather than let her be taken by anybody else, and Walter bluntly dares Rodolfo to go ahead. Desperately, Rodolfo plays his last hand. Either his father release Luisa, or he will tell everyone how Walter inherited the title! Shocked, Walter orders Luisa's release, to the amazement of the crowd.

Comment: The scene opens with a very eerie hunting chorus, sung antiphonally and offstage. Rodolfo's entry slices through this mood like a hot knife through butter. His declaration "Son io tuo sposo!" *("I am your husband!") is a cabaletta in a single line, a great achievement of Verdi's that he would refine for the rest of his career. When Rodolfo tells Miller he has a secret on the Count, the sneaky clarinet figures convey the unspoken information. As soon as the Count arrives, though, he's back to his heroic tenor self, throwing off some mighty lines in the grand manner. Usually Rodolfo wears all his emotion on his sleeve, and tends to be more impressive in vocal explosions than as a nuanced character. Luisa's voice, naturally, stands out in the subsequent ensemble, carrying the melody while the others support and decorate. The denouement of the ensemble is more hormonal outbursts from Rodolfo, even though we are supposed to imagine his threat to his father as an "aside." Only in opera are asides shouted at full voice.*

Act II

Scene 1: A room in Miller's house.

Laura and the villagers tell Luisa they have seen Miller dragged off to prison in chains, yet God always sees the sufferings of the wretched. Wurm bursts in, ordering the villagers out. Wurm tells Luisa that her father awaits execution for the crime of threatening the Count, yet she can save him. The Count requires a certain letter from her, and she will be rewarded with her father's freedom. He dictates: "I never loved Rodolfo. Ambition overpowered me. Forgive me. I must return to my first love." Luisa is aghast, but Wurm assures her Miller will be executed directly if she does not sign the letter and swear before the Count that she wrote it freely, and show a certain noble lady that she is actually in love . . . with Wurm! Miserable, Luisa agrees.

Comment: This scene is a clear-cut conflict of good and evil. Wurm remains pure slime throughout, while Luisa goes through the full cycle of feminine responses. In the opening recitative, Luisa approaches a heroic stature, and here must convey a certain heft in the lower registers if she is not to come across as another tedious operatic blushing virgin. Her cavatina, "Tu puniscimi, o signor," then soars in the other direction, finishing with (one hopes) floating piano high C's. Next comes some more recitative, and then the cabaletta, which is de rigueur for a soprano who is about to be raped by a bass. The final aria approaches but never quite becomes a duet, despite interjections from Wurm. The point is that these two have absolutely no common ground. Luisa's cabaletta, "A brani, a brani, o perfido," requires a huge range but also a subtle cohesion from top to bottom.

Scene 2: A room in Count Walter's castle.

Alone, Walter considers that his son must be mad with love. His own firmness will compensate for his son's lack of worldly wisdom. Wurm enters. Luisa will come to the castle shortly by the secret path to make her confession before Walter and the Duchess, and the letter has been sent to Rodolfo by messenger. Walter repeats that he only wanted Federica's riches for his son's benefit, while Wurm realizes he too is caught in this scheme. He had suggested murdering the old Count himself. Walter recalls the murder with terror, but Wurm assures him everyone thought highwaymen were the culprits. "Not everyone," says Walter. The old man named his assassins before he died. Wurm is terrified, and the two realize their fates are linked in the Devil. Federica enters, and Walter dismisses Wurm. Walter tells the Duchess that Rodolfo never really loved anyone else, and soon she will have proof. Wurm enters with Luisa, reminding her of her father's plight. Federica is impressed with the girl's innocence, but why will she not look into her eyes? She's a nervous village girl, stammer Walter and Wurm. Slowly, Federica interrogates Luisa. Is she in love? Yes. With whom? Wurm, answers Luisa, in anguish. She never loved Rodolfo. Luisa thinks this lie will make her expire, Federica is overjoyed that she will have Rodolfo, while Wurm and Walter gloat.

Comment: *The "not quite a duet" finale to Scene I is followed by an awesome and rare two-bass duet in this scene. The two basses lower the overall tonal atmosphere, so to speak, so Luisa will stand out even more in the rest of the opera as a beacon of light in an evil world. These two men trade off declamations before uniting their voices. It's very difficult to know which is singing, the dramatic implication being that the two are united in a bond of guilt, but the musical implication is that they are in fact the same person, which makes Walter's connection to Luisa disturbingly perverted. The others enter to various snippets of recitative, Luisa's being in the lowest extremes of the soprano range, and therefore often barked or indicated rather than actually sung. She doesn't soar again until the scene's final quartet.*

Scene 3: A garden in the castle.

Rodolfo runs in, followed by a peasant. He tells Rodolfo Luisa sent him with the letter to Wurm. Rodolfo dismisses him. He reads the letter, and is crushed by Luisa's treachery. Wurm enters. Rodolfo produces two pistols, and demands Wurm fight with him. Rodolfo fires into the air, and when a crowd comes to investigate, Wurm disappears. Walter appears, pretending to be contrite and saying he grants permission for his son to marry his beloved. Rodolfo tells his father she has betrayed him, and threatens suicide. Walter counsels revenge instead. Let him marry another. Rodolfo is miserable, but Walter advises his son listen to him, since a father's love cannot stray.

Comment: *At this point, sensible people might wonder why it is that tenors are so unfailingly stupid, self-pitying, and short-sighted. Perhaps the tenor voice, with its inherent intensity, is best suited to depict non-intellectual emotions, such as anger, arousal, and despair. In any case, this is one of the most magnificent scenes Verdi ever wrote for tenor. The cavatina, "Quando le sere al placido," is justly famous as a showcase for the tenor's voice. The wrap-up cabaletta is less well known but hardly less of an opportunity for the tenor to show off.*

Act III

Setting: A room in Miller's house.

Luisa is writing at a table. Laura and the village girls try to console Luisa, urging her to eat something, but Luisa refuses. She asks why the church is lit up, but Laura, not wanting her to hear of Rodolfo's wedding with Federica, says the Count must be celebrating his new position. Miller enters, and Luisa asks her friends to leave them. They depart. He embraces her. How noble she is! He heard everything from Wurm. He picks up the letter Luisa was writing, a confession to Rodolfo, and deduces that she plans to die. Innocently, she explains that death is only a terror for those who are guilty. For others it is a bed strewn with roses. He begs Luisa to reconsider and persuades her to remain alive and keep him company. They will leave this place and roam wherever destiny takes them. There will be tears and hardship, but God will bless them and they will have each other. Miller retires to his room. Luisa hears the organ of the church playing and says a prayer, her last in this place. Tomorrow she will pray elsewhere.

Rodolfo appears at the door, unseen by Luisa. He tells a servant to bring his father, and quietly pours poison into a goblet. Producing the fateful letter, he approaches Luisa. Did she write it? Yes, she admits. He demands a drink, and she hands him the goblet. He drinks, and tells Luisa to drink as well. She does. All is over, mutters Rodolfo. He accuses her of disloyalty, which she denies. The castle clock strikes. He tells her this is their last hour. They have drunk poison! Now Luisa feels free to tell him the story of the letter. Rodolfo is horrified, cursing the day he was born. Miller enters, and Rodolfo confesses what he has done. Luisa, already faint, asks for her father's blessing; Miller bemoans losing his only consolation; and Rodolfo asks forgiveness. Luisa dies.

The villagers enter the house with Wurm and Walter. With his last breath of life, Rodolfo runs Wurm through with his sword, and both die. The two fathers are left alive gazing on their dead children.

Comment: This act maintains a superb structural unity from beginning to end. The opening chorus is the yet another reworking of the music that forms the Overture, now denoting friendly affection. The long scene between Miller and his daughter is excellent and truly moving. She manages to maintain her aura of innocence through some emotional turbulence. At the heartrending end of their scene, the baritone sings the underlying rhythmic part while Luisa has the high and simple melody. She is still, throughout everything, the pure village girl, and the pathos of her optimism is affecting. The confrontation between Luisa and Rodolfo is also powerful. At first, the orchestra carries all the drama while the two skirt around each other not saying what they truly think. When the truth comes out, so do the voices, and Rodolfo conveys despair with the full tenorial arsenal. The final trio is highly prized by critics and public alike. At one point, Miller's line is composed of long notes held until he is blue in the face. The younger people have much athletic singing, but the father sounds as if he is moaning in a despair that is beyond words or even melody. Toye described this scene well as the culmination of the opera's "intimate pathos," something quite rare in Romantic opera and one of the reasons Luisa Miller, *once heard, always retains a place of affection in the listener.*

Stiffelio

PREMIERE: Teatro Grande, Trieste, 1850. Libretto by Francesco Maria Piave.

Stiffelio is an extraordinary opera with a strange history. Encouraged by the success of *Luisa Miller*, Verdi looked to create another opera about ordinary people rather than historical heroes. Piave sent an outline for an opera called *Stiffelius*, based on a French play called *Le Pasteur, l'Evangile et le foyer*, which told the story of a Protestant minister whose wife has been unfaithful and who must choose between the revenge he craves and the forgiveness his calling demands. Here were real people in real-life situations. It was a daring move on Verdi's part—too daring, as it turned out. Even *Luisa Miller*, as novel as it was for an opera, had the requisite young couple in love, with the ingenue pursued by a mustache-twirling bass. *Stiffelio*, by contrast, concerned the problems of a long-married couple and a pastor's internal battle, much harder to portray in Romantic opera than mere testosterone. And the setting was to be contemporary, something unheard of in all but comic opera.

Ricordi had the opera placed at Trieste, perhaps hoping a smaller theater would be a safer testing ground. The censors at Trieste, however, were particularly reactionary and went hog-wild with their scissors and blue pencils. Stiffelio could in no way be a minister, but only a member of a sect. The final tableau of the opera, a highly dramatic moment when Stiffelio opens the Bible while in the pulpit and lands on the passage where Jesus forgives the adulteress, was watered down beyond recognition, with no quotation from the Gospel and no church setting. At some performances during the initial run, the entire last scene was dropped altogether. At one performance, another act from another opera was substituted. So much for the dramatic integrity Verdi wanted. He fumed, even critics cried out against censorial abominations, and the public could not make much of the story. The opera closed. It was produced in altered form in Florence and in Barcelona, after which the score was withdrawn from circulation. In 1857 Verdi and Piave took as much as they could of the original music and story and presented *Aroldo,* an opera set in the Middle Ages, with much new music. (See "A Note on *Aroldo*" at the end of this chapter.)

When Verdi and Ricordi suppressed copies of *Stiffelio,* they did so thorough a job that the opera was as good as lost for over a century. Music scholars pasted together a definitive critical edition in the 1950s, and *Stiffelio* was produced at Parma in 1968. Famous singers jockeyed to record the opera since here was a unique opportunity to sing Verdi roles without being compared unfavorably to the legendary singers of grandfather's imagined golden age. There were important and successful productions in Venice, London, Los Angeles, and New York through the 1980s and 1990s. The world of our own time got the last thing it expected—a new opera by Verdi.

Common wisdom attributes the relative initial failure of *Stiffelio* to the interference of the censorship and the mystification of its first audiences. Toye set the tone when he wrote, "To begin with, a Catholic audience could not understand a clergyman having a wife at all." Excuse me, but does anybody else out there detect some racial condescension in that comment? Catholics don't have priestesses either, but Italians managed to comprehend Bellini's opera *Norma.* Toye also ignores the fact that the play had been successful in Italy. The score was available abroad, but it did not sell well in England or Germany. Nor did Verdi ever seek to produce it in a Protestant country. He would have faced similar censorship problems in England anyway. Yet program notes continue to say the opera initially failed because Italians couldn't grasp the notion of a married clergyman.

Toye went on to say the premiere audience, ". . . as Latins," could not relate to an outraged husband forgiving his adulterous wife. If we get beyond the baiting language, Toye is onto something. Any audience, even a Nordic one, would find an opera about forgiveness more elusive than a plain old revenge story. The fact is the opera remains startling even today. I am hard-pressed to think of another opera as internal as *Stiffelio,* let alone another opera by anybody, Latin or otherwise, where a husband forgives an adulterous wife and where she does not die for her sin. The whole of *Stiffelio* is unusual, daring, and interesting. The ending is monumental and utterly unique. The title character shares some interesting parallels with that other famous jealous husband of opera, Otello; *Stiffelio* might be thought of as *Otello* on the humblest scale.

CAST OF CHARACTERS

STIFFELIO *(tenor)* A minister of an imaginary Protestant sect known as the Assasveriani. Verdi and Piave decided to place their Assasveriani in the Austrian province of Tyrol, because as recently as 1837 there had been a similar sect in that area suppressed by authorities. We are, therefore, to think of Stiffelio as a man accustomed to persecution. When in hiding, he had gone by the name Rodolfo Müller. He is not a young man (very untypical for a tenor role), and should be able to portray a certain world-weariness. The word *stiffelio,* incidentally, is Italian for "overcoat," though I cannot find any deep significance in this.

LINA *(soprano)* Stiffelio's wife. Although the opera is based on a case of adultery involving Lina, it is imperative that she be able to portray a certain innocence and true love for her husband. Distant from her own parents, and married to an overworked community servant, Lina is a lonely woman who needs love, not a flaming floozy.

COUNT STANKAR *(baritone)* Lina's father, at whose castle the action takes place. The castle is a center for the Assasveriani. None of their piety seems to have rubbed off on the man, however, and he remains utterly bourgeois throughout the drama.

Jorg *(bass)* An elderly, pious minister of the Assasveriani.

Count Raffaele von Leuthold *(tenor)* Lina's seducer, and a real loser.

Federico *(tenor)* Lina's cousin, and a member of the community.

Dorotea *(mezzo)* Federico's wife.

THE OPERA

Prelude

Comment: *Various themes from the opera are played, as well as a couple of new themes not heard again in the opera. The big tune is a bouncy trifle that would not have disgraced Rossini's frothiest comedies. It is the theme the members of the religious community will sing to welcome Stiffelio back, but in that context it provides an ironic contrast with murky dialogue. Alone in the orchestra, it has nothing to do with anything. The problem is that it's one of those tunes that gets under your skin and never gets out; a musical form of scabies.*

Act I

Scene 1: A room in Stankar's castle. Early nineteenth century.

Jorg, alone, is reading Scripture. He utters a prayer that Stiffelio stay true to his calling and not be distracted by his marriage. Stiffelio enters with Lina, Stankar, Raffaele, Federico, and Dorotea. Dorotea tells him a boatman was at the castle looking for him. Yes, says Stiffelio. Walter the boatman was asking his opinion about something strange that happened. The boatman saw a man appear at a window by the water, looking as if he were seized by a terrible fear. This story makes Stankar suspicious, and unnerves Lina and Raffaele. Stiffelio continues. The boatman also saw a woman, clearly hysterical, beside the young man. The young man leaped into the water below the window. This happened eight days before. Raffaele worries that there was a witness to his deed. The boatman found a wallet full of papers belonging to the man who jumped, and Stiffelio produces the incriminating evidence. All ask to see the papers, but Stiffelio tells them his calling demands that he burn the evidence of sin and let the sin perish in the ashes. Jorg, Dorotea, and Federico praise Stiffelio's high-mindedness, Lina thanks God that she hasn't been discovered and promises never to fall into sin again, Stankar reviews his suspicions and vows vengeance on Raffaele if it turns out to be true, while Raffaele tells Lina he must see her again, and will leave a note in "their" book, the agreed-upon spot.

From outside the room, members of the community are heard welcoming Stiffelio back to the castle. All except Lina and Stiffelio leave for the banquet room. Stiffelio wonders that Lina does not have a single word or glance for him now that they're alone. She addresses him as Rodolfo, the name she knew him by when they first met and he was escaping persecution incognito. He tells her how he missed her when he was away, and she says he must have had pleasures in his splendid work. Pleasures? All he saw was sin, vice, and injustice. He asks her for forgiveness for his outburst, since when he looks at her, he realizes that there is still fidelity. Yet woe to her if he is deceived! She suggests that his great soul would pardon any offense, but he says only an unwounded heart can easily forgive. She is crying. He asks why, and reminds her this is their anniversary day. Lina is not wearing her ring. He demands to know where it is. She can only cover her face. Furious, he calls for lightning to strike him and the earth to swallow him whole if he has been deceived.

Stankar enters, surprised at Stiffelio's anger. Composing himself, Stiffelio goes toward the banquet room with Stankar, first telling Lina he will return soon. "Soon," repeats Lina, alone. And what will happen then? She is miserable and full of repentance, deciding to confess all in a letter. Stankar returns, snatching the just-begun letter out of her hand. "Rodolfo," he reads, "I am not worthy of you any more . . ." Stanker tells his daughter confession is cowardly. She will feel better, but it will kill Stiffelio. He himself will stifle his righteous anger and continue to call her his daughter to keep the secret. Lina protests that she was dragged into sin against her will, and now repents. Stankar is unimpressed, and insists she keep the affair quiet. Love may be lost, but family honor will remain. She agrees. They leave.

Raffaele enters the study, thinking he is alone, though Jorg sees him from an inside window. Raffaele slips a letter inside a locked book. Just then, Federico enters and says Stiffelio has asked for his copy of *Messiah* by Klopstock—the very book in which Raffaele has hidden the note! Federico leaves the room with the book, followed by Raffaele.

Comment: A lot of plot and character information is laid out in the first scene, which is shorter than the synopsis would suggest. The opera opens with a vocal solo (unheard of at that time) that establishes Jorg as a rock of faith and temperance. When Stiffelio tells the boatman's story and the others comment upon it, there is a brief but deft septet one wishes would last longer. When he is alone with Lina, the many dimensions of Stiffelio's character become apparent. He tells her of the sin he has witnessed in a weighty solo, much of it written in the lowest tenor range. But when he begins to suspect his wife of infidelity, he becomes typically tenorial, singing of revenge and fury in the usual throat-busting lines. Lina's solo aria is touching and lets us know that she still loves her husband. Stankar is also firmly established in his scene with Lina. He is all military declamation, concerned with surface appearance and incapable of anything deeper.

Scene 2: The banquet hall of Stankar's castle.

The members of the community have organized a little party to welcome Stiffelio back, praising him for the love he spreads among the people. Stiffelio enters with Jorg, who does not enjoy frivolous parties. Just a few moments before he saw a gentleman hiding a note in a locked book. Stiffelio asks who hid the note, and Jorg points to Raffaele, who is now talking to Lina. Stiffelio is lost in thought. Dorotea asks him what he will preach about in church that evening. Judas and all vile betrayers, answers Stiffelio; seducers who ruin homes, for example. He takes the locked book from Federico. Dorotea blurts out that Lina has the key, and Stiffelio orders his wife to unlock it. When she hesitates, he breaks open the clasp himself and sees the letter. Before he can read it, however, Stankar takes it from him and tears it up. Stiffelio is furious at Stankar, Lina begs Stiffelio to strike her but leave her father alone, Stankar tells Raffaele to meet him in the cemetery, while Raffaele pretends indifference. The others wonder what demon invaded Stiffelio's heart to rob them of their serenity.

Comment: *Stiffelio's solo describing the various kinds of betrayal is as weighty and low as his previous denunciation of the world was. This is the voice of righteous indignation (think of Zaccaria, a bass, in Nabucco) rather than the jealous tenor. That comes after he tears the clasp off the book and threatens Lina, which serves the further purpose of allowing the chorus to be shocked and therefore bring the curtain down amid a blaze of noise.*

Act II

Setting: An old cemetery.

Lina walks through the cemetery alone, plagued by guilt and fear. She sees the new tomb of her mother, so pure in life, and begs her to intercede with God for her. Raffaele appears. Lina tells him to speak quietly, since Stiffelio has deduced the situation. Raffaele is unafraid; Stankar tore up the letter, and Stiffelio can only suspect Federico, who was actually carrying the book. And what of remorse? asks Lina. She never loved Raffaele. Raffaele protests his love, but Lina tells him a true proof of love would be for him to return her ring and her letters and leave. Raffaele refuses. He will stay and defend Lina. This, she says, will destroy her and also Stiffelio when he finds out.

Suddenly, Stankar approaches from the shadows. Stiffelio will know nothing, he declares. He orders Lina away and challenges Raffaele to a duel, taunting him and threatening to tell everybody that the "noble" Count Raffaele is really a foundling. They fight. Stiffelio appears at the church door and orders the men to cease desecrating this sacred place. "Then we'll go somewhere else," says Stankar, but Stiffelio tells him God will be there as well. Any offense must be forgiven at once, whatever it is. He takes Raffaele's hand and holds it out for Stankar to shake, but Stankar blurts out that he is disgusted by the sight of Stiffelio grasping the hand that offended him. Stankar immediately regrets his outburst, and Stiffelio is shaken. Can it be true? Lina appears at the gate of the cemetery, begging for pardon. Enraged, Stiffelio grabs Stankar's sword and threatens Raffaele, who refuses to fight. The congregation, waiting for Stiffelio, is heard singing from inside the church. Jorg appears at the church door, and tells the minister to remember who he is. "Yes," he mutters, "I am a priest!" Yet his rage still boils over, and he curses Lina. Jorg leads him to the cross in the cemetery, reminding him that Christ forgave all mankind their sins. Stiffelio staggers toward the cross and faints.

Comment: The orchestral prelude to the act is wonderfully murky and amorphous, a perfect depiction of moral uncertainty. Lina's aria is remarkable for its glowing accompaniment rather than any vocal pyrotechnics. There is no great duet between her and Raffaele for the interesting reason that they're not really in love. Stiffelio's attempt at a reconciliation between Raffaele and Stankar develops into a superb quartet displaying the nobility of spirit in both Stiffelio and Lina. Stiffelio's journey through rage to inner conflict is sung against the offstage chorus, whose monotonous liturgical music only serves to provide contrast to the hero. It is a great challenge to a singing actor, who must sound convincingly angry, choked, and conflicted in turn.

Act III

Scene 1: A room in the castle.

Stankar, alone, ruminates his disgrace. He casts away his sword, no longer feeling worthy of it, and looks instead at a pistol on the table. Why not end it all right away? As he reaches for the pistol, Jorg enters, looking for Stiffelio. Jorg had found Raffaele, who is now in the castle. The old minister leaves to search for Stiffelio. Stankar is overjoyed that Raffaele is in the castle. He leaves to find Raffaele and fight. Stiffelio enters the room with Jorg, telling him he will join the congregation in a few minutes. Jorg leaves. Raffaele enters the room, expecting Stiffelio's wrath, which he will not resist. Instead, Stiffelio asks him a single question. What would Raffaele do if Lina were free? Raffaele evades the question. Stiffelio sends for Lina, and hides Raffaele in an adjacent room to listen in on what follows. Lina appears. Bluntly, Stiffelio offers her a divorce. Lina protests. She knew something awful would happen, but would have preferred being killed to this. Stiffelio bitterly says her tears must be false. Offended that he thinks her tears insincere, she signs the proffered divorce document, and does not hear his quick cry of surprise that she should sign so willingly. The marriage is over, she says. Now she demands to speak to him as a minister of the Gospel. The minister must hear the confession of a sinner. How coldly he offered her the divorce, as if her honor were what she cared about most. She loves Stiffelio, has always loved him! God knows this is true. She was seduced. And for that, he interrupts, that man must die! Stankar enters the room with his sword bloodied. That man is already dead, he declares, leaving the room. Jorg comes to bring Stiffelio into the church. Stiffelio agrees to leave the room full of nothing but sin and death, and seek guidance in the church. Lina despairs of finding forgiveness, even though her heart never sinned.

Comment: Stankar's two solos at the beginning of the scene amount to a very humble version of a grand scena. This man is completely obsessed with appearances and lacks the slightest interest in the true moral questions. Why he is hosting a religious sect in his castle is anybody's guess. The interesting ethical debate begins when Stiffelio interviews Raffaele. We know Stiffelio still loves his wife; thus the concern for her well-being after their impending separation. He also has Raffaele figured out. Completely stunned by Stiffelio's offer to divorce his wife, Raffaele reveals himself as a coward, a hypocrite, and a cad.

The interaction between Stiffelio and his wife is excellent. Stiffelio's lines are repressed and do not presume to reveal his true feelings. When Lina demands he hear her confession, she sings of her unfailing love for her husband in a sad, stately solo accompanied by a weeping English horn. This scene, like so much else in Stiffelio, *is unique in opera. In what other opera do a troubled husband and wife sit down like grown-ups and try to figure out what to do? Just where one might have expected a battle-to-the death sort of duet, we get a measured scene where subtlety and nuance express everything. The posturing extravagant phrases were stated by Raffaele in the previous act, and we now see that statements like "No! I will stay by your side and defend you!" are mere blather uttered by men who will say anything when they're horny. Real love can reside in dialogue as well as cabalettas. It was a discovery that would haunt Verdi for the rest of his career.*

Scene 2: The inside of the church.

An organ accompanies the congregations as they kneel, intoning a psalm asking for forgiveness and mercy. Lina, heavily veiled, enters on her father's arm. Lina puts her faith in God, while Stankar asks forgiveness for the sin of murder. Stiffelio, visibly upset, approaches the pulpit with Jorg, who tells him to be strong and have faith. The people need his guidance. They ascend the pulpit; Stiffelio opens the Bible and reads: "Then Jesus, turning toward the people that had gathered, pointed to the adulteress, who was at his feet, and said: 'Let he among you who is without sin cast the first stone.'" Lina looks at Stiffelio imploringly. Won't he continue the reading? Stiffelio reads on: "And the woman arose, pardoned." He repeats, "Pardoned! Pardoned! God pronounced it so." Lina falls at the steps of the pulpit as the congregation repeats, "Pardoned! Pardoned!" She stretches out her arms and cries out to God.

Comment: A musical and emotional austerity pervades the magnificent and brief conclusion of the opera. After a minute of organ introduction, the chorus chants, reducing the lines of the psalm as they continue to little more than soft breaths saying, "Have mercy" and "Don't punish me."

Stankar has something of a melody to sing, while Lina's lines expressing trust in God are severely simple. Each short line is sung on one note until the final note, which is a jump to an upper octave, all sung in the quietest voice possible. The sense is of a bogged-down soul seeking a transcendent faith. Stiffelio's reading of the Gospel is likewise spare, a near-monotone recitative over an orchestral cadence depicting breathy, unspoken emotion. He repeats the word "Perdonata!" on a single note, only rising into melody on the final repetition of the word. The severity of the music tells us that God's word is expressed in a different, more authoritative voice than human passions.

Much is left unanswered at the end of this opera. Stankar's fate, for example, is not decided, for the feminine singular of the word "Pardoned" tells us it refers to Lina and no one else. And the great unanswered question is: What happens to Lina and Stiffelio? Do they resume their marriage? One hopes so, of course, but Verdi and Piave are quite careful not to presume to answer that question. Directors, of course, hate unanswered questions, and you may see a little stage business depicting what he or she thinks happens to the protagonists. Verdi had censors to maul his operas; we have directors. The point of this story is not whether or not Mr. and Mrs. Stiffelio live happily ever after, but Stiffelio's spiritual journey from human passions to divine generosity.

A NOTE ON *AROLDO*

PREMIERE: Teatro Nuova, Rimini, 1857.

Although Verdi managed to persuade Ricordi to suppress any copies of *Stiffelio* he could find, the composer clearly felt that the opera had something of value in it. For the opening of the small Teatro Nuovo in Rimini, Verdi accepted a modest commission for a new opera, and presented *Stiffelio* reworked as *Aroldo*. He decided to cast the story back into the more conventional time of the Crusades. Piave rewrote details of the libretto, and the result is a story that makes considerably less sense. The title character became Aroldo, a crusader with no particular religious calling. The sight of a modern couple discussing their marital issues was novel and disorienting to the audiences in Trieste, but watching a marauding crusader suddenly become a model of Christian forgiveness was truly absurd. However, opera audiences, then as now, are quicker to accept absurdity than novelty, and *Aroldo* had a modest success for a time.

Musically, Verdi refined passages of the score for the new opera, but *Aroldo* remains fundamentally *Stiffelio* in medieval drag until the final scene. Here Verdi wrote an entirely new scene with some excellent music. Taking place on the banks of Loch Lomond (!) instead of in a Protestant church, the act opens with not one but two idiot choruses. After these, however, there is a remarkable storm scene, reminiscent of that in *Rigoletto*. The finale begins as a trio, becoming an exquisite quartet as the forgiveness is pronounced. Although *Aroldo* has, to our notions, many faults, it also has this beautiful music.

Rigoletto

PREMIERE: La Fenice, Venice, 1851. Libretto by Francesco Maria Piave.

Rigoletto is a miracle. From its opening night to the present day, it has thrilled audiences all over the world. Verdi himself always spoke of it as something special, even in his later years when he was willing to view his earlier creations critically. It is a dramatic masterpiece whose musical ideas unfold swiftly, seamlessly, and furiously. The entire musical texture changes every couple of minutes, and yet a single dramatic sweep is maintained.

In fact, *Rigoletto*'s popularity and its abundance of original ideas sometimes work against its being taken seriously outside of opera circles. Everybody on the planet knows many of its "hit tunes," and *"La donna è mobile"* is what witless people whistle when they want to mock Italian opera. People who think they know all the treasures of *Rigoletto* because they can whistle *"La donna è mobile"* have much to learn. As for its swiftness, musical and dramatic, this means that you will miss much of *Rigoletto*'s power if you're not paying close attention or if the performance you're attending is less than thrilling. Since opera houses know they can sell tickets to *Rigoletto* regardless of who is singing, it is often ill served musically.

No matter. *Rigoletto* has withstood every conceivable crime against it, and will live forever. The score can surprise you with its richness and inventiveness after hundreds of hearings. The role of

Rigoletto is the career goal of every baritone in the world. The appeal is based on more than music. Verdi and Piave finally hit on a drama whose many assets could be perfectly explored in the language of Italian opera. The source of the opera is *Le Roi s'amuse,* a scandalous play by Victor Hugo that opened—and was immediately closed—in Paris in 1830. The action concerned a hunchbacked jester named Triboulet at the profligate court of King Francis I of France. The King goes about seducing court ladies and commoners alike, while his jester makes light of it. Unbeknown to the court, however, the jester has a beautiful and pure daughter whom he keeps secluded from this evil world. When the daughter is seduced by the King, Triboulet turns on King and courtiers alike. (And in no uncertain terms. He names the great families of France, and tells them, "Amidst the hunting grounds, your mothers whored themselves to their lackeys. You are all bastards!" *"Au milieu des huées, vos mères aux laquais se sont prostituées! Vous êtes tous bâtards!"* The French language is unique for tossing off lines like that.) Verdi was thrilled with the play, and called Triboulet "a creation worthy of Shakespeare." But there was still the matter of getting approval from the authorities in Austrian-occupied Venice.

Verdi knew there would have to be a few changes, but neither he nor Piave expected the onslaught that came from the censors. Of course a king couldn't be murdered (or nearly so) onstage, of course he couldn't rape this jester's daughter just offstage while courtiers sang. But the police in Venice went further and deplored the entire subject's "repulsive immorality and obscene triviality." The libretto was rejected outright, with or without emendments. This time, Verdi was ready for war. The censors erred when they dared to suggest to Verdi that the opera was unsuitable because a hunchback as hero was tasteless and ineffective. "A hunchback who sings?" he stormed. "Why not? . . . Will it be effective? I don't know; but if I don't know, neither, I repeat, does the person who suggested the change." In the end, the much underappreciated Piave ran interference between the authorities and the Bear of Busseto, and the result is *Rigoletto* as we know it. For this we should be grateful, for while all of the names and the setting are changed, the basic issues of the play remain intact and even augmented in the opera.

CAST OF CHARACTERS

RIGOLETTO *(baritone)* A hunchbacked jester to the Duke of Mantua. One of the great creations of the stage, Rigoletto is a cruel, misshapen, hideous creature who has one beautiful thing in his life. This is his daughter, whom he nurtures and loves and tries to protect from the world.

GILDA *(soprano)* Rigoletto's only daughter and source of joy, a young woman who leads an extremely, and ultimately tragically, secluded life. The soprano must be able to portray youth, innocence, and dreaminess, but also grit and determination at times. She must also be light enough to be carried in a sack. Her name is pronounced "JEEL-dah."

GIOVANNA *(soprano)* Her maid. Another one of the fussy duenna characters who plague the operatic stage, Giovanna is firmly in the tradition of the servant who gets a vicarious thrill from love and is not above a well-timed bribe.

THE DUKE OF MANTUA *(tenor)* Ideally, the tenor should be able to convey good looks, gaiety, Renaissance refinement, and a permanent state of sexual arousal. In reality, we're lucky if we get any of these qualities from the singers who portray this role, since it is considered fairly agreeable to the voice and can be sung by lighter lyric voices as well as the more typical spinto varieties. Usually he is just portrayed, vocally and dramatically, as a pig.

THE COUNT MONTERONE *(bass)* The only courtier at Mantua with any sense of right and wrong. Budden calls Monterone's brief but key utterances "the voice of God." It is Monterone who gives the curse that is the catalyst of the drama.

MARULLO *(baritone)* A courtier.

THE COUNT CEPRANO *(bass)* A courtier.

THE COUNTESS CEPRANO *(mezzo-soprano)* Ceprano's wife.

BORSA *(tenor)* A courtier.

SPARAFUCILE *(bass)* A hired assassin, but a man with a strong sense of professional ethics. The role is written very deep in the bass voice, and is a favorite among former lead basses in the "golden sunset" of their careers. *"Sparafucile"* is Italian for "gunshot."

MADDALENA *(mezzo-soprano or contralto)* Sparafucile's sister. This poor woman is only in the final act, but she has some very important music to sing there, including the famous quartet and an equally important trio. She is a floozy (the name Maddalena was the preferred choice for easy women) who lures in the men her brother intends to kill. She is usually portrayed as a flaming slut with much cleavage on display.

THE OPERA

Prelude

Comment: *The Prelude is very short and packs an immediate punch. It is the theme of the curse, which will be referred to throughout the opera. The curse is represented by two sharp blasts from the trumpets and trombones, repeated to a single crescendo in the orchestra. This crescendo fades away, and with another repeat of the notes ("duh-DUM!"), the curtain rises.*

Act I

Setting: A hall in the palace of the Duke of Mantua, late sixteenth century.

In the midst of courtly festivities, the Duke tells Borsa about a young lady he has noticed at church and now wants to seduce. She lives in a quiet house down a dark alley, and is visited every night by a man. She does not know the Duke's real identity. Borsa points out the other beauties present at the court, and the Duke finds the Countess Ceprano the most attractive. But what, asks Borsa, if the

mysterious young lady should find out about the Duke's other philan-
derings? The Duke does not care. All women are the same to him.

Comment: *We are meant to understand the ducal court as a place of total
depravity. Not only honor, but lives are bartered cheaply here. The gaiety is
very superficial, almost hysterical. Verdi conveys this by use of the onstage
banda playing frenetic music while the orchestra in the pit remains silent
for much of this scene. When the Duke flirts with the Countess, the banda
plays an elegant minuet, evocative of the game the two are playing. Verdi
wrote out his banda music for "a few instruments" on only two staves of
music—in other words, the exact instruments and their number are left up
to the conductor of a performance, many of whom decide to reproduce the
Berlin Philharmonic onstage, appropriately tarted up in Renaissance drag.*

*When the Duke speaks of all women being the same to him, it is a brief,
light aria, "Questa o quella." This* arietta *is a frothy bagatelle, written
with a folksy 6/8 (clomp/clomp, clomp/clomp) accompaniment. Tenors
who include it in their "greatest hits" recordings do so at the risk of sounding silly, since this is one of the many moments in* Rigoletto *that sound
trivial out of context. The contrast of frivolity and genuine tragedy is at the
heart of this opera.*

The Duke leaves the party with the Countess Ceprano, who has
only resisted half-heartedly. Rigoletto enters quietly, pointing out to
Ceprano (and everybody else) how angry he must be to see the Duke
leave with his wife. The courtiers find this very droll, commenting
that the Duke is amusing himself well. "As always," remarks Rigoletto. With one last comment about the fretting husband, Rigoletto
leaves the room.

Comment: *Our first glimpse of Rigoletto is not the usual star entrance.
Instead of announcing himself, in the standard operatic manner, Rigoletto
merely insinuates himself into the scene, slimy and cruel.*

Marullo enters the room with the hottest piece of gossip imaginable. The courtiers draw close by. He has discovered that Rigoletto
has a mistress! Well, they respond, who would have believed that!

The Duke and Rigoletto come back into the room. Rigoletto recommends abducting the Countess Ceprano that very night. But what
about Ceprano, wonders the Duke. Rigoletto recommends prison,
exile, or his worthless head. Ceprano draws his sword on Rigoletto.
The Duke calms Ceprano and tells Rigoletto to be a little more moderate in his jests. Rigoletto, however, has complete trust in the Duke's
protection. Ceprano suggests to the courtiers revenge on the jester,
each of whom has a score to settle with Rigoletto. How? they ask. Let
them meet tomorrow and decide, advises Ceprano. They agree on
revenge.

*Comment: Everything that unfolds after Ceprano draws his sword is
sung in ensemble concertato. In other words, the Duke, Rigoletto, Ceprano,
and the courtiers all sing at the same time. There's no way you could
understand very word trying to read the in-house translations, but this is
opera, not spoken drama, and what is important is the overall effect. Hearing the courtiers sing "Si! Vendetta!" while Rigoletto and the Duke sing a
different melody conveys all the information you need to know.*

The Court Monterone bursts in, demanding to see the Duke and
hurling threats. Rigoletto approaches to speak to him, imitating the
Duke in walk and "speech," suggesting the Count forget about his
daughter's honor. Monterone notes this insult from Rigoletto, but
addresses the Duke. Yes, he swears, he will interrupt the Duke's
orgies, accusing him of dishonoring his daughter and his whole family
forever. Even beheading will not silence him, since his ghost will
return carrying his severed head crying to God and the world for
vengeance! The Duke orders Monterone arrested. Monterone curses
both the Duke and Rigoletto, to the courtiers' shock. Monterone
points at Rigoletto. Let he who laughed at a father's shame be
damned with a father's curse! While the courtiers leave to continue
their debaucheries, Rigoletto quivers in horror at the curse laid upon
him.

*Comment: A great deal of information and action has unfolded in this
scene, which lasts only about twenty minutes. If you look at the events*

schematically, it's clear that we are seeing a dramatic chiaroscuro composed of elegant yet silly court intrigues on the one hand and serious, menacing realities on the other. Musically, this is emphasized with the antiphonal dialogue between the thunderous chords in the pit orchestra and the tinkly court music of the stage banda. Musicians have always admired the compositional agility of this scene. For audiences, the effect improves each time it is experienced. The finale is Monterone's thunderous verbalization of the curse theme.

Act I, Scene 2 (sometimes Act II)

Setting: A dark cul-de-sac in Mantua. On one side of the alley is Rigoletto's house, with a walled garden visible. On the other side is the more impressive home of Count Ceprano.

Rigoletto is walking home, recalling how the old man (Monterone) cursed him. In the dark alley, he runs into a mysterious man. "Go," he says, assuming the man is a beggar. But the man asks for no money—he makes his living with his sword. He would eliminate any rival for a reasonable fee. "Even a nobleman?" asks Rigoletto. "That would cost more," is the answer. The man explains, quite matter-of-factly, that he'll kill anywhere his client wishes, but prefers to kill in his own home, where his sister lures and distracts victims. His name is Sparafucile. He can be found in this alley, every evening. Rigoletto sends him away.

Comment: Sparafucile is introduced in the orchestra with two solo cellos, muted bass drums, and cello and bass pizzicati forming a menacing and slightly comic ambience. The orchestra continues to provide the melody while the baritone and Sparafucile (a deep bass) "sing-speak" over it. This is a device derived from comic operas, when the "bad guys" are forming their plots. Here the sarcasm, while not devoid of comedy, is grotesque.

We are the same, muses Rigoletto after Sparafucile leaves. Sparafucile kills at night with his dagger, Rigoletto by day with his tongue.

The jester laughs, the assassin slays. He recalls the old man's curse again. Oh, men! Oh, nature! They have conspired to make him evil! To be deformed, to be a fool, with no duty, no capacity for anything but laughing! Everyman's consolation—crying—is denied him. That master of his, young, happy, so powerful, beautiful, tells him, "Make me laugh, fool!" And he must force himself to obey. "I hate you, sneering courtiers!" Rigoletto exclaims. "What a pleasure to sting you! If I'm evil, it's only because of you!" He looks at his small house, noting that here he becomes another person. But that old man cursed him! He can't stop thinking about that. Ah, no, that's madness! He rushes into his garden.

Comment: This narrative, "Pari siamo," challenges every ounce of musical and theatrical talent a baritone has. In less than three minutes, we must see and hear the full range of human emotions. He is, by turns, philosophical, resentful, self-pitying, envious, hateful, tender, frightened, and resolute. He thunders, he wails, he mocks, yet he must always sing. No one artist has sung the definitive "Pari siamo." No one human could encompass it.

When Rigoletto quotes the Duke, listen carefully. Baritones usually try to imitate the tenor's sound in this phrase. If the two gentlemen are not getting along well, it will be a parody.

The climax of the narrative is the great arching line where Rigoletto declares that it's madness to think about the curse, "E follìa!" The third syllable of the phrase is held, and the orchestra immediately rushes into the current of the following orchestral theme as the baritone hits the final syllable, assuming he's got any breath left. The conductor must pay very close attention at this point.

In the garden of the house, Gilda rushes to greet her father, who embraces her as his only joy on earth. She asks what saddens him, and asks to share his secrets. "Who is my family? What is your name?" the sheltered girl asks her father. He brusquely answers that she has none, reminding her never to leave the house. Gilda replies that she leaves only to go to church, and he compliments her on this, but she persists, venturing to ask who her mother was. Rigoletto does not want to remember such sadness. She was an angel, he tells her, who took pity on his deformity, and then died. Now he has nothing but his daughter. Gilda again asks her father's name, his country, his family, but he replies that it's no use to know. "Religion, family, homeland, my whole universe is in you!" he answers. She replies that she is pleased to be a joy to the unhappy man, but slyly asks if she might not be allowed to see more of the city where she has been cloistered for three months. Never! answers her father, who mutters to himself that they would abduct a jester's daughter in this city just for a lark.

Rigoletto calls Giovanna, asking if anybody saw him come home. No, no one, answers Giovanna. He bids Giovanna guard this gentle flower and return her unharmed to him. The Duke appears outside the garden walls, and Rigoletto runs to investigate the sound, finding nothing. Gilda is near exasperation at these suspicions. Rigoletto returns to remind Giovanna not to open the gate to anyone. "Not even the Duke?" she asks. "Especially not the Duke!" answers Rigoletto. Gilda bids farewell to her father, and the Duke, still hiding outside the walls, is surprised to learn her true identity. Rigoletto and Gilda embrace, and he leaves.

Comment: This scene, usually called a duet because it has a single overall structure to it, actually breaks down into five main parts, with interconnecting bridges. The scene begins in excitement, directly after "E follìa," as Gilda and Rigoletto embrace, the orchestra rushing through an excited melody over which the two singers "surf" their lines in uneven phrases of quasi-recitative. The orchestra plays a minor-mode bridge, and repeats its theme in very light scoring, achieving that eternal Verdian goal of variety but also preparing us for a more introspective section. When Rigoletto begs Gilda not to speak of her mother, "Deh, non parlare al misero," it is a beautiful, languid melody over a soft 3/4 beat that any other composer would have stretched into a full aria. Gilda responds in minor-mode phrases, suggesting that she is not "resolved" on the situation. His reply that she is everything to him, "Culto, famiglia, patria . . . ," is also like a complete aria in one line. The strings come in with needling little figures as she tries to get permission to go out more. After he calls Giovanna, he settles into an expansive symmetrical melody urging her to guard his daughter, "Veglia o donna questo fior." *Some commentators are put off by the simplicity of this melody. Simple, perhaps, but who other than Verdi could have written it? Gilda repeats the tune, they are interrupted by the sound of the Duke lurking in the alley, and they repeat it as a duet when Rigoletto returns. In the reprise, Rigoletto takes the melody and Gilda ornaments his line with vocal figures. The effect is stunning in its directness. Her line wraps around his like a vine around a tree, showing her complete dependence on her mysterious father, and also showing her as the only ornament in his otherwise dreadful life.*

Gilda confesses a tinge of guilt to Giovanna for not telling her father about the young man who has followed her to church. Giovanna replies that there's no reason to stop that harmless relationship, since the young man appears generous and noble. Gilda says she would prefer him poor and humble—and just then the Duke appears in the garden, bribing Giovanna away. Gilda tells him he must leave, but he protests that he cannot leave when his heart is on fire, and the love he bears will transcend all earthly considerations. Gilda is impressed with these words, and asks his name. Meanwhile, Ceprano and the other courtiers appear on the street outside the walls, noting Rigoletto's house. The Duke tells Gilda he is Gualtier Maldè, a poor student. He and Gilda bid farewell, and the Duke leaves by a back way.

Comment: *The Duke shows up full of standard tenorial hormones in this scene. His little wooing* arietta *is very symmetrical and standard. You get the feeling he's on automatic pilot. Yet insincere though he may be, his horniness is real enough. As his* arietta *concludes, the vocal line crawls up the scale by half-steps, through the passaggio and landing on a B flat—a classic "ascending" trope of Italian opera telling us he means business. Gilda answers his phrases with only snippets of his melody—she only half-understands what he's getting at. The concluding "Addio!" duet has been grist for the parodists for years, as the tenor and soprano repeat that word twenty-seven times while moving toward opposite sides of the stage.*

Gilda, alone, repeats the beloved name now engraved on her heart—Gualtier Maldè. She walks up to the terrace with a lantern, always basking in the name of her lover. From outside the walls, the courtiers comment on the beauty of Rigoletto's supposed mistress.

Comment: "Caro nome," *Gilda's only aria, a very familiar piece of music, is a lovely and elegant melody of cascading scales arranged in ascending order. It strikes many people on first hearing as old-fashioned, an impression augmented by years of interpolated high notes and additional fioritura. Actually, it is quite unusual. Verdi wrote that it is to be sung at a very slow pace and sotto voce. Whatever you do, don't applaud when you think the aria is finished—it isn't. Gilda walks upstairs to her bedroom for a reprise of the finale, trilling (one hopes) the whole way and usually adding another high E flat for good measure. Meanwhile, during this final part, the evil courtiers have been gathering around the garden wall. This is indicated in the score, where Gilda's final trills and high notes are, somewhat surprisingly, accompanied by trilling low strings, thudding tympani, and an ominous bassoon. It says, in effect, that trouble is brewing, which we will shortly see to be true.*

Rigoletto returns to the street, not sure what has made him go back there, and still fretting about Monterone's curse. Borsa tells the courtiers to be quiet, but Ceprano suggests killing the jester. Borsa and Marullo suggest a more amusing plan. Rigoletto bumps into them, complaining of the darkness of the night. They tell him they're going to abduct Ceprano's wife, and suggest he join them. They are masked, so must Rigoletto be. While they are slipping a mask over his head, they add a blindfold. The courtiers urge quiet in their mischief, and some proceed into the garden while Rigoletto himself holds the ladder. Gilda is gagged and abducted, dropping a scarf as she's carried away. She cries for help from a distance. Wondering what is taking the courtiers so long, Rigoletto touches his eyes and realizes he has been blindfolded. He sees the open door to his garden, spots Giovanna lying there terrified, and cannot speak. After spotting the dropped scarf, he cries out, "Ah, it is the curse!"

Comment: All right, let's face it right away. Confusing Rigoletto to make him think he's raiding Ceprano's house when he's actually abduct-

ing his own daughter not only sounds ridiculous, it IS ridiculous, and there's not much to be done about it. When the chorus sings to be quiet, "Zitti, zitti," one is confronted with one of those moments in Italian opera that seem written with the sole purpose of providing material for parody. In its favor, it can be said that the scene is short and moves very swiftly. Directors try to make it as believable as possible, and the courtiers usually spin Rigoletto around after they put a hood over him to convince you of his disorientation. His cry of "Il maledizione!" at the end of the act must be convincing and is belted out over the full orchestra.

Act II (or III)

Setting: A hall in the ducal palace, with a doorway in the background leading to the Duke's private rooms.

The Duke enters alone. She was stolen from him! She, whose modest gaze could have awakened a sense of constant and true love in him, was taken from him! He can almost see those tears she shed for her lover "Gualtier," who would now give his soul to make her happy.

Comment: *Here the Duke is all rage and sadness. The recitative "Ella mi fu rapita!" is loaded with oaths of vengeance on those who stole his "true love" from him. The subsequent, familiar aria, "Parmi veder le lagrime," is a stately apostrophe to Gilda's beauty and purity. It is firmly in the bel canto style, although built around a six-line structure that gives it an even broader feeling and challenges the tenor's ability to sing a beautiful legato line. Budden points out that this apparent about-face from the rake who had sung of "this one or that one" in the first act is an excellent psychological stroke. The Duke is that sort of spoiled child whose favorite toy is the one he can't have.*

Borsa, Marullo, Ceprano, and the other courtiers enter the hall, quite pleased with themselves. They tell the Duke how they discovered the beautiful girl in Rigoletto's house, then abducted her. The

Duke realizes they are talking about Gilda, and asks her where-abouts. When told she is in the palace, he determines to fly to her and show her that sometimes slaves of love are even found on thrones.

Comment: The courtiers recount their tale to a bouncy tune, a perfect example of an early Verdi idiot chorus. Of course, these men are supposed to annoy us. The Duke responds with a brief, furious cabaletta, "Possente amor mi chiama," once traditionally cut in performance because of its difficulty and because it was thought to be too dramatically clumsy and old-fashioned to watch the tenor stand front-center stage, declaiming how quickly he would fly to his love while not moving his feet. But "Possente amor" is exciting; thematically it associates the Duke's debaucheries with those of his depraved courtiers while adding a touch of serious menace, and it punctuates the end of the first scene of this act. Most important, it will provide a marvelous contrast with Rigoletto's subsequent, awesome scene. Like the end of "Caro nome" and a few other places in Rigoletto, *the logic of the structure is most apparent when read in reverse, so to speak.*

Rigoletto enters, feigning perfect calm. The courtiers mutter "Poor Rigoletto," but the jester walks about singing "La ra, la ra" while looking for signs of Gilda's whereabouts. Ceprano asks, "What's new, buffoon?" " 'What's new, buffoon?' " parrots Rigoletto. "Only that you're more tedious than usual." The courtiers laugh. Rigoletto congratulates Marullo on having escaped harm from the night air, but Marullo protests that he slept through the night and didn't go out. "Ah," replies Rigoletto, "then I must have been dream-ing." He continues looking for signs of Gilda, and sings.

Comment: There's really nothing to call this other than the "La ra" scene, and it requires great restraint and sophistication on the baritone's part. Many enter snarling and barking, but this is a mistake. How much more effective when the baritone parallels the accompanying violin, courtly, graceful, and pathetic. The emotional outburst is yet to come. The violin notes, a series of quick couplets working around a minor scale, are superbly nerve-wracking, like minor nicks from a razor blade.

A page enters to say the Duchess would like a word with her husband. Ceprano says the Duke's asleep, Borsa suggests he went out hunting, but the page is not to be fooled. The Duke was seen in the hall just a moment ago. "He cannot be disturbed!" thunder the courtiers. Rigoletto pales. Gilda is with the Duke! The courtiers tell him to find another mistress, but he attacks the Duke's door, raving "I want . . . my daughter!" "His daughter!" answer the shocked courtiers. Yes, says Rigoletto. Are you not pleased with yourselves? Give her back! He rushes at the Duke's door again, but the courtiers block him.

Rigoletto turns on them. Courtiers, vile, accursed race! Nothing is above money to them, but a daughter is a gem without price. Give her back! He hurls himself at the door, denouncing them all as assassins. They struggle with Rigoletto, who wearily gives up the direct assault. He weeps. He turns to Marullo, saying he has a kind heart, asking "Is it true? Is she there? Ah, not a word, silence." Turning to the other lords, he begs for mercy. It would cost them nothing to return Gilda to him, but for him it would mean the whole world. "Have mercy, lords!"

Comment: In three minutes, this narrative, "Corteggiani, vil razza," encapsulates a personal journey as vast as any in theater. It is a whole opera in one aria. There is no limit to the demands on the performer—it has room for any humanity the baritone can put into it. Musically, he begins in full voice, cast into the highest fraction of the baritonal range with hardly a chance to take a breath (and this while, in theory, flinging himself against a wooden door). The climax comes when he screams "Assassini! Assassini!" at the courtiers. Of course, he shouldn't actually scream here, but a great artist will make you think he did. Then he must plead with Marullo in abject, broken phrases. Finally, he begs pity of the lords in broad gorgeous lines built around an endless legato. Again, there's hardly any room to breathe, but if the singer can manage the final lines with true sweetness of tone, you will be convinced of Rigoletto's inner nobility. The effect is, frankly, heartrending.

This is why it's almost impossible for a young singer to portray the full emotional immensity of Rigoletto. Anger modulates into desperation, dis-

belief, and finally complete collapse. There are countless examples of vocal music that capture the essence of these emotions separately, but very few that can move from one to the other realistically. Yet this is what opera (so often accused of mannerism and unrealness) can portray, at its very best. And opera doesn't get any better than "Corteggiani, vil razza."

Gilda rushes out from the Duke's room into her father's arms. Rigoletto dares to hope that it was all merely a jest, but Gilda asks to speak to him alone of her dishonor. Rigoletto magisterially orders the courtiers away. Calling on heaven for courage, Gilda tells of the young man who had followed her to church, and how she had dared to dream of true love. He told her he was a poor student, and then she was carried by force to this place and to suffering. Rigoletto consoles her and she expresses gratitude for such a kind and understanding father.

Guards lead Monterone across the back of the stage on his way to prison. The old Count pauses before the portrait of the Duke, bitter at the ineffectiveness of his curse, and is taken away. Rigoletto calls out after him that he's wrong—he will be avenged! Gilda asks for pardon for the Duke. She was dishonored, but she knows he really loves her, and in spite of everything she still loves the Duke. Rigoletto will not hear of it. There will be bloody vengeance.

Comment: *The act ends with another protracted scene of short duets between Gilda and Rigoletto. When telling her story, Gilda sings in long phrases, beginning quietly but developing into a full and rather defiant statement of identity. She has become a woman. This scene requires an entirely different voice from the one used in "Caro nome." The idea that Gilda apparently enjoyed being raped is difficult to stomach, and has been for some time. (Queen Victoria disapproved of this scene, and it was traditional through the 1920s for the ladies of New York to turn their backs to the stage during it.) This is why it is imperative to draw a complete picture of Gilda in her first scene. She is smart, inquisitive, and brimming with life. While she makes it clear that her abduction caused her to suffer, the fact remains that it was the first life experience she has ever had. Thus she persists in her delusion that the Duke actually loves her. She has no other choice but to believe that.*

Monterone's brief appearance must be very impressive, accompanied by a thunderous outburst from the orchestra. This sets up the final duet between Rigoletto and Gilda, a rip-snorting double-time march that captures the two protagonists' rush of opposing yet related emotions. In context, it is a perfect finale to one of the finest acts in opera.

Act III (or IV)

Setting: A rundown tavern on the banks of the Mincio River, with Mantua in the background. Sparafucile is inside the tavern, nonchalantly polishing his leather belt.

Outside the tavern, Rigoletto asks Gilda, who is dressed as a man to aid her flight to another city, if she still loves the Duke. Always, she replies. But what if she were to see the Duke with another woman? Would Gilda still love him? Yes, she answers. Rigoletto swears vengeance, and Gilda begs pity. He leads Gilda to a crack in the wall, and tells her to look inside. All she sees is a man, not the Duke. Shortly, the Duke enters the room and tells Sparafucile he wants two things: his sister and some wine. Sparafucile goes into the next room to fill the order. Alone, the Duke sings about the fickleness of women, like a feather in the breeze. Women are pretty and lovable, but deceitful. Whoever trusts them is miserable, but whoever does not pluck love from that breast is never really happy.

Comment: Well, here it is, the aria "La donna è mobile," the piece people refer to when they want to trivialize Italian culture. First of all, let's face facts right away: "La donna è mobile" is truly a great tune, perhaps the most hummable melody there is. But is it great opera? Yes, it is. The gloomy final act of Rigoletto gets this ironic send-off, forming a contrast of Shakespearean deftness. Another great feature of this aria is its plasticity. It makes its effect no matter how it is performed. If the tenor lifts his wine glass and strikes a pose, then the Duke is a gushing braggart. If he opts for more refinement, then the Duke is a cynical rake. If he "whoops" the high notes, he is an artistic pig. All these interpretations work. Thus the aria cannot fail dramatically, which is impressive for a piece of music often dismissed as musical fluff.

Legend has it that Verdi withheld this music until the night of the final dress rehearsal, knowing that it would be played by every organ grinder in Venice after one hearing. Indeed, the night of the dress rehearsal, the bands in the Piazza San Marco were already playing "La donna è mobile" as the performers were leaving La Fenice. This may or may not be true, but it is undeniably true that those same Venetian bands have been massacring it ever since.

Sparafucile returns with the wine and his sister Maddalena. The Duke begins flirting with her immediately. She flirts back, but also protests that the Duke is too forward. He swears he wants to marry her, and she laughs. Meanwhile, Gilda, looking into the tavern, calls him a villain, and Rigoletto asks if she has seen enough. The Duke begs Maddalena to feel his beating heart. Gilda recognizes the same words the Duke had spoken to her, and wonders why her heart surrendered to such a man, while Rigoletto attempts to console Gilda by telling her she will be avenged.

Comment: The celebrated quartet is familiar from the radio and the concert hall, as well as television commercials. The first part, "Un dì, se ben rammentomi," is composed of recitative lines sung against an orchestral melody, much as in Act I but with a very different and more urgent feel. The orchestra plays an elegant rushing melody of the type Verdi often associates with flirting (as in Traviata). The formal quartet, "Bella figlia dell'amore," begins with the Duke, whose melody is long and stately. It rises in the scale, in the "upward" manner of all tenors in heat. Maddalena is choppy, frivolous, and sarcastic; Gilda's tune is long and sad (it crawls down the scale as a counterpoint to the "up" tenor); and Rigoletto's is a grim near-monotone. The cumulative effect is stupendous, assuming a good performance and a tenor who can relinquish the spotlight long enough to sing in ensemble. There are many examples of good ensembles in opera that compare and contrast the various characters' states in a given moment, but the miracle of this quartet is that the overall structure is so unified. The interdependent fates of the characters are implicit in their conflicting emo-

tions. Some critics have gone so far as to say this is the supreme example of the form in all opera. That may or not be true, but it is a major accomplishment in any case.

Gilda is sent on her way. Rigoletto goes around the tavern and returns with Sparafucile. Twenty scudi was the agreed wages for the killing. Rigoletto hands the assassin ten scudi, promising the balance on receipt of the body. Sparafucile says he can throw the body in the river for the same price, but Rigoletto asks for that pleasure himself. The jester leaves, promising to return at midnight. Sparafucile reenters the tavern. The thunder of an approaching storm is heard. Maddalena and the Duke are still flirting. Sparafucile offers the Duke his own room. The Duke whispers something to Maddalena and follows Sparafucile upstairs. Maddalena has a moment of pity for the poor man about to be killed. He's so handsome! From the upstairs bedroom, the Duke sings himself to sleep, repeating his song about the unreliability of women.

Sparafucile returns to the table with his sister, and both sit for a while, lost in thought. He drinks from the bottle left by the Duke. At last, Maddalena says that she finds the young man charming, and obviously worth more than twenty scudi. Sparafucile orders her to see if the victim is sleeping, and to bring his sword. She leaves the room. Gilda, meanwhile, reappears outside the tavern and listens through the crack in the wall. Maddalena returns, saying the young man is a regular Apollo. She pleads to spare his life. Sparafucile throws a sack at her and tells her to sew it up. The sack will be used to throw the body of Apollo into the river. Overhearing this, Gilda is appalled. Maddalena suggests they kill the man who ordered the murder (Rigoletto) instead, and take the other ten scudi from his corpse. Sparafucile is shocked at this suggestion. He is an honest tradesman who keeps his bargains! The storm is building. Maddalena tries to run upstairs to warn the stranger, and Gilda praises her as a good-hearted girl. Sparafucile suggests a compromise. If, before midnight, any wayfarer shows up at the tavern, they'll kill him instead and give that body to the hunchback. Gilda is tempted to die for her deceiver, and asks heaven for pardon. The bell strikes half past eleven. The storm is furious. Maddalena weeps. If a woman like that can weep, considers Gilda, then what is she waiting for? She knocks at the door. Sparafucile thinks it's the wind. Gilda asks for entry. Maddalena urges him to the deed, Sparafucile gets his sword, and Maddalena asks for heaven and her earthly father to forgive her. Sparafucile stands behind the door, Maddalena opens it, and Gilda enters. When the door is shut, all is silence and darkness.

Comment: *The storm scene is a stock feature of Italian opera, even as a background for a murder. Verdi loved to reinvent the standard features rather than eliminate them. No one melody encapsulates the storm; it keeps dissipating and re-forming, always threatening in new ways. The howling wind is represented by a non-verbal chorus, a startling effect noted, and overused, by the makers of B-movies of the mid–twentieth century. Meanwhile, a full trio forms with a straightforward unified melody. It is repeated just before Gilda enters the tavern and dies down with the storm.*

Rigoletto approaches the tavern. The storm is almost over. The jester gloats, soon to savor his revenge. Midnight strikes. He knocks at the door. Sparafucile opens and presents him with a heavy sack— the body. Rigoletto asks for a lantern, but Sparafucile insists on payment. Receiving it, he instructs Rigoletto to throw the body into the river a little upstream, where it's deeper.

Rigoletto sees the Duke's spurs. Avenged at last! Now, into the river with him. Just then, he hears the voice of the Duke from inside the tavern, singing his song. Rigoletto wonders if he is mad. That assassin is a robber! He trembles, cutting open the sack. A flash of lighting reveals it is Gilda. No, it's not possible! She's well on her way to Verona! A delusion! He pounds at the door of the tavern. No answer. He screams for his daughter. Faintly, Gilda speaks. It was her own fault. She loved too much. Now she must die for him. Rigoletto is horrified that Gilda was caught in his plan. She begs him to forgive her, and to forgive the Duke. She promises to pray for her father from heaven, where she will be alongside her mother. Weeping, all Rigoletto can do is beg Gilda not to die. She bids him farewell and dies. Grabbing her body, he remembers the curse.

Comment: This scene has some obvious difficulties in stage perfor-mance, and yet is full of genuine pathos if the director does not make it low comedy. Yes, Gilda must be carried around in a sack by Rigoletto—there's no practical way out of it. Naturally, this limits the number of sopranos who can be cast in the role. The sack schtick, beyond being a physical burden and the butt of many hoary operatic jokes, is actually a perfect symbol of Gilda's predicament. Notice that all of this story is about enclosed spaces within a larger context: the Duke's bedroom, the garden behind the wall, and the inside and outside of the tavern, not to mention Gilda's virginity, which Rigoletto is trying to save at all costs. Trying to do the right thing for the only beauty in his life, Rigoletto has cocooned Gilda to death. The trickiest moment in production is when the Duke reprises a few bars of "La donna è mobile." *It always cracks everyone up, since people seem to think there's something inherently funny about that tune anyway. No matter. The final duet, with Gilda's harp-accompanied "vision" of heaven and Rigoletto's sad cascading lines of* "Non morir, non morir!," *is a lovely denouement before the great cry of* "La maledizione!"

If Hugo's hunchbacked jester was, as Verdi said, a creation worthy of Shakespeare, then Verdi's treatment of the story is no less a masterpiece of tragedy. With the arsenal of melodic creativity at his command, Verdi was able to create a powerful story that ranks with any on the stage.

Il trovatore

PREMIERE: Teatro Apollo, Rome, 1853. Libretto by Salvatore Cammarano.

THIS IS THE OPERA your parents warned you about. *Il trovatore* is wild, uninhibited, and relentlessly intense. It could only have been written by Verdi, and only at one point in his career. It took the world by storm at its premiere and has hardly stopped a moment to catch its breath ever since. As *Dwight's Journal of Music,* a Boston publication, stated as early as February 1861, "*Trovatore* is almost the only opera. It stands for all operas."

Not that its popularity has helped its reputation. *Trovatore* is the Rodney Dangerfield of operas—immensely popular, but it gets no respect. Shaw defended it, but only as a parent speaks up for a deformed child. He never questioned that it needed defending in critical circles. Later, the Marx Brothers and Danny Kaye turned to this work for their opera farces as a matter of course. Apparently, the first thing a newcomer to the world of opera must learn is to laugh at *Trovatore.* The first target of derision is the story. It is said to be farfetched, insane, and hopelessly complicated. It is the first two, but not the third. The action revolves around a terrible crime that occurred a generation before, when a gypsy woman, driven to distraction by the cruel execution of her mother, sought revenge by killing the baby of the lord who ordered the execution. In her confusion, she killed her own baby by accident. OK, that's pretty far out, but so what? The newspapers feature almost daily stories about parents murdering their own babies, and Shakespeare gets just as wild. It is intended to be an outrageous crime. The gypsy woman tells the opera's hero the whole story in the second act, and even he doesn't believe it! That's exactly the point. As for having a confusing story, the crime was done years in the past and is recounted in two narratives. The rest of the story is not confusing in the least. Apparently, critics of this story never find themselves so confused that they actually read the libretto.

If they were to do so, they would find something else you never hear about this opera. *Il trovatore* has a great libretto. Salvatore Cammarano (who died before completing the third and fourth acts) wrote some of the most singable lyrics ever penned for opera. You wouldn't know this unless you listen to the Italian words, whether or not you understand Italian. Much of the venom aimed at the libretto of *Trovatore* should actually go toward its English translations, which tend to be horrid. Let one example, from as recently as 1963, suffice: "Trample my corpse on this cold floor, But pardon the Troubador." (In Italian the line neither rhymes nor makes mention of any floor, cold or otherwise.)

Then there's the music. It is a given that Verdi chose a very primitive orchestral vocabulary for this opera, usually justified because the majority of musical ideas in this opera are placed on the singers' shoulders. But there are many subtleties in the orchestral score, and familiarity with the score proves that Verdi was always conscious of the effect he was aiming for and was always dramatically correct in his orchestration choices.

The singers, likewise, bear a huge burden in this opera. Each of the four soloists must, at one point or another, step up to the lip of the stage and try to blow everyone's wigs off. But most of the time they are required to sing with a thorough knowledge of the Italian lyric tradition. *Trovatore* has been called the culmination, and therefore the death, of the bel canto form. In other words, it ideally calls for all the artistry needed to sing Rossini, plus something else. Too often, we get the something else alone.

Balancing the singers and knowing when to lay it on in the orchestra and when to pull back makes this opera a challenge for conductors. Alas, this opera's reputation as oom-pah-pah strings with vocal howling has made some consider it foolproof, and we often get less than first-rate conductors in the pit. On the rare occasion when all these considerations are rethought, *Trovatore* can turn even the most jaded audience on its head. It is time to stop apologizing for *Trovatore,* and start apologizing to it. It is as modern and urgent as anything written since. In fact, in its use of the orchestra to provide a driving rhythm, its frankly emotional vocalism, and its appeal to the primal rather than the intellectual senses, *Il trovatore* may be an unacknowledged source of rock and roll.

CAST OF CHARACTERS

MANRICO, THE TROUBADOUR *(tenor)* An officer in the service of Prince Urgel, who is at war with the Prince of Aragon. He is also a troubadour, which here means he strums a lute and sings love songs when he isn't at war. Historically, troubadours were nobles who entertained at court (usually their own), but the Romantics confused troubadours with minstrels, and people have remained confused ever since. What is important for us is that Manrico is both a poet and a warrior, though you often wouldn't know it in performance.

AZUCENA *(mezzo-soprano)* His mother (sort of), an old gypsy woman, one of the most fascinating creations, and coveted roles, of all opera. Azucena is the definitive Spanish gypsy name, although Verdi was probably not aware of that fact. In Spanish folklore, the mythical ur-gypsy Azucena is a sort of patron saint of secular music, as Cecilia is the patroness of sacred music.

LEONORA *(soprano)* A young lady-in-waiting to the Princess of Aragon. Leonora might appear from the story alone to be a fairly standard-issue ingenue, but musically she is the epitome of womanhood and all it stands for.

THE COUNT DI LUNA *(baritone)* The bad guy, supposedly driven to evil deeds by his insane love for Leonora. Di Luna is in the service of the Prince of Aragon, and therefore Manrico's rival in both the Courts of Venus and the Fields of Mars.

FERRANDO *(bass)* An old soldier of the Count's. He delivers the narration at the beginning and then hangs around for the rest of the opera, occasionally interjecting something. The roles lies very deep in the bass register.

INES *(soprano)* Leonora's attendant, a lady whose primary purpose is to stand there and be a sounding board for Leonora's feelings.

RUIZ *(tenor)* Manrico's henchman, a soldier who fetches swords, rallies the troops, and sounds the alarm.

The action is set in Aragon, Spain, in 1409, during a civil war between the Prince of Aragon and the Prince Urgel.

THE OPERA

Act I: "The Duel"

Scene 1: The atrium of Count di Luna's palace of Aliaferia. Ferrando and servants are lounging, while soldiers keep watch. Night.

Ferrando advises the soldiers and servants to be alert. The Count will pass this way to stand by the window of his beloved, where he spends hours keeping vigil. The Count is jealous of the troubadour Manrico, who serenades the maiden each night at midnight. The men ask Ferrando to help them stay awake by telling the story of Garzia, the brother of the Count.

Ferrando begins. The late lord, the old Count di Luna, had two sons. A nurse was sleeping by the second one, and upon waking discovered a hideous gypsy witch standing over the cradle. The nurse screamed, and servants threw the witch out. She claimed she had only been casting horoscopes for the infant, but soon the little boy grew sick and almost died. The witch was found and burned at the stake. The witch had a daughter, even more evil, who avenged her mother by kidnapping the sick infant. No one could find the poor child, but later, at the place where the witch had been burned, they found—alas!—the half-burned skeleton of a baby, with the fumes still rising! The father lived a few more days, but in his death throes began to imagine that his son was still alive. He made his surviving son swear that he would search for his brother. The witch has vanished, but Ferrando is sure he would recognize her even now. The men say she has been seen on the rooftops as an owl or a crow, but she always disappears by morning. A bell sounds midnight. All curse the infernal witch.

Comment: For many years this opening narrative telling of things past was considered one of the "problems" with the opera. The critics forgave Wagner, who used the same device, but not Verdi. At least Verdi made his narration bounce right along with a lot of musical interest. The entire opening scene is kept in minor keys, casting a tint of eeriness over the proceedings.

Scene 2: The gardens of the palace. Night.

Ines chides Leonora for stopping in the garden. It's late, and the queen has asked for Leonora. Ah, wonders Leonora, must she pass another night without seeing him? Ines demands to know more about Leonora's secret love. Leonora explains that she first met him at the tournaments, where he conquered all. But when the civil war began, he came no more, until one quiet night. She heard beautiful music being sung under her balcony by a troubadour—singing to her! Only angels could feel more bliss than she felt at that moment. Ines is disturbed by this story. Leonora must forget about this troubadour. She refuses. Of such a love words cannot even speak, but her fate is tied to him. Ines prays for her, and they enter the palace.

Comment: We learn a lot about Leonora in her first appearance, beyond whether or not she can sing. Her first aria, "Tacea la notte," begins in low eerie phrases. It is self-consciously old-fashioned, as she is still a rather innocent young lady. But she soon soars to a climax in pitch in what we realize later is merely an ascent up the scale. It is a beautiful technique

Verdi uses, generally with women, to show us a character laying claim to her own selfhood. The cabaletta "Di tal amor" is a galloping coloratura flash piece with all the usual trills and leaps. Many of the best sopranos, cast with an ear toward the spinto phrases of Leonora's other solos and ensembles, have choked on it, or at least dragged behind the brisk tempo and sparkle Verdi has indicated. If the soprano can manage to lighten the timbre of her voice for this solo, it is quite dramatically effective as well as a good tune. We sense that Leonora, underneath all her piety and courtly demeanor, is a cauldron of hormones about to boil over.

The Count di Luna enters the garden, musing on his love for Leonora. Just as he is about to approach her, he hears the voice of the troubadour singing to her. The Count wraps himself in his cloak. Leonora runs out to Manrico. Why is he so late tonight? Manrico sees that there is another man hiding, and accuses Leonora. She protests her love for Manrico. The Count steps forward and demands the troubadour's name. Manrico identifies himself, and the Count is stunned. Manrico has been convicted of treason. What madness to enter the palace! Manrico dares di Luna to call the guards and have him beheaded on the spot. Di Luna insists on killing Manrico himself, and challenges him to fight. Leonora pleads with di Luna to spare her love, but the jealous Count says her confession of love has condemned Manrico to death. The men depart with drawn swords, and Leonora faints.

Comment: Manrico sings his song offstage to harp accompaniment, indicative of the troubadours' lute we are to imagine filling his world with music at all times. It is a haunting melody, and a perfect setup for the more famous offstage lute song in the final act. The subsequent trio is raw to the point of near-hysteria. There needs to be some palpable element of wildness here, or the soloists are merely marking time until the next hit tune. As for the finale, we must accept on faith that women just used to faint easier in olden times. Must have been the clothes.

Act II

Scene 1: "The Gypsy Woman." A gypsy camp in the mountains. Dawn.

The gypsies greet the sunrise and get to their blacksmithing work. Hammering at their anvils, they sing of their gypsy maids. Azucena stares into the fire, hallucinating a shrieking woman being burned at the stake. Her thoughts, she says, are even darker than her song. Manrico notices the old woman's mysterious words. The gypsies go off to work, repeating their song.

Comment: It would take a well-funded archeological expedition to find a corner of the world where people have not heard the Anvil Chorus. Sir Arthur Sullivan parodied it beautifully for a Burglars' Chorus in The Pirates of Penzance. After the D'Oyly Carte Opera's tour of New York in 1929, Sullivan's version of the tune became popular among street urchins as "Hail, Hail, the Gang's All Here." People who complain that Verdi's music sounds like the cheapest popular tunes are not exactly wrong, they just have it backward.

Few people titter during the Anvil Chorus in performance, however, since it is brief and effective. Its insistent pounding on the off-beat sets a rhythm that beautifully depicts the off-kilter world of Il trovatore. Azucena's solo, "Stride la vampa," is written in 3/4 time, a rhythm that perfectly illustrates a person rocking back and forth while staring in a trance. The first note of each measure is heavily emphasized, like a stab. This character is clearest and most defined when she is lost in memory. Verdi also created an interesting effect by writing a sustained trill of four measures toward the end of the solo and putting harmonies in the orchestra, suggesting to some that Azucena is defiantly holding on to her obsession against all distractions.

Manrico asks Azucena to tell him the story she sings about. Sadly, she does so, picking up where Ferrando's narrative had left off. Her mother, accused of witchcraft, was led in chains to the place of execution. Azucena, with her child at her breast, followed, weeping. In vain did her mother try to reach out and give her a last blessing. Turning to Azucena, the mother cried "Avenge me!" These words have echoed in her heart ever since. Did you avenge her? asks Manrico. Azucena continues: She saw the Count's infant nearby, and noted the flames already burning. Manrico gasps. The flames? Could she possibly . . . ? The infant was weeping, continues Azucena. She feels her own heart breaking at what she is about to do, but then she sees her mother dying at the pyre, seeming to repeat "Avenge me!" The flames leap out before her—and she hurls the infant onto the fire! The madness departs, and she sees the flames consuming the struggling body of the child. She looks around her, and sees the son of the wicked Count on the ground where he had been, still living. What are you saying? asks Manrico. "My own son, I had burned my own son!" Manrico gasps in horror. Then who, he asks, is he, if not her son? Azucena reassures him. Of course he is her son. Her mind gets confused when she recounts that moment.

Comment: As soon as you wipe that smirk off your face, we can talk about why this narrative, "Condotti ell'era in ceppi," is one of the most dramatic moments in all theater. The orchestra begins with a soft strum punctuated by a sighing violin. The mezzo's regularly metered lines climb up the scale and back down for "Mi vendica, sclamò." So far, everything is quite formal. Verdi is seducing us into the story. When she lays eyes on the Count's infant, she feels pity for the child, depicted by flutes and piccolo. Azucena is never entirely insane or devoid of genuine humanity. A reminiscence of "Stride la vampa" is heard as Azucena recounts the flames' catching. Where previously she had held a trill at the end of the vocal line, she now leaps up in the scale. We might think this is the climax, but after another incremental climb up the scale, she hits the stratosphere again with a high B flat when in her memory she sees the Count's child still living. After Manrico's interjection, she stabs the air with a forte cry of "Il figlio mio!," also on B flat. In other words, the high notes are not sprinkled about for effect. They are the inevitable cries of a disturbed, yet very sane, mind. After the "explosion," the orchestra dies down in pitch and volume, and Azucena finishes her narrative in the lower reaches of the range, as the urgency of the memory fades. It is clear that Verdi was cherishing the outrageousness of the story, daring himself to bring it to life on paper and daring the singer to make us believe it in performance. If it still seems incredible, do not dismiss the opera yet. Remember that even Manrico finds the story too outrageous to believe at face value, even though naturally he would not want to believe it. This is key to understanding the opera. Verdi, with his musical talent and innate feel for the human condition, has managed to make this moment incredibly powerful and even convincing.

Azucena recounts her motherly devotion to Manrico. When people said that he had died in battle, didn't she search the fields for him? Didn't her tears bathe his wounds? Loftily, Manrico recalls his wounds as marks of glory, since only he held his ground on the field that day while his comrades fled. Then the vile di Luna attacked with all his contingent, and he fell as a hero! That, says Azucena, was how he repaid Manrico, who had spared the Count's life after they fought their duel. Why, she asks, did he show mercy when he held the Count's life in his hands? That he cannot explain. When the Count lay below his sword, a voice from heaven came to Manrico, saying, "Do not strike him." Azucena does not believe this. The word of heaven never spoke for such an evil soul as di Luna's. If ever Manrico has another chance, he must plunge his sword into the man's godless heart. A horn call is heard. Manrico answers on his own horn. "Avenge my death," mutters Azucena. A messenger approaches with a letter, which Manrico reads. The town of Castellor has fallen to Manrico's cohorts, and their leader has chosen him to command its defenses. Leonora, having heard that Manrico fell in battle, is planning, that very night, to take the veil in a nearby convent. Manrico cries out to heaven, arousing Azucena. He sends the messenger for his horse. Azucena begs Manrico not to go. His wounds are not yet healed. Manrico insists he must ride with all haste to Leonora. Azucena pleads, but to no avail, as Manrico rides off to find Leonora.

Comment: *This duet scene moves through a wide variety of feelings. When Manrico tells of sparing the Count's life, his music becomes tender* *and lyrical in the extreme, assuming the tenor can manage such a tone. Everything moves up a notch when Manrico arms for battle, and they sing a duet that is really a cabaletta for two voices singing in different but related keys (G minor and G major). It is a superb effect, showing us both the connection and the disparity between these characters. As she pleads with Manrico, Azucena's line reaches up to high C. Whatever else is going on in this complicated relationship, we are certain that her need for Manrico is genuine.*

Scene 2: The cloister of convent near Castellor.

The Count enters the cloister with Ferrando and several followers, wrapped in cloaks. Ferrando suggests that their venture is madness, but Di Luna turns on him. It is a case of both love and wounded pride. Manrico has been killed, now he faces another rival in the form of the convent. Leonora belongs to him! The flash of her starlit smile conquers the sun! One glance from her is the sunbeam that disperses the stormy darkness of his heart.

Comment: This dear, sweet, pretty romanza "Il balen," a staple of Victorian parlor entertainment and music boxes, is a terror from hell to sing. It is very high in the baritone voice, even by Verdi's standards, and is such a four-square tune that any fudging will be glaringly obvious. There's absolutely no place to breathe, and the slower it is sung (that is, the longer the vocal line), the more the audience is pleased. The bridge of the melody, when the baritone sings "Ah, l'amor, l'amore ond'ardo," is a real minefield. The phrase is stretched over seven measures, with an accent on the first beat of each measure. Tradition requires him to "emote" through these accents until they are almost little throbs in the voice. Lovely, except that the voice can go awry at any moment in this process, and then there is no distinguishing him from a tomcat in the moonlight. The romanza wraps up with a reworking of the bridge in jaunty 12/8 time, doubled by gushing strings.

Ferrando and his followers withdraw, and the Count hides himself, ready to abduct Leonora as she passes with the other nuns. From the cloister, they can be heard chanting about the peace of mind conferred by the veil upon the sinful daughters of Eve. Leonora enters with Ines and her companions. She asks Ines not to weep for their parting, but to lead her to the altar of God. The Count bursts upon them, swearing that Leonora shall have no altar other than the one of marriage. Suddenly Manrico appears. Leonora wonders if he is raised from the dead, while the Count assumes that hell has renounced Manrico to torment his life further. Manrico says that neither heaven nor hell own him yet; he is alive and full of indomitable power, as is the God who punishes the wicked. Ines and the women exclaim that Leonora's trust in heaven has been rewarded, while Ferrando and the Count's men urge the Count to withdraw, since fate always fights for Manrico. Manrico's soldiers rush in and disarm the Count. Manrico escapes with Lenora, the women withdraw to the convent, and Manrico's men hold the Count and his men at bay.

Comment: The nuns' chorus is background music, and Leonora's exchange with Ines is very modest and maidenly. The action really begins with the almost simultaneous appearance of the Count and Manrico. As complicated as it may appear to read about, it all unfolds in about five minutes on stage, and proves what dramatic wonders can be achieved in an old-fashioned concertato. Leonora leads the ensemble with a solo beginning in breathy couplets depicting her astonishment. These coalesce, however, into one of the boundlessly arching phrases that come so easily to this character. Di Luna and Manrico make their contributions, always wound around Leonora vocally. When the necessary stage business happens, there are some obliging flashes and cymbal-bangings from the orchestra, and then all stops again as Leonora repeats her soaring phrase. (Usually Manrico joins her in this fragment, although the score does not say to.) The phrase is a "close-up" technique, a focus on a human emotion outside of time, one of many to be found in Trovatore.

Act III

Scene 1: Di Luna's camp outside the Castle Castellor.

Soldiers are gaming, but looking forward to the battle. Reinforcements arrive. Ferrando tells the men they will attack Castellor at dawn, and there is fine booty in the castle for everybody. All are stirred in anticipation.

Comment: There are two Soldiers' Choruses here. The first is Verdi in his best "nervous" mode, rushing strings punctuated by orchestral thumps. After Ferrando's brief exhortation comes the more famous chorus, "Squilli, echeggi." It is another piece of music that everybody knows, a distinctly Trovatore melody constructed of couplets around a stressed off-beat. Structurally, this music bears an unfortunate resemblance to "Humoresque" and even, it could be argued, the Laurel and Hardy theme song. One senses directors are embarrassed by Verdi's tuniness at this point. Verdi wasn't embarrassed by it, however. The theme is repeated forte with full brass accompaniment. It is shameless and even vulgar, and should be played as such.

The Count enters, furious that Leonora must, even now, be in Manrico's arms. There is a noise outside the camp. Ferrando and the soldiers drag in Azucena, who was lurking beyond the tents. They assume she was spying. The Count questions her. Where was she going? Nowhere, she answers. It is the custom of gypsies to wander. Where does she come from? From the mountains of Biscay, poor, with but one son to console her. Now she looks for him. Ferrando seems to recognize her. The Count asks her if she remembers a child who was stolen from the old Count and never seen again. She asks who he is. The brother of the stolen child, answers di Luna. Azucena starts, convincing Ferrando that this is the same gypsy woman. The Count and the soldiers are overjoyed that they have found the murderess at last. She calls for Manrico to help her, and di Luna thanks God that he has both the killer and his rival's mother in the same person. Azucena threatens the worse son of the evil father with God's vengeance, di Luna swears to avenge all his wrongs on her, while the soldiers drag her away, promising to burn her.

Comment: *All the excitement in this scene is provided, predictably enough, by Azucena. When she is asked where she comes from, she sings a moody and effective solo, "Giorni poveri vivea." Subsequently, she pulls out the heavy artillery for her threats at the end, "Deh, rallentate." It is the perfect form of a grand scena, but woven so seamlessly that the change from pensive to ballistic has occurred organically rather than abruptly.*

Scene 2: A room adjacent to the chapel at Castellor.

Leonora hears the preparations for battle, but Manrico consoles her. The battle will come at dawn. Until then she must think only of love. The chapel organ plays. They urge each other to the altar, which will open all the pleasures of pure love. Ruiz enters. The gypsy woman has been captured by di Luna. Already the flames are lit. Manrico trembles. He tells Leonora that the woman is his mother, and he must save her though it cost his life. Ruiz departs to rally the troops. Manrico, crazed with vengeance, swears to save Azucena. Leonora says she cannot bear more blows of destiny. It would be better to die. Ruiz returns with the soldiers. Manrico inflames himself and them with the spirit of battle, and runs out, crying "To arms!"

Comment: *The arias "Ah! sì, ben mio" and "Di quella pira" represent the alpha and the omega of the tenorial experience. The first is a romanza, though quite different from the ones Verdi had written for tenors until this point. The scene opens with an air of menace (strums in the lower strings), not absent even from this brief moment of love. The romanza, then, is a very self-conscious attempt on Manrico's part to allay Leonora's fears. It must sound both calming and confident. Unfortunately, most tenors are cast in this role for their ability to sing the following cabaletta, and they tend to trash the romanza. There is the slightest indication of a love duet sung to a background of organ music, all the more poignant for its brevity.*

After the messenger's news, we have, structurally speaking, all the makings of a classic grand scena. "Di quella pira" is a balls-out cabaletta of the first magnitude, the acme of the draw-your-sword-and-cry-for-battle tradition. The bulk of the aria is a four-square breathy melody built around lines of five beats and accompanied by a rousing gallop from the strings and horns. Manrico has switched gears entirely. Few are the tenors who can be equally convincing at both.

Then there is the issue of the high C's. Tradition had added a few of these, one in the middle and another at the end. Apparently, a tenor in the years after the premiere wrote to Verdi for official approval of these additions. Verdi gave it, provided he sang a good high C. Both notes are expected to be held as long as possible. The final high C is especially perilous. Other tenors sing the aria as written, disappointing much of the audience but also positing themselves as refined artistes. The problem is we need something to distinguish this example of Manrico running to battle from the previous time he did so, at the end of Act II, Scene I. What is the best solution? The great tenor José Carreras offered very sensible advice, suggesting that opera companies advertise on the placards which performances would include the high C's and which would do without them.

Act IV

Scene 1: A wing of the Count's palace of Aliaferia, with a prison tower in the corner. Night.

Ruiz leads Leonora forward, both cloaked. He points to the tower containing di Luna's prisoners, including Manrico. Leonora dismisses Ruiz. She looks for protection to a ring she wears on her right hand. Leonora addresses the prison tower. She asks the tender wings of love to carry her sighs up to him, but not to let him know of the pain in her heart. Prayers are head from afar for the soul of the condemned man. Those sounds, those solemn dark prayers strike the air with terror and make Leonora's heart pound. She hears Manrico from the tower, awaiting death and bidding Leonora farewell. Ah, these dungeon doors will only open for him when his corpse is already cold! Again Manrico bids farewell, asking Leonora never to forget him.

Comment: Leonora's aria at the beginning of this scene, "D'amor sull'ali rosee," *is, in effect, the eleven o'clock ballad. Leonora is a different woman from the first act, more experienced and disillusioned but also less bound to convention and expectations. This aria reflects these changes. It is sad, with long haunting phrases and vertiginous descents down the scale. The subsequent "Miserere" is another of the opera's hits to make it into the communal unconscious. The soft but insistent strumming of strings sounds like the palpitations of which Leonora speaks. Her line, usually delivered full-throttle, revels in chesty low notes, while Manrico's antiphon is a lovely, harp-accompanied melody. The contrast is severe and interesting. In a sense, he's the damsel in distress and she the noble warrior to the rescue. All around them are the death-chanting monks pronouncing doom. Few would know it, but there is an additional cabaletta for Leonora after the "Miserere," a powerful aria, "Tu vedrai che amore in terra." It is generally thought to be too demanding on the soprano after the previous scene, but count your blessings if you happen to catch it.*

The Count enters with some attendants. He gives them their orders: the axe for the son, the fire for the mother. They depart. He wonders if he has overstepped the authority given him by his prince in ordering these executions. It is the woman who drives him to such desperate acts! Where can she be? Leonora steps forward, asking for mercy for Manrico. She throws herself at the Count's feet, but this only strengthens his resolve to make Manrico suffer. No price on earth could gain a pardon for the troubadour. Leonora says she only has one thing to offer the Count—herself. Astounded, di Luna asks reassurance that she means what she says and will carry through. She swears it by God. The Count calls a guard and whispers orders, while Leonora, aside, remarks that the Count will have her body, but only cold and lifeless. The Count says Manrico will live. He will live, she repeats, and thanks God for this gift that reinforces her resolve. They enter the tower together, Leonora protesting that she will keep her word.

Comment: The scene between Leonora and the Count builds splendidly in both pace and sheer volume. Again, Leonora must make the vocal and spiritual journey from genuine pleading to fiery determination, which should convince the Count of one thing and the audience of another. Not every soprano capable of living through the role can be expected to convey such duplicity through her vocalizing, but Verdi has provided the opportunity in his music.

Scene 2: The castle dungeon.

Azucena is lying on a pallet, and Manrico sits near her, urging her to sleep. She cannot. She hears the executioners approach, terrified at the thought of burning. She tries to relax and, half-asleep, thinks of their mountain home. Perhaps they can find rest there again, and she will hear Manrico's sweet lute song again. He prays that heaven may hear her plea and grant her rest, as she falls asleep.

Leonora enters the cell. Manrico rejoices that he may see her again before he dies, but she tells him he will not die. He must leave immediately. But will Leonora not follow him? No, she replies. She must stay. She urges him to leave for his own safety. He will not move, insisting she look him in the eye and tell him at what price she bought his life. Nothing to say? He understands. How evil to sell, yes, sell a heart sworn to him! Leonora protests the insult. Azucena remembers the peaceful mountains. Manrico curses Leonora, whom he now hates, but she asks him rather to pray for her at this moment, and falls to the ground. How rapidly the poison courses through her veins! Manrico repents that he dared to curse this angel. The Count enters, pausing at the door. Begging God's grace, Leonora dies.

The Count grasps Leonora's deception, and orders Manrico to the block. While being dragged out, he cries farewell to his mother, who wakes up and sees the Count. She tells him he must not kill Manrico, but the Count pulls her to the window to watch as Manrico is beheaded. "He was your brother!" cries Azucena. The Count is horrified. "Oh mother, you are avenged!" she declares, as she falls by the window. In horror, the Count realizes that he alone lives on.

Comment: *Although Azucena begins another narrative reliving the horrors of death by fire, this does not develop as it had in earlier scenes. Instead,* *her main music in this scene becomes a nostalgic duet with Manrico, "Ai nostri monti." Like the father's nostalgic "Di Provenza" in* Traviata, *it has all the feel of a lullaby. Soft pizzicato strings complete the picture. It is a very striking break with everything we have seen so far of Azucena.*

When Leonora enters, there is the inevitable trio, with Azucena contributing more of the lullaby and Leonora pouring out her emotions in another of those ascents up the scale that seem so natural in Verdi's handling. The actual finale is all rushing and fury, in the manner of events dictated by fate and beyond the realm of human sensation. Only Azucena's final cry, hitting a high B flat, is genuine feeling. It is a microcosm of the opera as a whole, depicting two separate levels of experience. There is the material world, with its insane, cruel, unmanageable facts, and there is the human response to that world, which is genuine, palpable, and often soaring and noble.

In mythic terms, the ending of Trovatore *is fascinating. Azucena's final cry, "Sei vendicata, o madre!," is both a victory shout and a cry of despair. Her love for Manrico is genuine enough, yet his death has fulfilled her life's mission, in a sense. She has, after all, completed the murder she botched a generation before. The lethal component of genuine parental love, so well explored in* Rigoletto, *is further probed here.*

La traviata

PREMIERE: La Fenice, Venice, 1853. Libretto by Francesco Maria Piave.

THE NAME

La traviata means "one who has gone astray," a very nice expression for a "fallen" woman.

La traviata might well be the world's most popular opera. After hitting its stride about a year after its less-than-successful premiere, it has grown in popularity and never stopped growing. It's said (although I'm not sure how this can be known) that for the last hundred years there has been at least one live performance of *Traviata* somewhere in the world every single night. In 1997 it received professional productions in sixty-two America cities, plus making appearances in workshops and other smaller programs. Its music pops up in movies, on television, and on radio in the most unlikely places. It has become part of the communal unconscious.

Much of *Traviata*'s popularity is due to the heroine. The tragic, beautiful, noble, young, and doomed woman has also become a figure in popular iconography. And Verdi was clearly in love with his heroine. In no other Verdi opera does the soprano carry the whole work so squarely on her own shoulders as Violetta. Vocally, the demands are incredible. The soprano must have brilliant coloratura, the ability to sing long legato passages in a faint pianissimo, and, at two points in the score, to give out a Wagnerian Niagara of sound. She must even speak convincingly at one point. No one woman has ever exhausted the vocal possibilities of the role. In fact, it has often been suggested (and only partly in jest) that four separate sopranos should be engaged for the part, one for each act, since an entirely different voice is required in each. All sopranos want to sing it at some point in their careers, whether they should or not. The opera always succeeds, no matter what approach is used or what vocal shortcomings are highlighted.

Vocal technique is only the tip of the iceberg. Violetta is the most desirable woman in a huge city famed for its feminine treasures. She is also a fully drawn, real woman. She must portray, in roughly the following order, frivolity, charm, reflectiveness, nervous hysteria, dignity, thoughtfulness, nobility and the capacity for sacrifice, raw love, confusion, vulnerability, despair, death, and redemption, often combining several of these at once. In order to better understand this work, which continues to fascinate the whole world, it is worth taking a look at the remarkable woman who inspired it.

Alphonsine Plessis was born in a village in Normandy in 1824. Her mother left home when she was six, and it appears that her alcoholic father started pimping his daughter at the age of twelve. So much for romantic idealizations of country life. Arriving in Paris at the age of fifteen, Alphonsine spent some time as a dance hall girl, but quickly rose through the ranks of prostitutes. By the time she was sixteen she had changed her name to Marie Duplessis, established a salon, and began attracting attention.

Everyone agreed she was beautiful, but Marie also had natural grace and refinement. Somewhere along the way she learned to read and write; she kept a private library of over 200 books and discussed literature with the leading writers of her era. She not only had style, she set the styles for all Paris. One admirer wrote, "She neither flaunts nor hides her vices." This is an important aspect of Marie's personality, crucial also to her literary and operatic incarnations. In a world of deceit, she was unequivocally honest.

She required huge sums of money to live. A quick sexual encounter with her cost 500 francs in a time when a schoolteacher earned 300 francs a years. If one wished to be seen with her beyond the bedroom, the price skyrocketed, and jewels, horses, and even houses were expected as payment. Her partiality for camellias was based on their expense. Each one cost three francs (the average daily salary for a laborer), and she packed as many as she could fit onto her dresses, hair, and even fan. Nor were those camellias always white. On the five appropriate days each month, Marie wore red camellias, announcing, in effect, that shop was closed. This is the Parisian genius for being utterly refined and totally gross at the same time. (When Violetta gives Alfredo the flower in Act I of the opera, telling him to return when the color "fades," it seems like a grand gesture of the chivalric era. In the novel, it is a very earthy and practical device.)

Marie had simultaneous arrangements with several different rich men for the next few years. In 1844 she met the serious young Alexandre Dumas *fils* and began a relationship that lasted a little under a year. At no time was her arrangement with Dumas monogamous. No one could afford Marie on his own, least of all the penniless Dumas. They parted ways in 1845. Far from languishing and dying, Marie then met the man she loved most, Franz Liszt, the ubiquitous stud of Romantic Europe. Meanwhile, there were other men: the eighty-year-old Count Stackelberg, a fabulously wealthy Russian who paid for her house on the Boulevard de la Madeleine; the Count Perregaux, whom she actually married on a quick jaunt to London and then promptly dismissed on her return to Paris; and several others.

Marie's spectacular rise, such as it was, was destined to be brief. An indeterminate illness made her thin and pale, which only added to her allure. It became apparent that she had consumption, which was the most fashionable terminal illness one could get in those days, giving the victim a frail beauty and an aura of irresistible doom. It was the nineteenth century's version of "heroin chic."

Dumas, traveling in Spain with his father when he heard of Marie's illness, wrote her a long letter asking forgiveness for past wrongs. No reply to this letter is known. He learned of Marie's death on his return to France in February 1847.

In July of that year he wrote (quickly, by his admission) *La Dame aux camélias,* an account of their relationship that falls somewhere between a novel and a memoir. It is preachy, whiny, and self-serving, with many of the facts changed. Dumas also personified his own ambiguities by inventing the figure of the bourgeois father who insists on the breakup. However, *La Dame aux camélias* also has a certain amount of honesty, if not accuracy. It gives insights into many of the questions of the opera. For example, in Act III, a great ensemble is built around the moment when Alfredo, as the hero is called, insults Violetta (Marie) publicly by flinging money at her, saying that she is now repaid for all the money he had disgracefully allowed her to spend on him. Throwing money at someone is rather crass, but what is so insulting about repaying money actually owed? In the novel the situation is quite different. Marguerite, as she is called, is living with a count but takes pity on Armand, as he is named in this incarnation. She goes to his small flat and assures him that she still has feelings for him, then makes the ex-lover's mistake of spending the night with him to prove it, and then returns to the bill-paying count. When she leaves, he is disgusted with himself for having slept with her, and sends her her "fee" for the night. This, apparently, was the insult that ended the relationship. Of course for the stage, the payment of a prostitute had to be changed to the repayment of expenses incurred.

The stage, it would appear, was where this story was heading from the time it began. Dumas morphed the novel into a play of the same name, telescoping a few characters and moving events around a bit to fit the theater. Verdi saw the play in Paris and immediately sent it off to Piave as an opera subject. Both composer and librettist were struck by the directness of the story and by its modernity. It was an opera waiting to happen. The management at La Fenice was also struck by the story's modernity, and insisted on resetting it in the remote and operatically conventional past. Who would want to pay money to see people on stage who look like people in the audience? Verdi acquiesced, although he sensed this would make the opera more difficult to understand. Marguerite's world is firmly in the Europe of the industrial era. There are complicated systems of credit and loans, there is a bumbling aristocracy that had lost its power base, there is a powerful middle class nervous about morals and appearances, and there is a new rich class of *arrivistes* ready to throw money around for such status symbols as rentable women. No matter. The censors and the management of La Fenice pushed the opera back to around the year 1700, with everyone running around in the (then) usual wigs and knee beeches.

The new setting didn't help. *Traviata* failed at its Fenice premiere, although it was not the fiasco Verdi's letters claimed it was. A year later, it was produced at the Teatro San Benedetto in Venice, with a few tinkerings in the score, after which it began its triumph around the world, a triumph that continues to this day.

It has become fashionable to see an analogy between Violetta and Giuseppina Strepponi. One article in a recent program at the Metropolitan Opera went so far as to call *Traviata* a love letter from Verdi to Strepponi. I would caution against taking this point of view too directly, since it smacks of rethinking history as it should have been in light of our contemporary sensibilities. Certainly Strepponi, as Verdi's live-in mistress with a gaggle of bastards scattered around Italy, had her conflicts with social expectations, but there was a difference between a woman of the theater and the card-carrying *belles horizontales* of Paris. Verdi, who was a prig despite his own irregular liaison, would have preferred to maintain that distinction.

CAST OF CHARACTERS

VIOLETTA VALÉRY *(soprano)* A young Parisian hostess: the Marie Duplessis of history and Marguerite Gautier of literature, stage, and screen.

ALFREDO GERMONT *(tenor)* A young man in love with Violetta: the Alexandre Dumas *fils* of history and Armand Duval of literature, stage, and screen.

GIORGIO GERMONT *(baritone)* Alfredo's father, a bourgeois landowner from Provence. This character, a personification of conventional morality, was invented by Dumas.

FLORA BELVOIX *(mezzo-soprano or soprano)* Violetta's flighty friend and fellow hostess.

GASTONE *(tenor)* A young spark about town, friend of Violetta and Flora and, curiously, Alfredo. Directors, or rather their assistants, sometimes make him out to be gay (since Dumas is clear that Gastone has never been Marguerite's lover, and these being Frenchmen . . .). Who cares? His job is to get Alfredo on stage and then fade into the wallpaper. Still, you will probably see him trying to convince you he's the Rex Reed of Orléanist Paris.

ANNINA *(soprano)* Violetta's maid.

DOCTOR GRENVIL *(bass)* A friend of Violetta's.

THE MARQUIS D'OBIGNY *(bass)* Flora's "protector."

THE BARON DOUPHOL *(baritone)* Violetta's sometime lover.

THE OPERA

Prelude

Comment: *The violins begin softly and slowly, giving a general feel of sadness and loss. We then hear the "big theme" of the opera, a full, lush, and stately cascade down the scale. It is undeniably elegant and a bit sad. This will be Violetta's big moment in Act II when she begs Alfredo to love her forever, no matter what. When the theme is repeated, this time by the cellos, the violins counter with a busy harmony, suggesting all the intrigue central to Violetta's world. The union of gossipy chatter and elegant sadness is a perfect depiction of Violetta.*

Act I

Setting: A large room in Violetta's home.

Violetta is relaxing on a sofa, chatting with Dr. Grenvil and other friends. Another group of friends come into the house, led by the Baron and Flora, on the arm of the Marquis. Violetta rises to greet the newcomers. Flora and the Marquis ask how Violetta can be partying. Violetta answers that she wants to, since having fun is the best medicine for what ails her. The other guests agree.

Comment: The curtain rises on a party in full swing. The orchestra obliges with some rather martial-sounding chords as the scene begins. That's all our ham-fisted directors have to hear, and we are usually treated to a loud raunchy scream from one or more of the female party guests in productions these days. It's as if we're being told that these people were, you know, like partying. This is a mistake. Marie (Violetta) was a great hostess as well as a whore, and knew the difference between a dinner and an orgy. It was one of her chief charms. Alas, the union of elegance and sexual license is something our era cannot grasp, but it was crucial to the world depicted here. For the comings and goings of the party guests, Verdi lets the orchestra carry the energetic melody while the vocal lines are interjections.

Gastone, a fashionable young party animal, presents Alfredo Germont, a man who greatly admires her, to Violetta. Servants set the table for dinner, and guests take their places, Violetta between Gastone and Alfredo. Gastone tells her that while she was ill, Alfredo called every day to inquire after her health. Violetta is surprised by such kindness, telling the Baron that he was less attentive. Flora finds Alfredo *simpatico*. Alfredo proposes a toast to love. Violetta joins the toast, calling for her guests to be joyful, since love is fleeting, flowers lose their bloom swiftly, and all in life is folly except pleasure. Life is only pleasure, she suggests. Only when one can no longer love, answers Alfredo. She warns him not to speak of love to one who does not know it. "Such is my destiny," he retorts. The guests drink to a night of wine and song.

Comment: The brindisi *(drinking song) is one of those stock features of Italian opera that we're not supposed to like. This one is irresistible, shameless in its "oom-pah-pah" accompaniment, familiar from movies, radio, and a hundred TV commercials. It works here. It even can't be accused of that supposedly cardinal sin of Romantic opera—stopping the action—since the action is a dinner party in progress. Moreover, it frames Alfredo and Violetta within the crowd, and makes their subsequent love scene more inevitable.*

Music is heard from an adjoining room, and Violetta invites the guests to dance. As they are going in, Violetta stops suddenly, turning pale. All ask after her, and she replies that she is fine, but must sit down. She insists they go dance—she will join them in a moment. All go except Alfredo. She looks in a mirror, and is frightened by her pallor. She sees Alfredo who says she will kill herself if she continues in this way. No one in the world loves her, he says, except him! Ah, yes, she had forgotten this great love. Does she laugh at him? Has she no heart? Perhaps, she says. And how long has he been in love with her? A year, he answers. One day she passed by him, happy and ethereal. And since that tremendous day, he lived in a love he didn't even comprehend, that love which is the heartbeat of the whole universe, mysterious, proud, the crucifixion and delight of the heart. Oh, she says, if this is true, then he must leave. She can only offer friendship, and could never accept such noble love. He must find another, and then he will be able to forget her.

Comment: *How little the battle between the sexes has changed! Alfredo's concern for Violetta amounts to a delusion that his love can cure her of tuberculosis. Given the opportunity to express his love, Alfredo begins haltingly, interrupted by plunks in the orchestra, beautifully depicting shy palpitations. When he hits his stride ("Di quell' amor!"), he sings of love in one of those beautiful, unforgettable romantic musical phrases that can be written by only a few Italians. This phrase will recur in the last act, played on a solo violin, as a sort of love theme. The Italian term for a bit of music that expresses this sort of emotional rush is* slancio, *something hurled out like a spear. This* slancio *falls down through the scale, depicting the inherent melancholy of "falling" in love. Violetta interjects with frivolous little coloratura frills, resisting Alfredo's seriousness, although they join voices for a brief moment at the end.*

Gastone pokes his head in at the door, asking what the devil the two are up to. "Joking," says Violetta. Well then they must continue, says Gastone, who quickly leaves.

So no more talk of love, chides Violetta. Alfredo obeys and prepares to leave. She gives him a flower from her dress, to bring it back to her when it fades, she explains. "Tomorrow!" he shouts. She agrees. They bid farewell to each other. The guests tumble in from the ballroom, thanking Violetta for the delightful evening.

Comment: When Gastone and his friends walk in on the lovers, we hear the party music in the orchestra. It is an effective shift in point of view managed by music in pre-cinematic days. The business of the flower has been addressed in the introduction to this chapter.

Left alone, Violetta is astonished how powerfully Alfredo's words have affected her. No man has ever made her fall in love. Perhaps this is the man who can make her abandon her present life, and let her feel that love which is both crucifixion and ecstasy. No, it's madness to think so! What could a poor woman like her, alone in the populated desert they call Paris, hope to find in life? There's only one course for her, to revel in earthly pleasures while she can! Alfredo appears outside her window, repeating his commitment to true love. Violetta repeats her resolve not to fall for such vanities, commanding her thoughts to new pleasures, new pleasures . . .

Comment: The first haunting aria, "Ah! fors'é lui," shows Violetta's tender side, daring to hope for love after all her disillusionments with life. Its musical climax is a repetition of the slancio *from Alfredo's little aria, showing her moving spiritually closer to him. After some rapid recitative, remarkable for its bitterness, Violetta launches into the fireworks aria of all time, "Sempre libera." This one includes runs and trills in the lowest as well as the highest reaches of a soprano's range. Toward the end, Alfredo's appearance outside the window prompts another rendition of the* slancio, *followed by a truly psychotic run of notes from Violetta. (A series of descending couplets amid this, if not executed to perfection, is indistinguishable from a yapping chihuahua.) The libretto doesn't make it any easier on her. The opening phrase, "Sempre libera degg'io folleggiare di gioia in gioia," is said to be as challenging as singing with a mouth full of peanut butter.*

Violetta's solo is obviously a grand scena. There is the haunting recitative, the cavatina, more recitative, and a peel-the-wallpaper cabaletta. There are, however, important differences between Violetta's scene and the standard grand scena. The issues at stake here are not war and patriotism but that very modern question, "What is the right way for me to live out my personal destiny?" The "messenger" who causes the mood change necessary for the big aria is a conflicting internal impulse rather than a changed external situation. This is the modernity of Traviata.

Act II

Setting: A room in a modest but pleasant country house.

Alfredo enters the home where he and Violetta have taken refuge from the whirl of Paris. He has no joy when she is not around. And she, who gave up all her admirers and friends to live with him three months ago, now lives only for him, and he seems to live in heaven.

Comment: Alfredo is the very picture of smug masculinity in this scene. His aria, "De' miei bollenti spiriti," however, is more sympathetic than the words would indicate. A steady, muted rum-tum-tum in the orchestra suggests all the passions lying just below the surface. Verdi did not indicate a tempo for this aria. A moderate tempo, allowing us to hear the pizzicato strings in the orchestra and the tenor's voice without either putting us to sleep or rousing us to arms, seems the most appropriate.

Annina the maid enters, and Alfredo questions her. Where has she been? To Paris, she answers, to sell the Mistress's carriage and horses. Alfredo is shocked at the news that Violetta must sell possessions to keep them. He resolves to go to Paris and cover her debts. He swears Annina to silence and she leaves. Alfredo expresses his remorse and shame at being little better than a kept man. He leaves for Paris.

Comment: So who did Alfredo think was paying the bills? The hero comes off looking even more naive than he has to here. Piave did some judicious cleaning up of Dumas's long digression into Marguerite's finances, and the result is not quite satisfactory. The scene ends with a standard cabaletta, "O mio rimorso," which shows us a tenor standing in one place telling us how he's going to run off and take decisive action. This is often cut, although the scene is unbalanced without it. The cabaletta is showy and difficult to sing, but it gives Alfredo a moment to display chutzpa in his voice, if not in his actions, filling him out better than leaving him with the bouncy "De' miei bollenti spirti" as his only full aria.

Violetta enters as Alfredo rushes off. Annina tells her he is off to Paris and will be back by evening. Violetta finds this strange. Annina gives her an invitation to a party at Flora's. Violetta tosses it aside. Flora doesn't realize how little such things now appeal to Violetta. The gardener announces a gentleman visitor. Violetta assumes it to be the agent who is handling the sale of her property, but a stern man appears at the door announcing himself as the father of Alfredo Germont, the boy she is ruining. Violetta replies that she is a lady and in her own home, saying she will withdraw to spare M. Germont, rather than herself, further embarrassment. Germont is impressed by her bearing, yet isn't it true that Alfredo wants to squander his inheritance on her? Violetta replies that she would refuse the offer. She hands him her business papers to show him the true state of things. Germont agrees that her actions are better than her past would suggest. She answers that God has erased her past because of her love for Alfredo. Noble sentiments, he comments, but he will ask of her a sacrifice in the name of these noble sentiments. She knew it, she says. She was too happy. He asks her to decide the fate of his two children. Two children? she asks. Yes, replies Germont. God gave him a daughter, as pure as an angel. The daughter's fiancé cannot marry into the family while Alfredo is associated with Violetta. Germont begs her not to be the cause of his family's unhappiness.

Comment: The confrontation between Germont and Violetta is a duet in the style of Rigoletto, *with brief exchanges and rapid developments rather than a single melody. Verdi's early publishers thought it too long, and some audiences still agree. Big mistake. This is the dramatic climax of the opera. It is best broken down into five parts to trace the development.*

Germont has the first extended solo, "Pura siccome an angelo," describing the angelic young daughter. It is a broad and lovely tune, meant to arouse sympathy in Violetta.

Yes, agrees Violetta, it will be hard, but she will separate from Alfredo until the marriage is contracted. No, replies Germont. It must be forever. No, never! says Violetta. Doesn't Germont know what genuine love binds them together? Doesn't he know that Alfredo offered her everything? Doesn't he know that she has a terminal illness, and will not live long? Leave Alfredo forever? Violetta would rather die.

Comment: Violetta's music, "Non sapete," becomes breathy and broken as she realizes what Germont is asking of her.

Hear me out, says Germont patiently. Men are fickle. One day, when her charms have faded, boredom will set in. What then? She admits this is true. Germont suggests Violetta assume a new role, as the consoling angel of the Germont family. She bitterly considers how there is no hope for a fallen woman. God may grant her mercy, but men never will.

Comment: Germont slows the musical pace down in this polite but manipulative passage, "Bella voi siete," where he insinuates himself into her worst fears.

Violetta, controlling herself, asks Germont to tell his lovely, pure daughter that a luckless woman who has only one good thing in her life will give it up for her. Germont urges her to weep, since he feels her pain and knows the sacrifice couldn't be greater, but he is sure her noble heart will prevail in the end.

Comment: Violetta's music, "Dite alla giovine," slows down even more than Germont's, as she represses her feelings and, in essence, agrees to his proposal. She sings quietly of her plight in the inherently poignant key of

E flat major. The effect sounds like the voice of one who is stunned, and only maintaining composure with great effort. Germont's cries of "Piangi! Piangi! o misera!" *are not consoling. She repeats her stately verse.*

Violetta asks what she must do. Tell him you don't love him. Alfredo wouldn't believe that. Leave him. Alfredo would follow. Then . . . Germont's voice trails off. Violetta understands. She asks Germont to embrace her as if she were his own daughter. This will give her strength. She sits at the writing desk. Alfredo will be heartbroken. His father must console him. How generous she is, he comments. What can he do for her? "I will die!" she says. "But don't let Alfredo curse my memory." When she is dead, Alfredo must know the sacrifice she made for him. Germont urges her to live and thrive, nourished by the knowledge of the nobility of which she's capable.

Comment: After a transitional recitative (all in minor keys), Violetta finally gives some vent to her emotions in "Morrò, la mia memoria."

They bid farewell. They may never meet again. Violetta reminds him to tell Alfredo everything one day. Germont agrees and leaves.

Comment: Germont, it is always pointed out, has been the more static partner in this scene, since he has one mission and carries it out, while she must basically change as a character. This is true, but Germont has also played a brilliant game of carrot-and-stick with her, moving from threatening, to pleading, to insinuating, to offering a degree of friendship and a great display of admiration. The baritone role requires as much emotional and vocal diversity as the soprano through this part.

Violetta writes a note and rings for Annina to deliver it. The maid is surprised by the address, but Violetta tells her to be silent and go. She finishes another letter and seals it. Alfredo enters, asking Violetta what she's doing. Extremely agitated, Violetta deflects his questions. He admits he, too, has a lot on his mind. His father is coming to see him. Violetta uses this as an excuse to get away. It would be better for her to meet his father after they've spent some time together. Then everything will be well, because Alfredo loves her—he loves her, doesn't he? Of course, he answers. Alfredo asks why she is crying. From joy, she answers. She will always be there, near him, among the flowers. "Love me, Alfredo!" she cries. "Love me as much as I love you." She hurries out.

Comment: This brief outburst from Violetta, "Amami, Alfredo!," makes or breaks the opera. If Violetta cannot project genuine love for Alfredo right here, then she may come off as the fickle whore Alfredo subsequently suspects her to be. The music, which appeared as an elegantly unforgettable theme in the Prelude, should be all raw emotion here. Sopranos with dramatic heft in their voices must let it flow in a cascade of sound at this point, and those with lighter voices must find some way of faking it effectively.

Alfredo is satisfied that Violetta's heart lives only for his love. It is late. Perhaps his father will not come. The gardener enters and tells Alfredo that Violetta left in a carriage, and Annina left a while before her. Alfredo knows. Not to worry, he advises. "What does that mean?" the gardener wonders. A messenger arrives, delivering a letter given to him by a lady in a carriage on the road. He leaves. The letter is from Violetta. Alfredo is filled with dread. He opens the letter and reads one line. It says, "Alfredo, by the time you read this . . ." He cries out in anguish. Germont enters from the garden and embraces his son, trying to console him. He reminds his son of his native home in Provence, and his family. He can return there and find solace. Alfredo doesn't know how his poor father has suffered worrying about him, but now they are reunited, and God has answered the prayers of a suffering father.

Comment: This set piece, the aria "Di Provenza," is famous from the usual round of recital encores, soundtracks, and even an appearance on television's The Odd Couple. *It is so formal and conservative that it demands attention. Two strophes of perfectly metered seven-beat lines with an A/B/B/A rhyme scheme, and a sweet statement of the theme in the woodwinds, make this aria worthy of Bellini or other composers who wrote a generation before* Traviata. *Germont belongs to the previous generation, and this aria is his statement of bewilderment at the "new ways." Also, legend has it that the tune of "Di Provenza" was a lullaby Verdi had heard in his youth. It certainly has that feel. Germont is attempting to lure his errant son back to the innocence of his youth.*

Alfredo barely hears his father. Baron Douphol is behind this! He swears revenge. Seeing the invitation to Flora's party on the table, he vows to go there and find Violetta. Germont runs after him.

Comment: Everybody agrees that this otherwise monumental act ends rather lamely after the aria "Di Provenza." Verdi originally wrote a cabaletta for Germont, but it didn't say anything the aria hadn't, and it has been consigned to the outtakes file. Also, the tail end of the act has more of the "someone's coming, someone's going" fuss that plagues the whole act. Notice how many letters and notes are passed around. This very intimate confrontation between three people can be as hard to manage as a huge choral scene.

Act III (or Act II, Scene 2)

Setting: The salon of Flora's elegant townhouse in Paris, during a party.

Flora is mingling with her guests. She tells them she has invited Violetta and Alfredo. The Marquis is surprised Flora hasn't heard the news. Alfredo and Violetta have split up. Flora and Dr. Grenvil are astonished at this. The doctor saw them only yesterday, and they looked so happy.

Ladies enter disguised as gypsies, singing of their power to tell fortunes. One group looks at Flora's hand and advises her she has many rivals. Another examines the Marquis's and pronounces that he will never be a model of fidelity. Gastone leads in a group of young bucks all dressed as Spanish matadors. They sing about a young matador who killed five bulls in one day to win his love's heart. Dancers perform a bullfight masque while the partygoers sing along.

Comment: The gypsies and the matadors constitute the "production number" of Traviata, *the frivolous music forming a severe contrast with the rest of the opera. Dramatists have always utilized the technique of comic relief to heighten tragedy, and in opera it can be even more crucial than in pure drama. This scene, unlike most other ballet sequences in Verdi operas, is never cut. Verdi knew what he was doing here.*

Alfredo enters, to the surprise of many guests. They ask him where Violetta is. "I don't know about her," he says. They cheer his sangfroid, and he sits down to play cards with Gastone and a few friends. Violetta shows up, escorted by the Baron. The Baron points out Alfredo, and tells Violetta she is not to speak one word to him. Flora pulls Violetta to a sofa and they chat in low voices along with Dr. Grenvil. Gastone deals the cards. Alfredo wins again. "Unlucky in love, lucky in cards," he mutters bitterly. He wins again, saying he'll return to the country with his winnings. Alone? ask Flora. No, he answers, with one who fled from him. The Baron challenges Alfredo to a game of cards. Violetta asks God for pity. Alfredo wins. A servant announces dinner. All go to the dining room, the Baron telling Alfredo they will continue the game after dinner. Alfredo says he will accept the challenge at any game the Baron proposes.

Violetta returns to the room, having asked Alfredo to meet her there. He arrives. What does she want? He must leave at once, she says. He is in grave danger. And does she think he is such a coward, or is she afraid he might kill the Baron? She merely repeats that he must leave. Only with her at his side, he answers. No, that cannot be. She took a sacred oath to leave him. He asks who compelled her to take this oath. "One who had the right," she answers. Douphol? Yes. Does she love him? "Fine," she says. "I love him."

In a fury, Alfredo calls all the guests into the room. Do they know what his woman has done? Violetta asks him to be silent. He continues. This woman squandered everything she had for him, while he, blind, vile, and miserable, was able to accept everything. But there is still time to cleanse himself of such a stain. Let all their friends be witness that he has paid her everything he owes her! He throws his money at her, and she faints in Flora's arms. Just then, Germont enters.

The guests are furious at Alfredo for hurting Violetta. Germont cuts through the crowd, and announces that offending a woman, even in anger, earns a man contempt. Where is his son? Germont can no longer recognize him. Alfredo berates himself for what he's done. Germont considers to himself that he alone knows the true nobility of Violetta's heart, yet must remain silent. The Baron threatens Alfredo, while friends console Violetta. She regains consciousness, and tells Alfredo wearily that he doesn't understand the extent of her love. The day will come when he does know, and may God spare him the bitter remorse that is sure to follow. She herself will be dead by then, but she will still love him. Germont leads Alfredo out, followed by the Baron. Flora and the Doctor help Violetta out to Flora's room, and the guests depart.

Comment: It is a given in opera that the chorus shows up and leaves as a single body. Here it must be accomplished very quickly, since the proceedings take on a very fast pace between the ballet and the concertato finale. Even Alfredo and Violetta's exchanges, where one might have expected a protracted duet, are dispatched in rushing phrases. When Alfredo calls everyone back into the room, he gets a quick declamatory solo that ends in a great cymbal-crashing chord and a unison chorus (sounding as martial as anything in Verdi) as Violetta faints, cash falling about her like confetti. Clearly Verdi was thinking of the stage tableau as he composed the music. The chorus is interrupted by the clarion notes of Germont, decrying in a typically Verdian high, legato line that hits its apex at "Dov'è mio figlio? Più non lo vedo."

Germont's solo is the beginning of the concertato finale, which is constructed one component at a time. Some scholars find it old-fashioned, while others say it emanates naturally from Germont and his point of view. After the solo, Alfredo has a few breathy broken phrases expressing, "My God, what have I done?," followed by sad and quiet descending phrases from the chorus. Violetta enters with her solo, sounding higher than it actually is written because of the low string accompaniment in contrasting key. Having fainted, she must now sound somewhat out-of-body, and the effect is of an angelic voice if done correctly. The chorus accompanies her in 3/4 time, the rhythm of forward motion. This is the glory of the concertato form, which can show an individual sentiment spreading through a crowd and becoming general. The final main theme, however, is left to Alfredo and Violetta. They sing a simple but poignant progression for ten notes up the scale, accentuating the words "rimorso" in his line and "amore" in hers. The chorus sings the accented 3/4 beat that propels Alfredo and Violetta's gush of honest emotion. This ensemble may be old-fashioned, but the music exactly suits the drama.

Act IV (or Act III)

Setting: Violetta's bedroom.

Violetta, very ill, is sleeping on her bed. Annina is dozing on a chair beside her.

Comment: *The prelude to the final scene is one of Verdi's most masterful orchestral essays, with the violins (alone) building and fading around no discernible single melody. It is more than sad—it actually sounds faded.*

Violetta awakes, asking Annina for a glass of water. Annina gives it to her, goes to the window, and sees Dr. Grenvil coming to call. Dr. Grenvil asks how she is feeling. Her body suffers, she replies, but her soul is comforted. She saw a priest a few hours before, and is at peace. The Doctor tells her she is improving, and promises to return soon. As Annina shows the Doctor out, she asks how Violetta is really doing. The Doctor tells her it will be over in a few hours. He leaves. Music and dancing are heard from the street. It is Carnival, Annina reminds Violetta, who considers how much suffering there must be in Paris amid all the revelry. She asks Annina how much money is left. Twenty louis. Violetta tells her to give ten to the poor, and then to see if there are any new letters. Annina leaves.

Alone, Violetta pulls a letter out from her bosom and reads it. "You kept your promise. The Baron was wounded, but will recover. Alfredo is out of the country. I myself told him of your sacrifice. He will come to ask your forgiveness. I will come too. Take care of yourself. You deserve a better future. Giorgio Germont." Too late! she cries. The Doctor advises hope, but there is none. She bids farewell to the past, her youth, and her life. She misses Alfredo's kiss, once a consolation. Asking God to forgive the sins of one who went astray, she realizes all is over.

Comment: Violetta's solo scene is a unique grand scena. She could hardly be expected to sing a cabaletta—besides, she already did in Act I. She speaks the words of the letter from Germont. This is a commonplace in opera. Speaking stands for reading, as singing stands for speaking, in the operatic world. Other composers had used the same effect and even provided light orchestral accompaniment for letter scenes, but Verdi tried something new. Seven strings play the slancio *from Alfredo's declaration of love in Act I while she speaks. This is, as Budden says, a "device which Hollywood has done to death." I would go further and say this is the unacknowledged source of all weepy soundtracks. What is surprising is that audiences never laugh at this moment in* Traviata.

The real test, anyway, is the subsequent slow aria, "Addio del passato." It is a haunting reminiscence written in a minor key, accompanied by a plaintive oboe. Occasionally the key shifts into a major, when she speaks of happy memories and hopes, but she always gets dragged back down to the sadder key. The ending is a series of five notes, repeated three times before finally resolving on a high A. This run sounds best sung on one breath. Done correctly, it sounds like someone fighting for their very life breath, and dying away in the process.

The revelers pass by the house, singing of the pleasures of Carnival and leading a fattened ox to the butcher.

Comment: The offstage Carnival music is, intentionally, I would imagine, banal in the extreme. This is a good example of Verdi's admonition that one must occasionally write bad music to create good opera, and the dramatic effect here can be tremendous.

Annina enters, obviously excited but begging Violetta to remain calm. Violetta immediately guesses the cause of the excitement, and rises. Alfredo? Yes! Annina opens the door and he and Violetta fall into each other's arms. He begs her forgiveness, but she insists there is nothing to forgive. They will be together now, that is all that matters. He promises to take her away from Paris, and her health will return. She repeats his notion.

Comment: *This duet, "Parigi, o cara," is so statically formal in its structure, with the tenor and the soprano trading melody and decoration in the second verse, and so chirpy in its tuniness, that we must question the sincerity of the emotions articulated. These are the brave words at the deathbed, as lovely and hollow as sending a get-well card to someone with a terminal illness. If the singers grasp this, it can be devastating.*

Violetta insists they go to church to give thanks for his return, and orders Annina to bring her dress. With an effort, she realizes that she is too weak to move. He is terrified at her pallor. No—it is only the excitement of Alfredo's return. "See?" she asks. "I'm smiling!" But she collapses. Alfredo tells Annina to get the Doctor. Violetta adds that the Doctor must know she wants to live now that Alfredo is back. Annina leaves. Violetta cries out at dying so young, now that life is worth living again. Alfredo begs her not to close her heart to hope. She sinks on the sofa. Annina enters with the Doctor and Germont, who greets her as his daughter "You see?" says Violetta to the Doctor. "I am dying among my dear ones." Only then does Germont realize the seriousness of the situation, and what harm he has caused. Violetta gives Alfredo a medallion with her portrait, so he may remember her. He begs her not to die, and Germont asks for forgiveness. She tells Alfredo that should a young girl capture his heart some day, he must show her the portrait and tell her an angel in heaven prays for their happiness. Suddenly, she rises, as if reanimated. Strange. The spasms have stopped. She feels new life in her body. With an exclamation of joy, she collapses. The Doctor takes her pulse and pronounces her dead.

Comment: *Germont, Grenvil, and Annina show up in time to form some vocal accompaniment to Violetta's death. It is an ensemble that never quite jells into static formality, since there is sadness but no actual* *emotional resolution. The death itself is portrayed by Violetta starting to speak her lines to string accompaniment, as in the letter reading at the beginning of the act, but she evolves into singing as the orchestra swells. The exclamation of joy is, of course, a high note, "Aaaah!," invariably sung with arms outstretched, and then a great collapse, diva-style. Violetta must really hit the floor with a thud to bring the point home here.*

Dead divas are nothing extraordinary on the operatic stage, yet there is much about this death that affects us uniquely. For one thing, Violetta's death is not a sudden event timed to bring the curtain down. She has been dying all night, and this is quite rare in opera. Then there is the love story. The whole fatality of love is explored throughout this opera, yet in very believable, approachable terms. Bills must still be paid. Family issues must be considered. Verdi makes love and death heartrending in their absolute realness.

I vespri siciliani

PREMIERE: Paris Opéra, 1855. Libretto by Eugène Scribe.

THE NAME

This opera was first written in French, and according to the current
mania for literal accuracy that would mean you'd call it *Les Vêpres
siciliennes*. Good luck getting just the right glottal fricative on that *r*
without eliciting howls of laughter. It's only rarely performed in
French, and almost all available recordings and scores use the Italian.
Better to stick to the Italian title, which is pronounced "ee VAY-spree
see-chee-LYAH-nee." The title refers to the Sicilian Vespers, a massacre of French soldiers in Palermo, Sicily, in 1282. Most opera people
call the work *Vespri* and leave it at that.

THIS OPERA was the first original work Verdi wrote for the Paris
Opéra, his previous *Jérusalem* having been a revision of *Lombardi*.
Around 1830 the Opéra found a formula for keeping the theater full,
and they kept to this formula with fervor and exactitude. A production at the Opéra had to be grand in scale, almost always five acts,
and with a brilliant ballet in the middle. Historical and religious subjects were the favorites, and rousing choruses were expected like
clockwork every few minutes to wake everyone up. In between, there
were bravura arias for each of the soloists—long showpieces that may
or may not have had any connection with the onstage happenings.

Musically, the formula had been launched by Auber, but it was Meyerbeer who set it in stone. If Meyerbeer was the heart of the Paris Opéra, then its soul was Eugène Scribe, a dramatist of great enterprise whose works run to several volumes. Scribe wrote and sold librettos by the pound, so to speak, all quite indistinguishable from each other except by details of setting. Scribe's public would have been as open to innovation as any Parisian now would be to a new recipe for café au lait. Even in his own day, people spoke of "Scribe's factory."

All this mechanization was anathema to Verdi, who preferred to torture his librettists to death over details, and who was always demanding novelty in operatic situations. Surprisingly, Verdi told everyone in Paris he was satisfied with the libretto when he arrived. Of course he assumed that details would be changed as the music was written and the opera staged. Verdi became increasingly dissatisfied as the work progressed and he realized Scribe had no intention of attending rehearsals or executing the necessary rewrites. Verdi also had troubles with the staff of the Opéra, and eventually things came to such a pass that he asked to be released from his contract. The Opéra declined, and the Bear of Busseto grumpily continued to work.

The result is an opera that has never wholly pleased anybody, despite many excellent qualities. The music is written with great care and attention to detail, and Verdi employs great subtleties of orchestration throughout. His mind was committed to the project, but his heart was only engaged intermittently. If anything is missing in *Vespri*, it's the sustained level of emotional truth so evident in his previous three operas.

Vêpres had a more than respectable run of fifty performances at the Opéra, and Verdi promptly had it translated into Italian. It found some success on the peninsula, although it had to be produced in various guises because of its potentially incendiary content. Verdi, however, was soured on the experience, and did not write for the Opéra for another decade. Besides the Scribe factory and the fossilized tastes of the audience, he was disgusted with conditions in Paris. The Opéra was run by the French government, as it still is today. The wasted time, the endless stage rehearsals, and the inevitable bickering were not at all congenial to him.

Vespri has its share of problems: long, uninspired recitatives to move the action along, flat characters who manage to offend both French and Italian sensibilities, a few pro forma choruses, and a grotesque massacre for a grand finale. Yet it has much to recommend it and more than a few sublime moments. Even Boito in 1864, while he was at the height of his iconoclastic phase, found much harmonic beauty to praise in the score. From the point of view of the general audience, the lead soprano role is particularly exciting and occasionally thrilling. A prima donna of the caliber of Maria Callas can bring the whole work alive for the people in the seats.

CAST OF CHARACTERS

MONFORTE *(baritone)* The French Governor of Sicily under Charles d'Anjou, King of Naples (another Frenchman).

ARRIGO *(tenor)* A young Sicilian patriot.

GIOVANNI DA PROCIDA *(bass)* A Sicilian doctor who has been in exile for many years because of his work for the Sicilian patriotic movement.

THE DUCHESS ELENA *(soprano)* A Sicilian patriot. Her brother, Duke Federigo, was executed by the French for insurrection.

NINETTA *(mezzo-soprano or contralto)* Elena's maid. Ninetta's job primarily consists of being near Elena when there is an ensemble to be sung.

DANIELI *(tenor)* A young Sicilian, engaged to Ninetta.

BETHUNE *(bass)* and VALDIMONTE *(bass)*, French officers; TEBALDO *(tenor)* and ROBERTO *(bass)*, French soldiers; MANFREDO *(tenor)*, a Sicilian partisan of Procida's.

HISTORICAL NOTE: The French, or more specifically the Normans, made their presence felt in Europe throughout the eleventh and twelfth centuries. The conquest of England in 1066 was the most famous example, but they also took Naples and Sicily around the same time. There were a series of riots against the French throughout Sicily in 1282, and they were eventually expelled. For generations, Sicilians have told stories of the Sicilian Vespers, when the bells for the evening prayer service (vespers) signaled the beginning of a massacre in which thousands of French were supposedly killed in one evening in Palermo. History cannot find any evidence of this event ever taking place, but it lives on in the popular conscience. The historical Giovanni da Procida was an adventurous Sicilian physician, but he apparently was not in Sicily in 1282.

THE OPERA

Act I

Setting: The main piazza of Palermo, 1282.

Tebaldo, Roberto, and other French soldiers are drinking and carousing in the piazza, while Sicilians walk by, eye them suspiciously, and mutter for the day of vengeance to come. Bethune and Valdimonte enter and join the soldiers, all praising the women of Sicily while the Sicilians are shocked by their audacity. Elena appears from her palace, leaning on Ninetta and dressed in deep mourning for her brother, the Duke Federigo, who was executed by the French. Valdimonte is struck by her beauty, respectfully greets her, and retires. Addressing her dead brother, Elena swears vengeance on the French occupiers. Roberto orders Elena to sing a festive drinking song. Ninetta protests, but Elena agrees, singing a song ostensibly about a foundering ship at sea, saved by God's intervention but also by the bravery of the sailors. The Sicilians understand her coded message. The Sicilians are about to attack the French with knives drawn, but just then Monforte appears from the Governor's palace and the crowd scatters. Elena, Ninetta, and Danieli tremble at the sight of the Governor, who laughs with scorn at the Sicilians' hatred. Arrigo runs in and greets Elena. Honest judges have set him free, despite Monforte. Monforte calls Arrigo ungrateful. Arrigo threatens Monforte while Elena and

Ninetta beg him to keep silent. Monforte reveals his identity, ordering the women to withdraw and Arrigo to remain. Who was Arrigo's father? He died in exile. Arrigo never knew him. And his mother? Dead ten months. But he has stayed at Duke Federigo's palace? Yes, in the hero's room! The traitor's! corrects Monforte. Arrigo expresses his admiration for the dead Duke Federigo, and how he wants to die for him, while Monforte, to himself, secretly admires Arrigo's lust for freedom. Monforte offers Arrigo a commission in the French army, but Arrigo refuses. The Governor gives Arrigo a piece of advice: He must never cross the threshold of Elena's palace. He knows Arrigo burns with an ill-omened love. It will be his undoing. Arrigo says he is free and his heart knows no laws. He defies Monforte with his very life, and Monforte promises the young man he shall have the death he seeks.

Comment: The opening scene, with a double chorus of swaggering French and muttering Sicilians, is very deft and greatly admired by musicians, but for all that it plays more like a lost opportunity in the opera house. Its restraint seems out of place. Elena's song, the most interesting part of the scene, is a great study in suspense and innuendo, suggested by trembling strings and an insinuating vocal line. It ends in a cabaletta as she exhorts "Courage!" to the islanders, a ringing call to arms for the inevitable explosion of an oppressed race. The quartet is also more admired by musicians than by audiences. Scribe originally had the Governor address the Sicilians as "race faible et poltronne" ("weak and lazy race"), which Verdi insisted be changed. On the other hand, for all his complaints on the subject to Scribe and the Opéra, Verdi seems to have accepted the portrayal of Sicilians throughout the opera as either wimps or sneaky assassins. This scene ends with a longish duet between baritone and tenor. Here the restraint is appropriate, since Monforte cannot tell all he is thinking, and the strings express what the baritone may not. Arrigo, however, is a tenor like so many others, and answers everything impulsively, culminating in a sustained high B flat as he bounds off the stage.

Act II

Setting: A pleasant seashore outside of Palermo, with the Shrine of Santa Rosalia nearby and the city in the distance.

A small boat is rowed ashore, and Giovanni da Procida steps onto his homeland, from which he has long been exiled and to which he now returns in secret. He greets his native city of Palermo, seen in the distance, and asks its inhabitants to rediscover their ancient valor. Everywhere he has traveled, trying to gain allies for the cause of Sicilian freedom, he has been told the Sicilians themselves must lead their own cause. Now let them rise up and regain their former splendor! He tells some companions to find Arrigo and the Duchess Elena. Let their vengeance surge in darkness and silence. The oppressors do not expect it. Procida advises caution, and the others leave.

Comment: Procida's boat is tugged onstage, accompanied by unmistakable "rowing" music. He then sings his great aria, "O tu Palermo," the big hit of the opera, a rare instance of a beautiful lyric legato for bass. When Procida dismisses the others, we have one of those operatic moments when people take a lot of time and make a lot of noise to say they are going silently and right away.

Arrigo and Elena appear from the shrine, greeting Procida with excitement. They ask him news of his travels, and he explains that Peter of Aragon will join their cause only if the Sicilians rise up first. The three try to think of a plan to ignite the people's anger. The young couples who are to be married will be coming soon to this spot to celebrate their engagements at the Shrine of Santa Rosalia. Amid such a crowd, one spark could enflame all. Procida withdraws. Alone with Elena, Arrigo confesses his great love for her. She offers herself to him if he will avenge her dead brother, which he swears to do. Bethune enters with some French soldiers, offering Arrigo an invitation to the Governor's ball that night in the palace. Arrigo refuses the invitation, which Bethune tells him is not permitted. Arrigo still refuses, however, and Bethune orders the soldiers to arrest him. He draws his sword but is disarmed and dragged away. Procida returns, annoyed at this obstacle to their plan. Elena demands Arrigo be freed as a point of honor, but Procida tells her to wait and see what unfolds.

The young couples approach, gaily attired. Ninetta and Danieli kneel for Elena's blessing, and dances begin. French soldiers arrive, signaling the dancers to continue. Among the French soldiers, Roberto and Tebaldo ogle the girls, urged on by Procida, who tells them he is their trustworthy friend. All things, he says, are permitted to the brave. Roberto recalls the rape of the Sabine women, and wonders why they shouldn't follow the classical example. The dances build. At a signal from Roberto, the French seize all the Sicilian girls, others drawing swords on the young men. Procida, now trusted by the French, tells them to respect Elena, and they do not seize her. The French gloat over their gallantry while the Sicilians mutter at their disgraceful conduct. The French leave with the women. Elena and Procida try to inspire Danieli and the others to vengeance. Meanwhile, a splendidly decorated boat passes offshore, carrying French nobles and Sicilian ladies to the Governor's ball. Lovely music floats ashore, insulting the Sicilians still further. Procida swears he will disguise himself and murder the Governor; the others agree to fall on the French soldiers with daggers.

Comment: The engaged couples dance to a tarantella while the French soldiers drool over the women. After the abduction of the women (accomplished very rapidly), the Sicilian men mutter breathy phrases indicative of their anger but also of their impotence. The violas drone throughout. This builds to a crescendo sliced, so to speak, by the songs wafting ashore from the ship on the way to the ball. The Sicilian men continue to mutter throughout the scene as they leave the stage. It is theatrically effective, but it makes them rather unsympathetic.

Act III

Scene 1: The study in the Governor's Palace.

Monforte sits at his desk, recalling the woman he took, against her will, as his mistress many years before. He now reads a letter from her, telling him to protect Arrigo, since Arrigo is his own son! Bethune enters, telling Monforte Arrigo has been brought to the palace by force. What punishment is ordered? Monforte tells Bethune that the rebel is to be given every honor, and sends for him. Bethune leaves, and Monforte looks forward to a future in which his paternal love can compensate for the hollow pomp of his office. Arrigo enters, asking why he is being treated with honor when he expected only death. Monforte asks if Arrigo still hates him single-mindedly, even after he has spared his life and tried to help him. He hands Arrigo the letter, and addresses Arrigo as his son. Arrigo is horrified that the monster is his father, knowing this means he must also lose Elena's love. He begs to flee, deaf to Monforte's offers of riches, glory, and honors. He remembers his mother, essentially killed by Monforte, and refuses to embrace Monforte, begging only to be allowed to leave the country. Monforte tries to hold Arrigo, but the young man breaks free and runs away, while the father gazes at him sadly.

Comment: So we discover (and not a moment too soon) that Monforte is Arrigo's father, and Arrigo is therefore a sort of proto–Luke Skywalker. The problem is we haven't really learned to care a lot for Arrigo. If anything, our feelings are with Monforte. His narrative at the beginning of the scene is lyrical and sympathetic, culminating in a lovely, spun-out "figlio!" that looks ahead to Boccanegra's rediscovery of his daughter. The aria is not thrilling in itself on first hearing, but gives the baritone a chance to display his voice. The duet develops into the broad, gorgeous vintage Verdi melody that is the main theme of the Overture.

Scene 2: A magnificent hall in the Governor's Palace, illuminated and decorated for the great ball.

Monforte enters with his pages and officers, taking a seat of honor. The Dance of the Four Seasons is performed.

Comment: The ballet, "Le quattro stagioni," is pleasant scenic music meant to portray the seasons. The most interesting part is not the bouncy spring flowers or the autumn harvest dance, but the melancholy summer heat wave, represented by a solo oboe. The ballet is only rarely performed with the opera, in which it is quite out of place.

The guests at the ball, including Elena, Arrigo, and Procida, cheer the splendid festivities. Masked courtiers continue dancing, while Elena and Procida anticipate the moment of attack. They and their conspirators wear ribbons to mark themselves. Arrigo is nervous, confusing Elena and Procida, who mingle among the dancers. Monforte approaches Arrigo. Is he tired of the unaccustomed festivities already? Arrigo tells him to leave him and to be careful, since there is trouble afoot. Monforte feels safe in his own house, and trusts his son to protect him, but Arrigo repulses him. He, too, has sworn to wreak vengeance. Monforte tears the ribbon from Arrigo and asks if he would deny his French blood. Arrigo tells Monforte he must fight for his homeland, but Monforte should leave immediately. Procida and his conspirators surround Monforte and Elena jumps at the Governor with her dagger drawn, but Arrigo steps between them and saves Monforte. Soldiers arrive, and Monforte tells them to arrest all who wear the ribbon, excepting Arrigo, who has saved him. The Sicilian conspirators are all dragged off to prison cursing Arrigo as a traitor.

Comment: The chorus states the first theme of the dance (a mazurka, presumably all the rage in medieval Palermo), which is then repeated more lightly by the orchestra throughout the scene. All the dialogue is recitative surfed off of the dance music, which we are to imagine being in adjacent salons offstage. Verdi had already used this device in Rigoletto *and* Traviata, *and would use it again with great effect in another conspiracy scene in* Un ballo in maschera.

The concertato finale begins as hushed exclamations from the Sicilians, who are as stunned by their own sudden disarmament (a few very quick crashing chords from the orchestra) as they are by Arrigo's supposed betrayal. Life tends to surprise these guys. Out of this, Elena, Danieli, and Procida sing a beautiful cantabile, which then develops into a theme that subsumes everybody. There is no attempt to differentiate the varying emotions of the people onstage, and while the effect is lush and gorgeous music, it makes no dramatic sense. The soprano, of course, is always able to individuate herself by sheer lung power; if we can identify her solo voice among the rush of sound, the dramatic situation will be improved, if not salvaged.

Act IV

Setting: A fortress courtyard.

Arrigo tells the soldiers he has been permitted to speak to the prisoners, and orders them to be brought to him. Alone, he considers his unhappy fate, cursed by those for whom he would die, and abandoned by his love. Elena is brought out, wondering what new torments the traitor has for her. He protests his innocence, finally telling her he saved not the hated Governor but his own father! He has refused all wealth and honor from Monforte, and only wishes to die with Elena. She expresses her love for him, overjoyed that she need no longer hate him. Procida is brought forth. Arrigo hides himself and dismisses the soldiers. Procida approaches Elena. Aragonese ships are approaching with gold and arms. Oh, to be in prison at such a time! He sees Arrigo. Elena tells him Arrigo is innocent, but just then Monforte enters with Bethune, ordering a priest and an executioner for Elena and Procida. If the populace stirs over the news of the execution, they are to be massacred. Bethune bows and leaves. Arrigo begs for the prisoners' lives, or demands to be killed with them. Procida pronounces the traitor unworthy of such an honor, and is stunned to hear Monforte call Arrigo his son. He will die now; Elena likewise bids farewell to her homeland; Arrigo swears they will not die, or he will die with them; Monforte gloats that the prisoners' deaths will take Arrigo's pride.

Monks are heard intoning the death chant *"De profundis."* Procida and
Elena kneel to pray for their souls, soon to be dispatched. Monforte
tells Arrigo he will pardon them if Arrigo will acknowledge him as his
father, but Elena says Arrigo is a traitor if he does so.

A great door opens to reveal a hall of justice, with monks chanting,
four penitents praying, and an executioner leaning on his ax. The
penitents lead Elena and Procida toward the place of execution. Various people fill the courtyard and beg for mercy, while Elena and Procida bid farewell to Sicily. Finally, Arrigo cries out "Father!" and
Monforte stops the executioner. The people cheer. Monforte declares
that Arrigo will wed Elena as a seal of friendship between the French
and the Sicilians. Elena refuses, but Procida urges her to accept. Elena
and Arrigo then express their joy. Monforte and the others anticipate
peace, while Procida anticipates vengeance. Monforte orders the
wedding that very night, at vespers. Joyfully, all cheer except Procida,
who continues to plot.

*Comment: Arrigo begins with a rather rambling recitative followed by a
pretty but vague cavatina,* "Giorno di pianto," *which builds in pace,
tone, and volume. A tenor who is a good singing actor can turn* "Giorno
di pianto" *into a personal triumph. He'd better do something, because
Elena is on her way to stealing the spotlight if she possibly can. The duet
scena begins with a maddening cliché of bad drama—a lover repeating*
"Forgive me! Forgive me!" *while neglecting to reveal the circumstances
that caused the injury in the first place. Eventually this nonsense is transcended. Elena shrieks* "'Iuo padre!" *on an appropriately stratospheric
note while the full orchestra thunders out. Her aria,* "Arrigo! ah parli a un
core," *can be a stunner, a very introverted moment, despite the floating
pianissimo notes up to high D. The idea is that she is relieved he is not a
traitor, but she still can't marry him, so there is no call for a joyous aria. In
the hands of an artist, this aria makes the time appear to stand still. The
duet is measured and subdued, all marked piano or pianissimo. They are
happy they love each other, but melancholy that they must part.*

   *This is followed by a quartet, which tends toward the restrained, like
so much of the rest of the opera. The music is spare to the point of mini-
malism. The monks chant offstage and provide little more than the rhythm*

for the plodding steps of the condemned. Elena and Procida float high piano interjections as they walk along, while the women's chorus intones "Mercy!" as an antiphon to the monks. If done right, it compensates with tension what it lacks in volume.

Act V

Setting: The gardens of the Governor's Palace.

Inside the palace, knights are heard toasting the wedding, while Elena and her maidens gather in the garden. She greets them and tells them of her joy.

Comment: Three short choral songs begin the final act, allowing Elena time to fuss with the train of her bridal gown while she finds a pose for her big aria. The aria itself, "Mercé, dilette amiche," is a frank showpiece, a bravura applause getter. In fact, it makes more sense in a recital than at this place in the opera. Yes, Elena is getting married and should be happy, but none of the issues that made her mope around the stage in high mourning at the beginning of the opera have been resolved. Still, it is frivolously brilliant. Written in the rhythm of a bolero, it contains coloratura, runs, and trills, including two trills held for nine beats followed by phrases marked "dolcissimo." The aria ranges from an A below the staff to a high C sharp. It concludes with a flashy cadenza with every note written out, yet some divas still add a few decorations to it.

Elena dismisses the maidens, and Arrigo enters the garden, pensive. He and Elena exchange vows of love and express surprise at the sudden turn of fortune.

Comment: Now, of course, would be a sensible time for a love duet, but instead we get another amorphous if lovely narrative by Arrigo interrupted by a few comments from Elena. These two just never seem to connect. In any case, it is traditionally cut, either because the evening is getting Wagnerian by this point or because of a nasty little high D written for the tenor.

Some men appear summoning Arrigo, who leaves with them, promising to return directly. Procida approaches Elena. Let her know the plan: As soon as she says "yes" at the altar, the bells will ring, and this will be the signal for the people to rise up and massacre the French. Elena is aghast. How can she compromise her honor so? Procida tells her he would lose everything, including honor, for his country. She protests that Arrigo is her husband, and he appears at that moment. Procida demands she denounce him to Arrigo then. This she cannot do, but neither can she betray her husband. Elena tries to delay the wedding, but Monforte and all the French knights and ladies appear and the Governor orders Arrigo and Elena to join hands. He pronounces them married. Procida calls for the bells to be rung. From every direction, Sicilian men and women rush in with daggers. They throw themselves on Monforte and all the French in a frenzy, and massacre them.

Comment: *The trio scena when Arrigo returns to the stage takes up most of the balance of the act. It is in the form of a grand scena à trois, the first part being slow and lyrical, the middle section agitated recitative with some big high notes for Elena, and the trio finale rushing and gasping. The bells are a good dramatic touch, beginning with one pealing in rhythm, followed by others as the orchestra crescendos. In the grotesque grand finale, the chorus repeats "Vendetta! A morte! Al terror!" as they massacre everybody. Even Wagner, no wimp when it came to onstage bloodshed, pronounced himself shocked at this carnage. We are not told what happens to the principals, but the original libretto left no doubt. Elena and Arrigo are killed along with Monforte, while Procida eggs on the killers, saying, "Sicilian or French, what does it matter? God will know his own." It says much for Verdi that he never set the "Kill 'em all!" line to music. In any case, we do have a mess at the end of the opera. Vespri's true glories are its ravishing solos and delicate ensembles, rather than the shambles at the final curtain.*

Simon Boccanegra

PREMIERE: La Fenice, Venice, 1857. Libretto by Francesco Maria Piave. Revised version: La Scala, Milan, 1881. Revisions to libretto by Arrigo Boito.

THE NAME

In Italian, the name of the title character is "Simone" (three syllables, "see-MOAN-ay"), and so he is called throughout the opera. For some reason the name is always written without the final *e* in English. Perhaps it looks too much like a feminine name. However, even in English, the name is always said with a long *o* and the accent on the second syllable, even though this makes it homophonous with the feminine name one was presumably trying to avoid in the first place. If you say "Simon" as in "Simon says," you will be laughed out of the opera house by know-it-all snobs. I cannot presume to explain this phenomenon, only report it.

Boccanegra has perhaps had a more checkered history than any opera in the Verdi canon. It failed entirely at its premiere, and only succeeded throughout the following generation on rare occasions when there was a great baritone to wow the audience. When Verdi revised it with Boito in 1881, the result was basically an entirely new opera. It was a critical success, and made the standard rounds, but the revised

Boccanegra didn't become part of the standard repertory until the 1930s. Even since then, the opera has proven to be more respected than adored by the public, and is primarily thought of as a vehicle for a star baritone. Verdi thought the role "a thousand times more difficult than Rigoletto." *Boccanegra* is popular today, but only when there is a true star in the role.

In his letters, Verdi makes repeated reference to *Boccanegra* as a dark and gloomy work. Perhaps he was describing the orchestral texture of his score, which is subtly reflective in a way his others are not. Also, there is a preponderance of low male voices, with only one soprano and a less-than-stellar tenor role to alleviate the tone. But there is also a superb airiness in parts of the score, especially those intended as breezy scene painting for the shore of Genoa. The lead character has a noble, lonely spirit. The recognition scene between him and his long-lost daughter is a triumph of pathos—perhaps Verdi's greatest father-daughter scene ever—but hardly the stuff of gloom. George Martin has suggested that the only reason *Boccanegra* might be considered unusually sad is because the character of Boccanegra is drawn out so fully that we really care for him as a human being. Certainly Simon's death scene is extremely touching, even if subdued by operatic standards, and can be devastating in performance.

Not that you would know this from reading a synopsis. The opera is based on a play by Antonio García Gutiérrez, the same Romantic playwright who wrote the source of *Il trovatore*. Like the more famous play, the Spanish drama *Simón Bocanegra* is loaded with outrageous situations but also leavened with commentary, color, and comic relief of a sort. All this was eliminated by Piave for the original incarnation of the opera in 1857, and even audiences who were quite accustomed to ridiculous plots were alienated by this one. When Boito arrived to perform surgery on the opera in 1880, he added the entire Council Chamber scene (Act 1, Scene 2), which ranks with Verdi's greatest achievements, and made several other changes to flesh out the characters on a human level. But the story in the 1881 version made less sense than ever. If you are the sort of person who can only digest operas if their plots are sensible, read no further. *Boccanegra* is not for you. There are no completely insane moments on the same level as throwing the wrong baby into the fire, but there is also less cause-and-effect logic.

One of Verdi's goals in revising *Boccanegra* was to bring it up to date, and for him that meant primarily the elimination of any cabalettas. There isn't one in the revised score, and there is no need for one. The drama flows from one moment to the next without stopping along the way for hit tunes. Yet much of the original music remains as well. Many complain that *Boccanegra,* even more than *Macbeth,* is therefore a hodgepodge of conflicting styles. That criticism will simply not hold water in performance, and few people indeed would be able to say for certain which parts are the older passages without the help of some scholarly guides. Even the original music was spruced up a bit by Verdi. In the Prologue, for example, the chorus originally screamed out "Simon Boccanegra, the pirate!" when his name is suggested as the new Doge. In the revision, the chorus sings the same notes, but the words "the pirate!" are whispered in pianissimo voices, depicting bewilderment far better than the conventional outcry.

In their correspondence for this project, which makes excellent reading, Verdi and Boito often used the metaphor of a shaky table that needed to be refitted. Boito originally complained that the table had only one good leg (the Prologue), but he worked with Verdi until they had a solid piece they were proud of. If there is a problem, it is the fact that the most obviously crowd-pleasing scenes are the first three. Stay tuned, however. The final scene can be quite touching, especially if the director has helped to create a community of emotion on the stage. If you're lucky enough to attend a production that follows and respects the score, you are in for a surprisingly powerful evening of theater.

CAST OF CHARACTERS

SIMON BOCCANEGRA *(baritone)* A privateer (a sort of official pirate) in the service of the Republic of Genoa.

JACOPO FIESCO *(bass)* Also called Andrea. A leading Genoese nobleman.

PAOLO *(baritone)* A Genoese commoner and leader of the people.

PIETRO *(baritone)* Another popular leader.

AMELIA GRIMALDI *(soprano)* Also known as Maria. An orphan girl adopted by the Grimaldi.

GABRIELE ADORNO *(tenor)* A Genoese nobleman.

A FEW POINTERS: (1) Fiesco is the family name. It becomes "Fieschi" (pronounced "fee-AY-ski") in the plural, when referring to the family. The singular "Fiesco" refers to Jacopo Fiesco. (2) Fiesco is hiding under the alias "Andrea" after the Prologue. (3) Maria is the name of Fiesco's daughter, whom we never see onstage. It is also rather inconveniently the name she and Simon give to their illegitimate daughter. To further complicate matters, Fiesco addresses his lamentation of Maria's death to none other than Maria, as in the Virgin Mary. (4) Maria Fiesco junior is taken by the Grimaldi family and passed off as their dead daughter Amelia Grimaldi. (5) The noble families who ruled the cities of Italy were divided for centuries into two groups known as Guelphs and Ghibellines. The Fieschi and the Grimaldi were Guelphs. (6) Don't feel bad if the Guelph/Ghibelline dispute confuses you somewhat. Half the time they confused themselves. By the time of *Boccanegra* the situation had degenerated into a blood feud well beyond political categorization. (7) There is a further division of the commune into patricians and plebeians—nobility and commoners, respectively. (8) "Doge," as we have seen in *I due Foscari*, is the name given to the elected leaders of the Republics of Genoa and Venice, the word being a form of the word for "leader." In English it is pronounced "doedge" (one syllable).

THE OPERA

Prologue

Setting: The piazza in front of the Church of San Lorenzo in Genoa, in the year 1338. Night.

Paolo and Pietro are discussing who should be the next doge. Lorenzino? Paolo suggests instead the brave man who defeated the African pirates and brought glory to Genoa. Pietro understands. And what is his reward if he backs Paolo's candidate? Riches, power, and honor. Pietro agrees to sell the people's support for such a price. He leaves. Paolo gloats that he, a lowly plebeian, will rise to the summit. Simon enters, asking why he has been summoned. Paolo offers him the doge's crown. Simon does not want it. Paolo asks him to think of his love, Maria. She languishes in the Fieschi palace as a prisoner. If Simon were doge, Fiesco could no longer deny his daughter in marriage. Simon agrees and withdraws. Pietro returns with sailors and workmen. They all support Lorenzino. Pietro tells them Lorenzino has sold out to the Fieschi, and they should vote for a brave man of the people—Boccanegra! And what will the Fieschi say? Nothing, answers Paolo. He points to the palace, telling the men of the innocent woman who is imprisoned there. Paolo has seen a strange flame pass by the window, like a soul in torment. The men cross themselves. They leave, promising to meet again in the morning and acclaim Boccanegra as doge.

Fiesco enters the piazza from his palace, which is now the cold tomb of his daughter Maria, who has died. He curses the vile seducer Boccanegra, and then turns to the statue of the Virgin over the piazza. Why did the Blessed Mother allow his daughter's virginity to be stolen so? He apologizes for his blasphemous outburst and begs his daughter to pray for him from heaven. Voices are heard from inside the palace, lamenting Maria's death. Simon returns, ignorant of Maria's death, and thinking only that he will be able to marry her when he is elected doge. Fiesco sees him, and Simon falls at the man's feet. Fiesco is unmoved. One of them must die. Simon bares his chest and begs Fiesco to kill him on the spot, but Fiesco refuses to commit a base act of murder. He demands his granddaughter, the child Maria had borne out of wedlock when Simon seduced her. Sadly, Boccanegra explains that the child is lost. She had been left in the care of an old lady near the coast of Pisa, but the old lady died, and three days later the child wandered off. Nobody knows where she is. Fiesco repeats that there can be no peace between them without the child, and walks away, hiding in the shadows. Boccanegra knocks on the doors of the palace, but no one answers. He enters the palace to investigate. Fiesco anticipates his revenge. Soon, Simon comes out from the palace, distraught at having learned of the death of Maria. From afar, he hears the people proclaiming him as doge. Fiesco seethes at the election. The people appear, and the bells ring, announcing that Boccanegra is the new doge of Genoa.

Comment: The Prologue is indeed dark and sinister in tone. Beginning an opera with a conversation was unheard of at the time, but is the perfect signal that we should listen closely for subtleties rather than expect bombast. The opera takes off with Fiesco's solo, "Il lacerato spirito," *an extremely compact display of emotion punctuated by brass and percussion thumps after each line. The offstage lamentations of a women's chorus mourning the death of Maria, and a chorus of monks offering a one-note* "Miserere," *are haunting. As the mourners exit the palace and disperse, there is a rather long and beautiful postlude in the orchestra with no vocal accompaniment. The real highlight of the Prologue is the duet, for lack of a better word, between Fiesco and Boccanegra. Each singer is completely individuated, never overlapping each other and expressing entirely different natures, yet it is organically indivisible. The music tells us these two conflicting natures are stuck with each other until death.*

Act I

Scene 1: The Grimaldi's garden outside Genoa, with the sea in the background. The year is 1363.

Amelia greets the breaking dawn over the sea, but why does the lingering night bring back memories of the small cottage where she grew up and of the old lady who died blessing her? Now she lives in a proud palace with a great family, but she cannot forget her humble home. She looks forward to solace from her lover.

From afar she hears the voice of Gabriele serenading her, and he appears and embraces her. She asks why he was so long in coming to her, and tells him of her fears. He knows he is caught in political intrigue with Andrea, whom she loves as a father, and Lorenzino and the others. He bids her be quiet and wary of informers. They gaze at the sea and at Genoa sitting proudly above the waves, and seek refuge in their love. Amelia sees a man outside the garden wall who has often been seen lurking. Gabriele suspects a rival. A servant enters and asks her to receive a messenger from the Doge. It is Pietro who asks if she will receive the Doge. She agrees. Amelia tells Gabriele the Doge will ask her to marry one of his favorites, and Gabriele must ask Andrea and arrange their own marriage immediately. She withdraws into the palace. Andrea appears. Gabriele tells him of his love for Amelia, but Andrea explains that there is much about the girl Gabriele does not yet know. She was born humble. The daughter of the Grimaldi died in a convent, and this common orphan girl appeared there the same day. Boccanegra, the new Doge, was trying to claim the riches of the great families who had no other children besides those in exile, so the Grimaldi substituted the orphan for their own daughter. Gabriele swears his love for Amelia, whoever she is, and Andrea blesses the union. The Doge's trumpets are heard, and they withdraw. Andrea looks forward to the day of vengeance.

Doge Boccanegra enters with Paolo and retainers. Boccanegra dismisses all, telling them to return in an hour. Amelia enters and is greeted by the Doge. He asks her if her exiled brothers don't wish to return to their homeland. She stammers. He understands. The proud Grimaldi refuse to bow their necks to a man like Boccanegra. Yet he will show them how he repays such pride, and presents Amelia with a pardon for all the Grimaldi. She asks why the Doge would do such a thing. Because of you, he answers. Wouldn't such a young and beautiful woman sometimes like to leave her seclusion? Impressed by his concern, Amelia answers that she does indeed love a young and pure man, but she is also courted by a wretch who wants the wealth of the Grimaldi. Paolo! cries Boccanegra. Yes, she adds, and since the great Doge shows such concern for her welfare, let him know that she is not really a Grimaldi, but a common orphan from Pisa. Pisa? he asks. Yes, where she was raised by a good old woman, who died and left her only a portrait of the mother she never knew. Simon, agitated, draws a locket out of his breast, and Amelia does the same. It is the same woman. "Maria!" he cries. "You are my daughter!" They embrace, swearing to create a joyful world for each other and give each other all the peace and comfort that has eluded their unhappy separate lives. Savoring the long-desired words "father" and "daughter," he walks her to the palace, and she enters.

Paolo rushes in, asking for an answer. Simon tells him to forget Amelia—she can never be his. Boccanegra enters the palace. Paolo fumes. Pietro enters and asks for news. Paolo tells him the Doge has forbidden the union. Has Boccanegra forgotten who made him doge? Paolo plans to abduct Amelia and carry her by ship to Lorenzino's home. If Lorenzino objects, Paolo will reveal all of Lorenzino's plotting to the Doge. Pietro swears his help in the adventure.

Comment: The scene opens with a marvelously evocative orchestral painting. What exactly it depicts is open to interpretation. Some hear a sunrise, others a seascape. Dramatically, the important point is the switch to "light and lovely" for introducing Amelia and separating her from the gloominess of the Prologue. The celebrated interaction between Boccanegra and Amelia is the highlight of the scene, and one of Verdi's finest moments. The two actually get quieter as they realize who they are to each other—an entirely novel approach. They finish with the respective simple words "Padre!" and "Figlia!" spun out at great length in an emotion-filled piano voice. They have each found missing pieces in their lives, and are close to contentment. The denouement of the scene, a simple dialogue between Paolo and Pietro, depicts the dangers lurking in seemingly peaceful moments.

Scene 2: The Council Chamber in the Palazzo degli Abati. The Doge is seated on a throne, flanked on one side by the Maritime Consuls and on the other by the Constables. On one side of the room are twelve plebeian councilors, and on the other the twelve patrician councilors.

Simon, from his throne, reads a treaty with the King of Tartary, announcing that the Black Sea is open to all Genoese ships. Gifts are presented. Does the Council accept the treaty? They accept. The

Doge requests a vote on another, more delicate question. He produces a letter from Petrarch, who pleads for peace with Venice. Paolo
interrupts. Let the poet of the blonde lady from Avignon worry about
his rhymes! The councilors cry for war with Venice. This is the crime
of Cain, cries Boccanegra. Adriatica and Liguria have a common
homeland! The councilors cry that Genoa is their only homeland. The
sounds of a riot are heard from outside the hall. From the window,
Simon sees Gabriele and a Guelph being pursued by an angry mob.
Pietro tells Paolo to flee the chamber, or he will be caught. At that
moment, Simon orders the doors shut. Anyone who flees is a traitor!
Outside the people cry for death to the patricians. The councilors of
both sides draw swords on each other. The people call for death to
the Doge. With dignity, Boccanegra orders the herald outside to tell
the people he does not fear them, and in fact will open the palace
doors to them. The herald exits. His trumpets are heard. There is a
long silence, followed by the people cheering Boccanegra.

The crowd, including many women and children, burst into the
chamber, dragging Gabriele and Andrea, the unidentified Guelph,
with them. They cry for blood. Boccanegra ironically comments on
the voice of the people sounding like thunder from afar but like
women and children from up close. He asks Gabriele why the young
man is brandishing his sword. Gabriele admits he murdered Lorenzino, who had abducted Amelia Grimaldi. The Doge is horrified, and
the people call Gabriele a liar. Before Lorenzino died, Gabriele continues, he confessed that a great man of power had put him up to the
abduction. The Doge asks Gabriele who was named, but Gabriele
ironically tells the Doge to relax, since Lorenzino died before he
could reveal the name. Pietro tells Paolo he is lost. Boccanegra,
offended, asks if Gabriele dares to name him as the abductor, and
orders him disarmed. Gabriele breaks free and attacks the Doge, calling him a vile crowned pirate. Amelia rushes in and throws herself
between Gabriele and Boccanegra, demanding that Gabriele stab her
instead. All are stunned, and Amelia now begs Boccanegra for
Gabriele's life. He agrees, and asks her to tell what happened. She
explains she was walking at the shore at sunset, when three men
seized her and threw her on a ship. She fainted and came to in Loren-

zino's room. Seeing that villain, she told him she would tell the Doge of all his plots if he didn't let her go. Terrified, Lorenzino released her. The crowd agrees that the villain deserved death. Yes, says Amelia, but there is one more powerful who deserves death even more. She glares at Paolo, whom she suspects, but cannot name without proof. The plebeians and patricians accuse and turn against each other.

"Fratricides!" screams Boccanegra, commanding attention. All they know is the ancient hate of the feuding Doria and Spinola families, while the sea calls them to glory and the olive branch blooms in vain on the hillside. He weeps for the lying beauty of the nation's flowers, and goes crying "peace," and goes crying "love!" The people feel their anger calmed as the sea by a breeze, Amelia repeats the call for peace, Pietro tells Paolo to flee, Paolo can only think of further misdeeds, Gabriele is joyful that Amelia is safe, and Andrea weeps that his proud city is led by a pirate. Simon continues his plea for peace.

Gabriele offers his sword to the Doge, but Boccanegra refuses it, asking only for Gabriele's word that he will stay in the palace a single night until the whole plot is uncovered. Gabriele agrees. Boccanegra calls Paolo forth, who approaches in terror. With great authority, Boccanegra tells Paolo he has the sacred task of keeping order in the city, and helping him find the villain who ordered Amelia's abduction. "Let him be cursed!" He orders Paolo to repeat the oath. "Let him be cursed!" repeats Paolo, horrified. The entire crowd repeats the oath, cursing the criminal.

Comment: This celebrated scene is dramatic tension and lyric effusion throughout, and (let's face it) good old theatrical corn where necessary. It begins with rapid declamations back and forth, as the various parties agree only on war with Venice. The riot is signified simply and effectively by a single crescendo offstage with high female voices prominent. The tension builds again without a single climax, and Amelia's narrative of her abduction is unornamented and seamless. The long-delayed emotional gush is reserved for the great ensemble led by Boccanegra, "Plebe! Patrizi!" The baritone's vocal line remains the centerpiece throughout the whole concertato, singing against the chorus, orchestra, and even the soprano the whole way.

His line culminates in the soaring phrase "E vo gridando: pace! E vo gridando: amor!," *a great line of classically Verdian lyric effusion. It is a quotation of Petrarch's patriotic poem* Italia mia, *in which he cries for peace among the warring states of Italy. The reference to the poet at the beginning of the scene, therefore, is much more than the splash of color many assume it to be.* Italia mia *stands amid several long love poems in which the poet explains how his unrequited love for Laura has broken him. The relationship of the personal and the political is key, since political and romantic strife yield the same result—dismemberment. The memories of Italy's past glories are like reminiscences of past love. Both are efforts to remember—literally, to put something that has been torn apart back together. Boccanegra's pleas for an end to civil war, like Petrarch's, carry weight because of his shattering experience of love. The Petrarch quotation, amplified by the reference to him at the beginning of the scene, brought this message home to the Scala audience of 1880 in a very direct way, yet the message still rings true. Thus, in the musical* Hair, *the ballad* "Easy to be Hard," *a plea for healing from a jilted lover, is followed by the anti-war song* "3-5-0-0," *with its graphic images of dismembered bodies. Clearly, those who have been mangled by love are best qualified to preach against the butchery of war.*

Verdi brings down the curtain with the curse on Paolo. Boccanegra's denunciation of the "unknown" abductor is melodic yet threatening, each line building with menace. It is a great vocal and dramatic challenge after the ensemble, culminating in an orchestral explosion at the line "Sia maladetto!" *Paolo repeats the curse (on himself, of course) to another unison fortissimo from the orchestra, followed by the entire chorus repeating the curse twice in a hissing stage whisper. If perfect unison is achieved, the effect is startling.*

Act II

Setting: The Doge's rooms in the Palazzo Ducale.

Paolo tells Pietro to bring the "two of them" to him by the secret passage. Pietro leaves. Alone, Paolo reflects on his terror, having cursed himself and despised by all Genoa. He curses the ungrateful Doge, who now treats him contemptuously but who owes him his throne. He empties a phial of poison into a goblet. Fiesco and Gabriele are shown in by Pietro, who leaves. Fiesco is barely able to hide his contempt for Paolo, but Paolo assures him he hates the Doge. Paolo suggests killing the Doge as he sleeps, but Fiesco's honor is offended by such a cowardly proposal, and he refuses to participate. Paolo orders him back to his cell. Gabriele agrees that Paolo's plan is beneath contempt. Paolo suggests Gabriele must not really love Amelia, since the old Doge plans to use her for his own infamous pleasures. He leaves, locking the door behind him.

Alone, Gabriele vents his rage at the old man. He killed Gabriele's father, now he steals his only treasure. He begs heaven to restore Amelia to him pure, or never let him see her again.

Amelia enters, asking Gabriele who it was that let him in through the secret passage. He accuses her instead of answering, and hurls abuse at the name of Boccanegra. She protests her innocence but begs to keep her secret a little longer. She hears the Doge coming and tells Gabriele to hide, but he refuses. Finally, she pushes him onto the balcony, while he continues to swear vengeance. Boccanegra enters, reading a document. They greet tenderly. Amelia confesses the name of her love—it is Boccanegra's enemy, Gabriele Adorno. Boccanegra tells her Gabriele's name is written on the document he is reading as a conspirator with the Guelphs. Boccanegra says he will consider a pardon if the young man will repent. He dismisses her. Alone, he wonders if clemency or severity is the proper path. He pours himself a goblet of water, and notes how even water tastes bitter to the man who wears the crown. He falls asleep on a couch. Gabriele quietly comes back into the room. What holds him back from killing the Doge? Finally, he draws his dagger and approaches. Amelia runs into the room and stops him. Would Gabriele kill a defenseless old man? Boccanegra awakes, bares his breast, and dares Gabriele to kill him. He demands to know who opened the secret door for Gabriele, threatening torture to find the answer. Gabriele refuses to answer. Boccanegra tells him he has already avenged his dead father, since Gabriele has stolen his most precious treasure—his daughter! Gabriele is stunned at the word. He asks Amelia's pardon, she prays for her mother's protection from heaven, while Simon considers that a display of mercy for Gabriele would be a good example for Italy. Shouts of a crowd are heard from outside. It is the Guelph uprising. Boccanegra tells Gabriele to go fight with the traitors, but he swears loyalty to the Doge. He and Amelia express their joy as the crowd calls for arms.

Comment: Almost anything would be a comedown after the Council Chamber scene, but the opera really does creak at times here. The final trio is the most impressive part of the act, with Gabriele all remorse and Boccanegra's sad music showing both ambivalence and weariness.

Act III

Setting: Inside the Palazzo Ducale. In the background, Genoa is illuminated for a celebration, and the sea lies beyond.

From within the palace, people are heard cheering the Doge. A soldier hands Fiesco his sword back, telling him that the Guelphs have been defeated and he is free to go. Paolo is led past by guards, on his way to the scaffold. He tells Fiesco he will die, but he has poisoned Boccanegra. Fiesco calls him infamous. Outside the palace, the wedding chorus of Gabriele and Amelia is heard. Paolo admits he was the one who ordered her abduction, and Fiesco is thoroughly disgusted with him. Paolo is dragged off. Alone, Fiesco considers that this was not the vengeance he had wanted for Boccanegra. He withdraws into the shadows. A captain on the balcony addresses the people, saying the Doge has ordered that the torches be extinguished as a sign of respect to all who died in the recent fighting.

Simon enters, his head burning. He gazes out at the sea, remembering his glorious life as a privateer. Fiesco addresses him from the shadows. Boccanegra's star is setting. He shall die amid the ghosts of those he killed. Simon recognizes the voice. Fiesco reveals himself, and Boccanegra is overjoyed. He can make the amends promised years before, producing the lost granddaughter. Amelia Grimaldi is

Maria Fiesco! Boccanegra asks to embrace Fiesco as the father of his beloved, and Fiesco feels remorse. Amelia and Gabriele enter, followed by their wedding party. Boccanegra reveals Fiesco as Amelia's grandfather. Amelia is hopeful. The bitter hatreds are ended. "Everything is ending," says Boccanegra, admitting that his death is near. He blesses the couple as the lights of Genoa are extinguished. Amelia and Gabriele beg Simon not to die, while Fiesco and the chorus comment on the sadness of life. Man must always weep. Simon's dying request to the senators is that Gabriele Adorno be made the next Doge. He charges Fiesco with the task of seeing this accomplished. Calling out for his daughter Maria, he dies.

Fiesco goes to the balcony and orders the people to hail their new Doge, Gabriele Adorno. The people cry for Boccanegra. "He is dead," announces Fiesco. "Pray for his peace!" As a bell tolls and all the crowd in the palace kneels, those inside and outside ask for peace.

Comment: The act begins with a murky prelude, followed by cries of the offstage chorus cheering the Doge. This revolution, apparently, was as quick as the poison is slow. While Fiesco and Paolo banter, the chorus morphs seamlessly into a wedding chorus for Gabriele and Amelia. Two dramatic plots are unfolding at once. Boccanegra's protracted death must be unique in all opera. He was poisoned in the previous act, and his life ebbs throughout the whole final act. His duet with Fiesco is superbly dramatic, beginning with the two uttering their lines on a single note, and Fiesco continuing as a messenger of death throughout the encounter until he finally evolves into genuine remorse. When Amelia and the others enter, she begins a final ensemble marked by her continuously soaring and rich vocal line. During this, the lights of Genoa, visible in the background, are extinguished one by one. The tolling bell, the extinguishing lights, and the hushed chorus make this ending one of the most poignant in all opera.

Un ballo in maschera

PREMIERE: Teatro Apollo, Rome, 1859. Libretto by Antonio Somma.

THE NAME

The important thing to remember is the accent is on the first syllable of *maschera,* "MAHSK-ay-rah." It means "A Masked Ball," and has nothing to do with eye makeup. Usually *Ballo* will do.

THIS OPERA IS one of Verdi's tightest and most consistent. It tells a relatively simple story of a love triangle against a background of political intrigue. The passions and situations are straightforward and comprehensible. The music is refined and economical. Humor and lightness of touch, in the words and the music, are never far from the tragedy, and elegance and evil exist side by side. The five main roles are very gratifying to the singers, and there are two vocal rarities for Verdi: a contralto role with plummy solos, and a very frothy *travesti* ("pants") role written for a lyric coloratura.

Ballo has its provenance in a historical event. King Gustav III of Sweden, a great patron of the arts and a monarch who still fascinates the Swedish people, was assassinated in 1792 at a masked ball held at the beautiful opera house he had built in Stockholm. The assassin was a Count Ankarstrom, something of a religious fanatic, who shot the King at close range using rusted bullets to ensure death by blood poisoning if not by gunfire. The story, in somewhat altered form, appeared in plays, ballets, and even two operas. Eugène Scribe, the librettist of *Les Vêpres siciliennes,* wrote a play called *Gustave III, ou le bal masqué,* in which he added the intrigue of an affair between Gustav and the Countess Ankarstrom. Scribe changed the shooting to a knifing, which is much more manageable on stage, and added the love story, making Ankarstrom the King's confidante and secretary.

Verdi readily saw how this play screamed for operatic treatment. The final scene, the assassination at a masked ball, appealed to him immensely. He recommended the play to Somma, who produced a libretto. Verdi completed the opera, to be called *Gustavo di Svezia,* and contracted for its performance at the Teatro San Carlo of Naples. But when the composer arrived in Naples he discovered that the censors were insisting on a stunning array of changes. Gustav could not be a king or even any other sort of ruler, but a mere nobleman; there was to be no assassination; the lady in question should be the sister, rather than the wife, of the second male character; her name must be changed from Adelia to Amelia (huh?); there could be no fortune-teller; the setting of the story could remain in the remote north, but must take place in pre-Christian times.

Verdi stood firm and refused any cooperation with the theater or the authorities. He was considered in breach of contract and was in serious danger of landing in jail. Then the most surprising thing happened. The censors in Rome, of all unlikely places, approved the libretto as it stood! Even though the Roman censors were notoriously reactionary, there was no king in Rome to offend. Alas, the Roman authorities later changed their minds. Too exhausted to fight any more, Verdi succumbed to Somma's proposed compromise: If the setting of the opera were changed to colonial America, where the king could be metamorphosed into a governor, all the other features of the drama could remain in place. This seemed infinitely preferable to the Neapolitan solution, which would have meant horn-helmeted Vikings frolicking their way through mazurkas and minuets at a masked ball.

The opera, set in colonial Boston but otherwise musically intact, was given at Rome and was a wild success. That Verdi was able to snatch triumph from such a near-disaster is a testament to his resilience as a man of the theater.

WHILE *Ballo* doesn't have the "multiple editions" issue that plagues so many of Verdi's other operas, productions are faced with choosing between the Boston and Sweden settings for the story. Companies in the United States have tried to make some hay out of the Boston setting, championing *Ballo* as Verdi's quintessentially American opera. The marketing departments got busy and emphasized how the familiar icons of colonial New England would help us, the masses, to like, you know, relate. Well, we didn't. The thought of a glittering masked ball in colonial Boston is too absurd to contemplate.

But the Swedish setting has problems, too. Program notes always point out the absurdity of the Boston setting but never point out that it's equally absurd to imagine the flamingly homosexual King Gustav III running off with anybody's wife. Verdi acquiesced to the Roman censors' Boston idea with uncharacteristic swiftness. He liked the idea of taking the story away from historical specifics and placing it in Neverland. And no place was as foreign to him as colonial Boston.

History, however, has a way of persisting through theatrical morphs, and nowadays some productions overemphasize Oscar, to the detriment of the opera's coherence. The best course is to accept the inherent ambiguities in a work that has had a long journey from newspaper headlines to the opera house.

Today, most productions set the story in Sweden yet retain many of the names (Riccardo and Renato, Ulrica, and even Sam and Tom) from the Boston setting. The movement is toward creating a new mythic space for this otherwise uncomplicated story, one where neither the realities of colonial Boston nor the inconvenient facts of King Gustav III's sex life will take over the opera.

CAST OF CHARACTERS

RICCARDO, EARL OF WARWICK AND GOVERNOR OF BOSTON (or GUSTAV III, KING OF SWEDEN, or, most commonly, RICCARDO, KING OF SWEDEN) *(tenor)* A ruler popular with most, but not all, of his people. He is obviously a fun-loving fellow, with more than a touch of recklessness in him.

RENATO (or COUNT ANKARSTROM) *(baritone)* The King's secretary and best friend. The baritone is a good and honest man who has been wronged, rather than a mustache-twirling bad guy bent on causing trouble. He must have vocal star power, having one of Verdi's most important baritone solo scenes.

AMELIA *(soprano)* Renato's wife. Although Amelia is not a vocal challenge of the same caliber as Aida, or Violetta in *Traviata,* she must still convey a wide range of emotions and be able to deliver some spinto sounds. She must also, like Lina in *Stiffelio,* be able to project a sense of innocence despite her adulterous proclivities.

OSCAR *(soprano)* A page at the Court. One of Verdi's most curious and interesting creations. Oscar is played by a high lyric soprano with good coloratura abilities, yet must also be able to hold her own in thick ensembles throughout the opera. It is a mistake to cast a canary in the role, although lightness of tone must be conveyed in the solo passages. Brightness is crucial.

SAM (or COUNT RIBBING) *(bass)* and TOM (or COUNT HORN) *(bass),* two conspirators. These two have no solos to sing, but they contribute some very important ensemble work.

ULRICA *(contralto)* A fortune-teller. Ulrica is described in both the Swedish and Boston versions as a "negress, a person of unclean race." Mercifully, this is usually changed in performance.

SILVANO *(bass),* a sailor; CHIEF JUSTICE *(tenor),* a JUDGE *(tenor).*

THE OPERA

Act I

Scene 1: A hall in the royal palace.

Officials, courtiers, and commoners await the arrival of the King. Most of the crowd praise him, but Sam and Tom and a few of their adherents grumble. Riccardo has lost wars and lives. Riccardo enters with Oscar the page. The King graciously grants the petitions presented to him. Oscar shows him the guest list for the forthcoming masked ball. Riccardo reads the name of Amelia, wife of his best friend Renato. How much he loves her! The petitioners comment on how hard the King works for their well-being, while the conspirators murmur that the time is not yet right to strike him down. Both petitioners and conspirators withdraw.

Renato enters, announcing that he has discovered everything. Riccardo is horrified, thinking he is referring to his own clandestine but unconsummated love for Renato's wife. Renato, however, has discovered a conspiracy against the King's life. Riccardo is so relieved that he drops the matter and advises Renato to do the same. The people support him, and so does God. Renato advises caution. If he were to be killed, what would happen to the country?

Oscar announces the Chief Justice, who asks the King to sign an order of banishment for the gypsy fortune-teller Ulrica. The King asks Oscar if he knows anything of this witch. The page gaily recounts the witch's hokey effects, praising her as a very entertaining fraud. Riccardo is amused. Despite the Chief Justice's pleas, he calls back the crowd of petitioners and blithely invites them to join him, disguised, to inspect this crowd-pleasing sorceress. Renato warns again of the dangers the King faces, if not from demons, then from conspirators. Sam and Tom see an opportunity for assassination. Oscar is thrilled at the charade. All agree to meet at Ulrica's den at three o'clock.

Comment: *A great deal of information is unfolded in this swift scene, typical of the economy of the opera as a whole. Riccardo, Renato, and Oscar each get brief solos that act as teasers for their subsequent big scenes. Riccardo's musings on Amelia are contained in a brief solo, "La rivedrà nell'estasi," a lovely and concise cavatina. Renato's warning to the King, "Alla vita che t'arride," is scored with low winds and horn. Some hear ambivalence in this. Later it will assume a different meaning for Renato. Oscar is all fluff and fun right from his first entrance. His little ballad "Voltea la terra" has laugher written into it. The final ensemble has all the individuals reacting according to character yet forming a unified whole.*

Scene 2: The den of the sorceress Ulrica.

Ulrica stares into the boiling cauldron. The crowd of amazed onlookers call for silence. Ulrica invokes the King of the Abyss. Riccardo enters, disguised as a fisherman. Ulrica returns to her trance. The onlookers applaud. Ulrica strikes the ground and vanishes.

A sailor named Silvano approaches the cauldron. He has served for three hard years in the King's fleet and would like to know if there's any chance for advancement in his future. Ulrica reappears. She foretells money and a promotion. Riccardo signs a commission slip for Silvano and, unseen, slips it into the sailor's pocket along with a bag of coins. Silvano reaches for a coin to pay Ulrica, and finds his future set. The crowd cheers. A servant enters by a secret door and requests an interview for his mistress, an important lady. Ulrica orders the others out, but Riccardo, who recognizes the servant, hides in the darkness.

Amelia enters. She seeks Ulrica's help in overcoming her guilty love for Riccardo. Ulrica knows the cure, a certain herb that grows around the gallows. Amelia must gather it at midnight. She promises to be brave and gather the herb at the appointed time. From his hiding place, Riccardo comments that he will be there too. The impatient crowd clamor to come back in, and Amelia leaves through the secret door.

The crowd reenters, swelled with the courtiers and conspirators from the first scene now disguised in both common and outlandish costumes. Riccardo, telling Oscar not to betray his identity, steps forward. He tells of his life as a fisherman, and asks Ulrica if the sea will be bountiful to him.

Comment: *Riccardo's fisherman's song, "Di' tu, se fedele il flutto," is a rollicking good chantey, offering the tenor wide scope for the long, undulating phrases associated with that genre. It can be found on many recordings of selected arias and is a great crowd-pleaser. Dramatically, it has absolutely nothing to do with anything going on.*

Ulrica is not fooled by the chantey for a moment. She reads Riccardo's hand. The hand of a great man, obviously, but she will not say more. Riccardo presses her. Very well. He shall die. Riccardo shrugs. If bravely in battle, then no matter. No, counters Ulrica, by assassination. Riccardo asks by whose hand. A friend, she answers. The next man who shakes his hand will be the assassin. Riccardo glibly offers his hand to any in the crowd. All refuse to touch it.

Just then, Renato rushes in and approaches Riccardo, grasping his hand. The courtiers breathe a sigh of relief. Riccardo tells Ulrica that Renato is his best friend, and gives her money for her troubles. She accepts the money, and repeats her prophecy. Perhaps there will be more than one conspirator, she says, looking at Sam and Tom. The two conspirators grumble guiltily. Riccardo is amused at these events, which are either madness or a big joke. Renato is dimly aware of trouble brewing. Oscar reflects on the sadness of the prophecy. Silvano the sailor sings in praise of the King, no longer disguised, leading the people on in proclaiming him their father and friend.

Comment: *Ulrica's scene (she does not appear again) is a half-hour of great contrasts. For the role of Ulrica, Verdi wrote true contralto music, low, long, and menacing. But the most impressive music of the scene comes not during the actual witchcraft moments, but when unpossessed people are commenting on those moments. After Ulrica's prediction of death for Riccardo, there is a superb quintet, "E scherzo od è follia." The* predominantly low voices of Sam, Tom, and Ulrica form the tonal basis, the tenor's amusement floats above them, and Oscar's genuine concern provides the tonal pinnacle.

Act II

Setting: A lonely spot with gallows, at midnight.

Amelia appears at the desolate gallows. The place fills her with dread, but she must be strong and gather the herb to cure her love. But then what will become of her? A bell strikes midnight. Amelia hallucinates a head coming out from the ground. She prays fervently for mercy.

Comment: The orchestral prelude is rushing and nervous. We can imagine Amelia running to this spot. Once there, her grand scena is a great opportunity for the soprano. She must depict determination within frailty. After the bell rings out midnight (six strokes, as in Rigoletto*), she begins to chew up the scenery, but this is accomplished in a few soaring phrases rather than a cabaletta.*

Riccardo suddenly appears out of the shadows, and Amelia begs him to leave and save her reputation. His love is too strong for him to leave her now, but she reminds him that she is his best friend's wife. Riccardo does not need to be reminded of that, yet still his heart breaks with love. How many times has he begged heaven to show him the same mercy she now prays for? She asks God for a miracle to end this strife, and tells Riccardo to leave her forever. He demands that Amelia confess her love. Yes, she says, she loves him. He is transported by her confession, and repeats "You love me!," savoring the words. That is all that matters. Amelia cannot pursue her love, but cannot escape it either. Wouldn't it be better to die then and there?

Comment: When Verdi's detractors say he never wrote a convincing love duet, his defenders often point to this one. True, a wide range of emotions are present here—guilt, resolve, aggression, even joy. But what's missing is longing. The result sounds a lot more like a call to battle than a call to bed. Perhaps it's fairer to say that Verdi didn't write superb duets about falling in love, but about the consequences of having done so.

Amelia realizes, to her terror, that Renato is approaching, and she covers her face with a veil. Renato tells Riccardo that assassins are lurking. The conspirators knew Riccardo was meeting an unknown woman at the gallows, and plan to kill him there. Renato gives Riccardo his cloak and tells him to escape down a side path, where the assassins will not discover him. He promises to stay and protect the veiled Amelia, but she begs him to flee. She threatens to remove her veil if Riccardo does not leave instantly. Riccardo asks Renato a great favor. He must escort the lady back to the city without glancing at her, removing her veil, or even exchanging a word. Renato agrees. Amelia and Renato urge Riccardo to flee. Riccardo prays for Amelia's safety, and finally leaves.

Comment: *Riccardo has been warned to flee, but lingers to sing for a bit. There is something rather self-destructive in this man. His blithe dismissal of Renato's warnings, his insistence on visiting the fortune-teller, and his careless offer of his hand to anyone who wants to assassinate him should make this hesitation to leave the gallows seem more in character.*

Renato tells the veiled lady not to tremble, she will be safe with him. Sam, Tom and the other conspirators appear. They are disappointed to find only Renato with a veiled lady. Sam grunts that they were less fortunate, they didn't have belles waiting for them at the gallows. Tom demands to see the face of Renato's mysterious lady. Renato defies them. The conspirators draw weapons on Renato, who also draws his sword. Just as they are about to fight, Amelia pulls the veil from her face. The conspirators are stunned. His wife? Sam taunts the gallant lover, courting his own wife in the moonlight. Sam and Tom cannot wait to spread the gossip in town the next day. Amelia wonders where she can turn for support. Renato, absolutely stunned, gazes down the path by which Riccardo fled. Is this how he repays him for saving his life? He asks Sam and Tom to meet him at his house in the morning. He has urgent business to discuss. They agree to meet, and withdraw, chuckling to themselves over the amusing situation. Renato turns to Amelia. He has sworn on his honor to escort her back to the city. She is terrified by her husband's menacing voice.

Comment: *The courtliness of the conspirators' "laughing music" underscores what evil and menace may hide behind elegant veneers, a very important issue in this opera. At the end of the act, when something rousing would be expected, we only hear the "Ha ha ha ha" of the pianissimo chorus dying away in the (offstage) distance. It is powerful, understated, and refined.*

Act III

Scene 1: A study in Renato's house. In the background is a portrait of Riccardo. Two bronze vases are on the mantelpiece.

Renato drags Amelia into the room. There is nothing she can say to mitigate this outrage. She must pay with blood. She admits that for one moment she loved Riccardo, but she never stained Renato's honor, and God knows this is true. Too late, he tells her. She must die. She agrees to die, but insists on one last favor. She must embrace her only son once again. If the wife is unworthy to do so, then allow the mother. He cannot look at her, but points to the door. She leaves.

It's not Amelia, Renato considers, who is guilty. He looks at the portrait of Riccardo, crying "It was you!" Riccardo was the cause of all this treachery, suffering, torture. He remembers Amelia's sweet embraces and their pure love. All that is gone forever, and only hate sits now in the bereaved heart.

Sam and Tom enter. Renato says he knows of their plot to kill Riccardo. Sam and Tom deny it, but Renato produces the papers proving the conspiracy. So Renato will disclose the plot? No, he counters. He is on their side, though he does not explain why. He pledges on his son's life that Riccardo will die. Sam and Tom believe him, and they join with him in an oath that Riccardo will die. But by whose hand? Tom claims the privilege. Riccardo stole his ancestral castle. Sam also claims the honor. Riccardo murdered his brother. Renato takes a vase from the mantelpiece and suggests they draw lots, quickly writing the three names on cards. Amelia enters. Oscar is at the door, with an invitation from Riccardo. Renato orders Oscar to wait outside, but Amelia must remain in the room. She will draw the name out of the vase. Trembling, she pulls a card from the vase. Renato takes it from her and hands it to Sam, who reads the name "Renato." He praises the sacred justice of heaven. Amelia is shocked by the proceedings, and Sam and Tom cherish Riccardo's imminent death.

Renato orders Oscar in. Gaily, Oscar approaches Amelia, inviting her and her husband to a ball that night. Amelia declines. Renato asks if Riccardo will be there. Of course, replies the page. Looking at Sam and Tom, Renato replies that he and his wife will be honored to attend. Oscar announces it will be a splendid masked ball. Sam and Tom agree to attend in disguise. Oscar describes the splendor of the preparations, Amelia understands that she is partly to blame if harm should come to Riccardo, Renato anticipates his revenge, while Sam and Tom look forward to the dance of death. Oscar says Amelia shall be the queen of the festivities. The conspirators choose costumes of blue cloaks with vermillion ribbons and scarves knotted on the left. Their password will be "Death."

Comment: This scene is one of Verdi's most perfect. The musical structure, from plaintive soprano aria to dark baritone aria, to trio, to quartet, to quintet, is apparent from reading the synopsis. The soprano aria, "Morrò, ma prima in grazia," shows Amelia's tender and loving side. Her pleas are doubled by the cello, which, in Verdi, often signifies sincerity. Renato's great baritone aria, "Eri tu," shows both the vengeful wronged cuckold and the loving husband. Of course he's not going to kill Amelia. There are limits, even in Italian opera. When Sam and Tom enter, the trio is menacing and martial. The subsequent quartet is even more sinister. The melody is the oath trio, but faster and with more aggressive orchestration, and with the soprano's voice surfing above it like an alarm. No one character knows the full extent of the situation. The tension lies in the unspoken and dimly perceived. No medium can convey a situation like this better than opera. When Oscar arrives in all innocence to announce the masked ball, the tension is not relieved so much as heightened. In the quintet, Renato and Amelia carry the longer vocal lines, Sam and Tom mutter rhythmically, sounding like an evil dance of death, and Oscar's elegant trills and coloratura, thus supported by the lower voices, become almost horrifying. Amelia basically repeats Oscar's lovely vocal line, but in a minor key and with her inherently darker voice. It is a moment of sheer dramatic genius, diagramming the intersection of the delightful and the terrifying.

Scene 2: Riccardo's study. Evening.

Riccardo is sitting alone at his desk. He is reading a decree naming Renato governor of Finland. Riccardo can hardly bear to sign the decree and thus lose Amelia, but he steels himself and signs, expressing his regret. The music from the ball, taking place outside the study, is heard. Oscar enters, bringing a note from an anonymous woman. The note warns Riccardo to avoid the ball—his very life is in danger. Yet how can Riccardo miss the ball, and miss seeing Amelia one last time as well as appearing to be a coward?

Comment: This is the "eleven o'clock ballad" of the opera. Before Riccardo signs the decree (which summons Renato and Amelia back to England in the Boston version), we hear the strings recalling warm love themes, which continue even after we hear Riccardo's resolution represented by blunt chords. His decision is taken, but the feelings remain. This is followed by a lovely romanza, "Ma se m'è forza perderti." When Oscar enters, we hear the stage band music from the ball. This is the same sort of proto-cinematic technique that worked so well in Rigoletto *and* Traviata. *After Oscar leaves, Riccardo gives full voice to his "love theme," the lovely tune from the Prelude that was the basis for "La rivedrà nell'estasi." The backdrop usually rises at this point to reveal the ball in progress. The effect of the private life being made glaringly public is impressive.*

Scene 3: A splendid ballroom, with a masked ball in progress.

Courtiers and guests are reveling in the splendor and gaiety of the ball. Sam and Tom, in blue cloaks and beribboned as agreed, walk among the guests. They approach another in their costume, and whisper "Death!" "Death!," answers the man, Renato, who adds that Riccardo won't come to the ball. The three disperse. Oscar, masked, approaches Renato and names him, unfooled by the costume. Renato pulls Oscar's mask away and names him. Oscar protests the outrage, but Renato asks the page if it's fitting for him to sneak into the ballroom while Riccardo is sleeping. Oh, protests Oscar, the King is at the ball. Where? asks Renato. Oscar plays coy and replies with a teasing rhyme song. He knows where the King is, but will never tell, tra la la . . . Renato pretends he has urgent business with Riccardo, and must find him among the masked revelers. Half-convinced, Oscar tells Renato that Riccardo is wearing a black cloak with a scarlet ribbon. The page disappears into the crowd.

Riccardo, dressed as Oscar described, enters the crowd, followed by Amelia, also masked. She urges him to flee or he will be assassinated. He asks if she is the lady who wrote him the note, and asks for her name, and why she is so concerned for his safety. Through her sobs, he recognizes the voice of Amelia, his angel. Desperately, she concedes that she loves him, but he must leave or be killed. He declares that her love helps him defy fate. At last, he tells her that he has signed papers sending her with Renato out of the country. Her honor will be safe. He bids her farewell for the last time.

Renato suddenly comes between them and stabs Riccardo. If this is a time for farewells, then let this be his to Riccardo! Oscar runs over and calls for help. The crowd asks who did it, and Oscar points to Renato, who is surrounded and unmasked. They demand his immediate death. Riccardo, gasping, orders Renato freed and beckons him near. He shows him the order he signed sending Renato and Amelia out of the country. Yes, he loved Amelia, but did not stain her honor. Amelia's heart gives way to remorse. Renato is stunned by his own action, while Oscar grieves for himself and the nation. Riccardo

able situation. The point of *Forza* (and, yes, there is one) is not how events unfold in real life but how passions dictate lives. The details of those lives are often controlled by events in the past—destiny, you might say. The self is defined by powers the conscious will cannot control. *Forza* looks at the "inescapability of the self" in a way that must have bewildered our ancestors. In fact, this opera may have seemed old-fashioned at its premiere because it was, in a sense, a century and a half ahead of its time.

What makes *Forza* exceptional (and, in a good performance, quite disturbing) is that it takes place on two levels, one of these being wild and surreal while the other is firmly rooted in the plausible world of everyday people. The outrageousness of the first is constantly underscored by the frequent returns to the latter. *Trovatore* presents a single world of heightened emotions, which one may accept or reject wholesale. *Forza* maniacally deconstructs the world as thoroughly as a cubist painting, and never allows the audience to relax into a complacent perspective. There is not one note in it that can be spoken, yelled, or otherwise faked. One must sing as if in church to communicate the impressions of hell. Few can manage it. A successful *Forza* production is a rarity these days.

Forza had a few productions after the 1862 St. Petersburg premiere, including one in Rome under the name of *Don Alvaro*. Verdi then made considerable revisions for an authorized production that was staged at La Scala in 1869 These days, the original version is creeping up on recordings and occasionally in performances.

CAST OF CHARACTERS

Don Alvaro *(tenor)* The only son of a Viceroy of Peru who rebelled against Spanish rule and married the last Inca princess, hoping to set up an independent kingdom. They failed and were executed, and Alvaro grew up in shame with a predisposition to fatalism. We are never told exactly why he is in Spain. Vocally, the tenor must be able to express heroism and nobility of spirit.

LEONORA DI VARGAS *(soprano)* The daughter of the Marquis of Calatrava, in love with Alvaro. Like so many great prima donna roles, Leonora is a woman whose conflict is with herself. She is noble, filial, honor-bound, and pious as well as extravagantly passionate. The role makes incredible demands on the soprano's voice as well as her person. As Verdi said in a letter to an impresario who was experiencing only a moderate success with the opera, "In *La forza del destino* you certainly don't have to know how to sing fancy passages, but you have to have a soul and understand the *word* and express it."

DON CARLO DI VARGAS *(baritone)* Leonora's brother and thus Alvaro's sworn enemy, the implacable agent of doom in the opera. Carlo has been seen as the embodiment of Alvaro and Leonora's death wish. The character must be by turns deceptive, insinuating, noble in spirit, sympathetic, and thunderously vengeful. The role requires a singer who can hold the stage during one of the great grand scenas in the baritone repertory. Beyond this, he must blend well with the tenor in three important duets.

CURRA *(mezzo)* Leonora's maid, a notably meddlesome one who is, mercifully, disposed of early in the proceedings.

THE MARCHESE (MARQUIS) DI CALATRAVA *(bass)* The father of Leonora and Don Carlo. The poor Marquis probably has the worst luck of any character in opera—a real *schlemazel.*

PREZIOSILLA *(mezzo)* A lively young gypsy girl. Nowhere in opera is the mezzo so different from the soprano as here, musically, dramatically, and temperamentally. This character has a habit of showing up unexpectedly and leading songs. Preziosilla tends to annoy audiences. Perhaps that's the idea. Incidentally, the name Preziosilla is the same word southern Italians use for parsley, and also what they call a busybody, since such a person is "in everything."

PADRE GUARDIANO *(bass)* The Father Superior of the Franciscan monastery of Our Lady of the Angels, outside the village of Hornachuelos. Besides his important duet scene with Leonora in Act II, Guardiano must impart a sense of serene authority and genuine religious grandeur whenever he appears.

Fra Melitone *(baritone)* A Franciscan friar. The very opposite of Padre Guardiano, Melitone has more in common with Friar Tuck.

Maestro Trabuco *(tenor)* A peddler, muleteer, and genial busybody.

The Mayor of Hornachuelos *(bass)* An affable, small role, one of the many splashes of color across the canvas of the opera.

THE OPERA

Overture

Comment: *The Overture is eternally popular in the concert hall, since it commands attention and effectively quiets a chatting audience. Three E's are played by the brass, there is silence, the notes are repeated, and the strings break into a revolving, self-perpetuating theme associated with destiny. The effect is of being knocked over the head and then carried away into a rush of events. The balance of the Overture introduces themes from the opera, always connected by the destiny theme.*

Act I

Setting: A room in the palace of the Marquis of Calatrava, near Seville. The room is decorated tastefully but in need of repairs.

The Marquis closes the balcony doors and says good night to his daughter Leonora. He is happy that she appears to have recovered from her inappropriate love for the basely born Alvaro. She is full of emotions, trying to tell him something, but cannot. He kisses her and leaves. The maid Curra goes to Leonora, who is in tears. Curra tells Leonora all is ready, but Leonora is distressed. Such a loving father! How can she betray him? Curra taunts Leonora. If she hesitates, Don Alvaro will be killed or at least imprisoned and probably hanged later. She must not love Don Alvaro after all. Leonora is aghast. Of course she loves Alvaro! She is about to leave everything she knows to elope with him. She will be an orphan and a wanderer in a strange land. An inexorable fate drives her on to remorse and tears. She bids farewell to her home and homeland.

Alvaro appears at the balcony and throws himself in Leonora's arms. She is upset—he was so long in coming! A thousand things, he says, kept him, but now all is ready. He tells Curra to throw Leonora's things below into the courtyard. Leonora hesitates, but he consoles her. A priest is waiting to bless their union. Tomorrow the sun, god of the Indies, lord of his royal race, will smile upon their union. Still she hesitates. Coldly, he tells her that he releases her from her vows. She may stay behind. This rallies her, and she determines to follow Alvaro to the ends of the earth, but must never be parted from him. They prepare to leave.

Noises are heard, and Curra announces that people are coming up the stairs. Leonora tells Alvaro to hide in the wardrobe. He draws his pistol. She asks if he would use it against her father. Against myself, he replies. The Marquis enters in a fury, sword drawn, followed by servants. Alvaro bares his chest and tells the Marquis to strike, since he alone is at fault. The Marquis refuses to duel with one so basely born, and orders the servants to arrest Alvaro. Alvaro draws his pistol on the servants, saying he will only die at the hands of the Marquis. He swears Leonora is pure. In a gesture of submission, he casts his pistol to the floor, but it fires and hits the Marquis. Dying, the Marquis curses his daughter. Servants attend his body as Alvaro and Leonora run for the balcony.

Comment: *The first act throws us immediately into this opera's unique swirling world, where human will takes a back seat to events and, above all, destiny. Yet the music is as controlled and refined as anything in Verdi, which is odd, considering what occurs. The Marquis is a conventional father, but Leonora's conflicted and broken music draws our attention immediately to her. She gives vent to some of her feelings in her aria to Curra after her father leaves. "Me pellegrina ed orfana" is a poignant, though self-pitying, farewell to her girlhood.*

Alvaro's approach is signaled by a crescendo in the strings, and he begins the duet as soon as he hops in the window. This man is all impetuous urgency, yet there is nobility in his music. Alvaro begins his slancio *expressions of love immediately, unlike Alfredo in* Traviata, *who had a full act to warm up to them. When Alvaro describes the rising sun, god of his ancestors, it is a great arch of music imitating a sunrise, beautifully supported by a shimmering orchestra. It is thoroughly convincing to the audience as well as to Leonora, who finally stops fretting and determines to leave with Alvaro. Their duet keeps moving forward: There is no unison restatement of the main theme, but overlapping phrases instead. The music says these two are actually already in motion, even though of course they must stand in one place to sing it.*

The grand gesture of throwing down the gun only to have it go off and kill the Marquis is rather a stretch, and the audience invariably howls at this point. But the whole work is about life as a stretch, and Verdi no less than Rivas is aiming for a dramatic enactment of Murphy's law. The curtain falls quickly after the accident, and we are meant to feel overwhelmed by the pace of events.

Act II

Scene 1: A tavern in the village of Hornachuelos, near Córdoba.

The innkeeper and his wife prepare food while various guests greet each other and dance. The Mayor of Hornachuelos announces dinner, and various muleteers, including Maestro Trabuco, approach the table. Don Carlo, Leonora's brother, disguised as a student, says grace in Latin.

Leonora, dressed as a man, appears at the door of the inn, sees her brother, and quickly leaves for an upstairs room.

Carlo compliments the hostess in Latin, but the Mayor says the lady knows cooking better than Latin. Carlo asks Trabuco why he eats nothing; Trabuco is observing the Friday fast. Carlo presses Trabuco about the little passenger who arrived with him at the tavern, but just then the gypsy Preziosilla enters, shouting hurray for war. War has broken out in Italy against the Germans. The crowd cry death to the Germans, eternal scourge of Italy. Preziosilla and the crowd combine in praise of the beauty of war. Carlo asks her to read his palm. She tells him many sorrows lie in his path. Leaning closer to him, she says she knows he is not a student. No one makes a fool of her!

A band of pilgrims is heard passing through the town on the way to a jubilee. Leonora, still disguised, appears at the door again. If only she could escape! The pilgrims pass, begging God for mercy. At the Mayor's suggestion, all the guests kneel and join in the prayer. Leonora says her own prayer. If God will not help her, who can save her from her brother thirsting for her blood? The pilgrims pass. Leonora returns to her room upstairs.

Don Carlo toasts the health of the company. Pressing Trabuco again, he asks if his passenger was also heading for the jubilee. Trabuco does not know. By the way, continues Don Carlo, was that a cock or a hen? Trabuco replies that he notices travelers' money, and nothing else. Don Carlo now presses the Mayor. Why did n't the stranger join the others at dinner? What refreshment did he take? The Mayor says nothing. Carlo asks Trabuco if the stranger straddled the mule or rode sidesaddle. What a bore! exclaims Trabuco, losing patience and escaping to the stables to sleep with his mules.

Don Carlo suggests painting a mustache on the stranger's face, but the Mayor says he opposes playing practical jokes on travelers. Better if the student told the company his own story, where he comes from and what his business is. Carlo identifies himself as Pereda, an accomplished student at the University of Salamanca. A man named Vargas took him from there to Seville a year ago, and they became great friends. A foreigner, the lover of Vargas's sister, murdered his father, and Vargas, brave fellow, swore revenge. They set out after the guilty pair, but everywhere they heard that the girl had perished with her father, and only the seducer escaped. Vargas sailed for America, swearing to track down the killer, and Pereda returned to his books.

Preziosilla reviews a few details of this story, repeating her line that no one makes a fool of her! The Mayor says it is late, and time for all the people to retire. All say good night, Carlo repeats parts of his student tale, while Preziosilla laughs. No one makes a fool of her!

Comment: *The violent contrasts of tone in* Forza *are found not only between scenes but often within them. Any single page of this scene's* score contains enough ideas for a full act. Instead, the various ideas are presented as a phantasmagoria of shifting moods, backgrounds, and situations. We begin with a brief dance, followed by some lightly scored conversation. Preziosilla bursts in and sings a rousing number about the pleasures of military life, with the repeating chorus "E bella la guerra." After this strange moment, she reads Carlo's palm and lets him know she is on to him with a descending coloratura line, a laugh set to music. It will be repeated later in the scene by both the mezzo and the orchestra. The pilgrim's chorus virtually slices across all this frivolity. Verdi conceived of this chorus as a faint and haunting theme sung by a mixed chorus of sixteen, imparting an effect on the people over whom it passes like a breath of the divine spirit. Leonora reappears for this part, and her vocal line is center of the concertato. The people in the tavern are having a conventionally pious moment, but Leonora is withdrawing within herself and farther from the everyday world. The people in the tavern, however, return to their pleasantries not visibly altered by the intrusion of religion into their lives. They, unlike Leonora, have assimilated life's contrasts. Carlo tells his (false) story, "Son Pereda," to lovely and superficially convincing music. The scene ends with Preziosilla's laugh motif.

Scene 2: In front of the Church of Our Lady of the Angels, outside of Hornachuelos. A convent is on one side.

Leonora appears, trembling. Her story is now known, told by her brother to everybody in the town. And Alvaro, whom she lost while escaping, did not die as she had thought, but has sailed for America, abandoning her! She falls to her knees, begging the merciful Virgin Mother to forgive her her sin and allow her to erase the memory of Alvaro from her heart. She hears organ music from inside the church, followed by the chanting of monks. She must take refuge in this sacred place.

Comment: Leonora's first great aria, "Madre, pietosa Vergine," is in the form of a prayer, beginning nervously and broken but climaxing in the big theme we have heard in the Overture. This Verdian arching phrase is a killer, beginning piano in the low notes, growing to a forte high climax, and descending again. Leonora sings it the first time doubled by a subdued orchestra. We then hear the chanting of the monks in the church as a sort of choral accompaniment. The sound of the monks strengthens Leonora's resolve, and she repeats the phrase, this time to full orchestral accompaniment. Of course the phrase is scored legato—all on one breath. Don't count on it. If it is accomplished, however, the simple phrase is a perfect expression of emotional release. All the power of Italian opera to depict pathos is in that phrase.

Leonora rings the bell at the monastery door. A small window opens, revealing the face of Fra Melitone. Leonora asks for the Superior. Melitone tells her the church opens at five o'clock—she should come back then for the jubilee. She insists, saying she is sent by Father Cleto. That holy man? asks Melitone. What for? An unfortunate soul . . . He interrupts her. Always the same story. Very well, he opens the door for Leonora, but she says she cannot enter. Oh, excommunicated? asks Melitone. Fine, he will announce the stranger to the Superior, but if he doesn't come back, then good night! She prays while waiting. Padre Guardiano returns with Fra Melitone, bidding the stranger speak. Leonora will speak only to the father. Guardiano dismisses Melitone, who grumbles as he goes. Always secrets, and these holy men always have to know them! They treat the brothers like so many cabbages! Guardiano asks the brother what he is muttering. Oh, only that the door is heavy and creaking, says Melitone. "Obey!" says Guardiano. "The Boss has spoken!" mutters Melitone, leaving at last.

Comment: When Melitone leaves Leonora alone, a melancholy clarinet repeats her prayer. She is profoundly alone in her sadness. If you haven't guessed by now, Melitone is the comic relief of the opera. In the hands of a veteran character actor-singer, the role provides an excellent contrast to the unbearably self-serious protagonists. A good place to judge the Melitone is in the line about cabbages, "Noi siamo tanti cavoli!" The score indicates no trill in the first syllable of the last word, but a ham will trill, bleat, and do backflips over it.

Padre Guardiano bids the stranger speak. Leonora identifies herself as a woman, to the father's great shock. She begs him to rescue her from hell. How can a poor monk do that? he asks. Father Cleto wrote to Guardiano about her. She is Leonora di Vargas! Yes, she admits. Does he tremble at the name? No, says Guardiano. He bids her come trusting to the cross. She genuflects. Returning to Guardiano, she now feels comforted, no longer tormented by her father's curse. Guardiano tells her Satan is powerless in this place. That, she says, is why she seeks to live out her days in the cave where another woman once lived alone. Cleto told her about it. Guardiano is skeptical. What if her heart should change? Where is her lover? He killed her father unwittingly, she answers. And her brother? Sworn to vengeance. But why does Leonora not seek refuge in a regular convent? Never! she replies. She must be alone, entirely alone, to finish out her days in penance and prayer. He asks if her decision is final. It is. Praising God, he tells her it shall be done. Only he will know who she is. She will find a cave among the rocky heights, with a spring nearby. Every seventh day, he will leave a simple meal for her. He calls Melitone, and orders him to assemble the brothers in the church. Guardiano tells her she will depart for solitary life at dawn, but now let her receive the holy bread she will need to strengthen her. She thanks God that her sin has been forgiven. Guardiano gives her the simple robes of a hermit, and both implore God's blessing.

Comment: *This duet between Leonora and Guardiano is extraordinary even by Verdian standards of great father-daughter scenes. Guardiano does not go through varieties of emotions but remains constant throughout the interaction. The shifting feelings and expressions are all in Leonora's part, who is visibly trying to fit herself into Guardiano's world. The different segments of the scene are all presented in a stately pace, as we watch Leonora attempting to adapt to a contemplative way of life.*

Scene 3: The interior of the Church of Our Lady of the Angels.

Comment: *This may not be a separate scene at all. The original instructions say that the doors of the church should be opened, with the monks* *already inside. Acoustical limitations, however, often dictate changing the scene.*

An organ plays while the brothers surround the candlelit altar. Guardiano extends his hand in blessing over Leonora, dressed as a simple hermit. He addresses the brothers. A soul has come to seek salvation in their hills. The sacred grotto is an inviolable asylum, he tells them. No one must ever go there. If any break this rule, let them be cursed by all hell. Guardiano addresses Leonora. Rise and leave, he bids her. No living person will see her again. There is a bell at the cave. It may be rung if danger threatens, or if her last hour approaches. Then they will hasten to comfort her soul before it returns to God. The monks ask Our Lady of the Angels to protect the penitent, and Leonora repeats the prayer. She kisses Padre Guardiano's hand, and walks alone toward the hermit's cave. The monks extinguish their candles and retire. Padre Guardiano extends his blessing in the direction of Leonora's path.

Comment: This scene is ritual and stasis, one of the stock routines of grand opera meant to impress those who are bored by vocal solos. It begins with an organ solo, followed by Guardiano's formulaic antiphons with the monks. They sing a simple prayer, "Madonna degli angeli," which is repeated by Leonora as a soaring piano legato. The juxtaposition is striking. Sung by the monks, it is a calming piece of music. Moved to the soprano's voice, it is a cri de coeur. The act ends on a quiet note that is as much a question mark as a finale.

Act III

Scene 1: A forest near the town of Velletri in Italy, during the War of the Austrian Succession.

Men are heard in the distance playing cards. Don Alvaro appears alone, in the uniform of a captain of the Spanish Grenadiers. Tormented, he seeks death in vain. He remembers Seville and Leonora, and that night when he lost her. He thinks of his own sad life. His father sought to free Peru from its Spanish masters, and he married the last Inca princess to win the crown, but all in vain. He himself was born in a prison and raised in the desert, alive today only because no one knows his real identity. His parents dreamed of a throne but finished under the axe! When will his sorrows end? He addresses Leonora in heaven, since he thinks her dead. He asks her to remember him, to have pity on him, and to help him find the death he seeks.

Comment: The big tenor aria in the opera, "O tu che in seno agli angeli," is as convincingly melancholy and disoriented as Alvaro himself, signaled with a startling key change in the opening measure. Listen for the sad meanderings of the clarinet throughout the aria—this is the sort of accompaniment Verdi usually reserved for sopranos, not tenors.

The sounds of an argument are heard from the direction of the card game. Alvaro runs there, and returns with Don Carlo, who thanks Alvaro for saving his life in a quarrel over the card game. Alvaro asks how one of such obvious noble bearing got caught up in such a matter, and Carlo admits he is new to the area, having arrived only the day before. He asks the name of the man to whom he is indebted for his life, identifying himself as Don Felice de Bornos. Alvaro introduces himself as Don Federico Herreros, Captain of the Grenadiers. The hero of the army! exclaims Carlo. They shake hands and swear friendship. Shouts and trumpets are heard in the distance, and the two friends run off to battle.

Comment: Technically, this brief scene is a tenor-baritone duet, but it is not one of the three colossal duets people talk about in Forza. *Those are yet to come.*

Scene 2: The drawing room of a house near the fields of Velletri. Battle is raging in the distance.

Soldiers and a surgeon look out onto the battle. The grenadiers, led by their Captain "Herreros," are sweeping the enemy from the field. Aghast, the surgeon sees Herreros fall, though his men are rallied and carry the day. Voices cheer Spain and Italy. Alvaro is brought into the makeshift hospital on a stretcher, attended by Carlo. The surgeon looks to the wound. It is serious. Alvaro begs to be allowed to die, but Carlo assures him he will live and be rewarded with the order of Calatrava. Never! cries Alvaro. Carlo is stunned that his friend should be alarmed at the name of Calatrava. Alvaro asks the surgeon to leave, and beckons Carlo closer. Carlo must swear one favor to Alvaro in this solemn hour. Carlo agrees. Alvaro gives Carlo a key. In his bag he will find a package containing a secret that must die with him. It must be burned. Carlo agrees, and tells Alvaro to trust in heaven. Alvaro says he can die in peace. The surgeon returns with soldiers who carry Alvaro out of the room.

Comment: This duet, "Solenne in quest'ora," is the first and most famous of the three important tenor-baritone duets in Forza. Here Verdi abandoned himself to a gorgeous and sensual intimacy noticeably missing in his actual love duets. This brings up the question of eroticism between tenors and baritones throughout Verdi, a question that is so readily dismissed by critics that there must be something to it. This is the love duet Verdi never wrote for tenor and soprano. While I wouldn't say that Verdi was depicting an overt sexual attraction between two men, it seems clear that he perceived the inherent eroticism in male competition, conflict, and death, as celebrated in sport and war culture the world over. Specifically, Verdi understands the eroticism of death, which may be the central issue in the opera after all. Nowhere in Verdi are the tenor and the baritone required to blend their voices as beautifully as here.

Carlo muses alone. What a tremendous thing for such a courageous man to die. But why did he tremble at the name of Calatrava? Does he know the family story and their dishonor? Suddenly, Carlo is seized by a terrible thought. What if this man, this hero, is the vile seducer? He rifles through Alvaro's bag, but stops. What is he doing? Didn't he swear a solemn oath? He owes the Captain his life! But then, the Captain owes him his life as well. And what if this is that accursed Indian who stained his family honor? He will open the package! No one can see him here. Ah, but he can see himself! He throws the package down, telling the fatal vessel of his destiny to leave him. Oaths are sacred. But might there not be other proof in the Captain's bag? He looks through and finds a portrait. By heaven, it's Leonora! The Captain is Don Alvaro! Oh, let him live, that he himself may kill him! The surgeon opens the door, tells Carlo the Captain will live, and leaves. He is saved! says Carlo. What joy! Now at last he can wreak his vengeance. Oh, where is Leonora now? Here, perhaps? His joy would be complete if he could consecrate his sword with a single blow that would send both their souls into hell!

Comment: *Carlo's monologue is an excellent "duet-with-self" recitative, full of punchy declamations and meandering thought processes. The aria "Urna fatal" is a beautifully broad Verdian baritone cantabile. Carlo is still a human being at this point. When he sees the portrait of Leonora among Alvaro's possessions, he loses his humanity and becomes a demon. The surgeon pokes his head in and functions as the classic "messenger" in a grand scena. Carlo exclaims "Oh gioia!!" and launches into the only cabaletta in the opera, "Ah! egli è salvo!" (It was at this dramatic exclamation that the great baritone Leonard Warren died on stage at the Metropolitan Opera during a performance of* Forza *in 1960.) In this crucial scene the baritone moves from reason to vengeful resolution, and he must have the capacity to take the audience through the journey.*

Scene 3: A military encampment near Velletri.

A patrol of soldiers on reconnaissance enters cautiously, looks around the campsite, and leaves.

Comment: *This brief four-part chorus and its accompanying orchestration are greatly admired by musicians. The music has a certain formlessness that depicts the passage of time. When Alvaro enters, we can be assured enough time has passed for his wounds to have healed.*

Alvaro enters, melancholy. He prays to heaven in vain for oblivion. Carlo enters and asks if Alvaro is feeling better. Yes, replies Alvaro, as strong as before. Strong enough to fight a duel? asks Carlo. A duel? With whom? Carlo snidely asks if the Captain has ever received a message from Don Alvaro the Indian? Alvaro calls Carlo a traitor who broke his oath. No oaths were broken, insists Carlo; the portrait revealed all. He tells Alvaro to tremble before Don Carlo di Vargas. Alvaro is not afraid, but hesitates to fight with someone to whom he has sworn friendship. He attempts to explain that the Marquis was killed accidentally, and he searched for Leonora for a year only to find that she had died. Carlo tells him Leonora lives, and Alvaro is over-joyed. Now he is certain he would never fight Carlo, but when Carlo insists that he will also kill Leonora, the two swear to fight to the death. They draw swords and fight furiously, but a patrol comes from the camp and separates them. Carlo is dragged off, still swearing death to Alvaro. Alone, Alvaro decides he must turn to the monastery to seek the peace that eludes him in the world.

Comment: Verdi uses a clarinet to portray Alvaro's sadness at his entrance, the same instrument that has colored some of Leonora's reflections and Alvaro's aria. He picks up where she leaves off, and both are united in their morbid natures, even if physically separated. The ensuing duet with Carlo is dramatic in every sense of the word. It recalls Leonora's scene with Guardiano in that one character remains constant while the other bounces off that constancy. Here, Carlo is not volatile, but chillingly measured in his obsession to kill. Alvaro is more ambivalent, wanting friendship and even forgiveness from Carlo, but then calling for death in impulsive flights of fury. When the patrol separates the men, Alvaro, as the more mercurial of the two, is able to calm himself, while Carlo is dragged off in a rage.

Daylight breaks, and bugles sound reveille. Italian and Spanish soldiers appear, tending to their gear. Camp followers of all types also appear. Preziosilla enters, offering to tell fortunes. The soldiers call for drinks from the women. Trabuco enters with a box of trinkets, announcing his great bargains—scissors, pins, soap, to buy or sell. Soldiers offer to sell him various pieces of jewelry, but he dismisses it all as trash. Like his face, they mutter. Trabuco calms them and offers deals. Peasant women enter asking for bread. The war has destroyed their fields. They are followed by young recruits, who are homesick. The women of the camp cheer up the young men with promises of love, while Preziosilla tells them the other soldiers will laugh at their little-boy tears. A dance begins. Fra Melitone appears in the midst of the madness, momentarily caught up in a dance with camp followers. He extricates himself and begins to preach. He came from Spain to bandage wounds and save souls, and this is what he finds? Is this a Christian camp, or are they a bunch of Turks? This army has more bottles than battles! The whole world has gone to chaos, and do they know why? *Pro peccata vestra,* because of their sins! The Italian soldiers shout him down, but the Spaniards encourage him. He turns on both groups, and tells them they're all heretics! There will never be peace because these sewers of sin keep stinking up the world! The Italian soldiers try to beat him, but he gets away and runs off, still preaching. Preziosilla tells the Italians to let him go. Not very brave of them to pick fights with monks! She picks up a drum to rally the crowd's spirits, and leads them in a martial chorus. Rataplan!

Comment: This rather jarring scene, derived from Schiller's play Wallenstein's Lager, *came earlier in the original edition of the opera. Directors still fiddle around with the order of the scenes as they see fit. Our friends from Hornachuelos reappear here. Verdi indicated that Trabuco was to be understood as a Jewish peddler. To emphasize the point, he wrote some "bleating" music for him, which nineteenth-century composers fancied signified Jewish music by its similarity to synagogue chanting. Oy. Verdi does not get called on the carpet for using this racial stereotype, as Wagner does for doing the same thing in* Die Meistersinger von Nürnberg. *Fra Melitone's sermon is a rollicking comic number. The bottles-battles pun works equally in German, Italian, and English. Preziosilla leads all in the final "Rataplan" chorus, a mostly unaccompanied rondo chorus with only side drums providing the instrumentation and Preziosilla's vocal line imitating the fife. Rousing though it may be, it's also a big trial on one's nerves and everybody hates it.*

Act IV

Scene 1: The courtyard of the Monastery of Our Lady of the Angels at Hornachuelos.

Beggars are crying for Fra Melitone to hurry in ladling out their soup. Grumpily, he tells them he's not a tavern keeper. One woman demands more since she has six children. Melitone tells her she wouldn't have that problem if she spent her nights whipping herself and reciting rosaries. Guardiano approaches Melitone, who complains of the fertility of the poor. The beggars surround Melitone, who threatens them with the ladle over their heads, despite Guardiano's admonitions to be charitable. A woman complains that Father Raffaele is kinder, and Melitone responds that the saintly Father Raffaele was so kind that he has now retired to his room and left poor Melitone to deal with the rabble. The people clamor for Father Raffaele, until Melitone drives all the beggars out of the courtyard.

Comment: Melitone's antics can be truly funny in this scene. Verdi has obliged with sparkling conversational music. Guardiano is always on a separate plane from Melitone, and Verdi reestablishes the Father Superior's serene authority with a few bars of unmistakably ecclesiastical music.

The gate bells rings loudly. Melitone opens the door, and Don Carlo enters, cloaked, asking Melitone disdainfully if he's the gatekeeper. "This one's weird!" says Melitone to himself. Don Carlo asks for Father Raffaele. Again with Father Raffaele! mutters Melitone. There are two by that name, he explains. One is fat and bald, the other has such eyes! Carlo requests the one from hell, and Melitone leaves to find the second one. Alone, Carlo muses that Alvaro sought the hypocritical robes of the church in vain. Blood, blood alone will end the feud. Alvaro enters in monk's robes, shocked that Carlo is still alive. Yes, he answers, and now he intends to kill Alvaro, whether the monk will fight or not. Alvaro tells Carlo to leave. For five years he has sought oblivion in penance and service. When Carlo calls him a coward, he gets angry, but prays to God to forgive him the sin of anger. He gives his word as a monk that he had never stained Leonora's honor, but Carlo will not relent, and calls him a half-breed coward. At this insult, Alvaro demands a sword, but casts it down again. Carlo slaps him in the face. Alvaro picks up the sword again, and they rush out of the courtyard threatening each other with death.

Comment: Worlds collide when Melitone and Carlo have their brief interaction. Melitone calling Carlo weird (goffo) must be unique in opera and underscores the gulf separating the two worlds of Forza. *The duet for Carlo and Alvaro recalls the previous one in that Alvaro must cover more dramatic and vocal territory than the obsessed Carlo. They run off crossing swords and singing a unison melody, since they have for the moment become indistinguishable in their rage.*

Scene 2: A hermitage in the mountains, merely a cave with a door on it. Above it is a bell.

Leonora prays to God for peace. All these years of mortification have not erased Alvaro from her heart. Could she not at least die and seek peace in heaven?

Comment: "Pace, pace, mio Dio!" is the big soprano aria, popular as a concert piece since it shows the soprano range at its widest scope. As successful as it may be as a set piece, however, the aria really comes alive in context. Verdi begins the scene with a repetition of the three-chord fate motif. Leonora, absent for an act and a half, reappears in her solitude, contrasting with the strife of the previous scene. The aria repeats phrases and motifs. She has withdrawn into an entirely self-reflexive world, both physically and spiritually. The cycles in the aria's structure let us know that this is a world of fixed obsession. The pleas for peace perpetuate the obsession rather than break it.

She hears sounds in the distance. Who dares violate the sanctity of the refuge? A curse upon him! She retreats rapidly into her cave and closes the door. In the distance a dying man calls for confession. Alvaro enters, staring at his sword dripping with the blood of a Vargas. He knocks at the hermitage door, insisting the monk inside hear the confession of a dying man. A voice from within refuses. Alvaro begs. Leonora rings the bell above her cave and cries for help, also telling the rash man at her door to flee and avoid the wrath of heaven. The sound of the voice startles Alvaro, and when Leonora appears at the door, they recognize each other. He tells her not to come near him—he is dripping with blood. He had tried to avoid the fight, but finally could not, and killed the man. And the man was her brother! She runs toward the grove from which the dying man's screams came. Alvaro decries the cruel destiny that mocks him. A scream is heard, and Leonora returns, supported by Padre Guardiano. Even dying, Carlo could not forgive, but stabbed Leonora with his last breath. Alvaro cries out damnations, but Guardiano admonishes him not to surrender to fury while Leonora's soul begins its flight to heaven. Leonora also orders Alvaro to weep and pray. Alvaro senses his own redemption. Guardiano orders Alvaro to kneel, and Leonora tells him they will meet again in heaven. Leonora dies. "Dead!" says the guilt-ridden Alvaro. "Ascended to God," corrects Padre Guardiano.

Comment: The finale, predictably, is handled very quickly and with a great economy of expression. Leonora rushes offstage to get stabbed with shocking swiftness. Her staggering return to the stage lets her at least declaim her feelings with some poignancy. The membrane that has separated her conflicting selves is broken at last. The final trio is magnificently simple and moves toward a place of resignation. Leonora contemplates heaven (harps, flutes, and sweet strings of course, but nowhere more effectively than here), and Alvaro lets all his passion, including his melancholy self-loathing, dissolve into phrases of acceptance. We can actually believe his change of heart. Many operas end with a portrayal of a woman ascending to heaven, but no other scenes depict the effect of heavenly intercession on the living quite so well as this.

Don Carlos

PREMIERE: Paris Opéra, 1867. Libretto by Joseph Méry and Camille du Locle.

THE NAME

If the opera is spelled *Don Carlos,* it's in French; if it's *Don Carlo,* it's in Italian. *Carlos* is pronounced with equal stress on the two syllables, making it sound like "Car-LOS." The French prefer to keep foreign spellings and wait until the pronunciation phase before doing violence to foreign languages. The Italians are perhaps more honest and just translate the whole name.

FOR MANY OF US, the world can be divided into two populations: those of us who think that *Don Carlos* is the Greatest Thing That Ever Happened To Art, and everybody else.

Don Carlos is what might be called a "problem" opera. It certainly does not have the smooth symmetry of *Aida* or the unflagging orchestral mastery of *Otello* and *Falstaff.* The story is as huge as the world, and it sometimes sags under its own weight. But the score reaches unique heights. For all its unmanageability, this story touched Verdi in places no other story did. The result is a sprawling, ambitious behemoth that attempts, and occasionally achieves, everything.

Don Carlos, based on the Schiller play of the same name, is essentially the story of the private intersecting lives of six individuals at the court of Philip II of Spain, around the year 1560. The fate of the entire world hangs on the details, emotions, and actions of the lead characters. Everything in this story, then, is actually bigger than life. It is Verdi's longest opera, running up to five hours in performance. Stylistically, it is a hybrid, and has therefore sometimes earned a touch of scorn from those scholars who prefer art they can file into neat categories. *Don Carlos* was composed for the Paris Opéra, which meant certain conventions had to be followed. There are set choruses, a ballet (almost never performed now), show-stopping arias, standard duets, trios, a quartet, and even a rip-snorting "production number." Most people concede that Verdi was generally successful within these forms, and the big arias he wrote for soprano, mezzo, baritone, and bass (the tenor of the title has no aria in this work, interestingly enough) are often cited as the best he ever wrote for each voice respectively.

In between the "hits," however, Verdi experimented wildly with unconventional forms. In some of these he was so successful that he appears to have scared himself. Most commentators now agree that the relative conservatism of the subsequent opera *Aida* was in large part a reaction to *Don Carlos*—an attempt to consolidate everything he knew before leaping into the unknown territory of his final masterpieces.

Be all that as it may, *Don Carlos* must please or fail on its own merits. One problem many people have with this work is its overall tone. The curtain rises on a chorus of starving, freezing, war-weary peasants. After a brief interlude of young love in near-bloom (about seven minutes), there follow four and a half hours of gloom, doom, and darkness. The characters pray to tombs, and the tombs occasionally answer. There are only two scenes that can be played in "daylight," and one is full of menace and the other is an auto-da-fé. Throughout much of the action, a chorus of monks insists that the only solace available to humans is the grave. Death may well be considered the true leading character. Whether you enter into the mind-set of this opera fully depends largely on how much you are able to meditate on death for five hours.

This is only the first of the problems with *Don Carlos.* During the long rehearsal process at the Paris Opéra, Verdi realized the work was running too long even by Parisian standards and made several cuts. Some of these passages, such as the peasants' chorus at the very beginning, have survived intact and can be used or discarded by productions today. Others are more difficult to splice into the score. One ravishing duet in Act IV, Scene 1, was lost until 1970, when it was discovered in a dusty Parisian archive. *Don Carlo* was first given in Italian at London's Covent Garden in 1867, just before the Italian premiere at Bologna. These versions used all of the music that had been produced in Paris including the ballet. *Carlo,* however, failed in Naples in 1872. Convinced the opera was simply too long for Italian tastes, Verdi dropped the first act and the ballet for a version that premiered at La Scala in 1884. For years this four-act version in Italian was standard. Another edition of the score, however, was issued in Modena in 1886, with much of the original Act I restored.

Until quite recently *Don Carlos* was seldom produced outside of France. For the past fifteen years or so, it has proven quite popular in the United States and England. The argument for *Don Carlos* in French is quite convincing and simple: It was written in French and should be preformed that way. Budden was adamant about this issue, citing several points in the score where the French setting is clearly more appropriate than the Italian. The Italian has much to recommend it, however. Every instance the francophiles can cite where the French text suits the music better than the Italian can be countered by an opposite instance where the Italian works better. *("Justice! Justice!"* cries the queen in the study scene [Act IV, Scene 1]—using a word with three, or, rather, two and a half syllables, over four notes of music, as in the Italian *"Giustizia!")* The fact is that *Don Carlos* works perfectly well in French or Italian. If your local company is performing it, go see it whatever language it's in.

CAST OF CHARACTERS

PHILIP II, KING OF SPAIN (PHILIPPE/FILIPPO) *(bass-baritone)* Philip ruled Spain from 1556 to 1598. He also ruled Portugal, the Spanish Netherlands (including modern Belgium), Milan, Genoa, southern Italy and Sicily, a chunk of eastern France, his eponymous islands the Philippines, and, at least in theory, the entire New World. He inherited the throne of Spain when his father, the Holy Roman Emperor Charles V, abdicated and retired to a monastery, where he presumably died. The role of Philip requires a bass who can portray magnificence and vulnerability.

ELISABETH DE VALOIS, PRINCESS OF FRANCE (ELISABETH/ ELISABETTA) *(soprano)* Daughter of Henri II of France, and from Act II on, third wife of Philip II, and therefore Queen of Spain. A truly regal role, our prima donna must convince us of her bloodline with her every gesture, sing a hell of a lot of exhausting music over the course of a marathon night, and appear young.

DON CARLOS (CARLOS/CARLO) *(tenor)* The Prince (Infante) of Spain, the only son of Philip II by his deceased first wife. Although Carlos famously has no aria to sing, this is one of the most challenging roles in the Verdi repertory, and many of the great tenors have choked on it. He sings a great deal of music, often in a frenzied state. Carlos is also, like Otello, a challenge to the acting abilities of the tenor. If we do not believe that this is a genuinely tortured individual, then we will be rooting to have him handed over to the Inquisition at the earliest convenient moment.

RODRIGO, THE MARQUIS (later DUKE) OF POSA (RODRIGUE/ RODRIGO) *(baritone)* A grandee of Spain, often just called Posa. Posa is an idealistic revolutionary amid Europe's most severe court. While some see Posa as the true hero of this drama, others point out that he actually causes at least as much trouble as the supposed bad guys.

THE PRINCESS EBOLI *(mezzo-soprano)* A lady of the Spanish court. Historically, the Princess Eboli was a famous femme fatale at the court of Philip II. She came from the great and notoriously proud Mendoza family, and wore an eye patch. Eboli is a vain schemer whose self-serving addictions cause a great deal of trouble. Verdi thought of her bluntly as a slut (his word, though he said it in French). The great challenge of this role is to win a measure of the audience's sympathy by sheer vocal chutzpa.

A MONK *(bass)* Although this might be called a comprimario role, Verdi was careful to request a premier bass for it, since he is at the center of the drama. The Monk should have a voice that immediately commands awe.

THE GRAND INQUISITOR OF SPAIN *(bass)* Also a role for a premier bass, the Grand Inquisitor should basically scare you to death with his very appearance, let alone his voice. He needs a voice every bit as commanding as the Monk, yet ideally they should have different timbres. Verdi intended the Grand Inquisitor to be played as a blind man of about ninety years of age.

TYBALT (THIBAULT/TEBALDO) *(soprano)* A young page of Elisabeth de Valois. A very rare case of a *travesti* ("pants") role in a Verdi opera, the other case being Oscar in *Ballo*. Tybalt's role is not quite as central as Oscar's, yet the high soprano voice is crucial in some of the ensembles to balance out the otherwise bottom-heavy cast. Verdi specified a prima donna for the role, which brings the grand total of star singers (in a perfect world, anyway) to eight.

THE COUNT OF LERMA *(tenor)* The good Count generally functions as a herald, although he too takes an occasional part in the ensembles. Ideally he has a pleasant and clear voice.

A HEAVENLY VOICE *(soprano)* A disembodied character, making a single appearance at the end of Act III.

THE OPERA

Act I

Setting: The forest of Fontainebleau in France, near the royal castle.

Foresters and peasants are at work, freezing in the snow and nearly starving to death. The winter and the long war with Spain have reduced them to misery. From afar, they hear the horns of the royal hunt. Elisabeth, Princess of France, appears on her way to the hunt, attended by her page Tybalt and others. The people approach Elisabeth. She addresses them as friends, and asks what they desire. The women ask for alms for one of their number whose husband has not returned from the wars and is presumed dead. Elisabeth gives the widow a gold chain and tells the people to take hope. The Spanish envoy has arrived. Peace should be concluded shortly. Looking forward to better days, the people pray for a young husband and a crown for their Princess. She smiles and moves on with her retinue. The people disperse.

Don Carlos emerges from the trees, where he has been concealing himself. He addresses the forest of Fontainebleau, to which he has come with the Spanish envoys, risking the wrath of his terrible father Philip of Spain. Now he has seen Elisabeth, his betrothed, and is filled with love for her. The hunting horns are now distant, and night has fallen. How will he find his way back to the palace? Just then, Tybalt appears, calling for help, with Elisabeth following behind. They have become separated from the hunt and are lost. Carlos bows deeply to Elisabeth, introducing himself as a Spaniard in the retinue of the Count of Lerma, the ambassador. Tybalt spots the lights of Fontainebleau in the distance, and Elisabeth sends him to the palace to fetch her litter. She will wait with the foreigner, since she has faith in Spanish honor. Tybalt leaves. Carlos gathers branches and starts a fire to warm Elisabeth. She anxiously asks him news from Madrid, especially of the Infante Carlos, to whom she will be married by the peace treaty. Will the Infante love her? Carlos gallantly tells her she has nothing to fear, the Infante already loves her, and she will be happy. He hands her a locket with the portrait of the Infante. Trembling, she opens it, and recognizes Carlos, who falls to his knees and declares his love for her. A cannon shot is heard, signaling the signing of the treaty and general rejoicing. Carlos and Elisabeth swear their love. Tybalt approaches merrily, followed by torchbearers, asking that he may never be parted from Elisabeth. She grants his wish. Tybalt salutes her as Queen, wife of Philip of Spain. She protests that she is to be married to his son the Infante, but Tybalt tells her Henri her father has awarded her to Philip. Elisabeth and Carlos are stunned and wonder if death would not be preferable.

The Count of Lerma and courtiers appear in the wood, followed by the peasants, all rejoicing at Elisabeth's elevation to the throne of Spain, while she and Carlos lament the fatal hour. Lerma formally announces the betrothal, but says the King of France insists that his daughter take this step of her own will. Does she consent to the marriage with the King of Spain and the Indies? The peasant women implore her to end their suffering. Steeling herself, Elisabeth assents to the marriage. The people rejoice as Carlos and Elisabeth bemoan their cruel destiny.

Comment: The opening chorus of starving peasants is often cut, since Verdi himself made the cut before the premiere, though it is effective and sets the tone of misery so crucial to this opera. In any case, we always see Elisabeth at least mime her charity to the widow. Carlos's recitative and arietta, "Je l'ai vue/Io la vidi" (his only solo), is sweet and pretty. This is a pleasant young love, but Carlos's passion only stirs later, when all are informed that Elisabeth will be wed to the King, Carlos's father. Musically, this suggests that the overriding passion of Carlos's life is not love for Elisabeth, as he says, but hatred for his father. His love seems to develop as a response to his father hatred. This was also a subject near to Verdi's heart.

When the entire Act I is cut, in one of the several heinous four-act versions around, Carlos's arietta is transferred to the next scene, in the gloomy cloister of San Yuste. If they interpolated the "Macarena," it wouldn't be a worse violation of tone.

In their all-too-brief moment of happiness, Carlos and Elisabeth sing a short and not very extravagant love duet. Verdi does not want to create so much joy onstage as to unbalance the opera as a whole. They are almost immediately confronted with the news that she is to marry the King. Thus the only remotely happy moment in the whole opera is cut short.

Act II

Scene 1: The tomb of the Holy Roman Emperor Charles V, father of King Philip II, at the Monastery of San Yuste in Spain. A grill separates parts of the chapel. Dawn.

From behind the grill, monks are praying for the soul of the late Emperor, who is now merely dust, and whose proud soul now trembles at the feet of the Lord. One Monk kneels at the tomb. He prays for the Emperor, who presumed to rule the world, but who forgot the One who rules even emperors. The monks' choir chants in prayer that God's anger be diverted from the sinning Emperor. God alone is great, cries the kneeling Monk, praying for mercy, while the choir repeats the cry that God alone is great. A bell tolls.

Comment: *If this scene doesn't make your hair stand up on end, something is seriously wrong. The Monk, who may or may not be a ghost, is clearly meant to represent at least a voice from the beyond. The solo is a gorgeous lyrical passage sung largely in the lowest reaches of the bass voice. The monks' chant is insistent and relentless, ending with the tolling of a bell signified with magnificent economy by two flutes each holding a note. Wagner would have taken fifteen minutes to create the same effect.*

Carlos enters, looking for peace from his torments of love in the place where his grandfather Charles V sought solace. The Monk complains that the world's troubles follow him even here, and tells Carlos the peace he seeks can be found only in God. He leaves. Carlos is amazed. The Monk seemed like Charles V himself, whose ghost, they say, wanders this monastery. The Marquis of Posa enters and embraces his Prince, who accepts Posa's consolation in this time of need. Posa says the hour has struck. The people of Flanders, suffering under Spanish rule, call on Don Carlos to save them, but what is the matter with the Prince? Carlos confesses that he is struck with an insane love—for Elisabeth. "Your mother!" cries Posa. "Great God!" Carlos worries that even Posa has turned from him, but Posa denies it. He suggests that Carlos go at once to Flanders, where the oppressed people will welcome him as a savior. A bell tolls. The King and Queen are coming to the chapel to pray. Carlos falters, but Posa rallies him and tells him to ask God for the strength to dedicate himself to a heroic struggle for the people of Flanders. Carlos and Posa swear blood brotherhood before God.

The King and Queen enter, preceded by monks. Carlos masters

his emotion under the suspicious glance of his father, and Elisabeth starts at the sight of Carlos. The King and Queen pray at the tomb while the monks chant for the soul of the proud Emperor. A bell tolls. Carlos cries out that he has lost Elisabeth, she belongs to the King, and stumbles, supported again by Posa, who tells him to be strong. The King, Queen, and monks leave. Carlos and Posa swear their undying love and devotion to freedom.

Comment: This is the oath duet of the opera, "Dieu, tu semas dans nos ames"/"Dio, che nell'alma infondere," *famous from concert programs and recitals. "Serious" musicians fault it for tinselly effect, but others rave about its nobility and humanity. The key to the duet is its context. Carlos and Posa swear loyalty to each other, and their music is deftly swept up into the magnificent fanfare of the royal procession. At the end of the scene, the two desperately return to their oath as a form of salvation. Individual concerns are swept into the political whirl throughout this opera, but death and loss remain at the center of everything.*

Scene 2: A lovely garden outside the gates of the Yuste Monastery.

The ladies of the court are enjoying the shade of the garden while the Queen, who alone among women is allowed into the monastery, prays. Tybalt enters with the Princess Eboli, who suggests a song to pass the time. Eboli sings the Veil Song, about the Moorish King Ahmet of Granada, who saw a veiled lady in his garden. Ahmet, saying he has tired of the queen, proposes the veiled lady join him. After protestations of love, Ahmet convinces the mysterious lady to remove her veil. By Allah, it's the queen! Tybalt and the ladies chime in at the refrain, singing in praise of veils and their importance to love.

Comment: In the Veil Song, we get to hear a mezzo sing roulades, trills, and strange faux-Moorish decorations in the lowest ranges of her voice, followed by a sprightly chorus. It's all very welcome after the gloomy previous scenes. The scenery should echo this "lightening up" effect, since it is clearly daytime and we have moved outside.

The Queen enters, clearly sad. Tybalt announces the Marquis of Posa, grandee of Spain. Posa bears a letter from Elisabeth's mother, the Queen of France, which he holds up to the ladies. He passes it to Elisabeth along with another note no one has seen, which he quietly urges her to read. The Princess Eboli flirts with Posa, asking him about the famed grace of the ladies of France, where the Marquis has recently been. Posa talks of a tournament at which the King of France is expected to joust, and gallantly flatters the Princess at the expense of the French ladies, the whole time keeping her away from Elisabeth. The Queen trembles reading the note, which is from Carlos, advising her by their sacred memories to trust Posa. Elisabeth composes herself and thanks Posa, permitting him to demand a royal favor. Not for himself, but for another, the Marquis replies.

The Infante Carlos is suffering from an undefined affliction. Though the King's heart is closed to him, he begs a word from his mother Elisabeth. The Queen wonders if she should receive Carlos. Eboli, meanwhile, comments to herself that she has seen Carlos go pale and tremble. There is only one possible answer—Carlos must be in love with Eboli! Elisabeth agrees to receive Carlos, who is announced directly. The ladies of the court retire, including Eboli, who is politely pulled away by Posa. The Countess of Aremberg, the Queen's lady-in-waiting that day, withdraws at a sign from Elisabeth.

Comment: *Posa's description of Carlos's affliction is a graceful, rather old-fashioned solo, except that it lies very high in the range. The baritone must convey courtly elegance while not choking on it. Eboli is rather ridiculous in this scene. Now that we have simultaneous translations in most opera houses, the audience usually explodes with laughter when she deduces, with zero evidence, that she must be the cause of Carlos's swooning. The mezzo will have her moment of revenge on the audience in Act IV.*

In a very melancholy state, Carlos asks a favor of the Queen. The air of Spain is killing him. He would go to Flanders, but the King will not hear him. "My son," she says, but he cannot bear that name. Addressing him as Prince, Elisabeth says she will ask the King to grant this, and starts to leave. Is that all she has to say to him? Not a word of pity, a glance? a tear? She asks him not to judge her heart, but rather to consider her commitment to duty. He declares his happiness dead forever, but asks her to continue speaking, since her voice is a paradise to him. She prays for his consolation, and bids him farewell in this life, further confessing that to be with him would be paradise. In joy at this disclosure, Carlos thanks God and suddenly falls to the ground. Terrified, Elisabeth goes to him, but her voice restores him. He defies the earth to swallow him and thunder to strike his brow. He declares he loves Elisabeth, and takes her in his arms. She retreats in a panic. What would he do? Kill his father and with his blood-stained hands drag his mother to the altar? He flees, and she falls to her knees in prayer.

Comment: For all its epic grandeur, we begin to realize in this scene that Don Carlos *is really a series of one-on-one confrontations punctuated by profound soliloquies and a few large ensembles. The problem is that neither the soliloquies nor the ensembles will make any sense, musically or emotionally, unless great attention is paid to these "duets." In this moment between Elisabeth and Carlos, every line or two is a new melody while building toward a single overriding structure. It is absolutely masterful. The historical Don Carlos suffered from many undefined illnesses, and most directors find it convenient to have him played as an epileptic. The tenor's acting abilities, if they exist, are greatly challenged in this scene.*

Tybalt hurries in announcing the King, who enters with Posa and the entire court. Why, asks Philip, was the Queen alone? Who was the lady-in-waiting on duty? Did she not know the rule of the court? The Countess of Aremberg approaches the King. Stiffly, he informs the Countess that she will return to France in the morning. The courtiers are struck by this insult to the Queen. Elisabeth approaches the Countess, urging her not to cry. Elisabeth will always hold her dear in her heart. The Countess will return to their beautiful homeland, but she must not reveal the outrage the Queen has suffered in Spain. Tearfully, all retire except the King and Posa.

Comment: Elisabeth's solo, "O ma chère compagne"/Non pianger, mia compagna," *is a long, plaintive* cri de coeur. *The romanza shows what a soprano is made of, since it requires an endless legato line floated over almost two octaves. (The really great sopranos make you think it has an even wider range.) Grief must be stated in oblique terms here, since Philip is still present onstage and the Queen is letting the whole court know of her unhappiness while not coming right out and telling the King to go to hell. She must convince you that she is wounded, yet still be regal. Vocal subtext is everything.*

The poor Countess never gets to sing a line. Expect her to compensate by wearing the loveliest gown imaginable.

Posa is about to withdraw with the others, but the King detains him. Why has the Marquis never asked a favor from the King? The proud Posa replies that he needs no favor, since he, at least, is protected by the laws of the realm. Philip notes Posa's audacity, but is there nothing the King can do for him? Not for me, replies Posa, but for others. "Speak," commands the King. Posa explains that he has just returned from Flanders, once so fair, now drenched in blood and suffering because of Spanish rule. Philip defends his bloody policy, saying it has bought the peace of the rest of the world. Posa asks if death can plant seeds for the future, and Philip counters that in Spain the people are submissive and faithful. He offers the same to Flanders. Such peace, exclaims Posa, is the peace of the grave! He begs the King to consider the judgment of history. Now Flanders is nothing but suffering, but with one word the King could change the whole world! Philip finds Posa a dreamer full of youthful naiveté, but not another word. The King has heard nothing. Posa need not fear him, but he warns the Marquis to beware the Grand Inquisitor. From now on the Marquis will be attached to the King's person. Posa begs to be left in freedom, but Philip insists. He needs honest and brave men around him amid all the sycophants. Perhaps Posa will also learn what personal agonies the King must endure. Posa is astounded by this intimate revelation from the cold King. Yes, says Philip, suspicions about the Queen, Carlos . . . Posa defends Carlos, but Philip cries that Carlos has taken his dearest treasure from him! Composing himself after this unseemly outburst, Philip grants Posa alone permission to speak to the Queen. But Posa must beware the Grand Inquisitor.

Comment: *The confrontation between Philip and Posa is really the heart of the opera in many ways, and is worth a close look since it contains many of the opera's glories as well as its problems. Verdi kept tinkering with this scene for years. As a result, we have three versions to choose from. The French version has an entirely different feel, with a much lighter orchestral accompaniment, while the Italian versions are less inhibited (or cruder, depending on your point of view). When Posa thanks God that he has been able to speak truth to the King, he does so in a gorgeous cascading line. In the Italian versions, the line is repeated by the orchestra. It is a heart-tugging but effective device more typical of his earlier works, and it can be more convincing than the French unrepeated vocal fragment. Later, after Posa's startling interjection "The peace of the tomb!," there is a hushed tension in the French. The Italian versions accompany Posa's outbursts with a tremendous minor chord thundered through brass, percussion, and sustained trilling strings. These variations reflect their texts. Compare:* "Arrière paix! La paix du cimetière!" *versus* "Orrenda orrenda pace! La pace è dei sepolcri!" *The French is sneering and disdainful. The Italian slaps you across the face. This work, sometimes to its detriment, has a foot in both French and Italian opera.*

In any version, the tension of the scene and its problems are based on the two characters in conflict. On the one hand, they are individuals who appear to like and need each other in some sense, and yet they are each representative of political and philosophical systems that will never reach concordance. The best productions embrace the impossible nature of this confrontation.

The ending of the scene is particularly problematic. Philip's hushed warning "Beware the Grand Inquisitor!" *strikes most people as an anticlimax. If the conductor and performers have managed to sustain the tension throughout, however, it is stark and haunting.*

Act III

Scene 1: Nighttime in the Queen's gardens.

Although the King is keeping prayer vigil on this night before his coronation, the court is frolicking at a great soirée in the Queen's gardens. Elisabeth appears, with Eboli. The Queen is already fatigued, and expresses a need to pray. Let Eboli wear her veil and mask, and be queen of the festivities. She retires. Eboli dons the Queen's mask and veil and delights in the role.

Comment: This scene is often cut, but the drama that follows makes more sense if we see the two ladies exchange costumes.

The revelers assemble for a great masque, "La Peregrina." In a beautiful fairy grotto, the Queen of the Waters appears, determined to punish a fisherman for entering her kingdom, but a page from the court of Philip II appears and informs her that the fisherman is seeking a pearl for the King of Spain. The Queen of the Waters offers all her treasures to the great Philip, but no pearl is worthy. They must all be combined to form one superb pearl. The pearls gather in a golden shell to form one, La Peregrina, excelling all pearls except Cleopatra's fabled one. The great pearl is, in fact, the Queen of Spain (actually Eboli), and all pay her homage while a Spanish national hymn is sung.

Comment: Never expect to see this very long and elaborate ballet performed. The excellent music is available on recordings.

The great pearl, La Peregrina, was part of the Spanish crown jewels, has an interesting history, and still exists. It was a gift from Philip II to his second wife, Mary Tudor of England. La Peregrina can be seen in Velaquez's portraits of the wives of Philip IV. It is one inch long. Joseph Bonaparte took it with him when he surrendered the crown of Spain, and it landed in the possession of his nephew, Prince Louis Napoleon, later Napoleon III. During his exile years in London, Louis Napoleon sold the pearl to get some quick cash. In 1969 it was sold at a Sotheby's auction to Elizabeth Taylor for $37,000. Although Ms. Taylor has sold many of her fabled jewels for the excellent charities she supports, La Peregrina has not been sold, since it was damaged some years ago when the dog chewed it. Or at least this is what I've been told.

All depart. Carlos arrives alone, reading a note he assumes to be from the Queen, telling him to be at the garden fountain at midnight.

Eboli arrives, wearing the Queen's veil, and Carlos, fooled by the disguise, expresses his love for her. She takes off her mask, and Carlos back off, terrified. Eboli wonders at this transformation. Then she understands—Carlos loves the Queen! He begs for mercy. Posa enters, telling Eboli that Carlos is mad and raving. She must not believe anything he says. She dismisses Posa. Even though he is now the King's favorite, she too is a powerful enemy. She thinks angrily of the Queen, that sly fox in a mask of saintly virtue. Posa pulls his dagger and aims for Eboli, but Carlos stops him. Bravely, she tells Posa to strike, since he will regret letting a wounded woman loose. Posa warns her of God's justice, while Carlos begs to be swallowed by the earth. Eboli leaves in a fury.

Posa tells Carlos he is in grave danger and should hand over any incriminating papers immediately, but Carlos hesitates to give his secrets to the King's new favorite. Hurt, Posa asks if Carlos can doubt his friendship. Handing over the papers, Carlos throws himself in Posa's arms.

Comment: *This is a difficult scene to pull off without laughter, though the vengeance trio before Eboli storms off should help restore the tone. Plainly, it is cruel to the Eboli character to cut the beginning of this scene. Unless we have seen her exchange costumes with the Queen earlier, at the Queen's request, she looks like even more of a scheming vengeful bitch than she needs to. The trio shows Eboli as a harpy, full of vengeful bloodlust. It's the first time a character in the opera has let go of all pretenses and just declared his or her true emotions. After she leaves, Posa and Carlos reaffirm their friendship to the strains of their oath duet.*

Scene 2: The plaza in front of the Cathedral of Valladolid. (Sometimes this scene is set in front of the Church of Our Lady of Atocha in Madrid.) Philip's formal coronation is taking place inside the cathedral, to be celebrated with an auto-da-fé, a burning of heretics condemned by the Inquisition.

The people greet the joyful, glorious day. A funeral march plays while monks lead the condemned of the Inquisition toward the pyres.

The entire court, including Elisabeth, Posa, Tybalt, and the grandees, process from the palace to the steps of the cathedral. The people turn to the cathedral, begging to see their King. Philip appears at the doors of the cathedral, beneath a canopy. The lords bow, the people kneel. Philip speaks, then descends the stairs, taking the Queen's arm. Suddenly Carlos appears with six Flemish deputies, who throw themselves at the King's feet. Posa and Elisabeth fear for Carlos. The deputies beg the King for mercy for their suffering country, but Philip dismisses them as rebels and heretics. Elisabeth, Posa, Tybalt, and all the people plead for clemency for the Flemings, while monks urge the King to judge them as traitors. Philip remains unmoved. Carlos demands Flanders as a personal fiefdom. Philip declares him mad, and tries to continue on his way. Carlos, raving, does the unthinkable and draws his sword on the King. The King orders the Prince disarmed, but no one dares to move against Carlos until Posa calmly walks over and asks for his sword. "You, Rodrigo?" asks Carlos, betrayed. Posa kneels before Philip and hands him the sword, which the King takes. He grants Posa the title of duke for this action, and the procession continues as Carlos is left in despair. The people again salute the glorious day, as the pyres of the heretics are seen blazing in the distance. A voice from heaven welcomes the souls of the unjustly condemned. The monks resume their death chant, and the people cry "Glory to God."

Comment: *The opening chorus is a very jolly tune for people who are quivering under an oppressive church, as we were told in the Philip-Posa duet. The auto-da-fé is a great sprawling spectacle that is always compared unfavorably with the Triumphal Scene in* Aida. *Despite an abundance of excellent music here, unclear issues and characters prevent us from getting a satisfying overview of the situation. How are we to understand Philip? Is he enjoying the ghastly spectacle, or is he under compulsion to attend? Carlos, too, is difficult to fathom here. When he draws his sword on the King, it seems less heroic than just the next episode in his unresolved and exhibitionistic Oedipal complex. Finally, there is the issue of the heavenly voice at the end, which many find to be the last word in schmaltz. In* *recent productions it has been typical to have everyone freeze and have Carlos alone hear the heavenly voice, as a projection of his delirious mind.*

Act IV

Scene 1: The King's private study in the Royal Palace. Candles are burning low.

Alone at his desk, Philip muses as if in a dream. She never loved him. Her heart is closed to him. He remembers the expression on her face when she first arrived from France and saw his gray hairs. He stirs and wonders where he is. The candles are spent, dawn is breaking. Another sleepless night has passed. The King can never sleep. Treason will brew and his wife will be taken from him. He will sleep someday, dressed in his royal mantle, in the stone crypts of the Escorial. Treason and faithlessness will triumph. She doesn't love him. She never loved him.

Comment: *In* "Elle ne m'aime pas"/"Ella giammai m'amò," *we at last see Philip the man venting his true feelings in perhaps the greatest bass aria in the repertory. It also gives Philip the humanity that makes this opera a real tragedy of individuals rather than a Manichaean conflict of good and bad guys.*

The aria is preceded by an orchestral prelude of rolling, repeating phrases in the strings, shivers in the winds, and an agonizing cello solo— the definitive insomnia music. Philip's ruminations on his wife's coldness are expressed almost in gasps. The vocal line does not broaden until he thinks about death, the only possible consolation. The sudden switches of focus from Elisabeth to the state of the realm are superb. This is the key to the opera: the nexus—here the identity—between the personal and the political.

The Count of Lerma announces the Grand Inquisitor and withdraws. The blind Inquisitor is led in by two monks, asking if he is before the King. Yes, Philip answers, addressing the old man kindly as "my father." Philip seeks counseling and advice. The Infante is an armed rebel against the crown! The Inquisitor asks what the King intends to do about that. All or nothing, is the reply. Let Carlos flee or else let the sword . . . "Well?" asks the Inquisitor. "If I strike down my son, will you absolve me?" asks Philip. "The peace of the world is worth the blood of a rebel son," is the reply. But can a Christian sacrifice his own son? God, explains the Inquisitor, sacrificed His. Can nature and blood keep silent? Yes, before faith. Very well then. The Inquisitor asks if Philip II has nothing more to say to him. No? Then let him speak to Philip II!

There is one who is even more dangerous than the Prince, a radical whose notions threaten the hard-earned peace of the land. And yet this one is protected by the King! Philip protests that the man is his only friend. By what right, asks the Inquisitor, can Philip call himself King if he seeks out equals? Furiously, Philip orders the "priest" to keep silent. But the old man only accuses more boldly. The spirit of the innovators has entered the King. Yet the church is a kindly mother, and accepts true repentance. Let the King hand over to the Inquisition the Marquis of Posa! "Never!" thunders the King. The old man hints that the King himself is not above being brought before the Inquisition. He will not let Philip destroy his life's work. Why, he asks, did the King call forth the shade of Samuel? What is he doing there? What did the King want of him? He pounds the floor with his staff, summoning his monks and preparing to leave. Philip asks that peace be restored between them. "Peace?" says the Inquisitor, leaving. Philip asks that the past be forgotten. "Perhaps," says the Inquisitor, from beyond the doorway. The King's pride, muses Philip, must bow before the priest's pride.

Comment: *Nowhere in the opera are the fear and gloom so central to this story painted in more vivid tones than in this scene. The orchestra plods through its deepest reaches, while the intimidating bass-baritone Philip is confronted by the even scarier bass-profundo Inquisitor. The man is not afraid of anything. He even manages to make the word "Sire" (two syllables in both French and Italian) sound disdainful, the way a New York cab driver can turn the word "lady" into an insult. The first time he says it, it ends on the lowest note he sings. (Verdi also wrote in an optional* note even lower—an E below the bass staff, which is generally only audible to some breeds of dogs.) The second time he sings it, it is his highest note.

Beyond its obvious symbolism as the epic battle of church and state, this scene also keeps sight of the individual characters who enact that struggle. The early part of the scene is the most formulaic. Philip asks questions about Carlos, and gets solid, if terrifying, answers from the Grand Inquisitor. Each question and answer rise a step in the scale. It's like an antiphonal catechism. Clearly, Philip is quite ready to dispose of Carlos. The real issue is Posa. The Inquisitor thunders forth his anathema of the Marquis, capped by a brass fanfare that has all the weight of God's own judgment.

The Queen enters, furiously demanding justice. Her jewel casket has been stolen! She will have justice! The King calmly replies that he has her jewel box. Will she not open it? Then he will. She asks heaven for help. Inside the box, Philip is furious to find a portrait of Carlos. Does she dare to admit it to him? Yes, she admits it. She was once engaged to the Prince, but came to Spain, pure and undefiled, in deference to her duty. Does the King dare to doubt a Daughter of France? A Queen of Spain? Philip notes her boldness, yet she has only seen his tender side. Let everyone beware his fury once it's stirred! And for what crime? asks the Queen. Betrayal, he answers. With contempt, she tells Philip that she pities him. Philip sneers. The pity of an adulteress! The Queen faints at the word, and Philip calls for help. Posa and Eboli run in.

Posa rebukes Philip. The King of Spain commands half the world, but cannot command himself. The Queen is reviving. How alone she is! Her only hope is in heaven. Eboli regrets her actions. Philip curses the demon of suspicion. Posa realizes the time for action has come. After a moment's hesitation, the King withdraws. Posa follows him.

Comment: *Elisabeth's cries for justice are in high relief to the previous scene, sounding literally like an alarm. When Posa and Eboli tumble in, we get the feeling they've been standing outside the room with their ears to the door the whole time. The four characters sing a quartet expressing their various states. Philip is conflicted, Elisabeth saddened, Eboli remorseful,*

*although we don't yet know for what. It is similarly not entirely clear why
Posa chooses this moment to begin a course of action, but it does save time.*

*The four conflicting characters are outlined in sharp contrast in the
libretto, but the music tells another story, sweeping all into one arching
lyrical statement. In the melodic unity of the quartet, there is an implication of sympathy among these characters, a moment of understanding that
everybody is doing what they must. These people are suffering together.
Life, the world, the human condition, and perhaps God are ultimately to
blame.*

Eboli, overcome by remorse, throws herself at the Queen's feet
and begs pardon. Elisabeth asks for what crime. Eboli confesses that
she stole the jewel casket and denounced Elisabeth to the King,
because she loved Carlos and was rejected, and gave in to jealous
vengeance. Elisabeth tells her to rise, she is forgiven, but Eboli has
another sin to confess. The unforgivable crime with which she had
denounced the Queen she committed herself . . . with the King. Icily,
the Queen orders Eboli to give her back her crucifix necklace. Allowing Eboli one day to choose between the convent or exile, Elisabeth
leaves.

Filled with shame, Eboli cries that she will never see the noble
Queen again. She curses her own fatal beauty, bestowed by a vengeful heaven in its anger. She cries, considering that she will never be
able to atone for her crimes. But what about Carlos? Perhaps he will
fall to the Inquisition tomorrow. Ah, she still has one more day. She
will save Carlos! She feels herself reborn. One day is left to her. She will
save Carlos!

*Comment: After Eboli's confession, the orchestra must express the feel-
ings the royal lips of Elisabeth de Valois cannot say. A full orchestral C
major chord makes the impact, followed by rotating figures in the cellos
and finally a progression of long high notes held by a solo horn. The effect
is one of being hit over the head by an iron skillet, reeling and spinning,
and finally numb awareness. Elisabeth's statement of Eboli's penalty
while she withdraws is a model of dignity amid calamity, loaded with
repressed tension.*

It is also a perfect prelude for a grand scena. "O don fatal/e" *(the Italian uses the final* e*) is probably the great mezzo-as-diva moment in all opera. As soon as Elisabeth leaves the room, Eboli explodes into a frenzy of emotion, supported by the orchestra, orgasmic after the repression of the previous scenes. The orchestra then provides five rapid notes followed by two terrific thumps, repeated twice, as an intro to Eboli's cursing her own fatal beauty. The central section is slow and sonorous, exploring the lower reaches of the mezzo range as well as the highest. Never before had Verdi allowed himself to explore the sheer beauty of the mezzo voice with such sensuality. The second turning point in the aria comes when Eboli thinks of Carlos. What in earlier years would have been a cabaletta (think of Abigaille in* Nabucco*) is now entirely encapsulated in Eboli's final two lines. She feels herself reborn at this chance to do something beyond considering her own vanity, and the vocal line requires a torrent of sound up to a high B flat. If it doesn't bring the house down, consider the performance a failure.*

Act IV, Scene 1, of Don Carlos *is a triumph of lyric architecture. Its structure (solo-duet-duet-quartet-duet-solo) is a huge arch, so deftly handled that it has been compared to Mozart. Characters who have been little more than stone symbols or plot conventions become full human beings here. This one scene is a journey through the human experience.*

Scene 2: A prison cell. Guards pace beyond the bars.

Carlos, in his prison cell, is lost in thought. Rodrigo enters the cell. They embrace. Carlos says he is entirely destroyed by his hopeless love for Elisabeth, and can do no more for the world or their cause. Posa tells him he has saved him from prison and the Inquisition, but at a high price. They must say farewell forever. Carlos is stunned by this news. Yes, says Rodrigo, this is his supreme day. They will love each other again in heaven. But why does Carlos cry? Death itself has charms, says Posa, when one can die for Carlos. Posa explains that he has set himself up, using Carlos's papers, as the criminal traitor who is brewing unrest. Even now there is a price on his head. Carlos offers to intercede with the King, but Rodrigo tells him to save himself for the oppressed. Carlos must reign, and Posa must die for him!

Immediately, Posa is shot by a soldier who has been standing unseen with a monk just outside the prison cell.

"The King's vengeance is quick!" says Posa, collapsing. He tells Carlos that Elisabeth will see him tomorrow at San Yuste. He fades, but sees a happy Spain in the future. Carlos will reign, and he will die for Carlos. He cries "Farewell," admonishes Carlos to save Flanders, and dies.

Comment: The orchestra introduces us to the sad scene of Carlos languishing in prison with hushed chords. Reminiscences of Fontainebleau are heard, which of course make no sense in the four-act version. When Rodrigo enters, his dialogue with Carlos is the most passionate in the opera—indeed, Verdi rarely allowed his librettists to show this much love between anybody. Rodrigo then launches into his great aria. "C'est mon jour/Per m'è giunto" is a pinnacle of the baritone repertory. It is difficult in a classically Verdian way—rising very high in the voice and built on long extended lines requiring an endless air supply. This aria is the moment when the idealistic Posa becomes fully human. The simplicity of the vocal melody is an opportunity for the baritone to reveal the full beauty of his voice, and therefore, in the world of Italian opera, his validity as a human being. A great baritone can rip your guts out here.

Posa invariably collapses into Carlos's arms after being shot, and, yes, he sings another solo, "Ah, je meurs/Io morrò." This is another heart-tugger, and is usually accompanied by the expected gasps, sobs, and staggers. The friendship theme is repeated in the flutes, and the solo melody is repeated. It is an ironic parody of a cabaletta, which would be expected after the long lines of the aria. Rodrigo's ultimate "action" is his death. Since the melody is the simplest in the opera, it's obvious that Verdi wanted the baritone to do something creative with the reprise. Many can think of nothing better to do than flail around the floorboards, but some will incorporate a "morendo" ("dying") in the voice and take half the audience with them to a better world.

Philip enters with his retinue, telling Carlos he is free and returning his sword to him. Carlos recoils in terror at the King, accusing him of dripping with the blood of Posa's murder. Carlos tells Philip he no longer has a son—let the King choose a new son in his own image from among the butchers in his court. Carlos throws himself on Posa's corpse, and he and Philip both mourn the one true hero in Spain. The courtiers note that Posa took the King's heart with him, and that Spain must now descend into long night.

Comment: This scene was cut from performance early on, was lost for over a century, and has only recently crept up in a few productions. It does stop the action in what is becoming a very long night, but it also provides a rare connection between Philip and Carlos. The music is sad, gloomy, and gorgeous. Verdi later used the theme for the Lacrymosa *section of the* Requiem, *where it is carried primarily by the mezzo.*

Bells are heard tolling, and the people are rioting outside the prison in protest of Posa's murder. The King bravely orders the prison doors opened. He will face his subjects. They swarm in, demanding vengeance. Eboli, masked, slips through the crowd and tells Carlos to flee. Suddenly the Grand Inquisitor appears. The entire crowd stops motionless. He calls them infidels to threaten God's chosen king, and orders them to their knees. They fall and beg forgiveness. The King and the Inquisitor call out "Glory to God," and the people, terrified, repeat the call.

Comment: By this point we are moving beyond plot logic and entirely into the realm of ideas. Why must Eboli appear to utter one line ("Flee!")? Carlos has already been pardoned. The libretto does not even tell us if Carlos leaves with her. In any case, the important function here is to show the King in need of the Grand Inquisitor's authority over the people, and the utter degradation of the masses. Verdi also needed an ensemble to bring down the curtain after the long grand scena.

Act V

Setting: The tomb of the Emperor Charles V at San Yuste, as in Act II, Scene 1. Night.

Elisabeth, alone, prays at the tomb. She addresses the Emperor, who knew the hollowness of the world's splendors and now, at last, is at peace. If tears are still shed in heaven, then let the soul of Charles V bear hers to God. Carlos will come soon. She promised Posa to protect the Prince. Let Carlos go to glory and forget her. As for her, her work is over, and so let her life be. She thinks of her homeland, and Fontainebleau, and the beautiful gardens of Spain. If Carlos should linger in their shade, let the trees, the flowers, the lawns, and the fountains sing her memory to him. She bids farewell to dreams and illusions. Nothing binds her to life any more. Her heart seeks one thing only, the peace of the grave. Yes, the Emperor knew life's emptiness. If tears are still shed in heaven, let him carry hers to God.

Comment: The prelude is extended, wrenching magnificence. The orchestra pounds out the chords of the monks' chant of death from the first cloister scene. The theme of "God alone is great," sung by the Monk, is here transformed into a motif of more general sadness played by the horns. The chant chords repeat. Instead of the restrained flutes punctuating the end of the phrase, which signified bells in the earlier scene, the strings play a dejected upward phrase. This repeats and engulfs the whole orchestra, including rolling tympani, straining to the point of unbearability before receding to the violins only. They play in their highest reaches until cascading down three octaves and fading away for Elisabeth's solo. It is the most frankly emotional music Verdi ever wrote for the orchestra.

Elisabeth's aria itself, "Toi qui sus le néant/Tu che le vanità," is divided into six major parts. The first part begins with her invocation of the dead Emperor. It is stentorian and regal. Once she has Charles's attention, so to speak, her voice becomes light and soaring as she contemplates heaven. In the second part, she thinks of Carlos and her vow to Posa (which we have to take on faith, this being based on a scene in Schiller never included in the libretto). This section is broken recitative. The third section, recalling Fontainebleau, is full of reminiscences of the brief love duet in Act I, here recounted mostly by clarinet and flutes. The fourth section addresses the gardens of Spain, and we hear the clarinet and oboe (indicators of memory) recount themes from her duet with Carlos in Act II, Scene 2, an unhappy encounter but a rare moment of closeness between the two "lovers." Nervous repeating figures in the strings introduce the fifth section, the farewell to dreams and illusions. The theme in the strings imperceptibly and magically transforms into the "agony motif," if we may call it that, of the prelude, while Elisabeth figuratively severs all her connections to life. The musical message is clear. Life is full of sound and fury, but it always adds up to suffering. If you're lucky, you die. The sixth section is a restatement of the first, though with a difference. She soars to a high A in fortissimo voice over the full orchestra before her contemplation of heaven leads her back, prayerfully, to floating pianissimos. This aria requires more than great singing. Like a very few other solos in opera, it is a pilgrimage through the trials of the human experience.

Carlos enters. Elisabeth tells him he must forget her and live as a hero, so that Rodrigo's death will not have been in vain. Carlos is eager to go to Flanders, save the people, and erect a great tomb for Posa. This, says Elisabeth, is the heroism worthy of their love, selfless, idealistic. Carlos says that a day before nothing could have torn him from the touch of Elisabeth's hand, but now he will gladly leave as a token of his love. Her love has ennobled him. But why does she weep? These, she says, are the tears women accord heroic men. They will meet again in a better world. At this solemn moment, let there be no weakness, no inappropriate names for each other. They bid farewell as mother and son, farewell forever until the next world.

Comment: *This brief scene runs through a great many emotions, but romantic love is curiously absent. The first part is a* marziale, *a warlike call-to-arms as Elisabeth rouses Carlos's fighting spirit. Trumpets and a march-like strumming form the accompaniment. The two lovers then settle into a*

farewell section. The orchestra pumps muffled chords, like sighs, while the
strings positively drag their cadences. The feel is one of extreme exhaus-
tion.

Yes, says Philip, entering with the Grand Inquisitor and officers of
the Inquisition, farewell forever! He tells the Inquisitor he has done
his duty, and the Grand Inquisitor promises his office will do the
same. Carlos draws his sword and threatens anyone who approaches
him. The grille of the cloister behind the Emperor's tomb opens up,
and the Monk appears. He gathers Carlos under his cloak. The
world's troubles follow even into this sacred space! All recognize the
voice of the Emperor Charles V. Carlos is drawn behind the grille,
which closes again. Philip, Elisabeth, the Grand Inquisitor, and the
others are stunned.

Comment: *The opera ends with surprising suddenness. Again there are*
some major departures among the various versions. In the French, Elisa-
beth mutters "Ciel!" and Carlos is quietly dragged into the cloister while
the monks repeat their hushed meditation on the ashes of Charles V.
Refined and lovely, but not much of a payoff after five hours in the theater.
In the Italian versions, the orchestra thunders out the monks' chant while
Elisabetta shrieks "Ahhhh!" on a sustained high A because, well, that's
what Italian divas do in such moments. Coarse, but it effectively brings the
curtain down.

And what, one may ask, exactly is happening at the end of this opera?
Nobody really knows. Not even Verdi knew. Perhaps the Monk, who is
definitely Charles V in some form, is alive and brings Carlos into the
sacred cloister, never to be disturbed again. Or this may be the ghost of
Charles V, escorting Carlos into death. Verdi, for better or worse, decided
to end this sprawling epic with a question mark. Directors, on the other
hand, often feel compelled to provide answers. One recent production in
Paris had Carlos impale himself on the Inquisitors' swords (?) and end up
being transfixed in a cruciform. When all else fails, crucify the hero. Better
to accept that there are never any pat answers in this opera. Mystery and
irresolution pervade even the conclusion. Carlos is outside of the conflict,
one way or another. The battle is over. Everybody lost.

A NOTE ON HISTORY AND *DON CARLOS*. History, as we have seen in *Giovanna d'Arco* and *Un ballo in maschera*, gets trashed in opera, and *Don Carlos* is no exception. Let's begin with the Emperor Charles V, whom we met in *Ernani*. After a thoroughly exhausting life, Charles retired to the monastery of San Jerónimo at Yuste in 1558, leaving his son Philip as King of Spain. The monastery's not spooky in the least. It looks a bit like a shopping mall in Coral Gables. He held a "funeral" for himself to symbolize his retirement from the world, and attended it dressed as a monk. This was not unheard of in that time.

The war we hear of at the beginning of the opera was real enough, with France and the Hapsburgs slugging it out in a debilitating conflict. Philip's army (of which only slightly more than one tenth was Spanish) fought a great battle at St. Quentin, and peace negotiations followed. Later, the monastery at El Escorial was built as a memorial. The peace was signed at the village of Chateau-Cambrésis (not Fontainebleau) in 1559. Don Carlos was in Spain at the time. Philip, then in Flanders, married Elisabeth de Valois by proxy and arrangements were made for her to leave for Spain, where Philip would meet her. She was thirteen years old, he was thirty-two and twice widowed (but hardly the gray-haired old goat of *"Elle ne m'aime pas"*).

Don Carlos, a year younger than Elisabeth, was a sickly and disturbed child, especially notorious for his cruelty to animals. There is every evidence that Philip tried to be a good father to the boy, but no one in sixteenth-century Europe would have batted an eyelash if the king had chosen to execute his son publicly. It is true that Elisabeth de Valois did have a curious rapport with Carlos. They both died in 1568.

The Inquisitor General of Spain at this time was a man named Fernándo de Valdés, who was seventy-eight years old in 1560. He was appointed by the king, who could have removed him at any time. In fact, Philip kept promoting de Valdés and expanding his powers even though they differed on many policy issues. Philip once told an advisor not to worry about de Valdés, since the old man would surely die any day. De Valdés fooled everybody and lived until the ripe age of eight-six, becoming the chief spook of Spain in the process. The Opera's Inquisitor threatening Philip is preposterous Romantic revisionism. In Spain, the Inquisition was a state office, and Philip was clearly the boss.

When Posa is flirting with Eboli in the monastery garden scene, Eboli asks for news of the court of France. Posa tells her that there will be a tournament, at which the King himself will joust. In reality, King Henri II jousted at a tournament, celebrating the proxy marriage of his daughter Elisabeth to Philip of Spain, and was killed in that tournament when a lance pierced his eye, leaving his fifteen-year-old son François (husband of Mary, Queen of Scots) as king. Elisabeth was in Paris at that time. Posa's grotesque small talk is paradoxically a reminder of both the presence and the absence of historicity in this work. Incidentally, Posa's excuse for approaching the Queen is to bring her a letter from the Queen her mother, which he displays ostentatiously. The *bonne maman* in question was Catherine des Médicis, a woman who thought nothing of ordering a massacre of thousands of her subjects while enjoying a hearty breakfast and not even burping. If we were supposed to take Elisabeth's sentimental memories of France at face value, it would have been better not to mention her mother at all.

In *Don Carlos,* history and art live in opposition to each other, yet are closely related, like the worlds of Life and Death in which the opera takes place.

Aida

PREMIERE: Cairo Opera House, 1871. Libretto by Antonio Ghislanzoni.

Aida is so popular, so often performed, and so accessible that it has become synonymous with Italian opera in the minds of many people. La Scala has had over forty separate productions of it, and it holds the Metropolitan Opera record for most number of performances— 1,033 to date. It is an unforgettable spectacle of huge proportions that whacks the spectator over the head on first viewing.

To those who are easily swayed by first impressions, *Aida* is only spectacle. Such people have missed the point entirely. The grand choruses, ballets, and the once-heard-never-forgotten Triumphal March all serve as an architectural framework for a very simple love triangle that may have been the most intimate story Verdi ever told. It is certainly the most symmetrical. It begins and ends very quietly. The ensembles and choruses build logically and organically, always as part of the drama. The masses never tumble in willy-nilly. The score never loses sight of the principals.

Yet, for all that, there's no denying that *Aida* is grand opera, in every sense of the term. The individuals in question are not just anybody. The two women are each the heiress of mighty rival kingdoms, and their fathers the kings are often nearby to remind them of this. The fate of all the Nile (the whole world in that cosmology) hangs on their actions and choices. The hero faces the choice between power/duty and love, chooses love, and accepts the inevitable results. We receive the story through all the magnifying powers of grand opera, but the achievement of *Aida* lies in finally serving up grand opera in human-sized bites. The passions of the principals may be bigger than life, but never so unwieldy that they cannot be comprehended. *Aida* is *Don Carlos* brought into extremely sharp focus.

Musically, *Aida* has the reputation of being more conservative and less daring than *Don Carlos*. This is only partially true. The music of *Aida* is deceptively approachable, but hardly simplistic. The more one hears it, the more one finds innovations and marvelously creative touches and, yes, subtleties in the score. Those who dismiss it as big hit tunes are eventually forced to eat their words, as Hans von Bülow and others have discovered. *Aida* has become the all-time warhorse of opera for the simple reason that it never gets old.

CAST OF CHARACTERS

THE KING OF EGYPT *(bass)* A rather statuesque monarch, given to lofty pronouncements.

AMNERIS *(mezzo)* His daughter. Along with Azucena in *Trovatore*, one of the great mezzo roles.

AIDA *(soprano)* An Ethiopian slave, serving Amneris.

RADAMES *(tenor)* Captain of the Guards. The hero.

RAMFIS *(bass)* The High Priest of Egypt.

AMONASRO *(baritone)* King of Ethiopia and Aida's father.

THE HIGH PRIESTESS *(soprano)* This lady gets some lovely music to sing, but, alas, all offstage.

A MESSENGER *(tenor)*

The action takes place in Memphis and Thebes, Egypt, in "the Time of the Pharaohs," which narrows it down to a mere 3,000 years.

THE OPERA

Prelude

Comment: The gorgeous Prelude contrasts two themes, one depicting repressed emotion and the other later associated with the (evil) priests. The personal is smothered by the institutional right from the opening notes, although we are not yet fully aware of the meanings of these themes. Verdi demonstrates the intersection of the two by giving both melodies to the strings, and primarily to his signature instrument, the cello.

Scene 1: A hall in the Egyptian royal palace at Memphis.

Yes, says Ramfis the High Priest to the warrior Radames, the Ethiopians have rallied after their recent defeat and are preparing to invade the Egyptian homeland again. Ramfis has consulted the goddess Isis, who has named the supreme commander of the Egyptian forces. The man named is fortunate indeed, exclaims Radames. Ramfis leaves to inform the King of the goddess's decision.

If only I were the chosen warrior, says Radames. He could lead men to victory to return to Memphis and tell the beautiful Aida that he fought for her. He muses on the heavenly Aida of the divine form, dreaming of taking her to her mountain home and enthroning her near the sun.

Comment: The recitative between Ramfis and Radames is extremely formal, with orchestral chords punctuating the dialogue. The harmonies of the chords make it clear to Western ears that Ramfis is a priest, but the stiff dialogue and music also imply that he and Radames are on distant terms.

The celebrated aria "Celeste Aida" is a nightmare for tenors, and often for audiences, in actual performance. The score is marked "con espressione" for the singer and "piano" for the orchestra. Besides a typically Verdian legato that puts neon lights around any harsh breaths or quick gasps, the sweet vocal line calls for a heavy dose of portamento that sounds like a tomcat in heat if the tenor is not in absolute control. The final phrase is marked "pianissimo" over the series of F's (in the dreaded passaggio), *climaxing on a B flat below high C for six beats, further marked "morendo," or "dying." In other words, Verdi is asking a tenor, of all people, to be extremely ethereal in precisely the place where he is trained to be bombastic. Most tenors ignore the score markings and wham out the best loud high B flat they can muster. Most of the audience will at least applaud this, though the know-it-alls will cluck with disapproval. Verdi wrote an alternative ending to the aria, merely hitting the B flat for one beat before dropping a full octave to repeat the phrase. Audiences invariably think the tenor has choked when they hear this, no matter how many explanatory articles appear in the evening's program. It just doesn't sound right. A perverse truth seems to be that the best tenors in this role often have the worst times with this aria. (The great turn-of-the-century tenor Jean de Reszke simply refused to sing it, and cut it from his performances.) Listen for the portamento, the expression, and the control of the overall aria, and then prepare yourself for anything—absolutely anything—at the finale.*

The Princess Amneris enters, commenting on the joy on Radames's face. He tells her of the coming war, and his hopes to be named general. No other dreams and hopes? she asks. Radames notes the interrogation. Amneris swears vengeance on any rival for Radames's love. Aida enters, dejected. Radames is visibly moved by the sight of her. Amneris marvels that her handmaid might be a rival. With exaggerated kindness, she tells Aida to confide her troubles in her as a sister. Aida says she has heard of the coming war, and is anxious for her country, her family, and for Amneris. To herself she adds that she also sheds tears over her secret love. Amneris tells the slave to tremble before the daughter of Egypt, who sees her secret betrayed by her blushes. Radames notes the anger on Amneris's face. Woe if she should discover his and Aida's secret love!

Comment: *Amneris enters to a lovely theme in the cellos that will accompany her at various times later in the opera. This tells us that Amneris is beautiful and graceful and a viable rival for Aida when she's* *not being bloodthirsty and vengeful. The meaner side of Amneris doesn't take long to surface, however, signified by nervous figures in the strings.*

Ramfis, the King, priests, officials, and others enter, heralded by trumpets. The King calls for the messenger. The Ethiopians have invaded the sacred soil of Egypt, wasting the crops and fields, and are now attacking Thebes. The invaders are led by the fierce warrior Amonasro, their king. "My father!" exclaims Aida to herself. The invaders spread war and death. "Then let war and death be our cry!" says the King. The crowd calls repeatedly for war. The King interrupts to tell them Holy Isis has named the Egyptian general—Radames! He exults in his election, Amneris rejoices with him, and Aida expresses her fears. Now to the Temple of Phtha, urges the King, to invest Radames with the sacred armor. He leads the people in a war anthem. Ramfis exhorts all to remember that the gods alone grant victory or defeat. Aida bemoans that she loves the enemy of her country. Radames anticipates glory. Amneris hands him a banner. "Return victorious!" she commands him. The crowd repeats the call. All leave except Aida.

Comment: The intimacy of the first scene rapidly morphs into the sort of monumentalism that most people mistake for the essence of Aida. *The brief interjections by the various principals are subsumed into the massive chorus. It is imperative that Aida, Radames, and Amneris (and even Ramfis to some extent) establish their characters effectively before everyone gets lost in an operatic equivalent of the flooding Nile.*

"Return victorious!" repeats Aida bitterly. Her own lips said the traitorous words! Victorious over her father, who battles to free Aida from her slavery in Egypt and restore her regal dignity? Over her brothers? Yet how can she wish for the destruction of her lover? Never has anyone known such anguish. Aida begs the gods for pity on her suffering, and to let her die.

Comment: This famous narrative, "Ritorna vincitor," is best understood as a dialogue, or even a duet, with its contrasts of tempo and key modulations depicting Aida's inner battle of love and duty. Neither wins.

Aida's only conclusion is that she is miserable and wants to die. At this point in the narrative ("Numi, pietà!"), a single, plaintive, gorgeous melody forms, which Aida varies until walking offstage while sustaining a (one hopes) pianissimo final note. Scene I has therefore been a great arc from quiet to volume and back to quiet, as is the opera as a whole.

Scene 2: The interior of the Temple of Vulcan (Phtha).

The High Priestess leads the prayer of the people to Phtha, life-giving spirit of the world, echoed by the priestesses and the priests. Radames is led into the sanctuary. The priestesses perform a dance around him as they invest him with the sacred armor of Egypt. Ramfis reminds Radames of the sacred trust he has undertaken. The High Priest prays that the god lift his hand over the holy land of Egypt, Radames begs protection for his homeland, and the people pray for victory. Radames and Ramfis invoke the awesome name of Phtha the Immense.

Comment: The opening of this scene is pure stasis. The High Priestess is offstage. This always confuses a large part of the audience at the curtain calls following the act, when a lady in a tasteful modern dress takes a solo bow at the footlights. During the act, she sings three ethereal prayers to the god Phtha (the Egyptian Vulcan). Each prayer ends in the chorus of priest-esses singing "Noi t'invochiamo" ("We invoke thee"). These prayers are answered antiphonally by the priests, in very hushed chants. The men sound like a Russian liturgical chorus. It may not be authentic Egyptian religious music, but it gets the message of "exotic" and "religious" across beautifully. The dance that follows is a lovely melody carried by the flutes that we will hear again at the end of the opera.

Act II

Scene 1: Amneris's apartment in the royal palace.

Amneris is being dressed by her maidens and slaves for the victory celebration. Radames has vanquished the invader. Amneris dreams of

Radames returning to Egypt and her love. Moorish slaves dance for
Amneris's pleasure.

Aida enters and Amneris dismisses the others, saying that Aida is
a child of the defeated and her pain is sacred to Amneris. As soon
as she sees Aida, however, she wonders if the slave can really be a rival
for Radames's love. She determines to find out with a ruse. She
tells Aida she sympathizes, but encourages her to look toward the
future. Time is a great healer, and love, even greater. The word *love*
sets Aida dreaming, and Amneris pursues. The slave should trust in
the Princess's friendship and confide in her. In all the Egyptian
army, wasn't there one man who caught Aida's heart? After all,
most are alive, and not all shared the fate of their general, Radames.
Aida's outburst betrays her love for Radames. Amneris tells her
that she was lying—Radames is alive! Aida thanks the gods,
but Amneris tells her to beware. She herself is the rival for Radames's
love! Aida momentarily stands proud, about to tell Amneris that
she too is . . . but she gathers herself before revealing her royal birth,
and grovels before Amneris, imploring mercy. Yes, she loves
Radames, but she will keep her love secret and tremble before the
happy fortune of Amneris. Amneris is unmoved. Trumpets and choruses in the distance announce the beginning of the victory celebra-
tions. Amneris exits in triumph, ordering Aida to attend her,
groveling in the dust, at the parade. Alone, Aida repeats her plea of
mercy to the gods.

Comment: *This scene opens with feminine elegance, as the women sing
of their menfolk returning from the war. War is depicted by strumming
harps, which stop when Amneris, dreaming of Radames, floats some pretty
notes over the others. The Dance of the Moorish Slaves is fast and effective—just about a minute of fussy, then pounding, music. The great cat
fight begins when Aida enters. Amneris's faux-friendliness is extremely
slimy. They each get some stentorian proclamations of their own self-
worth, and Amneris exits in triumph. The ending of the scene is a direct
repeat of the end of "Ritorna vincitor."*

Scene 2: The gates of the city of Thebes.

The King, Ramfis, the priests, and officials all enter. Amneris enters, attended by Aida. The people sing a hymn of praise to Egypt. The women offer lotus and laurel crowns to the victors, urging the girls to dance as the stars dance around the sun. The priests urge the people to give thanks to the gods, arbiters of fate. Trumpeters lead the victorious troops in procession before the royal entourage, followed by dancing girls who carry the trophies of war. Finally, Radames enters to the acclaim of the crowd.

Comment: This is the Triumphal Scene, containing the Triumphal March, one of the most recognizable pieces of music in the world. Its recognizability is assisted by the fact that Verdi uses only five notes, in various configurations, to create it.

The March is immediately followed by the ballet. Verdi wrote some very virile music for this, and most productions will include some sort of ritual reenactment of the battle. Predictably, he extended the ballet music for the Paris production of 1880. Apparently he liked what he heard, because he instructed Ricordi to include the new ballet music in all subsequent publications of the score. The music is remarkably versatile, and works equally well with traditional European ballet steps and the wilder and (supposedly) more African-influenced choreography one is likely to see today.

The King salutes Radames as the savior of the country, directing him to receive the triumphal wreath from Amneris's hand. The King swears by his crown that whatever Radames asks on this day will be granted. Radames calls the prisoners forth before he makes his request. They are led in while the priests intone their invocation of the gods. The last prisoner is Amonasro. Aida cries out that she sees her father, the crowd is amazed at this coincidence, Amneris exults that Aida's father is in Egyptian hands, and Amonasro tells her not to betray his true identity. The King orders Amonasro to identify himself. "Her father," replies Amonasro. He fought, was defeated, and sought death in vain. He defended his king and his country. His king lay dead at his feet. If love of one's country is a crime, then they are all guilty and ready to die. But, he continues, the Egyptian king is a mighty lord who should look with mercy on the captives. Today they are struck down by fate. Tomorrow it may be the Egyptians' turn. Aida repeats his plea, echoed by the Ethiopian prisoners and slave girls. The priests warn the King that clemency would be madness for these barbarians. Their death is preordained by the gods. The people beg the priests to calm their bloodlust. Radames gazes on Aida, more beautiful than ever in her compassion, and Amneris notes this with bitterness. The King muses that mercy is good in the sight of the gods.

Comment: When Amneris crowns Radames with the victor's laurel, she does not sing, but is indicated with her lovely theme music. Count on the mezzo to vamp it up at this point.

Amonasro's narrative begins in halting phrases, befitting the defeated state he is trying to project. After the first two lines, the silence is punched by one of the fierce beats on the bass drum that punctuate the score of this opera. He then launches into a broad aria of typical Verdian baritonal glory. This is repeated first by Aida, then by various parts of the chorus as they plead for mercy, contrasted with the priests who, as always, demand death and slaughter. Radames's and Amneris's asides ornament the overall picture without receiving any special attention. It is scandalous how many tenors will keep their mouths shut for this gorgeously balanced ensemble. Any cheating by the soloists makes this scene the hollow noise critics complain of. A great conductor is also needed to plumb the full depths of this ensemble, with its six solo and fourteen choral parts. On the nights when it all comes together, this scene justifies all the excesses and bombast of Italian opera.

Just at the moment of the ensemble when all vocal parts are in full gear, the orchestra abruptly quiets down and all singers except Aida stop singing. Aida alone continues her line without lyrics, from the forte demanded by the ensemble diminishing into a piano and floating up and down the scale in heartbreaking lyricism. This is another excellent use of the operatic "close-up," refocusing our attention on an individual.

Radames reminds the King of his oath, and asks life and liberty for the Ethiopian prisoners. "*All* of them," notes Amneris to herself. The priests cry out for slaughter while the people ask mercy. Ramfis interrupts. The Ethiopians are proud and brave, and must be planning vengeance even now. He suggests that Aida and her father remain as pledges of good faith. The King favors this plan. He grants Radames the hand of his daughter Amneris, acknowledging that one day Radames will rule Egypt with her. Amneris exults—let the slave now dare to steal her love!

The King leads anthems in praise of Egypt, and the priests thank the gods. Aida wonders what she can now be living for. The prisoners and slave girls praise the clemency of glorious Egypt and her king. Radames considers that the throne of Egypt is not worth the loss of Aida, Amneris rejoices in her triumph, while Amonasro whispers encouragement to Aida. The day of Ethiopian vengeance is near. The people praise Egypt and Isis.

Comment: The huge Act II finale raps up neatly, with a basically unified chorus punctuated by a few decorative outbursts from the various principals, and a rousing restatement of the Triumphal March.

The second scene of Act II is often compared favorably with the auto-da-fé scene of Don Carlos. *All the same elements are there: the parade of unfortunate victims, evil bloodthirsty priests, a crowd crying for mercy, a vacillating king, and sympathetic soprano voices. (Remember that in Verdi's cosmography, women are always inclined toward mercy and priests are always hateful, history notwithstanding.) There is no doubt that it is all handled a lot more smoothly here than in the previous opera, where the situation was more complicated. None of the characters, not even Aida, are divided against themselves the way they are in* Don Carlos. *The Egyptian people are monolithically joyful about winning a war, while the Ethiopians are defeated and want to live. Despite its massive size and twenty vocal parts, the scene is manageable dramatically.*

The monumentality of the scene is an opportunity for the production team to go hog-wild. One can expect anything in the larger houses— horses, phalanxes of extras, and, yes, even elephants. The scene has been staged at night, which permits a groovy torchlight parade, prized by the tone-deaf, but destroying the chiaroscuro contrast with the subsequent two, more intimate, acts. Basically, a staging of Act II, Scene 2, can man-

age several levels of production as long as the principals can always be found—visually, aurally, and dramatically—amid the massive goings-on.

The scene comes to a tremendous close with a grand choral unison leading into a restatement of the *Triumphal March*. Maria Callas, apparently, once felt that this was insufficiently dramatic, and decided to highlight herself by carrying the vocal line up to a full-throated sustained E flat above high C. It is neither subtle nor pretty, but it is powerful and convincing. The "Mexico City E flat" has become famous in opera circles; it is currently available as a sound bite off the Internet and can be used as a strident way of saying "You've got mail."

Act III

Setting: The banks of the Nile, by the Temple of Isis. Ramfis and Amneris alight from a boat and enter the temple to keep vigil.

Comment: The orchestral prelude to Act III, depicting the moonlit banks of the Nile, is one of Verdi's great moments. Scholars often point to this passage when they feel the need to persuade naysayers that Verdi really was a great musician. Violinists surf the full tonal range of their instruments in soft pulsing figures while the other muted strings play triple-piano tremolos. The fingering for the violins is not possible to accomplish in the course of playing, and must be set beforehand. A flute plays trills, figures, and a melody belonging to no discernible (European) key. If the moonlit Nile doesn't actually sound like this, it should.

The offstage chorus sings a spooky-sounding chant when invoking Isis. One contemporary of Verdi wrote that the composer was walking through the market place of Parma one day with Teresa Stolz, and was very impressed with the cry of a vendor selling cooked pears, "boien-ti, boie-e-e-en-ti!" That's one story. Another version of the legend says it was a bean-seller, hence "fazoo-li, fazoo-o-o-o-li!" Yet another insists it was boiled beets. Whether the vendors ever sang this tune or not is lost in history, but I can inform you that you should not expect to hear it today. You're lucky if you hear anything in the market place of Parma today besides dreadful Italian pop radio.

Amneris and Ramfis traditionally enter off a boat, or at least a cool triangular sail indicating a boat, floating along the river. Amneris's brief musical exchange with Ramfis shows her in the "nice, lovely princess" mode, rather than as the dominatrix bitch she becomes when sharing the stage with Aida.

Aida enters furtively. Radames will come to this spot, but what will he say? Sadly, she thinks of her homeland, which she will never see again. She thinks of the beautiful mountain land, the forests, the cool valleys, the perfumed streams . . . No, she will never see them again.

Comment: *Aida's solo soliloquy here, "Qui Radamès verrà," is her big moment, the kind that, if done right, will linger in the public memory for generations. Verdi has provided the soprano with a splendid opportunity to show her full range, both musically and emotionally. Throughout the aria, "O patria mia," her lines are introduced, echoed, and occasionally doubled by a long plaintive melody for solo oboe. This feels like a dialogue between Aida and her memories, represented by the oboe. Much of the aria is written piano or even pianissimo, and the ascent high C right before the end is as notorious among sopranos as "Celeste Aida" is among tenors. Done effectively, she will carry the entire audience with her "over the top."*

Amonasro appears, confronting Aida. He knows of her fatal love for Radames, and of Amneris's jealousy. But Aida has the power to defeat her conquerors, and return triumphant to the balsam forests and golden temples of her homeland. Aida is thrilled by the idea of returning home. She remembers the horrible time when the Egyptians invaded and destroyed their country, and now prays for a return of peace. Amonasro joins her prayer for an end to war, and tells her revenge and victory are close by. The Ethiopians are armed and ready. All they need to know is the route the enemy will take. But how could they discover that? asks Aida. Amonasro says Aida could help. Radames loves her, he is the Egyptian general . . . Does she understand? Never, she cries! Amonasro turns on his daughter. Then let their cities drown in blood, and the dead will point to Aida, saying they are ruined because of her! What does he see now? A specter, the ghost of Aida's mother, cursing her. Aida begs pity of her father, but he repulses her. She is not his daughter. She truly is the slave of the Pharaohs! She relents. She will be worthy of her name and her country. Amonasro sees Radames approaching, and hides among the palms. Alone, Aida cries out, "My homeland, how much you cost me!"

Comment: This scene is the climax of Verdi's long list of father-daughter confrontations, a trope where he has no equals, not even excepting Shakespeare. This is the emotional crux of the work, the only place in the opera where there is an actual character transformation. The scene begins in slow and pensive phrases, thunders in the middle, and concludes in an andante—a very untypical structure. Amonasro begins to manipulate Aida with a pleasant invocation of their homeland and its cool balsam forests, which she echoes note for note. His music turns fiercer as he reminds her of the wars that devastated Ethiopia. When Aida refuses Amonasro's suggestion of duping Radames, he thunders curses at her in the name of her countrymen and finally her mother's ghost in short, fortissimo phrases. His final insult, that Aida has truly become a slave, has its effect. Apparently love may be stronger than duty in this opera, but it's no match for the power of identity. The supremacy of selfhood as expressed in this scene, rather than all the elephants and what-not in the previous act, accounts for much of the emotional power and enduring popularity of the piece.

Radames enters, carried by love to see Aida again. She keeps him at a distance. He is betrothed to another. He reassures her. The Ethiopians have begun the war again. He will conquer, and then tell the King everything. And what of Amneris's jealousy? asks Aida. No, there is only one hope. Let them flee this burning desert. She will show Radames a new homeland of virgin forests where they can forget the world. Yes, he answers, but how can he leave his homeland, the land where their love was born? She tells him of the cool valleys of her land. He hesitates. She tells him to run to Amneris, but he insists he will cast his lot with Aida. Aida asks how they will avoid the Egyptian army. They will take another route. Aida asks which route the army is taking. The pass at Napata, replies Radames.

Amonasro appears. Then his army will meet the Egyptians at Napata! Radames is stunned. Amonasro reveals his true identity. Radames
lashes out at his error. He is dishonored! No, says Amonasro. He was
duped but not dishonored. It was the will of fate. Hurry, let them
leave, and Radames will be welcomed as a hero in Ethiopia, but
Radames is so filled with shame he cannot move. Amneris and the
priests come forth from the temple. She understands the situation at
once, and calls Radames a traitor. Amonasro runs to stab Amneris,
but Radames stops him, telling Aida and Amonasro to run. Casting
down his sword, Radames offers himself to the priests for arrest.

*Comment: Radames blows on the stage with all guns blasting here. He
is excited, and when he's excited he always sounds as if he's calling the
troops to war. His brash entrance is completely at odds with the previous
scenes, which were always full of subtleties and nuances. Aida is already
in intrigue mode, trying to burst his enthusiasm and make him comprehend matters. Radames answers with a short aria, for lack of a better
word, outlining his military solution. He can only imagine his sword saving the day. Two trumpets provide the martial beat for this outburst. It's a
subtler version of "Di quella pira" without the high C's.*

*Aida's proposal is much cannier, psychologically and musically. After
Radames recoils in horror at the suggestion that they flee, she sings in flat,
measured tones of the inhospitable desert. Then she breaks into melody,
describing the Ethiopian land, full of virgin forests and cool breezes. The
melody she sings is meandering, languid—and sexy as hell. She is backed
by a choir of three flutes, caressing her voice and our ears the whole time.
She is seductive in an erotic way, but Radames needs more convincing.
When she reaches the end of her phrase, she promises a paradise like no
real place on earth, where they can "forget the world." The flutes play a
charming figure that functions here the way the deliberately old-fashioned
aria "Di Provenza" (which was, you may recall, said to be based on a
familiar lullaby) functioned in La traviata at a similar moment of crisis
for the tenor. He must be coddled like an infant.*

*Radames, who does not appear to have brains among his functioning
organs, tries to protest in his usual bombastic tones, but he's no match for*

Aida. She floats her melody over him a second time, and this time he sings the flutes' melody when they arrive at the word "forget." Aida's plan is working. He, however, is that peculiar brand of macho who can never act when there is a real decision to be made. (Throughout the opera, Radames only reacts.) She must threaten him with leaving before he can finally be persuaded to flee, and the duet that closes this part of the scene is sung in the "Rally the troops!" spirit he can comprehend.

Radames also tempts us to laughter when we watch him figuring out in plodding phrases what he has done. At last he does something forthright when he stops Amneris's murder, and the end of the act features him nobly offering himself to the priests. It is a single stentorian line that must impress the audience if he is to elicit any sympathy whatsoever.

Act IV

Scene 1: A hall in the palace.

Amneris, alone, struggles with her conflicting feelings. Radames can't be a traitor, and yet he was going to flee with Aida, who has escaped. Yet Amneris still loves Radames, and decides to save him. The guards bring him forth. Amneris warns Radames that the priests are deciding his fate even now. He should defend himself, and she will ask a pardon from the King. Radames refuses. Though he feels neither traitorous nor guilty, his words gave help to the enemy, but his honor is unstained. Let the sentence be passed. No, insists Amneris, he must live, since she lives only for him. Without Aida, he protests, he has no desire to live. And Aida is dead, perhaps because of Amneris. Amneris says Aida is not dead. When the Ethiopian hordes retreated, only Amonasro was killed, but nothing is known of Aida. Radames prays she reach her homeland in safety, and never find out about his execution. Amneris says that execution can be avoided, if Radames will swear to love her and forget Aida. He refuses. Does he then insist on dying? Very well. Let the priests have their prey. Radames is led out. Immediately, Amneris accuses herself of betraying her love and handing him over to death.

Comment: Verdi's instincts were right on the money in this scene when he decided against giving Amneris a self-pitying romanza to sing. His solution of disjointed exclamations and reminiscences is much more effective in depicting the Princess's conflicted state of mind. It is a huge challenge to the mezzo, however, since she must switch personalities on a dime. First she is imperious, trying to sway Radames with her authority. In the course of the action she threatens, pleads, tries being seductive, and ends in a fury that quickly morphs into remorse. Throughout, Radames is entirely passive. His time of action—even reaction—has passed.

From inside the priests' hall, Ramfis is heard reading the three accusations of treason against Radames. Each time, the high priest challenges Radames to defend himself, and each time Radames is silent. The priests declare him a traitor while Amneris, alone, protests his innocence to the gods. The priests decree that Radames will be buried alive under the temple of the offended god. Amneris is shocked at the bloodlust of the so-called ministers of heaven. As they enter the hall, repeating the verdict of treason, she tells them that they commit a crime and offend heaven in killing the innocent. They are unmoved. He is a traitor. He will die! Amneris curses the priests. Let heaven's vengeance strike their whole unholy race forever!

Comment: The actual trial in this Judgment Scene is offstage. All we see is Amneris reacting to it, another precinematic close-up technique. It is extremely symmetrical in form, illustrating the inflexibility of the theocratic state. The form is as follows: Ramfis, singing a capella, calls out Radames's name three times. A horn choir ("da-da-daaaah!") punctuates the naming of the accused. Ramfis (again a capella) reads the sentence, ending with "Discolpati!" This means "Defend yourself," but is even more accusatory in Italian, as in "Unguilt yourself." The priests repeat "Discolpati!" and there is a tense, quiet kettle-drum roll. "Egli tace" (He is silent), sneers Ramfis. "Traditor!" cry the priests in ascending notes. Amneris then screams her head off and begs the Numi for pietà. This whole process is repeated (you guessed it) two more times, each a step higher on the scale. Amneris's exclamations are the human emotional reaction to a (literally, as we shall see) stifling society. These, and her gasps of "Numi, pietà!" *make clear what we have suspected all along—that she and Aida, rather than being opposites in conflict, are really mirror images of each other.*

Amneris gives full vent to her impotent rage at the end of the scene, cursing hypocrisy and entitlement and priests in general. Expect vocal blood and thunder, after which the mezzo will probably swoop front-center stage and demand an ovation. In all fairness, they usually deserve one.

Scene 2: Interior of the Temple of Vulcan (Phtha), split into two levels. Above, the temple is resplendent. Below is a dark vault, with Radames seated alone. Priests are sealing the vault with a large stone.

Radames ponders his fate. He will never see the light of day again. Worse, he will never see Aida. In the darkness he cannot make out forms. What does he see? A phantom? A vision? It is Aida! In this tomb? Yes, she answers. She had sensed the outcome of his trial, and ran to share Radames's fate. Radames protests. To die, so young and pure—she must not! But it is too late, and Aida is already seeing the angel of death coming to bear them to eternal light and joy.

In the temple above, the priests and priestesses invoke the gods. Aida tells him it is their funeral hymn. Radames tries in vain to move the stone that seals the tomb. Aida tells him all is finished for them on earth. They hold each other while they bid farewell to earth and greet the heaven of pure light. Amneris enters the temple above, and implores peace, while the priests and priestesses invoke almighty Phtha.

Comment: The celebrated Tomb Scene is a masterpiece of restraint and threatrical effectiveness. Radames's musings as he is sealed into the tomb are appropriately diaphanous and nearly monotone. He croons when he mentions the name of Aida, and his only outburst comes when he realizes she is with him in the tomb. The chorus sings music from the first temple scene, with variations. The simple finale, "O terra addio," *is repeated twice. Somehow, the singers must portray running out of air without, well, running out of air. Done well, the audience will be transported. The only variation occurs when Amneris enters the temple above and repeats the line* "pace t'imploro." *At the very end, when the full chorus sings* "Inmenso Ftah" *in pianissimo voice, the effect is of a soul very quietly taking leave of the body.*

The split-level stage was Verdi's inspiration. Set designers are forever trying new variations, but they never seem to work as well as the split-level temple. One reason is that there is an acoustical element to this stage design. Amneris's very simple lines can wash over Aida and Radames and blend perfectly even when sung in a pianissimo.

The Requiem

PREMIERE: The Church of San Marco, Milan, 1874.

THE NAME

Officially, it is *Messa da Requiem,* or *Requiem Mass.* Since it was composed in memory of the author Alessandro Manzoni (who died in 1873), it is also often called the *Manzoni Requiem,* which is quite proper. However, if you were attending a performance and told people you were going to the *Manzoni Requiem,* you would be considered hopelessly pretentious. Just a warning. When not in the middle of a discussion or book about Verdi, you will usually call it the Verdi *Requiem,* and let the pedants howl.

WHAT IS THE *Requiem?* Good question. "*Aida* in church," sniff some. Much of what is written about the *Requiem* is a debate about whether it is opera by nature or church music. Verdi wrote it as a tribute to Manzoni, to be performed in a church but not as part of a service. After its first performance it moved to La Scala, where it was cheered and encored just like any opera. It then went on a triumphal tour of Europe, always performed in theaters or concert halls. Today it is performed in concert halls or occasionally in churches being used temporarily as concert halls. The *Requiem* is not appropriate as musical accompaniment to an actual Mass, nor did Verdi ever intend it to be.

Any prayers for the dead can be set to music and called a Requiem, but Verdi chose, with some alterations, the traditional Catholic funeral service, in Latin, used for individuals whenever appropriate and also used on all Souls' Day, November 2. This service includes a medieval poem, the *Dies irae,* or "Days of Wrath," a vision of the Last Day when heaven and earth will split open, the dead will rise out of their graves, and Jesus will return to earth to separate the blessed from the damned. The poem, although not Scriptural, is based on the vision of the Day of Wrath in the first chapter of Zephaniah. After the *Dies irae,* there is also a last optional section, the *Libera me,* or "Free me," a separate poem often included in this service because of its beautiful text. It is not part of the official service of the Mass, being used as the prayer when the coffin is closed and censed. Verdi had written a *Libera me* for the projected Rossini Requiem of 1868, which was never completed. This was the seed, substantially reworked, that eventually became the present *Requiem.*

Of the texts used, the *Dies irae* stands out among these as intense, personal, and primal. The poet makes no effort to hide his fear or express it in any but the most direct terms. The meter of the poem, a relentless trochaic tetrameter (DUM-duh DUM-duh DUM-duh), augments the sense of menace—repeat the rhythm rapidly to yourself and you will hear the famous "shark" theme from *Jaws.* The final section is a poem in blank verse into which Verdi chose to splice bits of the *Dies irae.*

What makes appropriate religious music? In Mozart's time, the general feeling was that good music was good wherever it was played. Mozart, Berlioz, Schubert, Rossini, and Brahms all wrote religious music that has since been consigned to the concert halls. Franz Liszt, who was somehow both a sensualist and an ascetic, wrote austere church music as well as music so extravagant it borders on camp. The church reacted, and has been reacting ever since. The basic notion is that music should serve to aid the worshiper in devotion, not become the object of devotion. Music is sensual by definition—it is experienced by means of the senses, and therefore is imperfect. Overemphasis on music is therefore a form of sensual idolatry—worshiping the created rather than the Creator. At the beginning of the twentieth century, this notion was outlined in a papal encyclical that specifically banned any music that might be considered "theatrical" from use in church services. In other words, the Catholic church, one of history's most important promoters of music, has deliberately removed itself from that position. One Catholic commentator of our own day, Jeff Stone, has compared the Church to a fabulously wealthy family that stores priceless heirlooms in the attic and puts paper plates out on the dinner table.

The church's stated attitude toward "theatricality" in music fails to consider that drama and religious ritual appear to have common roots and perhaps even common goals. Both are enactments of the larger questions and problems of the human condition played out before the entire community and intending to have an ultimately uplifting effect. The intersection of the liturgical and the operatic in the Verdi *Requiem* shows us something that was difficult for most Europeans and Americans of a century ago to understand, namely, that in its ability to remove us from the bondage of ego and to explore the unconscious outside of the usual strictures of time and logic, opera itself is essentially a spiritual experience. The greatest master of Italian opera was able to apply his genius to humanity's most persistent existential questions and elucidate them for people in a direct and gripping way that has eluded theologians, philosophers, and scientists alike. Call that theatrical if you like. As Charles Osborne said about this piece, in perhaps the finest phrase of his career, "If this is music more suitable for the theatre than the church, then so much the worse for the church."

The *Requiem* is not opera, since it is not staged, but it uses the musical techniques of Italian opera to explore the issues at stake in the Requiem Mass. Nor does the church—any church—have a monopoly on those issues. Although using the language of Christian imagery, and in particular the *Dies irae* with its anxiety about the fires of hell, the issues are common to all people. Verdi is looking at the fear of death, the fear of retribution for human shortcomings, and, most of all, the ancient primal fear among humans that the sun won't come up. People all over the world practiced sacrifices to appease the cosmic powers and ensure the continuation of life. Christianity offers

Christ as the sacrifice whose death and resurrection defeat the powers of hell (darkness). Verdi does not presume to tell us the outcome of the ancient struggle. What matters for him is the emotional state of humanity as it considers these questions. The imagery he uses is the powerful language of the Middle Ages, for whose people the fires of hell were a very real, literal eventuality. Our primal fears of death, darkness, and the innate wretchedness of the human psyche continue to haunt us every bit as much as they terrified the cave men and the medieval flagellants. The basic issues remain the same. Is there an order to the universe, or is chaos inevitable, and where do I fit into all this? And what if it all ends tomorrow? Assuming God exists, does He care enough to intervene for me? For us? If you think the modern mind has transcended primal fears about the end of the world, consider the neurosis surrounding the entirely manufactured concept of the millennium. The Y2K Bug was nothing but a very elaborate analog of the *Dies irae*.

The *Requiem* is performed by a large chorus, orchestra, and four soloists: soprano, mezzo-soprano, tenor, and bass.

I. Requiem

Grant them eternal rest, oh Lord, and let eternal light shine upon them. A hymn in Zion is fitting to you, God, and a vow will be made to you in Jerusalem. Hear my prayer, all flesh will come to you. Grant them eternal rest, oh Lord, and let eternal light shine upon them.

Lord, have mercy. Christ, have mercy. Lord, have mercy.

Comment: *The chorus begins this section quietly and in a deceptively standard liturgical voice, asking for rest and light in the familiar words. The solo voices enter individually in the "Kyrie eleison" section, combining into a very lyrical quartet backed by the chorus. The finale of the section, however, is a return to the hushed voices of the chorus.*

II. *Dies irae*

Dies irae

That day, the day of wrath will dissolve the age in ashes, as David and the Sybil prophesied. How great the terror will be when the judge is coming, and everything will be thoroughly reviewed.

Comment: Four great G minor chords are pounded out by the orchestra as the chorus swells up to what amounts to a prolonged cry of all mankind seized by terror, followed by four more orchestral pounds with bass drum on the offbeat. All hell is breaking loose, and those who were lulled into any sort of complacency, musical or spiritual, by the opening section are abruptly roused from it by this unforgettable music. The pounding chords and bass drum are an analog of the poetic meter (DUM-duh) and have a liturgical provenance. At Tenebrae, the ancient traditional service for midnight of Good Friday, music is replaced by the slamming of large books in the choir loft to represent Christ's harrowing of hell. Verdi's music is a sort of Tenebrae on LSD. There is no mistaking what is intended here—fear, on the universal level. When the end of the world finally comes, the soundtrack will already have been written. The reference to the Sybil, the seeress of pagan Rome, may strike us as odd for a medieval Christian poem, but medieval monks were great admirers of the classic texts.

Tuba mirum

The trumpet, scattering its astonishing sound through the graves of all the lands, will herd all before the throne. Death and Nature will be stupefied when all creation rises again to answer to the judge.

Comment: Four trumpets in the orchestra begin the call, answered by four trumpets that Verdi specified to be unseen. The entire orchestra builds into a great fanfare and the basses of the chorus sing the first sentence in appropriately stentorian phrases. Startlingly, all becomes silent in an instant, and the solo bass practically whispers the second sentence ("Mors stupebit . . ."), reflecting the stupefaction of Death and Nature as their usual laws have been reversed.

Liber scriptus

The written book will be brought forth in which everything is entered from which the world will be judged. *("Dies irae.")* Then, when the judge takes his seat, whatever is hidden will appear. *("Dies irae.")* Nothing will remain unpunished. *("Dies irae,"* etc.*)*

Comment: *This section is superbly dramatic, with the mezzo singing an intense solo sounding, in fact, a lot like Amneris in* Aida. *The interesting scoring in the orchestra and the whispered punctuations of "Dies irae" from the chorus, however, give the sense that her terror is inward while she is standing silent before God, who is reading the book of her life. Not to be frivolous, but it is not unlike sitting across the desk from the big boss as he reviews your work and decides if you will be fired or promoted. The mezzo twice utters the last line of the text, "Nil inultum remanebit," the second time blasting it out. This frightening moment is the cue for the chorus to erupt into a full-voiced restatement of the* Dies irae, *which underscores the connection between individual anxiety over the fate of the entire universe. The* Dies irae *will subside in volume and lead into the next section without a discernible break.*

Quid sum miser

Then what am I, a wretch, to say? To which protector will I appeal, when even the righteous man is hardly safe?

Comment: *The mezzo also begins this section, which develops into a trio with the soprano and the tenor. The music is remarkably gentle and lovely, the feeling being more one of shame than fear. This is reinforced by a prominent bassoon accompaniment punctuated by a wailing clarinet.*

Rex tremendae majestatis

King of awe-inspiring majesty, you freely save those who are to be saved, save me, fountain of pity.

Comment: The basses boom out the salutation, echoed by the whispering tenors. The soloists sing the phrase "Salva me" as an intricate quartet, again punctuated by the booming basses and then reinforced by the whole chorus. The prayer, then, functions on both the cosmic and the personal level. The basses acknowledge the sheer grandeur of God, while the individuals put forth their very personal concerns for salvation.

Recordare

Remember, holy Jesus, that I am the reason for your journey, do not destroy me on that day. Seeking me, you sat down weary, you saved me by suffering on the cross, don't let such labor be in vain. Fair judge of punishment, grant the gift of remission before the day of accounting.

Comment: This graceful duet for mezzo and soprano seems like an interlude amid all the cowering self-loathing of the rest of the Dies irae, *and indeed the text represents what Dr. Elizabeth Kubler-Ross calls the "bargaining" phase of death. "Seeking me, you sat down weary" is a quote of Saint Augustine commenting on Jesus and the woman at the well. Augustine emphasizes Jesus' enthusiasm to save each and every soul, and here the individuals are using that notion as a sort of bargaining chip at the supreme moment.*

Ingemisco

I groan like a guilty man, my sins redden my face. Spare the supplicant, God. You who absolved Mary and listened to the thief have also given hope to me. My prayers are not worthy, but you, who are good, make them good, lest I be cremated in the eternal fire. Save me a place among the sheep, standing at your right side, and separate me from the goats.

Comment: The Ingemisco *is the only complete solo for tenor in the* Requiem, *and as such is quite frankly an aria. It is lyrical, but not symmetrical in the bel canto sense. When the soloist asks for a place among the sheep,* "Inter oves locum," *the music lightens considerably and there is even a prominent oboe part that seems like an almost jocular reference to shepherds' music. The tenor sings more passionately as he considers the possibility of salvation (being counted among the sheep rather than the goats, who always get a bad rap in Scripture and mythology), one of the few places in the work where salvation seems like a distinct possibility. The cellos repeat the pastoral theme, and the tenor rises to a sustained B flat at the word* "dextra," *referring to being on God's "right" side (in both senses). The note is marked as a decrescendo, but don't count on it.*

Confutatis

When the damned are overthrown and consigned to the burning flames, call me with the blessed. Supplicant and bowed down, I beg, my heart almost burned out with contrition, help me at my end. (*"Dies irae,"* etc.)

Comment: The text has quickly shifted from the possibility of salvation back to consideration of the fate of the damned, and Verdi quite rightly changed voices from tenor to bass. More "profound" than the tenor voice, the bass's melody is on a level of grandeur with those in Don Carlos. *The musical phrase continues to what seems like the very last notes of a final cadence before being cut short by the* Dies irae *again in all its fury.*

Lacrymosa

On that tearful day, when the guilty man rises again out of the ashes to be judged, spare him then, holy Lord Jesus, grant them rest. Amen.

Comment: The mezzo leads this section, joined primarily by the bass but also the other soloists as well as the chorus. It is a stunningly sad piece of music, depicting true inner grief rather than outward panic, and very effective after the recapitulation of the full "Dies irae" strophe that precedes it. The Lacrymosa was a slight reworking of the tenor-bass duet written for Don Carlos but discarded and not found until 1970. Amusingly, Toye, who knew nothing about the lost Carlos duet, singles out the Lacrymosa as ". . . one of the few pas sages in the work whose character is definitely liturgical." This must prove once and for all how arbitrary these divisions of "operatic" and "liturgical" really are. In any case, it is stunning as music, as evocative of the sadness of death in its own way (vocal) as Chopin's or Beethoven's funeral marches.

III. Offertorio

Domine Jesu Christe

Lord Jesus Christ, King of Glory, free the souls of all the faithful departed from the punishments of hell and the deep pit. Free them from the lion's mouth lest hell engulf them and they fall into darkness, but let Saint Michael the standard-bearer lead them into the holy light, as you once promised to Abraham and his seed.

Comment: *The shift in texts, from the hair-raising* Dies irae *to the more detached words of the Requiem Mass itself, is reflected by a lyrical warmth in the music of this movement. While there are still "punishments of hell" and a longing to be led toward "light," the narrative voice has changed from the desperation of "Save me!" to "Let them be saved." The soloists invoke a new sense of self-worth when challenging God to remember the promise He made to Abraham and his descendants.*

Hostias

Sacrifices and prayers we offer in praise to you, Lord. Accept them for those whom we remember today. Make them go across from death to life, as you once promised to Abraham and to his seed.

Comment: *The tenor leads this section, but not in a lyrical aria like the* Ingemisco. *The haunting melody of the* Hostias *is restrained and a bit distant. In fact, the tenor here is a priest performing a ritual—the sacrifices he speaks of are the literal animal slaughters performed in the time of the Temple and repeated in the eucharist with Christ as the "lamb" whose death is reenacted at every Mass. While the tenor's melody is plaintive, at least he is able to approach his God rather than collapse in terror as in the* Dies irae. *There is hope in this section. The* Hostias *is rarely set in music, generally being muttered by the priest to himself while the chorus sings the* Domine Jesu Christe. *In fact, it's called "The Secret Prayer." The repeat of the line "as you once promised to Abraham and his seed" is Verdi's addition.*

IV. Sanctus

Holy, holy, holy Lord God of hosts! The heavens and the earth are filled with your glory. Hosanna in the highest! Blessed is he who comes in the name of the Lord. Hosanna in the highest.

Comment: *The magnificent double chorus of this section sounds more like other composers' church music than any other part of the* Requiem. *The angels are the singers of this section, and indeed they are unaffected by the Day of Wrath, since they exist in the space between temporality and eternity. The scoring is deliberately brilliant and joyous, in great contrast to the rest of the work.*

V. Agnus Dei

Lamb of God, you take away the sins of the world, grant them rest. Lamb of God, you take away the sins of the world, grant them rest for ever and ever.

Comment: *This section is another respite in the cataclysm. The mezzo and soprano first introduce the theme unaccompanied, then it is repeated by the hushed chorus with spare orchestration. The* Agnus Dei *is also, like the* Sanctus, *intoned at every Mass, and its familiarity invites the audience to remember religion as a consolation.*

IV. Lux aeterna

Let eternal light shine on them, Lord, with your saints forever, for you are compassionate. Eternal rest grant them, Lord, and let perpetual light shine upon them, with your saints forever, for you are compassionate.

Comment: *The mezzo, tenor, and bass sing this section, allowing the soprano a respite in preparation for her prominent role in the subsequent part. "Light" is the primary motif of this section, and the scoring calls for shimmering strings and even a piccolo.*

VII. Libera me

Free me, Lord, from eternal death on that terrifying day when the heavens and the earth are stirred, when you come to judge the age with fire. I become fearful and trembling at the trial at hand and the wrath to follow when the heavens and earth are stirred. (*Dies irae.*) That day, that wrathful day of calamity and misery, a great and bitter day, when you will come to judge the age with fire. (*Requiem.*) Grant them eternal rest, Lord, and let perpetual light shine upon them. (*Libera me.*) Free me, Lord, from eternal death on that terrifying day when the heavens and the earth are stirred, when you will come to judge the age with fire. Free me.

Comment: *This long movement begins with the soprano desperately telling God to save her, a recitative as furious as that of any operatic soprano about to be violated by an evil baritone. Before this can be developed into a cohesive aria, the* Dies irae *sounds again with full force, and herein lies the scandal, from a religious point of view, of the whole work. Christianity may threaten with the fires of hell, but offers the chance of salvation. Jesus' journey, through death and hell but ultimately to heaven, is reenacted in the Requiem service. Verdi's manipulation of the text implies that the reassuring postapocalyptic vision is not necessarily a safe haven. Shifting again, the consoling opening phrases of the* Requiem *section are* *then offered, now sung quietly by the soprano and chorus. It culminates, one hopes, in the soprano's pianissimo B flat. The general prayers of the beginning of the work have now become the genuine supplications of the individual who has truly seen what is at stake. The chorus then bursts into a fast fugue that gives a feeling of confusion. What is one to believe? Toward the end of the fugue, the soprano again soars over the now forte chorus, this time running up the scale to another B flat as loud as she can manage it. She needs to take the audience with her over the top, so to speak. The merits of various sopranos' B flats at the end of the* Requiem *are debated by fans with such enthusiasm and seriousness one would think their own salvation depended on them. The forte B flat, however, is the climax, not the end. The last line is basically whispered by the soprano over the likewise hushed chorus. She is saying, in effect, "I need help—NOW! Are You there?" It is a genuine human request, unadorned and heartbreaking in its authenticity. If there is a divine answer to her question, we are not told it. All that is left, in the end, is the immenseness of the human desire and need for salvation.*

Otello

PREMIERE: La Scala, Milan, 1887. Libretto by Arrigo Boito.

As DIFFICULT AS it may be to write about music and opera, language fails entirely when trying to encapsulate *Otello*. This masterpiece is as great in its own way as any other work of art. It commands the respect of artists, audiences, and scholars equally—something that can be said of very few other operas. It is a revolutionary work that makes its artistic statement by using, and rethinking, every cliché in the war chest of standard Italian opera.

In *Otello,* Verdi achieved his goal of transcending the limits imposed by traditional forms of aria, duet, ensemble, and so on. Each act of *Otello*— indeed, the work as a whole—has a single structure. One idea gives way to the next, each arising organically out of the dramatic situation at hand. As we saw in *Aida,* the mature Verdi did not mind using the traditional components of Italian opera where they were appropriate, and in *Otello* every one of those forms is discernible if one looks. There is a storm, a drinking song, a love duet, an oath duet, a mad scene (in a sense), and a suicide to bring down the final curtain. The achievement lies in their masterful construction. Furthermore, there is not a single point in the opera where Verdi draws attention to his innovations for their own sake.

Musicians and experts praise this work for its profuse invention, but perhaps the real miracle is that general audiences love it as well. However, there is no need to worry that performances of *Otello* will become too familiar. The role of Otello is much too difficult to cast for that to happen. Otello has the reputation of being the heaviest tenor role, vocally speaking, in the Verdi canon, but that's only part of the story. The role calls for a secure bottom register, often sung against a blasting orchestra, but a huge amount of the higher segments are written right in the *passaggio,* a minefield for any tenor. Beyond this, the tenor must be able to act convincingly. Small wonder that a great Otello is a rarity. In fact, to say that there have been ten men in history who have made a credible mark on the role is generous For our purposes today, this means that any production of *Otello* is an event.

Shakespeare's play *Othello* tells the story of a heroic Moorish general in the service of the Venetian Republic who marries Desdemona, the daughter of a Venetian senator who does not approve of the match. Sent to defend the Venetian colony of Cyprus from the Turks, Othello unwittingly falls into the traps set by his ensign Iago, who artfully convinces Othello that Desdemona is unfaithful to him with his captain, Cassio. Spurred on by Iago's insinuations and his own tragic flaw of jealousy, he murders Desdemona before he discovers the truth and kills himself.

The problems in the play are familiar to many high school English students. What is Iago's motivation for destroying Othello? Why is Desdemona so utterly and fatally passive? How can we have sympathy for Othello, who deteriorates so rapidly from hero to villain? Indeed, a summary of the opera plot accentuates these problems, and Otello's deterioration is so swift we must wonder if he was waiting for the first convenient opportunity to snuff his wife. But that is only when reading about the opera, and these problems are surmounted gloriously by the opera itself.

Much of the credit for this must go to Arrigo Boito, who brought the art of the librettist to new heights with this work. He sought the inner meanings of the various scenes and situations, and reconstructed them as he saw fit, discarding some, adding others, with a savvy eye toward the strengths and weaknesses of the operatic stage. Many of our creators of opera today, who revel in setting masterpieces of stage drama as operas, would do well to memorize their source material a little less, and to study the methods of Boito a little more. Most radically, Boito manipulated the overall structure of Shakespeare's play. Shakespeare's Act I is dropped entirely, along with Desdemona's father Brabantio and Cassio's mistress Bianca. The lengthy denouement of the play is likewise jettisoned. The action, then, unfolds in a single place within, possibly, a single twenty-four-hour period. The concentrated and inexorable pace of the libretto compensates superbly for the loss of detail and color. The result is extraordinary. *Otello* is, in all probability, the pinnacle of the art of Italian opera.

CAST OF CHARACTERS

OTELLO *(tenor)* A great soldier in the service of the Venetian Republic, recently named Governor of Cyprus, Venice's largest and most vulnerable colony. Otello is a Moor, which means different things to different people. From the reminiscences in the love duct, it is apparent that Otello is a black African who was enslaved by Europeans. Otello won his freedom through military service, becoming greatly honored by the Venetian Republic. While in Venice, he met and basically eloped with Desdemona, daughter of a senator. He is about forty years old at the time of the opera—a magnificent man, entirely self-created in a hostile world, always an outsider but utterly awe-inspiring to his troops as well as his wife.

IAGO *(baritone)* Otello's ensign. The psychology of this character is the subject of countless tracts and essays. In Boito's conception, Iago is the personification of envy, as Otello is of jealousy. Their respective natures are lethal to each other. "Iago" is a Spanish version of "James," the patron saint of Spain, whose name was invoked in the long wars of the Christian *Reconquista* of Iberia as Santiago Matamoros, "Saint James, Killer of Moors."

CASSIO *(tenor)* A Venetian platoon captain. A young, handsome, popular fellow, whom everybody likes. Vocally, the role is a lighter tenor, easily distinguished by the ear from Otello, but not so *leggiero* that he gets lost in ensembles. It is common to cast up-and-coming lyric tenors in this role.

RODERIGO *(tenor)* A Venetian gentleman. Boito imagined him as young and rather foppish, with a passive nature easily manipulated by Iago. Roderigo is hopelessly, and rather ineffectually, in love with Desdemona. The role is usually given to the warhorse house comprimario tenor in the golden sunset of his career.

LODOVICO *(bass)* Ambassador of the Venetian Republic. Musically and dramatically Lodovico is the very embodiment of official Venetian *gravitas.* Producers like to cast the tallest bass they can find.

MONTANO *(bass)* The previous governor of Cyprus. Poor Montano doesn't have a lot to do plotwise, although he's there at the very beginning and the very end.

DESDEMONA *(soprano)* Otello's wife. A woman surrounded by "love, purity, nobility, docility, ingenuousness, and resignation," according to Boito's notes. But this is the same girl who defied her father and the whole Venetian establishment to leave her cushy life and marry Otello. She is also much younger than Otello. Vocally, she must convey all of Boito's impressions of her, but is also called upon to slice through Verdi's most elaborate concertato. She is invariably trooped out in a blond wig. The great diva Leontyne Price avoided the role because of its "*bianca, bionda* ambience." In Italian, the name "Desdemona" is pronounced with the accent on the second syllable, and the *s* sounds like an English *z.*

EMILIA *(mezzo)* Iago's long-suffering wife and Desdemona's companion. Vocally, Emilia carries important music in ensembles in Acts II and III, and finally gets to let all the cats out of the bag at the end of the opera.

THE OPERA

Act I

Setting: The harbor of a town in Cyprus. The castle is in the background. A storm is raging.

Guards spot a vessel heading toward the harbor through the storm. A trumpet alarm is heard from the sea, then a cannon shot. Cassio and Montano recognize the tossed ship as Otello's. Soldiers and other men come down to the quay, wondering how the ship can survive the storm. Lightning, thunder, whirlpools! The waves, the winds, the depths and the heights of the universe all convulse, and the very ether is ripped apart! More trumpet alarms sound, and the women of the town run to the quay, terrified. All turn to God and insist He save the ship. Iago and Roderigo cry out that the ship's sail has burst, and it's rushing headlong toward a rock. The Cypriots cry for help, while Iago prays in an aside to Roderigo that the ship be buried at sea. But the ship passes the reef and is saved. Men lower ropes and boats at the quay, others cheer the salvation of the ship now at the quayside.

Comment: The curtain rises directly onto the Storm Scene, with a dissonant chord played fortissimo by the full orchestra (including rattles, gongs trilled with padded drumsticks, and an organ), then dissolving into quick, rushing figures in the winds and strings. The first voices heard are four tenors, followed immediately by four basses. A larger chorus interjects, Cassio and Montano blurt out lines, then all the men comment in terrified wonder at the convulsing universe. Finally all the women join the prayer to cosmic order, and the full forces of the opera house have been employed, one by one, in less than four minutes. The effect of this scene is unlike anything else in opera, perhaps in art. Verdi depicts the storm as wild, anarchic—a rupture in the order of the universe. There are crescendos to fortissimo, but there are equally terrifying near-silences as well, and everything in between.

Otello has gone to sea to battle the enemy. If his ship is lost, the town will be overrun and plundered. The people's lives depend on the outcome of the storm. But, of course, there is more. When the full chorus of men and women address God directly, at the very singable line "Dio, folgor della bufera!," *every instrument in the orchestra is marked* "tutta forza" *("all power.") The people are not praying in supplication, but demanding salvation from a negligent deity. The issue at stake is the same as in the* Requiem. *Is there a God, or rather, does He have any power to save?*

Otello steps ashore. "Rejoice!" he exclaims. "The proud Mussulman is buried at sea! The glory is ours and heaven's. After our might, the hurricane conquered him."

Comment: "Esultate" *is the most famous entrance in opera, and, well performed, the best. It's a mere twelve measures long, very lightly scored against sustained chords in the horns and the organ still in the background. This means the vocal line is fully exposed. The tenor surfs the* passaggio, *rising up to an A below high C and down to F two octaves below, always forte. Don't try this one in the shower. Besides the musical impression, Otello's mere presence must also command awe. Note how he presents the news. The glory is "ours" (first) and "heaven's" (second), "our might" conquered the enemy, then the hurricane. The words and the music make one thing clear—Otello is, if not a divine entity, then at least superhuman. His very arrival at the harbor seems to have calmed the storm and saved the situation in a way God couldn't, or wouldn't.*

The people cheer Otello, who withdraws into his castle with Montano and Cassio. Thrilled by their military salvation, the people also note that the storm has passed. All is calm.

Comment: In "Vittoria! Sterminio!" *the divided chorus rushes through expressions of glee in very rapid, brief expressions. When they note the storm is calming, the organ finally stops playing. The effect is rather sudden and surprising. It is time for individual stories to emerge from the cosmic battle we have just experienced.*

Iago approaches Roderigo, who is melancholy over his hopeless love for Desdemona. Iago urges patience. She will soon get tired of the loathsome kisses from the thick-lipped savage, and Roderigo may move in on her then. Iago himself will help, for though he pretends to love the Moor, he really hates him, and he has reason to. That over-dressed Cassio was promoted to captain over him, despite Iago's qualifications earned in a hundred battles. Let Roderigo follow Iago's advice.

The people light a bonfire to celebrate the victory, commenting on the fire's ephemeral nature.

Comment: The musical structure of this famous chorus, "Fuocco di gioia," is very hard to summarize, since the singers and orchestra imitate fire, tapering off rather than resolving. Musicians rave about it, since it's probably the most evocative imitation of fire in music. Other opera commentators complain that it's not dramatically compelling and it stops the action. This misses the point. "Fuocco di gioia" exists precisely to stop the action, or rather to separate the action of the Storm Scene from the rest of the act.

Iago invites Roderigo and Cassio to join him in a drink. Cassio says no, since he's had enough already, but Iago insists on a toast to the marriage of Otello and Desdemona. This Cassio cannot refuse, and he raises his cup to Desdemona, the ornament of Cyprus. Cassio praises Desdemona, and Iago tells Roderigo to beware of this youthful, wily seducer, who will disrupt any hopes Roderigo still has of winning Desdemona's love. And when Cassio drinks, he is lost.

Iago leads the people in a drinking song, constantly refilling Cassio's cup. Cassio revels in the wine, and the people cheer his drinking. Iago urges Roderigo to start a quarrel with him.

Comment: In Iago's rousing drinking song, the vocal line is all evil insinuation amid the bravura. Cassio's interjections show him getting progressively drunk and belligerent (a process reflected in the orchestra), and the festive chorus contrasts with a steady, four-square melody.

Iago ends his little "Drink with me!" lines ("Bevi, bevi!") on A below high C, a rather high note for anyone, especially a baritone. Don't be too shocked if the baritone you see in performance sings "bev-" and then indicates "-i!" with a hand gesture. They do this all the time, and apparently have ever since the premiere.

Montano returns and tells Cassio it's time to stand watch. Cassio staggers, much to Montano's surprise. Iago whispers that the Captain gets this way every night. Cassio rallies to stand watch, but stumbles, and Roderigo and the people laugh at him. Roderigo calls Cassio a drunk, and Montano urges calm since Cassio is clearly impaired. Cassio draws his sword on Montano. Iago quickly urges Roderigo to sound the alarm at the harbor. Iago begs calm from the people while causing as much confusion as he can. Fights break out spontaneously. The women run and general melee ensues.

Otello enters and orders all to drop their arms. There is instant silence.

Comment: The orchestra grows in nervous figures while Iago stirs up trouble and the divided chorus cries for help in this masterful, brief riot scene. We get the feeling, hinted at in the storm and fire chorus, that anarchy is ready to erupt at any point in this world, sweeping everything before it unless controlled by a greater force.

That greater force is, of course, Otello, whose entrance here is hardly less impressive than in the "Esultate." There, his appearance seemed to calm a storm. Here, similarly, he stops human storms in a heartbeat. His a cappela cry of "Lay down your arms!" is sung on F and G (that is, in the passaggio.) The final syllable is followed directly by a full orchestral fortissimo "thud" for one quarter-note (the flutes shrieking their highest possible notes), then complete silence. You probably won't be able to discern every detail in performance, but the idea is clear: This man can command.

Otello asks if the people have "turned Turk," ready to slaughter each other. He asks "honest Iago" what has happened. Iago, all confused innocence now, replies that he doesn't know. They were all courteous friends, when suddenly everyone fell on each other. Otello asks Cassio for an explanation, but the befuddled Captain can only ask for pardon. And Montano? Wounded. Otello is furious. He strips Cassio of his captain's rank (causing Iago to crow to himself). Desdemona enters, and Otello apologizes for her disturbed night. He orders everyone back to their houses. He himself will stand there until the town is quiet once again.

Otello turns to Desdemona. Now in the dark night every noise stills. Let war thunder and the whole world collapse, if, after immense fury comes this immense love! Desdemona tells her proud warrior that much suffering and many sighs have led to this sweet embrace. Does he remember how he first told her of his long exile and great sufferings, and how she listened with a ravished soul? Then he told her of the bright deserts of his native land, and of the chains of slavery. He recalls that her face ennobled his story with tears. And you loved me, he says, for my misadventures, and I loved you for your pity. Let death come, he exclaims, and take me in the ecstasy of this embrace. The sky clears. Otello fears that he will never again know such perfect joy in his uncertain future. Desdemona prays that cares be driven from him, and their love never change through the years. Let the celestial powers say "Amen" to her prayer. Otello leans against the wall. Such intense joy deprives him of breath! He asks for a kiss, a kiss, and yet another kiss. He looks at the sky. Already the burning Pleiades are sinking into the sea. The night grows late, says Desdemona. He leads her slowly toward the castle. Come, he says. Venus is blazing! She murmurs his name as they walk.

Comment: *This splendid duet, "Già nella notte densa," is Verdi's most celebrated love scene. There is no denying its power and brilliant craftsmanship. It differs from every other love duet in opera because of the circumstance of the lovers. They are not meeting for the first time and acknowledging their passion, like in* Traviata, *nor are they duking out the terms of their passion, like in* Ballo. *These two are happily married and reveling in their perfectly legal, if somewhat unconventional, love.*

There is no one melodic structure in the duet. Each line unfolds out of the previous line in a perfectly organic pattern. Otello and Desdemona tend to sing separately rather than at the same time, as in all of Verdi's great confrontation duets, but there is no great conflict between these two characters yet. Their opposition consists in their natures. The "big theme" is played by the orchestra as Otello sings of the "kiss" ("un bacio"). He sings over the theme, and she merely mutters his name. Throughout the duet, his voice continually dominates hers, or, as one lecturer put it, she is constantly consumed by his more intense nature. After the "kiss," the orchestra fades into a sustained note in the highest reaches of the strings, triple pianissimo. He rises to an A flat below high C for his climactic line "Venere splende!" The orchestra comes in with sustained chords in the winds, harp arpeggios, and trilling flutes just as he says "splende," which has the effect of a great sigh followed by tingling. Desdemona waits a beat and a half after this, and says merely "Otello!" on the comfortable note F, and they hold their respective notes for another measure and a half. They are a chord, and he is the dominant note.

I invariably nod off at some point during "Già nella notte densa." That is not to say it's dull—quite the contrary. It is transcendental. The beginning of the act literally raises your blood pressure, and the duet brings it back down—not to where it was when you walked into the opera house, but to a whole new and mellowed plane of existence. The effect is shocking to the body. It is exactly like sitting down after an intense anaerobic workout. The body must shut down completely for a brief moment before continuing on an endorphinal high. And some people still think dozing at the opera is a sign of boredom. . . .

Act II

Setting: A room in the castle, with a garden in the background.

Iago tells the downtrodden Cassio not to worry, everything will soon be back to normal and Cassio will be able to forget everything in the arms of his mistress, Monna Bianca. Iago suggests he rely on Desdemona, who is the Leader's leader. Cassio should wait for her in the garden and plead his case. "Go now," he advises. Cassio leaves.

"Go now," Iago repeats, "I see your end already." Alone, Iago considers that Cassio is driven by an evil genius, and Iago is that evil genius. And Iago's evil genius? Inexorable God, in whom he places all his faith. He believes in a cruel God in Whose likeness he is made and on Whom, in hate, he now calls. From the vileness of some germ or atom he was born, evil, because he is man, and he still senses the primordial slime in himself. Yes, this is his faith, and he believes as firmly as any widow in church! Evil is his destiny. An honest man is a fool, and everything in him a lie: tear, kiss, looks, sacrifice, and honor. He believes man is a plaything of an evil fate, from the germ of the cradle to the worm of the grave. And after such a joke comes Death. And then? And then? Death is Nothingness, and heaven an old wives' tale. He shrugs his shoulders and watches the garden.

Comment: *This "Creed," like the Apostles' Creed, begins with and repeats the word "Credo" ("I believe"). The references to "germ" and "atom" are a nod toward Darwin, whose theories were being furiously debated at this time. Boito is playing with the fear that mankind must reconsider its capacity for divine aspiration if it must now understand itself as descended from primordial slime. Note that Boito's stage instructions call for Iago to shrug his shoulders and move toward the back of the stage. Don't expect this in performance. Baritones live for years on the hope that they will someday sing Iago, and they can hardly be expected to contain themselves after their big moment. Tradition calls for an evil laugh to punctuate the end of the narrative (something along the lines of "Moo-hoo-ahh-hah-hah" and sometimes even embellished with a twist of the mustache à la Snidely Whiplash). We are, thankfully, beginning to see the end of this cliché.*

In the garden, Desdemona is walking with Emilia. Cassio approaches her and bows deeply. Iago notes that his plot begins. Let Satan come to his aid! Desdemona and Cassio walk in the garden. Otello enters, but Iago gazes into the garden, pretending not to have seen Otello, and muttering, "I do not like that." Otello asks him what he's saying, but Iago pretends to be flustered and says nothing. Otello asks if that was Cassio speaking to Desdemona. Iago says he doesn't think so. With great insinuation, Iago asks Otello if, in the first days of his love, Desdemona and Cassio knew each other. Yes, answers Otello. Why? Just a vague thought, answers Iago. What thought? demands

Otello. Did Otello confide in Cassio? Cassio would often take a present or token to Desdemona. Oh, really? asks Iago. Yes, really. Why, doesn't Iago think him honest? Honest? repeats Iago. Otello asks what Iago is hiding in his heart. What am I hiding in my heart, sir? Yes, what are you hiding in your heart? How Iago's words echo Otello's! Let Iago speak his mind, if he loves Otello. Iago assures Otello of his love, but will not speak more even if Otello commanded his very soul. He warns Otello to beware of jealousy, a dark, evil, blind hydra that poisons itself on its own venom. Otello cries out but gathers himself. Before doubt comes inquiry and then proof. After proof, let love and jealousy be resolved together.

Desdemona enters the garden again, surrounded by sailors, women, and boys, who offer her flowers and sing her praises. Otello and Iago stand by in the room while Desdemona receives her gifts and praises in the garden.

Comment: Iago's exchanges with Otello are their most important character signifiers. The subsequent choral scene is long and, for many people, problematic. Each of the various groups, sailors, boys, women, etc., presents Desdemona with songs in the most rustic manner, including mandolin accompaniment and an Italian bagpipe. Iago and Otello sing nothing throughout the scene. Many commentators decry stopping the action for all this plunk-plunking. Truly, the choral music is annoying, especially when the boys sing an insistent 6/8 beat in their high voices. Otello's character transformation must occur during this scene, and he must communicate it with gestures, since he doesn't say anything. More than anywhere else in the opera, this is the place where the tenor's acting abilities are put to the test.

Desdemona and Emilia enter the room. Desdemona brings a petition from one who suffers under Otello's displeasure, Cassio. Otello asks if she was with him just now. Yes, she replies, and asks that he be pardoned. Not now, says Otello. She asks again. Not now! he snaps. How terrible his voice sounds. Let her wipe his forehead with her handkerchief. He tosses it on the ground. Desdemona guilelessly asks if she has offended her lord in some way. Let him tell her how, and she will beg pardon. Otello complains he does not understand the subtle deceits of love, or perhaps his advancing years are to blame. Meanwhile, Emilia picks up Desdemona's handkerchief, but Iago demands she give it to him. Emilia asks her husband what evil he is up to now. He orders her to obey him as a slave, and, though she resists, wrests the handkerchief from her. He commands her not to say a word. Desdemona asks pardon again from Otello, but he orders her out.

Comment: The repartee of this scene evolves seamlessly into a quartet without our being conscious of it, an effect Verdi had been moving toward since his earliest operas. Desdemona's vocal line soars above the broken and nervous phrases of the others. We should get the feeling that she is simply on a different level from the others—above them, in a sense, and therefore incapable of grasping their baser machinations. Thus the music tells us what the words never quite do—neither Boito's words nor Shakespeare's.

Desdemona guilty? What a horrible thought, says Otello. Iago notes that his poison is taking effect. Blithely, he tells Otello not to think of it any more. Otello explodes at Iago, who has nailed him to the cross. Was he so blinded by her beauty that he didn't see her deceit, and didn't feel Cassio's burning kisses on her lips? And now . . . And now . . . Now and forever farewell, sacred memories, enchanted thoughts, shining legions, victories and songs of battle! This is the end of Otello's glory!

Comment: Otello's solo, "Ora e per sempre addio," is written as a march, with pizzicato strings, trumpet rhythms, and plucking harps. His military glory is passing in front of his eyes, so to speak. Traditionally tenors have delivered this solo in a forte voice appropriate to the character's heroic past. Recently it has been more popular to sing it in a restrained voice, a mezza voce. There is no direction for this in the score, which merely says "larga la frase," or "broad phrase," but the effect is stunning. The march in the orchestra thus becomes truly mocking of Otello's present condition, and he himself is aware that his heroism is disintegrating before his demons. It takes much more breath control and technique to deliver this solo in a mezza voce *than full-voiced, and only a truly great tenor would risk it before the upcoming explosive duet. If he can manage it, however, the duet will be orgasmic rather than blustery.*

Iago tells Otello to be calm, but this prompts a fury from Otello. Throwing the ensign to the ground, he orders Iago to find proof of the crime, or beware his wrath. Rising and begging defense from heaven, Iago calls the world to witness that honesty is dangerous. He starts to leave, but Otello bids him stay. Perhaps Iago is honest after all. Better, says Iago, if I were a scoundrel! Otello is divided. He thinks Desdemona honest, but not, and thinks Iago true, but not. He must have proof and certainty. Iago asks what certainty Otello requires? To see them perhaps embrace? Death and damnation, shouts Otello. Iago can offer no proof, nor would he want to, but there have been indications that are all but certain. Listen. One night, Cassio was sleeping, and Iago lay beside him. Cassio spoke as he dreamt, and said, "Sweet Desdemona! Let us be careful and hide our love! I curse the bitter fate that gave you to the Moor!" Then all was quiet.

Comment: Iago's solo, "Era la notte," is scored for muted strings, triple pianissimo. The vocal line begins mezza voce, *and becomes lighter as the baritone continues. It is also very high in the range, being almost entirely written above the staff. When he is supposedly quoting Cassio, the score is marked* sotto voce *parlate, or "spoken under the voice." In other words, whispered.*

What a monstrous crime, mutters Otello. It was only a dream, says Iago. But he has another proof. Has Otello ever noticed in Desdemona's hand a handkerchief, embroidered with flowers and finer than gauze? Otello knows it well. It was his first gift to her. Yesterday, says Iago, he saw that handkerchief—in the hand of Cassio!

Ha, cries Otello, let God grant Cassio a thousand lives, since one will not satisfy his fury! All his love is gone. He calls for blood, blood, blood. He kneels. Yes, he swears, by marble heaven, by death, and by the vast dark ocean, let his raised hand flash with rage and fury. Iago kneels with him. Let all creation witness that he swears his arm, heart, and soul to Otello and to the bloody work at hand. They both raise their fists to heaven, imploring the God of Vengeance.

Comment: *All hell, literally, breaks loose when Otello launches the recitative introduction to the duet, "Ah! Mille vite." The effect after Iago's whispering, insinuating narrative is explosive—the storm of anarchy and destruction has erupted again, this time entirely within the person of Otello.*

The celebrated duct, "Sì, pel ciel," starts with Otello trumpeting thirteen E's (in other words, right in the passaggio*), up to an A (on the word "Morte"("Death")), then falling down the scale to C sharp below middle C, all marked "con forza." By that low C sharp that finishes the phrase, the orchestra has miraculously died down to pianissimo winds, trumpet, and violin trill. The tenor is fully exposed, and more fake this low note than all the high notes in the duet. But listen closely for it. It's the anchor of the whole passage.*

Iago repeats Otello's notes in a lower setting, and the two sing the final verse together, with Iago singing a different melody and revealing the first two verses as a relatively monotone harmony. The effect is obvious: Otello's brash actions are motivated by more complex, lower machinations, represented by Iago. The orchestra, meanwhile, is a miracle of sustained string trills, whirling woodwinds, and explosions from the brass and percussion, like artillery or flags whipping in the wind. It is beyond the militarism of Otello's character. In fact, the storm of the opening scene, the cosmic battle of light and dark, has been subsumed into his person at this point, and Otello is exploding. This is well beyond the standard oath duet of earlier Italian opera.

"Sì, pel ciel" often appears on concert programs and, in the opera, usually brings down the house to tumultuous applause. Musicologists sneer at the duet, but it offers the inherent thrill of a great tenor singing at the extremes of his faculties. For all the difficulties of subtle phrasing, artistry, and musicianship required in much of operatic singing, there is nothing quite so demanding on a gut level as this duet. It is thrilling not only in itself, but as the culmination of Act II, which is a microcosm of the whole story. Otello falls from greatness to evil banality in the course of Act II alone. Act I and the subsequent acts are, in terms of the hero's character development, prologue and epilogue, respectively.

Act III

Scene 1: A hall in the castle.

Otello and Iago are alone. A herald enters and tells Otello that the ship bearing Venetian dignitaries has been spotted in the harbor and will land soon. Otello dismisses the herald. Iago promises to bring Cassio to the hall and get him to talk about his new mistress, Desdemona. Otello should hide and listen, paying close attention to Cassio's gestures and manner. As he is about to leave, he whispers "the handkerchief" to Otello, who dismisses him brusquely.

Desdemona enters, graciously greeting Otello as the sovereign of her soul. Otello, feigning equal grace, takes Desdemona's white hand. How lovely it is! She says her hand is still ignorant of pain and age. And yet, he says, the pretty demon of bad advice resides in that hand, lighting it as it poses in prayer and piety. Still, she protests, that is the hand that gave him her heart. But she must speak to him of Cassio . . . He cries out at this and asks for a handkerchief. She offers him one, but he wants the one he gave her, which she does not have. Otello becomes menacing. Let her beware if she has lost it! He orders her to fetch it. She protests that she will, but surely Otello is toying with her to avoid discussing Cassio. He demands the handkerchief. But Cassio is his best friend! The handkerchief, he insists. She finally realizes the threat in his voice. He seizes her, and demands she look in his eyes and tell him who she really is. Otello's loyal wife, she insists. He tells her to swear it and be damned. What does Otello think her? Otello thinks her false. She is terrified by his awful glance, and sheds tears—her first ever. Otello almost believes her—even her demon would think her innocent if he saw her now. Desdemona asks what she has done wrong, but he counters that she doesn't need to ask—it's written all over her face. Is she not a vile courtesan? No, she protests, truly shocked, she is not the thing that foul word expresses. Suddenly changing to an ironic calm, he asks for her ivory hand, and begs forgiveness. He had thought she was that vile courtesan that married Otello! She runs off, horrified.

Comment: The scene opens with extremely lyrical music, which is Otello being sarcastic and Desdemona being herself. When she begins nagging about Cassio, half of the audience usually roars with laughter. There's nothing to be done about it. The same lines are equally difficult in Shakespeare, and Shakespeare had a lot more opportunity to show Cassio as an old friend of both Othello's and Desdemona's. Here we must believe that Desdemona is really too innocent and pure to comprehend that she's saying anything out of the ordinary. In the opera, it's an impression she must convey vocally, with a certain ingenuousness in the voice. The lyricism of the music gives way to outbursts from Otello, so we have an opportunity to see him struggling, not with her, but with himself. The word "courtesan" was Boito's solution to Shakespeare's plainer "whore," which Verdi did not like.

Alone, Otello tells God it would have been better for Him to torture him in any other way—poverty, shame, defeat. All these Otello would have borne patiently as the will of heaven. But this one radiance that made life a joy is gone. Now let Forgiveness cover her holy face with the horrible image of hell. Damnation! Let her confess her sin and then die! Confession! Confession!

Comment: This great soliloquy, "Dio! mi potevi," is the whole role in a nutshell. It begins in a pianissimo monotone marked "voce soffocata," a hint to directors that Otello suffers from epilepsy or other physical ailments. He then sings "dolcissimo" when recounting the beauty of which he is now (so he thinks) deprived, landing on a high B flat for the word "raggio" ("ray"). The mounting fury is a great crescendo of broken figures, again indicating almost gasping or choking. It is a great journey in barely two minutes.

Iago reenters and tells Otello to hide. Cassio approaches. He is looking for Desdemona to find how his case is going with Otello. Iago suggests he wait with him in the hall, and tell him of his love adventures. "With whom?" asks Cassio. "With Bianca," whispers Iago. Laughingly, Cassio says he is already quite tired of his mistress. Iago taunts him playfully, while Otello, the whole time, thinks Cassio is speaking of Desdemona, and becomes furious. Cassio asks Iago to help him figure out a mystery. Iago, pulling Cassio in various directions so Otello can only hear snippets of the conversation, tells Cassio to confide in him. He produces Desdemona's handkerchief, telling Iago he found it in his room. Otello sees the handkerchief in Cassio's hand, and calls for death and damnation. A fanfare of trumpets is heard from inside the castle, followed by a cannon shot. The ship from Venice has docked. Cassio, on Iago's advice, leaves, not wishing to run into Otello in the hall. Otello approaches Iago. How shall they kill Desdemona? Outside, the Cypriots cheer the Venetian delegates. Iago suggests they smother Desdemona in the bed where she sinned, and this justice pleases Otello. He prepares himself to receive the ambassadors, and Iago leaves to bring Desdemona to the hall, to keep suspicion to a minimum.

Comment: The plot creaks most in this scene, where Otello hears words like "kisses" and "fleeting loves," but conveniently misses "Bianca" and "I found this handkerchief in my room and I don't know how it got there." Furthermore, didn't Cassio deliver Otello's gifts to Desdemona in Venice? Wouldn't he recognize the handkerchief? (Perhaps it was tastefully gift-wrapped.) Again, as in the previous encounter with Desdemona, the music must cover the plot flaws. Iago and Cassio sing marvelously light and "chummy" music, a superb relief from the overall descent into tragedy. It also demonstrates both Iago's ability to change character in an instant and Cassio's basically agreeable nature. Otello's interjections, usually exclaimed from behind a pillar or some such silliness, further manifest his separateness from the others and his tortured state.

Lodovico enters, followed by Roderigo, heralds, dignitaries of the Republic, ladies and gentlemen, soldiers, trumpeters, and Cypriots. At last Iago enters with Desdemona and Emilia. The courtiers and Cypriots cheer the Lion of Saint Mark.

Comment: The entrance of the Venetian ambassadors and the others is managed very quickly and impressively, a jarring shift from the private to the public spheres. Expect a lot of red and gold on stage. This was the point

at which a ballet was inserted for the Paris premiere of the opera in 1894.
Verdi complied with some lovely ballet music, now available on record-
ings but never used in performance, even in France. As we will see, the
personal tragedy of the protagonists continues unabated, and the shift to
the public sphere is a change in backgrounds, not in narrative point of
view.

Lodovico hands Otello a written message from the Doge and the
Senate, and Otello kisses the seal of state in respect. Emilia notes
how sad Desdemona is. Iago greets Lodovico, who asks where Cassio
is. Otello is displeased with him, explains Iago. Desdemona remarks
that she thinks Cassio will return to grace. Otello snaps at her. Is she
sure of that? Iago says Cassio may return to favor, and Desdemona
says she truly hopes so. She is truly fond of Cassio. Otello calls her a
demon and tells her to hold her tongue. All are shocked at this outburst. Otello orders the herald to bring Cassio to the audience.
Lodovico wonders if this Otello can be the courageous warrior,
famous everywhere. Iago whispers that Otello is what he is, but slyly
refuses to say more. Cassio is brought in. Otello reads the pronounce-
ment of the Senate and the Doge, but keeps interrupting himself with
savage asides to Desdemona. The Doge recalls him to Venice, and the
Doge chooses Cassio as governor of Cyprus in Otello's absence.
Lodovico tells Otello to comfort Desdemona, who is obviously upset.
Instead, Otello announces that he and Desdemona will sail the next
day. Seizing her, he forces her to her knees and tells her to weep. All
are stunned.

Yes, she says, on the ground, in the slime, she weeps. Once her
smile brought hope and kisses, now there is only anguish in her heart.
Emilia admires Desdemona's noble suffering, Cassio wonders at the
fateful hour, bringing him honor he had not sought, Lodovico marvels at Otello's behavior, Roderigo bemoans that Desdemona will
leave the island, while the ladies call for mercy and the gentlemen are
astounded. All are absorbed in their thoughts and reactions, and do
not notice Iago speaking to Otello. Let Otello rouse himself to the
deed at hand. Iago himself will kill Cassio and dispatch his guilty soul
to hell. Otello agrees. Iago speaks to Roderigo, who is lost in self-pity.

If something were to happen to Cassio, suggests Iago, Otello and Desdemona could not leave.

Comment: *This is the great ensemble of the opera, a concertato that gathers all the various characters into a single tableau. It is the most complicated concertato Verdi wrote. It begins with Desdemona's appropriately low-lying phrases describing her present degraded state. She soars up higher with two arching melodies, not unlike Violetta, another wronged woman, at the analogous moment in* Traviata. *Pizzicato strings create a curiously disjointed subtext to the vocal line. Emilia, Cassio, Roderigo, and Lodovico provide a moment of ensemble harmony, sung a capella, before the divided chorus enters, first in short phrases, then long ones. The strings move almost imperceptibly from pizzicato to bowed. The final restatement of the big theme utilizes the full orchestra and chorus, building incrementally and seamlessly.*

Verdi keeps Iago well outside of the unified ensemble, making interjections to Otello and Roderigo. The original directions for this stage business are elaborate. This keeps the drama moving forward, but, paradoxically, Verdi's insistence on having Iago run around the stage and make asides now seems old-fashioned. Their comments keep the moment in real time, emphasizing that the others standing on stage are standing still. Fortunately, little of this matters in performance. The ensemble is, ultimately, entirely centered on Desdemona. It is a great vocal challenge to the soprano. Much of this passage lies low in the voice, which makes it hard to hear through the orchestration. Even when she soars, the orchestra and chorus soar with her, doubling her line, and ideally she should be heard through the whole ensemble. At such a point, one need hardly worry about whether the baritone is advancing the action.

Otello orders all out of the hall. Iago says to Lodovico that Otello has taken leave of his senses. Lodovico begins to escort Desdemona out of the hall, but she breaks away and runs toward her husband. Addressing her as his very soul, he curses her. All are aghast, and the hall empties except for Iago and Otello. The crowd outside cheers the Lion of Saint Mark and its representatives. Otello realizes he cannot flee his own wrath. The handkerchief . . . He faints. Iago notes

his poison is working. The crowd cheers Otello. Iago wonders who can stop him now from crushing the hero's face under his heel? The crowd cheers, cries glory to Otello and the Lion of Saint Mark. With a gesture of contempt and triumph, Iago points to Otello's writhing body. "Behold the Lion!" he sneers.

Comment: *Verdi and Boito went through hell trying to figure out a way to bring the curtain down on Act III. They knew there needed to be something after the concertato, but should it be a denouement or another climax? When Boito confessed himself stumped, Verdi suggested that the Turks should suddenly attack, and Otello would rouse everybody to arms and lead them again to victory. Boito diplomatically replied that such a resurgence of Otello's heroism at this late point in the drama would run counter to Shakespeare. The solution reached is quite effective In Act IV, Scene 1, of the play, Iago repeats "handkerchief" and "confession" to Otello as incantations, causing Otello to "fall into a trance." He then mutters, "Work on, my medicine. . . ." When Verdi was first discussing the possibility of setting* Otello *as an opera, he pointed to this moment as being supremely suitable for operatic treatment. He remembered it now and put it to use.*

Act IV

Setting: Desdemona's room. Night.

Emilia is preparing Desdemona for bed. She asks if Otello was calmer. He seemed so, says Desdemona. She asks Emilia to lay out her white wedding gown on the bed. If anything should happen to her, let her be buried in it. Emilia tells her to forget such ideas. Desdemona sits in front of the mirror and thinks of a poor pretty maid her mother had named Barbara. She loved a man who abandoned her. Barbara used to sing a song, the Willow Song. Now she can't stop thinking about that song. Barbara wept while she sang at the hearth, "Oh willow! Willow! Willow! Let's sing. The weeping willow will be my garland." Desdemona gives Emilia a ring from her finger, telling her to put it away. Barbara's song should have ended with the simple line "He was born for glory, and I to love." She jumps at a noise. Emilia tells her it's only the wind. "And I to love him and to die," she repeats, singing of the willow again. She bids Emilia farewell and good night. As Emilia is quietly leaving, Desdemona cries another desperate farewell to her friend. Emilia leaves.

Comment: This passage is often referred to as Desdemona's mad scene, though she is quite sane and, in fact, somewhat more in tune with her surroundings than usual. If anything, Desdemona seems to be in a state of shock. Most of the coloring in the orchestra is created by winds and muted horns. She is more haunted by memories than made insane by them, as her frequent comments to Emilia make apparent. At no point does her state of mind permit her vocal line to coalesce into a single lyric structure. She repeats "willow" ("Salce! Salce!") and her grief is echoed by the English horn or by silence. It is a superb study in emotions that must be repressed if they are not to consume the individual. The catharsis at the end is achieved in a single line, "Ah! Emilia, addio, Emilia, addio!," beginning on a passionate high C but dying down to F an octave and a half below. Scholars have pointed out that this line performs the function of a full cabaletta, and the soprano must communicate an entire cabaletta's worth of passion in the single, sobbing line.

Calmly, Desdemona prays to Mary, chosen among matrons and virgins, asking her to pray for all, sinners and righteous, who kneel before her and bow their heads beneath outrage and misfortune. She goes to bed. Otello enters the room through a secret door, putting out the light on Desdemona's table. He gazes at his sleeping wife and kisses her three times. On the third kiss, she awakes.

Comment: Desdemona's state of shock continues in her prayer, a paradoxical combination of repressed emotion and arching lyricism. Muted strings accompany her as she sings a single repeated note while reciting the standard lines of the Hail Mary, but soars in the interpolated lines. (The text was a setting of the Ave Maria incorrectly attributed to Dante.) The strings sustain their highest notes as she finishes her prayer and gets into bed. As the high strings die away, the basses take over in their lowest range, moving toward their highest notes, where they have an especially poignant sound. The whole conflict of natures between Otello and Desdemona is apparent in these few bars of orchestral writing. After he gazes on her for a moment, a new and very menacing theme is played by the oboe as he extinguishes the light, a moment where Shakespeare had Othello recite a memorable monologue. As he kisses Desdemona, we hear the "kiss" theme, the great unresolved orchestral swelling from the Act I duet.

He asks her if she has said her prayers. Yes, she replies. If she has any sins she has not yet confessed, she must do so immediately. He does not wish to kill her soul. But why, she asks, does he speak of killing? He tells her to think of her sins. She says her only sin is love. And for that, he replies, she must die. Because she loves Otello? Because she loves Cassio. She denies it. The handkerchief, he says. He saw it in Cassio's hand. She denies that she gave it to Cassio. He warns her to beware of perjury, since she is about to die. She protests her loyalty, and asks for Cassio to be brought in to prove it, but Otello tells her Cassio is mute forever. Does she dare to weep for him? She begs for her life, at least a little while longer, but he casts her down, calling her a prostitute. Without giving her time for one last prayer, he strangles her and looks at her limp body. It is as quiet as the tomb.

Emilia pounds at the door, which Otello opens. Cassio has killed Roderigo! And what of Cassio? asks Otello. He lives. Desdemona groans from the bed. Emilia runs to her. Who has done this? Nobody, replies Desdemona. "I myself. Commend me to my lord. I die innocent. Farewell." She dies. Otello calls her a liar, since he killed her himself. She was Cassio's mistress. Just ask Iago. "Iago!" gasps Emilia, calling Otello a fool to believe him. She runs to the door, screaming that Otello has killed Desdemona. Lodovico, Cassio, Iago, and Montano all run in, followed by soldiers. Emilia asks Iago if he believed Desdemona unfaithful. Truly yes, he thought her so. Otello says Desdemona gave Cassio the handkerchief he had once given her, and Emilia understands everything. Iago orders her to be silent, but she refuses, and tells how Iago took the handkerchief from her. Cassio adds that he then found the handkerchief in his room, and Montano adds that the dying Roderigo confessed all of Iago's schemes. Iago runs out the door, and is followed by soldiers. Otello picks up his sword, asking if heaven has no more thunderbolts, but Lodovico orders Otello to hand him the sword.

Otello says no one need fear him, even armed. This is the end of his road. Otello is finished. Dropping his sword, he goes to Desdemona and speaks to her directly. How pale she is, and tired, and mute, and beautiful. She was a pious creature born under an evil star, now cold as her chaste life and risen into heaven. Ah, Desdemona, Desdemona, dead, dead, dead! Suddenly he draws a dagger from his belt and stabs himself. Crawling to her on the bed, he tells her how he kissed her before he killed her. Now, dying, in the darkness where he lies, a kiss, a kiss, yet one more kiss. He falters before he can kiss her body the third time, and dies.

Comment: Otello's confrontation with Desdemona is handled very swiftly and with a minimum of reflection, as the situation dictates. When he strangles her, he comments, "Quiet as the grave," in a curiously detached phrase. He is neither triumphant nor yet defeated. Emilia's entrance and the subsequent revelation of facts is likewise very swift. The real drama resumes with Otello's final narrative, "Niun mi tema." Rather than challenging the tenor with heroics, as we saw in the earlier acts, Verdi has provided heart-wrenching music that challenges the tenor's soul as much as his talent. There is no faking it here, emotionally or artistically. Boito, too, must receive kudos for the words he wrote for this exquisitely economical "suicide aria." Note the use of words like "quiet" and "mute" throughout this scene. The opera began with the anarchic forces of nature represented by great noise. It ends with the death of individuals, represented by silence and its symbols.

Falstaff

PREMIERE: La Scala, Milan, 1893. Libretto by Arrigo Boito.

THIS IS Verdi's final opera, written when he was approaching eighty years of age. It is a comedy, a warm look at humanity and its foibles, with an undeniably life-affirming message. The libretto was created by Boito, who took the basic outline of Shakespeare's *Merry Wives of Windsor* and augmented it with lines from *Henry IV, Parts I* and *II* to fill out the title character. Verdi was impressed, and loved the idea of setting a comedy for his final opera. During the composition, he insisted to his wife and Boito that he was only writing for his own amusement, with absolutely no thought for the opera's fate on the stage. This should not be taken too literally. Still, it is clear that there is something extremely personal in the score of this opera; its musical language is introverted and seemingly indifferent to applause.

It is also Verdi's most technically admirable work. It has astounded musicians and experts from its first performances. Although *Falstaff* is appreciated by general audiences and is becoming ever more popular as the years go by, it has never been adored by them in the manner of *Traviata* or *Aida*. The usual explanation for this is that it is too rarefied for average tastes. There are no arias in the standard sense, no set pieces, and no melodies to hum on the way out of the opera house. The music is welded, rather than wedded, to the text from beginning to end. It builds and dissipates without any noticeable divisions. However, the musical and structural language of *Falstaff* is powerful and magical, even if one doesn't hear every nuance the first time. Boito's brilliant libretto is brought to life with an attention to detail unsurpassed in the opera house, not even by those who wrote their own librettos. Nor is this mere "word-painting," that genre of twentieth-century lyric writing that makes singers enliven such mundane phrases as "Pass the salt!" in dissonant exclamations above the staff. One never gets the feeling that Verdi is avoiding four-square melody in this work. The overall impression is of a story that simply could not be told any other way than the way he wrote it.

The understandable reverence in which *Falstaff* is held by musicians has served to create a smokescreen of highbrow piety around the opera as a theatrical experience. Such a situation would have made Verdi gag. He fastidiously avoided all theorizing about music and said an opera should be judged exclusively by the box office. Boito, too, who had been "spherical" a half-century earlier, was by the time of this work a practical man of the theater. *Falstaff* is a colossus from the technical point of view, but it is also a great opera, and its greatness is not all that different from any other great opera. It engages our attention by using music to penetrate places where words alone do not go. Ultimately, *Falstaff* entertains.

CAST OF CHARACTERS

SIR JOHN FALSTAFF *(baritone)* A gross, drunken, thieving, fat man who is also, let us not forget, a knight and quite at home with courtly pleasantries. He is also a philosopher.

BARDOLFO *(tenor)* and PISTOLA *(bass),* Falstaff's followers.

FORD *(baritone)* A successful middle-class man of Windsor, married to Alice. Ford is, for reasons not given here, disposed to jealousy.

MRS. ALICE FORD *(soprano)* Ford's wife, a smart, lively woman who gets her way in the end. She is also wise, and mature, and physically attractive. Her first name is pronounced "ah-LEE-chay." Verdi wrote that Alice, not Falstaff, is really the lead role of the opera, although she makes no grand gestures, musical or dramatic, and sings most of her music in ensembles. The role requires excellent musicianship and an ability to meld with others. Divas who are known as grand bitches often seek to repair their reputations by taking on this role. It confers credibility.

NANNETTA *(soprano)* The Fords' daughter, in love with Fenton.

MISTRESSQUICKLY *(mezzo-soprano)* An aging busybody of the town.

MRS. MEG PAGE *(mezzo-soprano)* The Fords' neighbor.

FENTON *(tenor)* A young buck in love with Nannetta. The role calls for a tenor of tremendously sweet sound, yet distinctly a full tenor. It is a mistake to cast a male canary in the role, since he must compete against several voices most of the time, and the excellent balance of the ensembles will suffer.

DR. CAIUS *(tenor)*

The opera takes place in and around the town of Windsor, England, during the reign of King Henry IV (1399–1415). Sort of. Falstaff makes references to the East and West Indies, which places the action firmly in Elizabethan times, where most productions are set.

THE OPERA

Act I

Scene 1: Falstaff's room in the Garter Inn.

Falstaff, writing letters at a small desk, is interrupted by a raving Dr. Caius, complaining that the fat knight has broken into his house and abused his servants. Falstaff breezily dismisses these charges and calls for more sherry. Caius then berates Falstaff's cronies, Pistola and Bardolfo, accusing them of getting him drunk and pilfering his pockets. Bardolfo, Pistola, and Dr. Caius exchange a rapid litany of insults, until Pistola threatens the doctor. Falstaff calms him, saying he doesn't want Pistola to shoot off in the room. Falstaff urges Dr. Caius to leave while he can, advising him to drink less in the future.

As the door closes behind the doctor, Bardolfo and Pistola intone an "Amen."

Falstaff looks over his tavern bill and Bardolfo searches their purse for money, finding only a few coins. Falstaff complains that the two lackeys cost him too much. They are eating his very flesh, and he is wasting away. He calls for a liquid dinner of sherry and orders his lackeys to proclaim his greatness. They hail Immense Falstaff the Enormous. He points to his paunch as his kingdom, saying it must be aggrandized. He has a plan. Master Ford is a man of wealth whose lovely wife controls the accounts. He praises the beauty of Ford's wife, Alice. Once, as he passed her window, she smiled at him, sighing at his obvious virility, with a sigh that seemed to say, "I belong to Sir John Falstaff!" But there's yet another woman at Windsor, called Meg, and Falstaff is sure that she, too, controls her husband's money and is taken with Falstaff's charms. Very well, he shall apply the charms of his life's Indian summer, and woo both the wives! He has written letters to each, and Bardolfo and Pistola must bear the letters to the ladies in question. They decline such pandering. Furious, Falstaff calls a page boy, and sends him on the errand. He turns on his lackeys. These two thieves are bound by honor? Not even he himself can always live by it! Occasionally he is even forced to use lies, ploys, and stratagems! Yet these two louse-bags stand upon honor! What honor? Can honor fill the stomach? No. Can it set the broken bone? It cannot. Honor is not a surgeon. What is it then? A word, flying on air. Can it hear who is dead? No. It lives with the living? Not even that, since it is inflated by vanity, corrupted by pride, debased by calumnies. Yet these scoundrels stand by it? He regally dismisses his lackeys, and when they hesitate, he chases them out of the room with a broom.

Comment: *In the first scene we are introduced to the musical vocabulary of* Falstaff, *with its swift repartee, darting orchestra, and wisps of melody that evaporate before coalescing. The curtain rises immediately and the action begins. The whole beginning, until the point where Caius is dispatched, might be called an overture, having a unity in the orchestra and setting the mood. Still, there are no themes, per se, set forth; it is curi-*

ous that Falstaff himself never has what might be called a signature theme. He changes with the situation. When Bardolfo and Pistola pronounce "Amen," it is a miniature fugue with their clapping hands beating out the time. An episode has ended. The only narrative comes when Falstaff discourses about honor. Commentators rave about Boito's deft touch in splicing different lines from the various Falstaff plays to construct this little character depiction. Although it's heretical to say so, this is the one place where I would quibble with Boito. In Henry IV, Part I, *the monologue occurs in a battle, amid windy comments about glorious death in battle. Its relief and wisdom are superb. Here, it is given as a portrayal of Falstaff's character, but gives a different impression when recited to thieves. Still, Verdi liked it, and his musical handling is fascinating. The orchestra appears to breathe under Falstaff's rhetorical questions, answering softly in the negative to accompany the negative answers. We hardly notice that a seed of melody has been planted, bursting out at the end as he dismisses the whole idea of honor.*

Scene 2: The garden of Ford's house.

Mistress Quickly and Meg greet Alice and Nannetta as they enter the garden. Meg and Alice compare love letters they have received from Sir John Falstaff. They are amazed to find them identical. All the women decide Falstaff must be undone, publicly, and with merriment. They make fun of his fat, his vanity, his deceits, his sins, and his greasy appearance. They leave.

Ford enters, surrounded by Dr. Caius, Bardolfo, Pistola, and Fenton. They complain to Ford about the scheming, lying, gross Falstaff, and insist on wreaking revenge for past wrongs. Pistola even suggests to Ford that he might find himself wearing the cuckold's horns, since Falstaff has written Alice a love letter. Ford agrees that no woman can be trusted.

The women come back and decide to begin their plot. All leave except Fenton and Nannetta, who take the opportunity to exchange a few furtive kisses. As they hear the others returning again, they bid a sweet farewell, he saying, "Kissed lips do not lose fortune," and she answering, "Instead, they renew themselves, like the moon." Fenton hides among the trees at the back of the garden. Alice, Meg, Quickly, and Nannetta hatch their plan. Quickly will go to Falstaff and invite him to Ford's house. Alice, Meg, and Quickly scamper off. Fenton playfully chases Nannetta around the garden, finally catching her. They hear the others returning again, and part with the same words as before.

This time, it's the men hatching a plan of their own. Ford will go to Falstaff incognito, and ask him to plead a lover's suit for him with Alice. The women come back into the garden. All remark on the coming adventure, Fenton alone being less interested in the plots than in his love for Nannetta. The men leave. The women come together and laugh. They'll swell Falstaff's vanity until he bursts! They part, still laughing.

Comment: In a direct defiance of operatic convention, all four women enter together and indulge in marvelously chatty music written in a loose 6/8 time. They summarize their disdain for Falstaff in a little scurrying pianissimo quartet that Verdi indicated should be a capella if they can manage it without falling out of tune with each other, or accompanied by quiet oboe and clarinet if necessary. The men then enter, sharing roughly the same vocal lines but in different pitches and with slightly different inflections within 4/4 time. Everyone has his own gripe about Falstaff, but they are only variations on the same theme, so to speak.

Amid these comings and goings, suddenly the stage is empty except for the young lovers. They only have time to tell their love with one line each, Fenton beginning and then answered by Nannetta, who holds a high A flat (which an oboe also has been sustaining throughout the exchange) on the first syllable of "luna" for ten beats. So it appears Verdi could write a duet about beautiful young love after all, he just waited until he was eighty to do it and dispatched it in six measures. The bit of poetry, incidentally, is a quotation from Boccaccio, not Shakespeare. The Decameron *story in which it appears tells the tale of a young woman who remains a virgin despite being captured and lusted after by eight men in a row. Anglo-Saxon critics are usually mystified that Italian audiences found Ford's quick jealousy so funny, but perhaps the allusion to feminine virtue caused them to look on Ford more sceptically than those who were unfamiliar with its source.*

Both groups return to the stage and chatter in one of the most remarkable passages in the opera. The women sing in 6/8 time, with variations, while the men return to their 4/4, roughly. The only focal point is Fenton, who stands behind the men and waxes lyrical. Onstage it sounds perfectly natural, and many in the audience might have to be told that they have just experienced a passage of music that causes orgasms in the conservatories. The men depart, and the women get the last word in a wonderfully fluffy quartet, with all four trilling in unison. The image of Falstaff being inflated and then bursting is, naturally, accompanied by a crescendo in the orchestra. After the "burst," the woman share a unison "ha ha" and leave. The whole scene is little short of a miracle.

Act II

Scene 1: Falstaff's room in the Garter Inn.

Falstaff is sprawled in his chair while Bardolfo and Pistola pound their breasts and plead repentance for their earlier disobedience. They admit a lady who wishes to speak to the knight. It is Mistress Quickly, who bows with great ceremony and addresses Falstaff as "Reverence!" Bardolfo and Pistola leave. She comes from Alice Ford. Ah, what a great seducer Falstaff is! "I know," he says, bidding her continue. She reports that Alice is madly in love with Sir John, and wants him to know that Ford is always out of the house from two to three. "From two to three," marks Falstaff. Yes, says Quickly, and Alice is dreadfully unhappy, watched over by a jealous husband. "From two to three," mutters Falstaff. Then tell the lady he shall not shirk his duty, and she may expect him. But Quickly has another message. The lovely Meg also loves Falstaff. Ah, what witchcraft does he employ to conquer these ladies? Not witchcraft, he protests, but merely a certain personal fascination. He hands a disappointingly small coin to Quickly for her troubles, and dismisses her. She bows and leaves.

Comment: Mistress Quickly is invariably played by a grande dame of opera past retirement age and a year or two shy of the glue factory. The

*line "Reverenza!" therefore is usually milked beyond all endurance, its
low tessitura allowing the lady to indulge in the few resonant notes she
has left. It will also be played in the orchestra at later points to indicate
Quickly bowing. Another noticeable "motif" is introduced here when she
tells Falstaff to visit Alice "from two to three" ("Dalle due alle tre"), a
sprightly couple of triplets recalled again later.*

Alone, Falstaff addresses himself as "Old John," urging himself on
his path. This old flesh still has some pleasures left in it. Bardolfo
announces a Master Brook *("Fontana")*. Ford enters, disguised. He
introduces himself as a man of means. Falstaff is delighted to meet
him. "Brook" wants a word in confidence, and Falstaff dismisses Bardolfo and Pistola, who are commenting on Ford's excellent deception. Ford jingles a purse of gold coins at Falstaff. He is in love with
Alice Ford, but she is not the least bit impressed by his protestations,
not even when he serenaded her under her window. Falstaff begins to
sing a love madrigal, which Ford joins. Ford flatters Falstaff's ingenu-
ity, courage, and experience, and says the gold is his if he can conquer
Alice for him. Falstaff accepts—in fact, he will be alone with Alice in
half an hour! Ford is shocked, but controls himself. Falstaff excuses
himself to change into his courting clothes, and leaves the room.
Alone, Ford gives vent to his fury. Is he dreaming? Dishonored by a
faithless wife and a tainted bed! Oh marriage, it is hell! Better to
leave his beer with a German or his brandy with a thirsty Dutchman
than his wife to herself! He will have revenge! Falstaff returns,
dressed in his finest. He and Ford bow at the door, each insisting the
other pass first. Finally, they exit together.

*Comment: Falstaff indulges both his vanity and his melancholy in the
little narrative "Va, vecchio John," snippets of which will be heard again.
Ford's jingling of the gold is depicted in the orchestra with triangles and
piccolos. Ford's solo monologue is on the grand scale, but he is so quick to
play the wounded husband that we must wonder how much of this fury is
projected fantasy. Expect Falstaff to return in all the comic splendor the
costume department can produce, even though the libretto merely indi-*

cates a *"new jacket."* *The business at the door is also generally camped up by directors into a major Alphonse-Gaston encounter.*

Scene 2. A room in Ford's house.

Alice and Meg prepare the scene for Falstaff's humiliation. They will coerce him into the laundry basket and have him dumped into the river with the wash. Quickly tells them of her interview at the inn. Sir John is coming, from two to three. It's almost two now. Alice calls downstairs for the laundry hamper to be brought in. She caresses Nannetta. Why is the girl not laughing with the rest of them? Nannetta explains that Father insists she marry Dr. Caius. That pedant? gasps Alice. She tells her daughter not to worry. The servants bring in the laundry hamper, and Alice directs them to dump it into the river on her order. They leave. The women set up a screen in one corner of the room, and put a chair and a lute by the table in the center. Alice tells the women that they will rally by the banner of merriment to spread joy in the air and the heart. Quickly goes to keep watch. Nannetta hides. Alice encourages them. The laughter of honest women is true, unlike the moping of hypocrites. They take their places, Meg outside the door and Alice in the chair, strumming her lute.

Falstaff enters, singing that he will pluck the enchanted flower. Alice flirts, but is coy, marveling that a man of his size should quake with love. Sir John tells her of his youth. When he was a page to the Duke of Norfolk, he was nimble, a mere specter, lovely, light, and graceful. That was the springtime of his life, so limber and slender he could slip through a ring. Alice asks him if he will not betray her with Meg. That ugly face? asks Falstaff. No more delays—a kiss!

Quickly bursts in. Ford is coming, furious! Falstaff hides behind the screen. Meg rushes in with the same news, and Alice tries to stifle her laughter. Meg insists she is serious, and Quickly tells her she really sees Ford coming through the garden. Ford bursts in, followed by Dr. Caius and Fenton. Bardolfo and Pistola run in, looking in the corners for Falstaff but not finding him. Ford asks Alice what's in the hamper. Dirty linen, she replies. Ford tells her she's taking him to the cleaners, and rifles through the dirty clothes. Ford runs off with the others to search the house. The women hide Falstaff, who barely fits, in the hamper, covering him with dirty linen. Alice leaves to round up the servants. Nannetta and Fenton sneak behind the screen to kiss. Meg and Quickly pretend to fuss with the laundry as the men return, not having found anything. Suddenly, they hear a kiss from behind the screen. The men hurl threats, believing it to be Falstaff and Alice, and prepare to storm the citadel. From inside the hamper, Falstaff complains that he's suffocating. Meg and Quickly close the lid on him. Ford pulls the screen aside, discovering Nannetta and Fenton, who run off. Alice reappears with the servants. Bardolfo imagines he sees Falstaff out on the landing, and all the men run up the stairs. Alice directs the servants to empty the laundry hamper out the window and into the river, near the rushes where the women are doing wash. The servants struggle with the hamper but manage to dump its contents, including Falstaff, into the river. The men come back in, and Alice, laughing, takes Ford to the window to show him the condition of his presumed rival in love.

Comment: *Alice's lute strumming is occasionally accomplished by the prima donna herself. Otherwise it is played by a guitar in the orchestra pit. Falstaff's brief solo describing his youth, "Quand'ero paggio del Duca di Norfolk," is delicate to the point of preciousness, a reminder of the courtly aspect of the fat man's personality. The balance of the scene is a furious montage of simultaneous action, based on nervous staccato notes that build to a great C major climax as Falstaff is dumped in the river. It is an excellent sweep of finely constructed music, and is also downright funny if staged correctly.*

Act III

Scene 1: The courtyard of the Garter Inn. Evening.

Falstaff, drenched and shivering, yells for some hot wine. Thieving, dishonest, wicked world! To live for all these years as brave and

upright cavalier, only to be tossed in the river with dirty laundry as if he were a bag of blind kittens! Wicked world! Everything declines. Go, old John, on your journey until you die. Then all virtue will be lost from the world. He notices gray hairs. The taverner brings him hot wine and leaves. Taking a sip of the wine, he feels its warmth course through his veins. He recovers his spirits, praising the great trill wine causes, trilling every fiber of the being, a trill that reverberates throughout the world.

Comment: *The act begins with a prelude, the strings sawing away to the rushing music they had played in the previous act, when Quickly ran in to tell Alice that Ford was coming. This builds in the orchestra until it climaxes in a cadence of trumpet and trombone chords. It is an entire Rossini overture boiled down to less than a minute. Falstaff's solo scene is justly celebrated, and here Boito's mosaic of lines culled from the various plays is beyond criticism. The entire character is here: melancholy, afraid of death, comically cynical, yet (and this is key) able to rally and face life yet again. The process of pouring the wine, drinking it, feeling it, and praising it is brilliant, and the example commentators and teachers use to explain the whole methodology of* Falstaff. *The strings shimmer as we imagine Falstaff tasting the wine. He describes the process deliciously—wine is a cricket ("grillo") that flits in the body of a drinker ("brillo"), creating a trill ("trillo"). The flute begins a cricketlike trilling theme, which passes to the violins at "brillo," which augment it one at a time until the whole orchestra is subsumed into the trill. Falstaff's spirits have thoroughly revived.*

Quickly appears, bowing deeply again and pleading for the lovely Alice. Falstaff has had enough of the lovely Alice. Alice, Meg, Nannetta, Ford, Dr. Caius, and Fenton peek out from behind a house, one by one, and hide again. Quickly insists Alice still loves him, and produces a letter. Alice and the others comment. Falstaff reads. She will meet him at Herne's Oak in Windsor Park at midnight. He must disguise himself as the Old Black Hunter. Quickly points out that Alice must be truly in love to agree to meet at such a time and place. Falstaff invites her into the inn to discuss details, and Quickly begins to tell of the spirits that wander the park at midnight.

All the others come out from their hiding places, and Alice continues to tell the story of the park's spirits in a comically spooky voice.
Nannetta and Meg confess that they're spooked, but Alice assures
them they are all just nursery tales. Alice continues to tell the story of
Herne the Hunter, who is growing horns on his head. Ford laughs
that these are horns he can appreciate. Alice chides her jealous
husband, and they make plans for the farce. Nannetta will be Queen
of the Fairies, Alice will collect the neighborhood children to play
elves and sprites, Quickly will be an old witch. All will wear fantastic
costumes and disguises. They will frighten Falstaff into confessing his
sins, beating it out of him if necessary, and return to their homes at
dawn. All except Dr. Caius and Ford depart. Quickly comes out of
the inn just in time to hear Ford promise Dr. Caius that Nannetta will
marry him—that very night in the farce at Herne's Oak. "You think
so?" says Quickly to herself, running off to find Nannetta and Alice.

*Comment: Quickly enters again with her "Reverenza," and the action
resumes. The score instructs Alice to tell her tale of Herne's Oak with an
altered voice. It's interesting to see what sopranos do with the moment.*

Scene 2: Herne's Oak in Windsor Park. Night.

The wardens' horn calls are heard in the distance. Fenton appears
alone, pining for Nannetta. "The kissed lips do not lose fortune . . ."
Nannetta's voice answers him. "Instead, they renew themselves like
the moon." She runs on, dressed as the Queen of the Fairies, and
they embrace. Immediately, Alice appears with Quickly, carrying
masks, robes, and disguises. She helps Fenton into his disguise as a
monk, advising him to follow her lead. She asks Quickly who will play
the bride in their deception. A merry thief who hates the doctor, she
answers. Meg enters, dressed as a naiad. Everything is ready. The fat
one is coming. They hide.

*Comment: Fenton's love soliloquy is haunting and apparently formless.
This young man sounds more genuinely in love than most of the posing,
strutting tenors in opera. The climax of the aria is the line he was singing to*

Nannetta in the garden scene, and we realize to our surprise that the aria, which seemed so meandering, had been aiming toward this resolution the whole time. I can't think of another instance in opera where the punchline, so to speak, of the love theme has been sung repeatedly before the body of the love aria, and the effect is stunning. He keeps singing through Nannetta's soaring rejoinder, and we are presented with the possibility of Verdi's first-ever depiction of young love in all its poetry, innocence, and sensuality. Just then, however, they are interrupted by Alice and Quickly, and the whole thing has been a superb tease. Slyly, Verdi has let us know, at this late stage in his career, that he was quite capable of writing the sort of love music that we now associate with Puccini.

Falstaff, wrapped in a cloak and wearing a helmet with enormous antlers, appears as the bells sound midnight. He counts, and asks Jove's help, since the god knows how love turns men into beasts. Alice runs up to him, agitated. Meg followed her! There is trouble afoot! Twice the fun! replies Falstaff. Meg calls for help from afar. She has seen goblins! Asking God's forgiveness for her sinful assignation, Alice flees. From a distance, Falstaff hears the songs of fairies and elves. He throws himself on the ground and buries his head in his arms. Even to see the spirit creatures means sure death for humans! Nannetta leads on a group of little girls, dressed as fairies. They form a circle around Falstaff, who remains motionless. Nannetta leads a song about the lithe spirits of the nights, tripping from flower to flower. All the others appear in costumes and disguises. They cry out that a mortal is spotted in their ethereal realm. A huge, horned ship of a man! They order Falstaff to rise up, but he remains motionless. Alice tells Nannetta to hide, since Dr. Caius is already trying to make a move. Nannetta hides nearby. Alice, Meg, and Quickly lead the children in poking, punching, and kicking Falstaff's enormous flesh. All hurl insults at him individually, naming each of his crimes and offenses. He confesses his guilt. The women chant for God to make Falstaff repent and live well. Falstaff adds a prayer to save his own abdomen. Finally, as Bardolfo hurls insults at Falstaff, Falstaff realizes this night spirit reeks of alcohol, and recognizes Bardolfo. Quickly quietly sends Bardolfo away to change into a bridal veil. Ford bows ironically to Falstaff. Who

now is wearing the horns? All unmask, and Master Brook is revealed as
Alice's husband. Falstaff admits he has been an ass, but, regaining his
composure, points out that he has provided a splendid time for all. His
own wit creates the wit of others. All cheer.

*Comment: Nannetta's song is appropriately diaphanous and lovely,
invariably staged with charming lights and children dancing. The mood
descends to the earthly as the "spirits" discover the prostrate Falstaff.
Verdi keeps the harassment of Falstaff from descending into sadism with the
lightest scoring imaginable, and Boito has obliged with excellent words for
this moment:* "Pizzica, pizzica, pizzica, stizzica, spizzica, spizzica, pungi,
spilluzzica" *("Pinch, pinch, pinch, bite, nibble, nibble, punch, peck"). Say
that three times fast and you earn a certificate in Italian phonetics.*

Ford says the time for revenge is over, now for pleasantries. He
will preside over the wedding of the Queen of the Fairies. Dr. Caius
approaches with the veiled Queen. Alice says another young couple
begs to share in the festivities, and they are brought forth. Ford
declares both couples married, and orders them unmasked. Dr. Caius
realizes he's married Bardolfo! Ford sees that Fenton and Nannetta
are likewise married. Alice soothes him. Falstaff says he and Ford are
even. And who is the ass now? Ford points at Caius. Caius points at
Ford, Bardolfo and Fenton point to both Ford and Caius. "Us," they
admit. Alice points out how happy their daughter is, and Nannetta
asks for forgiveness. Ford gives them his blessing as all cheer. Falstaff
suggests ending the play with a chorus, and Ford invites all to supper.

Falstaff leads the chorus. Everything in the world is a prank. Man
is born a prankster. Faith and reason deceive him. All are fooled!
Everyone laughs, but he who laughs last laughs best.

*Comment: The famous fugue that ends the opera is devilishly difficult,
yet creates a marvelous feeling of lightness (like the opera as a whole).
Some have found the final fugue "gimmicky." Yes, exactly. Verdi and
Boito are drawing attention to the illusions, not only of life, but specifically of the theater. As Verdi's farewell to the public, it is also a poignant
invitation for us to submerge ourselves in the whole deception of art.*

PART THREE

Exploring Verdi

Verdi Recordings

Aida Riccardo Muti made a name for himself in the seventies with clean readings of scores, correct to the point of pedantry. This much we know. What we don't know is why his 1974 *Aida* with God's own cast (Caballé, Domingo, Cossoto, Cappuccilli, and Ghiaurov) is so damned *fast* Either Muti was taking uppers or he had only two hours of studio time. If you are a day trader or other type-A personality, this recording may be ideal for you. The singing is unsurpassed. Muti also recorded the opera with Domingo and Dame Gwyneth Jones, but this recording is strictly for the ghoulishly inclined.

Conversely, Leontyne Price is given full rein in her most celebrated role, in Sir Georg Solti's luxuriant 1962 recording. Vickers is appropriately heroic as the one-dimensional Radames, and Merrill is a mega-lyrical Amonasro. Rita Gorr hemorrhages as Amneris. This recording remains a very good first choice. Claudio Abbado picked up where Solti left off in luxuriousness for his early-eighties *Aida*. The Scala orchestra is the aural equivalent of aged wine, and Verdi's partiality for the cello voice is fully explored. That's the good news. Conversely, while Domingo and Obrastzova are both "on," Ricciarelli is distinctly not in the title role. Still, it's interesting to hear how much Abbado learned about the score since his earlier recording with Martina Arroyo (terrific vocal presence), Domingo, and Cossotto. Herbert von Karajan's version with Freni, Carreras, Baltsa, and Cappuccilli somehow made nobody happy, even though Freni is good and Baltsa is superbly fierce. Carreras is still apologizing for it, even though he has some great moments. Still, Karajan fans (and anyone else interested in a rip-snorting *Aida*) would do better to go with his earlier recording from Vienna with Tebaldi, Bergonzi, Simionato, and MacNeil.

More recently, James Levine recorded his cast (Millo, Domingo, James Morris, Ramey, Zajick) from a great Met production in the late-eighties. I cherish this recording primarily for the excellent balance Levine demanded—and got—from his lead singers. In no other recording are Verdi's nuances for the big ensembles as well drawn as here. Millo may not have been the perfect Aida, but she has vocal presence and means what she says. Domingo actually sounds *younger* than on earlier recordings (i.e., the tenor entry in the Ramfis/Radames ensemble in Act 1, Scene 2). Lorin Maazel conducted Pavarotti in a 1990 recording featuring Pav's great discovery, Maria Chiara, who never quite caught on outside of Italy. Dimitrova's portrayal of Amneris is as vast as the Nile in flood season. Callas fans already have the Mexico City recording (only available in highlights at this point), featuring the notorious high E flat, but a better all-round performance was recorded at La Scala in 1955, with Tucker, Gobbi, and Barbieri all in fierce form trying to one-up each other. Serafin, as usual, conducts.

Alzira If you want to impress people as a real Verdian, you will have to buy the recording of Alzira made in 1938, featuring Elisabeth Schwarzkopf and a bunch of people you've never heard of. This recording is bizarre on a number of levels, primary of which being that it was made at all. It's in German, by the way. For years, the only available recording was a live one made (not well) at the Rome Opera in 1967 with Virginia Zeani and Cornell MacNeil. Now, there is a recording of Verdi's "worst" opera with Ileana Cotrubas, Francisco Araiza, and the ubiquitous Renato Bruson proving once again that there really is no boring Verdi music, only boring Verdi singers. Snap it up if you find it. The indomitable Lamberto Gardelli beats time efficiently and lets the singers soar.

Aroldo Well, this one's a no-brainer. Even if you're not ready to fatten up your CD collection with obscure early Verdi recordings, you should run out and buy the only commercial available recording of this opera. It was recorded by the indomitable Eve Queler and her Opera Orchestra of New York, a vital ensemble who have given the world many historic performances, often of lesser known operas, over the last quarter century. Caballé is sublime, Juan Pons his usual intelligent self, and tenor Gianfranco Cecchele, a workhorse Italian tenor, better than usual in this recording. The opera is not as good onstage as *Stiffelio,* but on recording it is in many ways better, with a luscious fourth act quartet, rousing storm scene, and some additional moments for the soprano to shine. The quality of the recording is fairly crude.

Attilla Before Ramey decided to make a career out of this opera, Raimondi was earning praise in the role. He is featured on a recording conducted by Gardelli in 1973, with Deutekom as a fierce Odabella, and Bergonzi and Milnes, both very good. Muti conducted two other available *Attila*s. One features an excellent Raimondi, with Antonietta Stella as a relatively dull Odabella and Cecchele as Foresto. Go ahead and buy the other recording, featuring Ramey in his most celebrated Verdi role. Odabella is sung by Cheryl Studer, a singer whose very name can start a deadly argument among opera people. There is no doubt that she eats this role up along with the scenery, while Neil Shicoff is infinitely the better Foresto.

Un ballo in maschera This intimate opera records well, and it's hard to go wrong. You're probably best off buying the Pavarotti recording with Solti conducting, Margaret Price as a stellar Amelia, Bruson in top form, Christa Ludwig vamping it up as Ulrica, and Kathleen Battle as one of the most memorable Oscars ever. Pav's voice is glorious and the acting irrelevant. Although it looks tempting, skip the earlier recording he made with Tebaldi in 1970, since she is past her prime and he had not yet hit his. Domingo is captured well on two recordings that are, however, uneven in the other roles. Karajan led the Vienna Philharmonic on one with Josephine Barstow, Nucci in one of his more forgettable moments, Florence Quivar as the Ulrica from hell (in a good sense), and Karajan favorite Sumi Jo as the world's most punctilious Oscar. Detached as Jo may be, she is all "fire and music" compared with the frosty Edita Gruberova in the same role on Abbado's recording with Domingo, Ricciarelli, Bruson, and a completely out of control (in the bad sense) Obrastzova.

La battaglia di Legnano God bless Gardelli, Carreras, and their friends for their intelligent and often impassioned recordings of the lesser-known Verdi canon. Their recording of *Legnano* is one of their best, with Carreras crying out *"Viva Italia!"* as if he means it, and Ricciarelli and Matteo Manuguerra also giving this score the respect it deserves without hedging on the passion or emotionalism. Buy it. One honorable mention live historical recording is Gianandrea Gavazzeni's Scala production of 1961, which is all about Corelli in unbelievable form.

Il corsaro It's hard to dismiss this opera since Gardelli and Carreras teamed up on this recording, with the impressive forces of Jessye Norman and Caballé duking it out for the tenor's love. Norman steals the show—no mean accomplishment. Carreras tosses off high notes and heroic moments with perfect ease, tempting you to imagine him singing a great Otello with a sensitive conductor, but it was not to be.

Don Carlo/s Any recording of this opera will represent a fairly hefty investment, so consider your needs carefully before plunking down the cash. The famous Carlo Maria Giulini recording (five acts, in Italian) featuring Vickers, Gré Brouwenstein, Fedora Barbieri, Gobbi, and Boris Christoff holds up well and has some excellent moments (especially for Christoff), but much has been learned about the score and the feel of the opera since this was made. Giulini's more famous recording from 1971 was the standard choice during the "Carlomania" of the 1970s, and remains popular. It is lyrical and refined in the extreme. Domingo is the phenomenal Carlo, Caballé never takes a breath, Milnes is Milnes, Raimondi had only begun to explore the nuances of Philip, while Verrett is focused like a laser beam. Her rendition of *"O don fatale"* can cut diamonds. Abbado made the first full-length recording in French, with Domingo (exquisite—he actually conveys neurosis), Ricciarelli (not ideal), Nucci (pretty creamy, this time), Raimondi (marvelously evolved in the role), an over-extended Lucia Valentini-Terrani as Eboli, and Ghiaurov (excellent, with a little help from the recording engineer). Abbado went for the full spooky effects in this recording, but some people find that the result is cold in the wrong way. A bonus is the extra disc of "outtakes" from the standard score of the opera, so with this recording you get such nuggets as the Elisabeth/Eboli duet, the Carlos/Philippe duet, and even the ballet *La Peregrine*—all of it! More recently, Antonio Pappano is the conductor of Luc Bondy's celebrated production for the Théâtre du Châtelet in Paris, with newcomer Roberto Alagna, Karita Mattila, Thomas Hampson, José van Dam, and Waltraud Meier. It is an excellent and unusual recording, with much scholarship given to the edition of the score. (You'll hear some of Abbado's outtakes as an integral part of the score here.) If you've been put off by the hype around Alagna, dismiss your fears. He is a Carlos to be remembered, and the rest of the cast is superb as well, with the possible exception of Meier, who annoyed everybody for some reason with her interpretation of Eboli. Karajan's recording is, on the whole, unsatisfactory for a lot of reasons. Carreras thought his own interpretation of the title role was a "mistake," and although Freni is reliable as always, this is one of the recordings that gave Karajan the reputation of crushing his singers in favor of the orchestra (which is awesome. The prelude to the final scene sounds like the best mini-symphony Bruckner never wrote). He chose to record the four-act Italian version, twenty years after anybody else on the planet thought this was the way to go. Bernard Haitink conducts this score well, but his recent recording with Galina Gorchakova, Olga Borodina, and a very lyrical Dimitri Hvorostovsky is compromised by the lack of depth in Roberto Scandiuzzi's Philip and Richard Margison channeling Ethel Merman in the title role.

I due Foscari There are two really good *Foscari* recordings to choose from. The standard choice is conducted by Gardelli and features Cappuccilli, Carreras, and Ricciarelli in one of her better performances. Some of the shrill coloratura in the early part of the opera is scary, but she manages to achieve that thing she does best—wounded femininity—by the end of the performance. There is also an interesting live recording conducted by Maurizio Arena that features (you guessed it) Bruson, Nicola Martinucci, and Lorenza Canepa, from the Teatro Regio in Parma. As you might expect, the performance was steeped in Verdi style and that elusive "idiom" they claim to have a monopoly on in Parma. Bruson is Bruson, while Martinucci is more difficult to love (and this is a difficult to love role to begin with). As for whether Cappuccilli or Bruson is the better baritone, all we can do is sigh for the days when we had to choose.

Ernani Buy the award-winning Muti recording. Even though it was recorded live in 1982, it has a great sound to it. (Muti famously browbeat the Scala audience beforehand, even forbidding them to cough.) While the conductor remains as precise as ever, he temporarily lapsed his anal-retentiveness and indulged in some high-romantic sounds and even a few moments of glorious schmaltz (e.g., the refrain of *"De' miei verd'anni"*). The Scala chorus and orchestra are indescribably superb. Freni admittedly has problems early on in the big aría, but gets it together in spectacular fashion for Acts III and IV, while Domingo, Bruson, and Ghiaurov give career defining performances. Italian opera—in fact, life—doesn't get any better than this.

Falstaff The standard choice for this opera was conducted by Giulini and featured a special cast he assembled solely for the recording in Los Angeles, of all places. The "L.A. *Falstaff*" in fact put that city on the operatic map, and within a few years America's number two city finally had an opera company of its own. Giulini's conducting is refined beyond the point of civilization, Bruson is brilliant in the lead role and the voice was in good shape. Ricciarelli and Nucci take their share of knocks from critics, but their respective interpretations of Alice and Ford were beyond reproach. Ricciarelli was said to play her own lute during her live appearances as Alice, incidentally. The rest of the cast is filled out in a top-rate fashion. Barbara Hendricks, Lucia Valentini-Terrani, and Brenda Boozer warble magnificently. The tenor is the silver-voiced Dalmacio González, one of the few recordings he made during his brief career.

Perhaps the most praised recorded performance of the title role was Sir Geraint Evans's ingenious rendition for Solti, featuring Ilva Ligabue, Freni, Kraus, Rosalind Elias, and Simionato. Evans not only gets the timing exactly right on the "Honor" monologue, but also makes it come alive with subtle expression. Karajan made two famous recordings of the opera, the earlier one with Gobbi, Rolando Panerai, Luigi Alva, Elisabeth Schwarzkopf, Anna Moffo, Barbieri, and Renato Ercolani. It is superb, although you might notice that Schwarzkopf as a "merrie English goodwyfe" is more than credulity will permit. The later recording is with Giuseppe Taddei (who sang the title role into his eighties, I believe), Panerai, Francisco Araiza when his voice was still fresh (that is, pre-Wagner), the lovely Janet Perry, and Christa Ludwig milking *"riverenza"* as if she were singing Brangaene on a slow night. Uneven, but interesting. Those who get bleary eyed over the great singers of the 1950s will prefer Serafin's recording with Gobbi, Tebaldi, Anna Moffo, Simionato, and MacNeil. This cast represents the triumph of style over scholarly exactitude, and proves that *Falstaff* has a heart, after all. The intellectual approach was attempted in Leonard Bernstein's recording with the ever elegant Dietrich Fischer-Dieskau, Panerai, Regina Resnik interpreting Quickly as Klytemnestra, Ilva Ligabue as a strange Alice, and Gabriella Sciutti a pretty but not astounding Nannetta. No one is completely satisfied with this mid-sixties recording, although I find it better than its reputation. Still, not a good first choice. Sir Colin Davis made a more recent recording with Panerai finally promoted from Ford to the title role, Alan Titus, Sharon Sweet, Frank Lopardo, and Marilyn Horne outdoing both Resnik and Ludwig in her chesty Quickly. The excellent Bavarian Radio chorus and orchestra back up this clean and crisp recording, which has some excellent moments, but falls short of the others in overall stylistic soul.

The historical recordings conducted by Toscanini are important and authoritative (it's hard to argue with someone who learned the score from Verdi himself), but the balance of modern recording engineering is missing. Save these for later.

La forza del destino While I usually recommend newer recordings for the simple reason that they have better sound production, for this opera I think you should go back to the fifties and sixties. They had more vocal individuality and sheer chutzpa in those days, and *Forza* is best with heavy doses of both those qualities. Any of the earlier Price recordings will be great, especially the one with Tucker, Merrill, Giorgio Tozzi, and a brilliant Ezio Flagello. There is an exciting recording with Serafin conducting Callas, Tucker, Carlo Tagliabue, and Nicola Rossi-Lemeni, but Milanov and the short-careered Anita Cerquetti deliver the goods as well.

The 1862 version of the opera has recently hit the shelves conducted by Valery Gergiev featuring the Kirov orchestra and chorus of St. Petersburg and a slew of Russian singers. The notion is that the St. Petersburgers have a special relationship to this version of the opera, and there was much hype about this recording's air of authenticity. I'm not sold on that—Verdi used all Italian singers at the Petersburg premiere in any case, but the recording is clear and exciting and a welcome addition.

The best performance of this opera I have ever experienced is, I believe, available only on video. Normally, I don't even open the whole video can of worms, but an exception must be made for the 1958 *Forza* from Naples's San Carlo, with Tebaldi, Corelli, Gobbi, Simionato, and Renato Capecchi. Even if you don't own an audio recording of this opera, get your paws on the video and play it daily for the rest of your life. In fact, you can even turn the picture off your TV and just let the glorious sound fill your house, since the production is absurd (the backdrops flop around in every breeze) and Corelli wears the goofiest looking hairnet throughout the opera. Ah, but the singing! Warning: Listening to this performance will turn you into one of those bitter old opera people who complain that all singers today are lousy.

Un giorno di regno Jessye Norman must just hate singing Verdi roles everybody else sings, so we are grateful that she was making records right about the same time "obscure" Verdi became popular. You get no extra credit points for guessing that Gardelli conducted this recording or that the tenor is Carreras. The singers (also featuring Cossotto on her best behavior and Ingvar Wixell) wisely do not try to make this opera anything more than it is, and while Norman's voice occasionally overpowers the material, Carreras is perfect for the gentle lyricism in the music.

Giovanna d'Arco The standard choice is Levine's recording (it was his first complete opera recording) with Caballé, Domingo, and Milnes. Hard to beat. Caballé has no trouble letting you know when she is communing with the angels. A popular connoisseur's recording, but harder to find and not well recorded, is from the San Carlo and features Tebaldi sounding as if she has already ascended into heaven. Gino Penno survives the rather thankless role of King Charles the Pathetic, while Alfredo Ugo Savarese is the bad daddy.

I lombardi alla prima crociata Three years after Pavarotti was choking in this role onstage at the Met, he must have eaten Wheaties for the studio recording. The Levine recording also features June Anderson, Richard Leech, and Samuel Ramey, and is much better than anyone in the Met audience could have thought possible. Carreras owned this role for a few years, and Gardelli conducted the Royal in an interesting recording with Hungarian momentary sensation Sylvia Sass. One self-appointed critic I know dubbed Sass's performance here as "dog time" (a direct quote), but others found her wildness appropriate for this insane role. Her cry of *"Non è da Dio!"* sounds like a pedestrian hurling insults at a reckless New York City cab driver. Your pick. There is also a fun live recording of this opera with Scotto and Pavarotti when they were still talking to each other (many moons ago), but it's better to buy this one after you own a studio recording. My personal favorite is Gardelli's very underrated (and increasingly hard to find) version in 1971 with Christina Deutekom, Domingo, and Raimondi sounding like the world's most sophisticated murderer/hermit. Grab it if you see it.

Luisa Miller Katia Ricciarelli is featured on a few thousand Verdi recordings, and was roundly blasted by the critics for almost every one, but this is one role where she shines. Any early recording (early seventies) of her in this role will be powerful. The easiest to find is the Turin recording with Carreras (superbly romantic) and Bruson (heart-wrenching), Previtali conducting. If you can find any early recordings (same era) with Domingo, snap them up. The later Levine recording is conducted brilliantly and Domingo is still musically impressive as always, but less ardent. Millo is quite good in the role, but Chernov does not bring you over the top in his Act III scene. The Caballé/Pavarotti/Milnes recording from London, conducted by Peter Maag, is, of course, solid, and she does some marvelous things, but the voice is so beautiful that Caballé does not need to work any extra at the characterization, and that necessary air of pathos is a bit elusive. Anna Moffo is right on the money, as are Bergonzi and Mac-Neil, on their recording conducted by Fausto Cleva.

Macbeth Buy the Abbado recording, with Cappuccilli, Verrett, Ghiaurov, and Domingo. If La Verrett's rendition of the Letter Scene doesn't transform you on the cellular level, give up and never waste your money on another opera recording. This art form is not for you. Listen to Cappuccilli's voice change "character" from the beginning to the end. When people complain that today's opera singers always sound the same, what they are bemoaning is the dearth of exactly what the two leads do so resplendently on this recording. Not that it's the only good *Macbeth* out there. In fact, the same cast (with the exception of Ferruccio Tagliavini for Domingo) can be found on an earlier live recording from Vienna. Thrilling moments, but some infuriating lapses of sound at key points. Leonie Rysanek also made quite a name for herself as Lady Macbeth, and can be heard on a good recording with Leonard Warren (who is solid but hardly explores the complete range of the character), Jerome Hines, and Bergonzi. Leinsdorf conducts the Met orchestra and chorus before they were the celebrated ensembles they are today. Muti uses all of his control issues to keep Cossotto from spontaneously combusting in his recording, and you can sort of tell it's killing her. Milnes is her Macbeth, and he opts for a few quirky choices in his reading of the role. Raimondi and Carreras complete the cast. Milnes was on better behavior when conducted by Karl Böhm in Vienna with a chilling Christa Ludwig, a scary Karl Riddersbusch, and Carlo Cossutta. Speaking of Rysanek, the legendary lady she replaced for her Met debut, Callas, also felt rather territorial with this role. Victor de Sabata recorded a performance at La Scala in the mid-fifties with a dull Enzo Mascherini in the title role, Italo Tajo, and good old Gino Penno. This performance is all about Callas eating up the scenery magnificently rather than a good take on the whole opera.

I masnadieri Gardelli, of course, is responsible for the only currently available recording of this wild opera. Caballé is marvelous in the role written for Jenny Lind, with trills and pianissimi galore. Bergonzi, Raimondi, and Cappuccilli complete the awesome cast.

Nabucco There are three standard choices for this opera. The first was made in 1965, Gardelli conducting Elena Suliotis and Tito Gobbi in the lead roles. People debate Suliotis's pros and cons with vehemence, but Gobbi is fascinating in the Indian summer of his career. *"Dio di Giuda"* shows him at his best and worst, breathy and chopped yet always married to the text and still capable of great emotion. The second recording was Muti's contribution to the field, his professorial style exploring the "morning after bel canto" nature of the opera. Scotto scared everybody with her Abigaille when this was issued, but it sounds better in retrospect. If you prefer excitement to a pretty voice, this may be a good choice for you, although some of the high notes can kill a bowl of goldfish. Manuguerra is the lusty Nabucco. A more recent, and very popular, entry is the Gardelli recording featuring Bulgarian typhoon Ghena Dimitrova in her most celebrated role. Cappuccilli sings the lead role as a very internal sort of experience, while Russian bass Evgeny Nesterenko almost steals the show as Zaccaria. Tower Records once put this recording on sale under a sign reading "Our loss is your Ghena." Tsk tsk.

Oberto, conte di San Bonifacio The two available recordings of Verdi's first opera are exact opposites of each other. Gardelli conducted Panerai, Bergonzi, Ruza Baldani, and Dimitrova in the more conventional of the two, exploring the blood-and-thunder of this work. Conversely, Sir Neville Marriner (the early music expert) conducted the newer recording, exploring the opera as a more four-square bel canto piece. Although Marriner's recording is fascinating and Ramey and Guleghina are terrific, the Gardelli is probably more useful at first.

Otello In theory, the Levine recording with Domingo, Scotto, and Milnes should be an ideal choice, but it was recorded before Levine achieved his recent mastery over the score and Domingo's performance, while excellent, is only a hint of what he has accomplished onstage with this role. You get more Domingo in the 1993 recording conducted by Myung-Whun Chung and the Bastille crew, but Cheryl Studer is a very specific sort of Desdemona (cold, you might say). Sergei Leiferkus is more convincing if no less bizarre as Iago. The Karajan recording with del Monaco, Tebaldi, and Protti is still a good choice if you're not too hip for the tenor. He is ringing and clarion—too much for many people, but definitely exciting. Del Monaco also follows the dynamics and markings of the score to an excellent degree—something he is rarely given credit for. Tebaldi is superb in her scena, but of course Herr Karajan dominates everything with his orchestra (the Vienna Philharmonic, in this case). Karajan was among the first conductors to grasp that the storm scene is about more than a climate condition. Protti is nobody's favorite Iago. Vickers is of course many people's favorite Otello, and his recording conducted by Serafin with Gobbi and Rysanek remains a standard choice for many people. I don't recommend it. Vickers was only thirty-five years old and had never sung the role on stage, so I don't think it does justice to his reputation in the role. True, *"Dio, mi potevi"* is among the most heartfelt things Vickers ever recorded, and the final *"O gioia!"* is the true roar of a wounded animal. That's the good news. If there's love or tenderness in the Act I duet, I'm too dense to hear it.

Skip the movie soundtrack recording. Domingo is great, of course, and Ricciarelli and Justino Díaz sound appropriately doomed and slimy, respectively, but conductor Lorin Maazel was either on drugs or trying to please director Zeffirelli. The results are quirky. There is also the recent Solti recording with Pavarotti tackling the lead role, which has some lovely moments but is generally considered a mistake.

Requiem There are 148 available recordings of the *Requiem*. They are all good. Most of them are great. Choose a conductor, orchestra, and soprano you like and go with that one. (The tenor, alto, bass, and chorus almost always sound terrific). Leontyne Price was revered for her *Libera me*. If you opt for the 1970 recording conducted by Fritz Reiner, be warned that the maestro was in a very slow mood when he made this one. If you want the opposite effect, go with any of Muti's recordings. My favorite is Zubin Mehta's recording with Caballé, Domingo, Bianca Berini, and Paul Plishka. It is that conductor's greatest success in Verdi. Caballé's *Libera me* is truly transcendental.

Rigoletto There's no shortage of good *Rigoletto* recordings, but it's a little trickier than just picking your favorite baritone and going with that choice. How the soprano interprets the role affects the overall meaning of the opera as well. (The tenor role is more agreeable. Any well-sung interpretation will work.) Callas was among the first to realize the dramatic potentials of Gilda, and her recording with a resplendent Tito Gobbi in the title role (Serafin conducting) is exciting from beginning to end. If you want to know the many meanings of *"Corteggiani, vil razza,"* Gobbi's rendition is a good place to start. The voice changes character on every line. In the same exciting vein is a live recording featuring MacNeil, Scotto, and Tucker, Previtali conducting, from Buenos Aires in 1967. (Did MacNeil ever rest in 1967?) Although this recording has all the usual sound problems, it is thrilling. Scotto never approached Gilda as a canary role—more like a condor—but in this performance she also had the voice to back up the interpretation. Richard Bonynge conducted his wife Joan Sutherland in his recording of the opera, along with Milnes and Pavarotti as a sort of afterthought. Milnes is always reliable and solid, although his mannerisms annoy many people. (His spinning out of *"Quel vecchio maledivami"* is certifiably loony.) Pavarotti is a delight as the Duke. James Levine used Pavarotti again for his recording with Cheryl Studer (good and solid, although some weird pitch issues) and the recently ubiquitous Vladimir Chernov. Levine conducts beautifully but Chernov is no one's favorite Rigoletto. In addition to these, Pavarotti is featured on a decent recording by Riccardo Chailly, with June Anderson as a Gilda of the aviary variety and Nucci working hard—a bit too hard—to summon the varied emotions of the title role. Cappuccilli's best outing in the role is found on Giulini's predictably elegant reading of the opera, with a solid Ileana Cotrubas and Domingo working overtime to put his personal imprint on a role he has usually been content to have associated with Pavarotti's name. Recently, I have been addicted to the recording featuring Bruson, Andrea Rost, and Roberto Alagna, conducted by Muti in 1994 at one of his famous "don't you dare sneeze" performances. Muti has been microanalyzing this score for thirty years, giving quirky readings of it all over the world, but on the night captured in this recording it all came together. Bruson, though well past his vocal prime, is a revelation, further proof that this role is better given to a world-weary baritone with half a voice than a young whippersnapper with ringing high B's. Rost can play the canary, but becomes a full-voiced woman at the exact right moment, just as she informs her father that she will stand by the Duke even though he raped her. It is a character transformation in one note. Alagna is all hormones conveyed by superb breath control (the single breath for his climbing scale in the duet with Gilda is the perfect, and graphic, vocal depiction of male sexual arousal).

Simon Boccanegra All things considered, the best choice is Abbado's studio recording of the Scala production with Cappuccilli, Freni, Carreras, Ghiaurov, and Van Dam. Hard to argue with that cast, and the maestro was at his most lyrical when he made this one. There is also a live recording from Vienna with Abbado, Bruson, Ricciarelli, and Raimondi. Although Bruson occasionally reaches his heights, it is not as even and lush as the studio recording with Cappuccilli. Gobbi can be heard in the role on two recordings, neither of which is well made, one from Rome with Victoria de los Angeles and Boris Christoff, and the other live from Naples with Leyla Gencer and Mirto Picchi. In one of his last recordings, Sir Georg Solti cast Romanian baritone Alexandru Agache, Kiri Te Kanawa, Michael Sylvester, and Roberto

Scandiuzzi, with the orchestra and chorus of the Royal Opera, Covent Garden. Agache has a powerful voice, but the tender side of Boccanegra is missing. One major historical recording stands out for honorable mention. The "Live From the Met" *Boccanegra* of 1939 with Tibbett, Rethberg, Martinelli, and Ezio Pinza, conducted by Ettore Pannizzi, is unbelievably good. If you only have one "ancient" recording in your collection, make it this one.

Stiffelio Gardelli, Carreras, and friends are at it again in this 1979 recording, with Sylvia Sass as a marvelously emotional Lina and Manuguerra and Wladimiro Ganzarolli filling out the cast. Carreras does a great job of conveying all the internal conflict of the title character. Domingo has made more of a mark on this role on stage, but you're in fine hands with Carreras on the recording.

Traviata Basically, choosing a *Traviata* depends on which soprano you prefer in the role. This is an intensely personal decision, one that should be made with the counsel of a therapist or a spiritual advisor. Be wary, however, of advice given by other fans. They will try to convince you that their choice is the only one. Also, virtually every soprano has recorded at least one rendition of this opera, some many more. Eventually you will need several different recordings, and don't even think of cheating with the "highlights." (Excuse me, but what are the "lowlights" of *Traviata*?) I can only say that *Traviata* is best considered as a life-long process, and offer the following guidelines. Callas is justly famous for the role, and fans swoon over her live recordings from La Scala and Convent Garden, London (and not the Lisbon recording, which despite the exotic name, is not considered top-notch Callas). The Milan and London recordings are a bit fuzzy technically, but capture the "performance" well. Sutherland is a technical marvel, probably the best "sung" Violetta available, though some find her detached. While Alfredo is usually an afterthought in this opera, special mention must be made of Pavarotti on this recording. He is superb. Anna Moffo was the butt of many drag queens' jokes through the 1960s, but her Violetta is damned good and stands up to time. Rosa Ponselle has an endless line and a vocal intensity that occasionally descends into sobbing, weeping, whooping, and so forth, but it is unforgettable (as is Tibbett's rendition of *"Di Provenza."* One friend of mine asks, "Why did the audience *ever* stop applauding?"). Caballé is probably the prettiest sounding Violetta, Scotto's among the most intense. Cotrubas's achieves heft where she needs it. The list goes on. Just take the plunge and buy your first *Traviata* knowing full well that it will not be your last.

Trovatore There are hundreds of *Trovatore* recordings, and the confusion is compounded by the fact that about a dozen singers, in various combinations, are featured on most of them. Leontyne Price loved to sink her teeth into Leonora, and while her early recording with Tucker and Warren is notable, she really lets loose on a recording with Corelli, Simionato, and Bastianini. Karajan conducted this live performance from Salzburg, and it is a testament to Price's regal essence that even that unbending autocrat allowed her so much room for interpretation. (Her whoop at one point in the Act I trio would not disgrace David Lee Roth.) Corelli is a perfect Manrico—all hormones and urgency, while Bastianini turns *"Il balen"* into a cascade of dreamy lyricism. Warning to amateur baritones: Even though it sounds so pretty, don't try to sing along or you can wrench your back. This I tell you from experience. Simionato is demented. The single word *"sclamò"* in her Act II narrative does not reverberate from the chest, it echoes straight from hell. Price also recorded the role with Mehta conducting, Domingo, Milnes, and Cossotto filling out the cast in grand style. It is a good, if slightly less insane, recording. Karajan also conducted Domingo in the role in the mid-seventies, with Raina Kabaivanska as Leonora, and Cappuccilli and Cossotto. Truly magnificent. It's hard to make people believe that Karajan can conduct briskly and let his singers shine, but this recording is proof. If you still aren't convinced, then go to Karajan's famous Scala performance with Callas, Di Stefano on a superb night, Panerai, and Fedora Barbieri. Callas apparently decided that Leonora, not Azucena, was the real loony of the opera. It is a much more satisfying overall performance than Callas's recording with Serafin conducting, Giacomo Lauri-Volpi, Italo Tajo, and Cloë Elmo completing the cast, although many "All that matters is how Callas sounds" people rave about the latter one.

Need more Leontyne? The obscure recording of choice is from Buenos Aires, with Bergonzi, Cossotto, and Cappuccilli, all of whom are beyond demented. (That's a compliment in this world.)

Now to finish up, Domingo. Although Domingo has never been a classic *tenore di caglioni* in the Corelli sense, people now forget what a fine Manrico he once was. In addition to the recordings with Price and Kabaivanska, he can also be found on Giulini's almost delicate recording, with Rosálind Plowright, Brigitte Fassbaender, and Zancanaro and the chorus and orchestra of the Santa Cecilia Academy in Rome. For years this "un-*Trovatore*" was the standard choice, but it now seems a bit too "nice" and is not a great first choice. You can also get your Domingo fix on Levine's Met recording with Millo, the incomparable Dolora Zajick, and Vladimir Chernov. This was made years after Domingo had hit his peak as Manrico, Levine is clearly not in love with the score, and Chernov is a total drag. Millo aquits herself decently, but you're better off with one of the earlier recordings.

Many people's definitive Manrico was Mario del Monaco, whose recordings of the role are hard to find. There is a good one usually available conducted by Alberto Erede with Tebaldi, Simionato, and Ugo Savarese from Geneva. Do not expect great sound production values, but do expect the rafters of your house to shake. Björling, Milanov, Barbieri, and Warren deliver the grand style (and plenty of old-fashioned schmaltz) in their recording conducted by Renato Cellini. Pavarotti is said to have given some fine performances of the role in his younger years, but the available recordings are hard-pressed to prove this. Mehta's performance from Florence's Maggio Musicale Festivale with Antonella Banaudi, Shirley Verrett, and Leo Nucci is the preferable choice for Pavarotti groupies. There are only four words for Sir Richard Bonynge's recording with the Pav and Joan Sutherland: What were they thinking?

I vespri siciliani Gavazzeni conducted two performances available on recording, one with tenor Gastone Limarilli and soprano Leyla

Gencer, the other and much more important one with tenor Gianni Raimondi, Scotto, Cappuccilli, and Ruggero Raimondi from La Scala in 1970. While the tenor Raimondi falls into a bit of barking (almost inevitable in this very long work), he also does some good ensemble work. More important is Scotto, who keeps up the level of excitement right to the end. (Her octave leap in the final aria is downright unnerving and will cause you to drop whatever you're holding in your hands at the time, but it's not dull. Put the cat on the floor and get ready for a great ride). Bass Raimondi has both authority and lyricism. It's a live recording, with some hilariously bad pickups. At one point some engineers or stagehands can be heard yelling abuse at each other. Still, this was one of those performances that proves the worth of *Vespri*. A young James Levine also recorded this opera with Martina Arroyo, Domingo, Milnes, and Raimondi. This version is well recorded and conducted and is much easier to take, if less exciting, than La Scala is. In between these two is perhaps the best choice available, another great Eve Queler and the Opera Orchestra of New York performance captured live. It features Caballé (who makes that same octave leap sound like the most natural moment in music), a very fresh-sounding Domingo, Díaz at his most menacing, and Pons. All in all, perhaps the best first choice. Muti recently marshaled the Scala forces for a recording featuring the ever-controversial Cheryl Studer, tenor Chris Merritt, Giorgio Zancanaro, and Furlanetto, who steals the show. Save this one for the Studer maniacs (and you know who you are). One interesting historical recording was made by Mario Rossi, with Anita Cerquetti, Mario Ortica, Carlo Tagliabue, and Boris Christoff. I don't know anyone who actually listens to this recording, but many like to talk about it. If intermission chatter is your main goal, make sure to drop this one around and earn major points from the cognoscenti.

Productions:
What You Might Expect to See

WHAT IS the best way to stage a Verdi opera?

Throughout the twentieth century, and especially since the end of the Second World War, stage design and direction have evolved to such a point that the director and the designer might well be considered the true stars of most opera productions. It's what the newspapers talk about in their critiques, with perhaps a sentence or two given to the singers. Few opera critics these days even know a lot about singing technique. It is a visual, rather than an aural, world at the moment.

Opera has been responsible for the most daring and influential innovations in stage design and production techniques throughout the last hundred years, and drama and musicals have been playing catch-up. Of course, try telling this to the guy on the street. Americans would have a hard time believing opera can be radical, all evidence notwithstanding. To be fair, many opera productions are old-fashioned, especially in the larger companies, which are seen on television more frequently than the smaller ones. Verdi's operas bear a large responsibility for this. They are performed constantly and have had a difficult time being reinterpreted by directors. As such, the operas themselves have a die-hard (and spurious) reputation for being old-fashioned. New and different productions are tried, but it has been harder to make a go of Verdi operas served up in new ways than it has been with other composers' work.

Verdi's operas tend not to take place in the psyche, nor in the intellect, but in the gut. The question, then, should be how to deliver the gist of Verdi's art to the emotional gut of the audience. Intellectual concepts may help to accomplish this, but more often they will simply get in the way of the optimum Verdi experience.

To produce a Verdi opera, certain facts must be regarded as givens. Everybody on the stage must be able to see the conductor at (almost) all times, because of the abundance of ensemble singing and the rapid, sudden changes in tempo and volume. This severely limits the acting the singers can do. From time immemorial directors have been trying to deploy the singers in a more fluid fashion to avoid the effort of three, four, or more singers standing idiotically at the footlights singing their respective lines (the "row of artichokes," as Rossini called them), but a certain stiffness must be expected.

The tension between musical and dramatic needs is one of the great challenges of Italian opera, and it is rarely satisfied perfectly. First, there is the issue of acting. Acting in an opera is not the same as acting in a play. The acting must first take place in the voice; any body gestures may be regarded as secondary, the body contorting a certain amount merely to produce the sounds. When Manrico sings his part of the *"Miserere,"* he is not on stage, yet he must be able to break our hearts when he sings *"Leonora, addio!"* If she is standing in the spotlight with the back of her hand against her forehead in a parody of a stock operatic gesture, it may annoy some people, but it is not as important as what emotion—what *acting*—Manrico puts into his line.

Verdi set all of his operas in the past. Most of them are set in the medieval or Renaissance eras. The fifteenth and sixteenth centuries are especially well represented by nine operas. Nor are the remote historic settings gratuitous. A whopping fourteen of Verdi's operas are built around specific historical events, such as the fall of Jerusalem in 587 B.C., the battles of Legnano and Velletri, the trial of Joan of Arc, the coronation of the Emperor Charles V, and so on. Traditionally, then, Verdi operas have inhabited the realm of women in big skirts, velvet, and silk, and men in doublet and hose. A wise director of my acquaintance once said that the most important thing a Verdi tenor needs to know is how to walk with a sword at his side (which is no easy accomplishment). Even today, Verdi operas are usually left in their original settings. There are several reasons for this. First is the relation to specific historical moments, as mentioned above. Second is the frank emotional, rather than didactic and intellectual, thrust of Verdi's operas. A third consideration is the unnaturalness and inherent stiffness of singers' bodies when attempting to deliver the musical phrases of the Verdian style.

Wagner's operas are so compromised by their association with Third Reich propaganda and iconography that it was necessary to reinvent them if we were ever to be able to sit through them again. With Verdi, there is very little real need to do this. True, the Italian Fascists did attempt to co-opt Verdi for their propaganda as the Nazis had done with Wagner, but the Italians were much less successful. For one thing, Verdi had already been uncontroversially popular with audiences since 1842. Wagner, on the other hand, had made himself plenty of enemies, as much by his offensive personality as by his difficult music. This provided propagandists with the element of paranoid victimization that is crucial to totalitarian planners. They were able to pose that they were "rescuing" Wagner's sublime art from Jewish and other conspirators. Nobody ever needed to rescue Verdi from anybody. While Italian Fascists were running to overblown performances of *Aida,* so were audiences all over the rest of the world.

If Verdi's operas don't need to be rescued from past associations like Wagner's, then neither do they need to be rescued from the historical distance of baroque opera. The conventions of eighteenth-century Europe are so foreign to people today that they might as well be from outer space. By Verdi's time, Europe was, anthropologically speaking, very much like today's world. Verdi wrote primarily for an urban, middle-class audience and judged the success of a work the same way a Hollywood studio does today—by the box office.

Still, there is a great desire on the part of directors and designers to "do something" with Verdi's operas. While the urge is laudable, and one always likes to see the classics done in a refreshing way, it is very easy for a concept to take over an opera and interfere with, rather than enhance, an audience's enjoyment of it. This happens when the score is compromised. Alas, few directors and designers have a great sensitivity to the music. Many "star" directors and designers in opera today do not have operatic backgrounds. Actually, it's considered almost a point of honor to be completely unfamiliar with opera. As we will see, some of the greatest productions in operatic history have been achieved by letting in the fresh air, so to speak, of talented people from outside the world of opera (Margaret Webster, Luchino Visconti, and Patrice Chéreau, for example). This has led many to believe that only by hiring the operatically ignorant can one hope to repeat those successes. The notion is that only those untainted by the musty conventions of opera can bring truly new ideas to the operatic stage. The problem is that such directors and designers will generally rely solely on the libretto (in translation, it need hardly be added). While opera is a form of drama, the "story" is told more through the music than through the words, especially in the case of Verdi. Therefore, many of these potentially interesting productions become comments on the libretto rather than on the music.

In a recent production of *Otello* in Germany, the director had an idea to add a visual touch to the hero's chilling entrance in Act IV. After Desdemona said her prayers, Otello was seen approaching the bedroom, bent on murder, wandering through a maze of undulating black rubber walls. The idea was to depict a loss of moral compass, a Munchian vision of the soul on its way to perdition. It was a wonderful idea, but does one even want a visual effect at such a moment? The cello theme gives way to the "kiss" motif, and the basses pour forth with an unforgettable depiction of total emotional collapse. There is not a visual concept in the world that would be worth a nanosecond's distraction from the music Verdi wrote for that moment. Verdi told Boito that it was sometimes necessary for the poet to write less-than-great poetry and the musician to write less-than-great music in order to create great opera. Perhaps the formula could be extended to directors and designers as well.

One of the most abused mantras in productions is the word "relevance." Of course a director must try to make a production relevant to the audience, but beware of those who suggest to you that you wouldn't be able to identify with the characters of Rigoletto or Aida unless you actually saw them pouring bowls of Corn Flakes and drinking Cokes. Violetta, as the prototypical modern woman, gets a lot of the relevant treatment. In all fairness, the sheer number of *Traviata* productions dictates that chances will be taken with this work, and yet is dying of AIDS somehow more profound than dying of tuberculosis? Is it a whole new way of looking at things? Isn't it a more powerful message to show that young death is always tragic?

For the past generation or so, updating the setting has been the favorite technique of directors who wish to be known as progressive. Unfortunately, updating has been overused. Far too often productions have tried to cover their paucity of new ideas simply by updating the action to the present century. That being said, there certainly is a great deal of leeway for settings in many of Verdi's operas. While some historical settings are relevant to the story (*Don Carlos, Lombardi,* etc.), others are not. We are told that *Il trovatore* takes place in 1409. There's nothing in the story of *Trovatore* that has 1409 written all over it, and the true setting of the opera is that place in ourselves where we keep all of our passions hidden. In other words, it could be any time when people are driven to extremes. To the best of my knowledge, this has never been fully explored.

Even more pervasive is the use of political symbols in opera. There seems to be a need among directors who approach opera from other arts to distance themselves from any suspicion of collusion with the establishment, as if stepping into the opera house were one of the early warning signals of impending totalitarianism. German and Italian directors have faced this problem for half a century, and many Americans have gullibly assumed the same delusion, that tradition equals political conservatism, and innovation of any sort (whether good or bad) must therefore equal enlightened liberalism. This also has the superb advantage of lifting one's work above any criticism, since you certainly don't want people thinking you're a crypto-fascist because you didn't see the wisdom of dressing Radames, say, in the uniform of Rommel's Afrika Korps. Bad guys are often dressed as fascists, in *Macbeth, Don Carlos,* and God knows what else. One is tempted to point out that the new and young audiences these productions purport to be seducing are as remote from Fascist Italy as they are from medieval Scotland or Renaissance Spain. If relevance to young audiences were as important as we are told it is, and only in such a direct manner, then every opera would be staged in a suburban mall.

Agitprop directors have a field day with *Macbeth*. All those oppressed masses—who could resist? Typical of this was the 1998 New York City Opera production, where Macbeth donned more and more black leather on his imperial uniforms in each successive act. The chorus *"Patria oppressa"* was sung by ragtag starving peasants who tottered and clung to each other on a severely raked stage, looking like everybody's worst nightmare of Ellis Island. Of course, they made a lot of noise as they fell all over each other, and missed a few of the conductor's cues. In other words, the pictorial notion came before the music. A more effective staging of *"Patria oppressa"* was done at the San Francisco Opera in the early 1980s. Each of the peasants stood perfectly still at various intervals on the stage, faces obscured by large hoods and each looking like an avatar of the Grim Reaper. The country was *paralyzed* by strife. More important, the choristers were able to watch the conductor without looking as if they were, and were free to focus on the unforgettable, and difficult, music. The huddled suffering masses of the City Opera production may tweak audiences at *Ragtime,* but that doesn't make it innovative. Nothing is less shocking than last year's avant-garde.

It is currently thought that a new setting for a Verdi opera—*any* new setting—is desirable because it forces audiences to look at the work in a new way. There is actually a certain amount of truth to this. *Rigoletto* is an opera everybody on the planet thinks they know, even though it bears a lifetime of study. To make people look at it as something new, even if one must annoy them in the process, will at least force a level of dialogue and thought about the work. This was the success of Jonathan Miller's production for the English National Opera in 1982, broadcast with much fanfare on American television shortly after. The Duke was a big mafioso, the courtiers his mobster henchmen, and so forth. Why a mafioso should employ a jester is left to our imagination, but the setting of the opera in New York's Little Italy (a pizza parlor, in fact) caused audiences to do a double take. Much tittering ensued, but the beauty is that people talked about

Rigoletto. However—and this is a crucial point—the Miller *Rigoletto* was a success because it was a good production, working with rather than against the score and trying to rediscover the characters anew. It was not a success merely because it was updated.

The emergence of the director as the star of a production was a post–Second World War phenomenon. While Wieland Wagner was busy at Bayreuth stripping his grandfather's operas of militarism, racial specificity, and Nuremberg-like monumentality, directors elsewhere were likewise seeking out new directions. Luchino Visconti was invited by La Scala to direct *La traviata* in 1955. Although the famous director had made a very operatic film, *Senso,* in 1951 (see "Verdi Films" below), he had never directed an opera. Yes, he updated the setting to the end of the nineteenth century, and, incredible as it may seem to us now, this elicited howls of protest. But Visconti was not merely being naughty. He thought the *belle époque* designs suited his star, Maria Callas. He also spent a great deal of effort working on the gestures and movements of the principals, and derived blocking and lighting from the given emotional situation. All of this was, we are told, accomplished with his unerring and legendary sense of taste. In a way, this was more subversive and radical than imposing some loopy concept on the drama. Visconti radically dared to take Verdi's characters seriously as people, and in doing so allowed their full humanity to flourish. Of course, he had Maria Callas to work with, which didn't hurt.

Across the ocean, an analogous situation was occurring at the Metropolitan Opera, an institution not noted for inventiveness in direction. Sir Rudolf Bing raised eyebrows when he announced that he would inaugurate his regime with a production of *Don Carlo,* which he adored and considered unjustly neglected. He caused further titters when he informed New Yorkers that the director would be Margaret Webster, a Broadway director with no previous operatic experience. Webster kept the settings in their traditional historical context, but took great pains to underscore the humanity of the characters, as Visconti would do at the Scala *Traviata.* The Met *Don Carlo* of 1951 was a great success, launching that opera's virtual triumphal march through the balance of the century, but it was not without controversy. In fact, it was greeted by demonstrations, protests, and picket lines. The opera, as we saw in the chapter on *Don Carlos,* had never shed its anti-Catholic reputation, and people who considered themselves instructed by the actions of Senator Joseph McCarthy were moved to denounce it as pro-Communist. It is a big leap from the anticlericalism of *Don Carlos* to Stalinophilia, but such were the times. Artistic choices are indeed all intensely political, even without jackboots and swastikas onstage. Perhaps the fact that Webster's ideas were paralleling those of such Marxists as Visconti was disturbing in and of itself. Or perhaps Webster penetrated to the core of *Don Carlo,* which is all about daring to see world history as a conflict of flesh-and-blood individuals. It is my theory that the McCarthyites who protested the Met *Don Carlo* were actually quite politically perceptive. Allowing Verdi's humanity to shine through the big skirts, heavy sets, epic situations, and conflicting historical currents is immensely powerful, and a threat to any stifling political ideology. Verdi's respect for individuals among communal situations is more radical than all the jackbooted indictments of fascism on the stages of our modern avant-gardists.

Visconti directed a few more operas, sometimes annoying people and sometimes thrilling them. Perhaps his greatest success was at London's Covent Garden in 1958 with, significantly, *Don Carlo.* As in Webster's Met production, Visconti succeeded with *Don Carlo* not by reshaping it (the sets and costumes were traditional and lavish) but by explicating the story through the individuals. More recently, director Luc Bondy scored a success with *Don Carlos* at the Théâtre du Châtelet in Paris. It would be hard to describe the production as either traditional or revisionist, since it had something of both genres. One felt the grandeur of the Spanish court and the terror of the Inquisition, without which there's no point to the opera at all, but the extreme simplicity of the largely black-and-white designs kept the pageantry to a minimum and for dramatic purposes only. The characters came alive as never before.

Many of the best Verdi productions are those that, like Bondy's *Don Carlos,* cannot be neatly categorized in one genre or other. Special mention must be made of Giorgio Strehler's legendary work at

La Scala, particularly in the 1970s. This great director sometimes permitted abstractions in the sets, sometimes opted for grandeur, often went minimal, but always concentrated on the dramatic story as indicated primarily by the score. His *Macbeth* of 1975 was almost perfect. The storm was indicated by a huge single waving piece of silk, menacing but also beautiful. The stage was bereft of sets for the pageant of Duncan's retinue, with the Macbeths front and center the whole time. The banquet had the guests arranged as if in an amphitheater, watching Lady Macbeth act carefree while Macbeth cannot keep up appearances and unravels spectacularly. Every detail, then, accentuated the protagonists' situation of the moment.

Each of Verdi's operas has its own personality, and each has its own set of issues and problems. Yet the same guidelines of good production will work for all, even the warhorse of all time, *Aida.* The big houses like to go all out for *Aida.* Audiences expect it, and, let's face it, Verdi wrote it as a grand opera. Big is fine for *Aida,* as long as directors remember that the principals must not get lost onstage in this ultimately intimate work. Small houses have had success with it, and even the terrarium theater of Busseto has produced it. I remember an extremely clever production at La Fenice in the 1970s, where the split-level motif of the Tomb Scene was used throughout the opera. All the hierarchical power structure of the society in question, so crucial to the human story of the opera, was portrayed without any of the massive monumentality usually deemed necessary for the depiction of that world. And, most important, the principals—and the issues they represented—were beautifully highlighted. The score was enhanced, not relegated to a subservient position.

The Metropolitan production of 1988 by Sonia Frisell, with sets by Gianni Quaranta, took a back seat to no one in terms of grandiosity on the Cecil B. DeMille scale, but still kept the principals at the forefront. In Act I, Scene 2, Radames is dressed by the priestesses in armor taken from the altar of the temple while the high priestess and the chorus chant. The Tomb Scene in Act IV, Scene 2, had the traditional split-level setting, but the upper part was the same set used in the first temple scene. While Radames and Aida expired elegantly on the lower level and the Amneris implored peace on the upper level,

the priestesses slowly put the armor back into the altar, according
honor to the symbols of Radames's office while he himself died in disgrace. The cue for this excellent touch was the flute cadenza that
plays in both the first temple scene and the final Tomb Scene. Somebody gave Verdi enough credit to trust his musical ideas as worthy of
dramatic consideration.

Ultimately, it's ideas like that one that make or break a production
of a Verdi opera, rather than whether it's updated, political, hip, conventional, musty, or abstract. A given production may be any of those
things or not, but its success will depend solely on how they illumi-
nate the score, and thereby the drama.

Verdi in Print

Biographies

Verdi: a Biography, by Mary Jane Phillips-Matz, with a foreword by Andrew Porter. New York: Oxford University Press, 1993. 941 pp.

This is currently the standard biography on Verdi, and it is superb. Ms. Phillips-Matz, affiliated with the excellent American Institute of Verdi Studies at New York University, has painstakingly researched every jot and tittle of Verdi's life, including giving fair due to the oral traditions of the people around Busseto. In fact, Phillips-Matz's research is almost detective work: She leafed through the records of practically every orphanage and convent in Lombardy to hunt down Strepponi's illegitimate children. Such thoroughness is typical of the book as a whole. She takes Verdi seriously and without apologies. There are very few digressions on conditions in nineteenth-century Italy. This is the book to go to when you want the facts, without confusion or hedging.

Verdi: His Music, Life, and Times, by George Martin. New York: Dodd, Mead, 1963. 633 pp.

Unlike Phillips-Matz's exhaustive tome, Martin's book is written in an erudite yet chatty manner, and includes long and informative digressions on tangential subjects. The church in Italy, habits and customs of the peasantry, and great stories about debauched aristocrats all get the Martin treatment. This is a good place to start if you need to be seduced into the world of Verdi. The operas are also reviewed in the course of the biography.

Verdi: A Life in the Theatre, by Charles Osborne. New York: Knopf, 1987. 360 pp.

Although Osborne included a great deal of biographical information in his *Complete Operas of Verdi,* this volume is a straight-on biography. It presents all the usual information clearly and conscientiously, but lacks the casually elegant charm of George Martin's study while falling short of the masterly scholarship of the Phillips-Matz book. One area Osborne avoids nimbly is sex. Granted, Verdi did not flaunt his sex life (unlike many other composers of the Romantic era), but sex must have played some role in his life.

The Man Verdi, by Frank Walker. Chicago: University of Chicago Press, 1982. 526 pp.

Originally published in 1962, this was for a long time the best Verdi biography in English. It still makes for great reading because of its insights into Verdi's character, although Phillips-Matz's tome has more nuts-and-bolts information in it.

Guides to the Operas

Verdi: His Life and Works, by Francis Toye. New York: Knopf, 1946 (written 1930). 414 pp.

Toye's book is considered the mother of all Verdi studies in English, written at a time when Verdi's reputation among musicologists was just crawling out of its low-water mark. It contains a good brief biography and character analysis before going through all the operas, one by one, and analyzing them in a personal yet erudite manner. Toye was considered quite daring to bother to write about Verdi's minor works, which were considered hopelessly old-fashioned at that time.

The Operas of Verdi, by Julian Budden. 3 volumes. New York: Oxford University Press, 1978, paperback ed. 1984. First published in Great Britain in 1973 by Cassell.

Budden's massive work provides study material for a lifetime, and Verdi fans refer to it time and again. Every version of every edition of Verdi's operas is assiduously looked at and compared through the eyes of an expert musicologist, providing invaluable help for those of us who must muddle through the various productions of *Forza, Don Carlos,* and the others.

That's the good news. The bad news is you'd better be able to sight-read a full orchestra score if you want to get the full effect of this work. Furthermore, some people complain that Budden is reductive— he will tell you what a certain passage is "about," and allow of no other interpretation. I don't find this to be true. Budden's points are so well argued that they sound like messages from God, but that doesn't mean we have to take them as such. My advice is to read the work in small doses and plan on rereading it for the rest of your career as an opera fan.

The Complete Operas of Verdi, by Charles Osborne. New York: Knopf, 1970. 468 pp.

Osborne's book came out just before Budden's massive study, which has overshadowed it somewhat. Even though I often complain about Osborne, this volume deserves credit for taking each of Verdi's operas seriously. Most of the necessary information is there, including the biographical, tangential, and anecdotal, all arranged in relation to each specific opera. Osborne clearly likes Verdi, and his enthusiasm, especially for the lesser-known works, is welcome. Also, you don't need to have three degrees in music to get through it.

Verdi Studies

Encounters with Verdi, edited by Marcello Conati, translated by Richard Stokes, with a foreword by Julian Budden. Ithaca: Cornell University Press, 1984. 417 pp.

This is a fascinating collection of contemporary articles, reminiscences, and interviews, all with our favorite Bussetano as the subject. Writers include Massenet, the playwright Giacosa, Ghislanzoni, the composer Pietro Mascagni, and many others. One gets the feeling

Verdi was very hospitable to guests but didn't like to talk too much. The notes are thorough and helpful.

The Verdi Baritone: Studies in the Development of Dramatic Character, by Geoffrey Edwards and Ryan Edwards. Bloomington: Indiana University Press, 1994. 193 pp.

The authors (a director and a singer, respectively) of this interesting little volume rightly consider the baritone to be the very essence of Verdi's art, and look at the baritone roles in seven operas (*Nabucco, Ernani, Macbeth, Rigoletto, Traviata, Simon Boccanegra,* and *Otello*) to make their case. One of their premises is that Verdi's baritones were far removed from the reality of their audiences even when they were new. In fact, that was and is their power.

The Verdi Companion, edited by William Weaver and Martin Chusid. New York: Norton, 1979. 366 pp.

This excellent collection of essays on all aspects of Verdi's life and works makes for good, erudite reading in manageable doses. Almost all the great Verdi scholars are represented.

Aspects of Verdi, by George Martin. New York: Dodd, Mead, 1988. 304 pp.

This book is a collection of essays by Martin, ranging from the serious and academic (including an inquiry into the orchestration of *Traviata* and an analysis of the role of Franz Werfel in Verdi studies) to the "strictly for fun" (an article on Verdi and food).

Correspondence

Verdi's Otello *and* Simon Boccanegra *(revised edition) in Letters and Documents,* edited and translated by Hans Busch, foreword by Julian Budden, 2 volumes. Oxford: Clarendon Press, 1988. 891 pp.

This is a fascinating collection of documents concerning the period (1879–87) when Verdi and Boito were revising *Boccanegra* and creating *Otello.* The first volume focuses on letters and telegrams between Verdi, Boito, Giulio Ricordi, Faccio, Strepponi, Muzio, and various singers and theater people. The second volume includes contemporary reviews of the pieces in question. The result gives great insight into the people involved and their respective characters. Busch had previously written *Verdi*'s Aida: *The History of an Opera* (1978), which is also interesting but difficult to find.

The Verdi–Boito Correspondence, edited by Marcello Conati and Mario Medici, English-language edition prepared by William Weaver. Chicago: University of Chicago Press, 1994. 321 pp.

This highly recommended collection of correspondence focuses exclusively on Verdi and Boito. Other protagonists are relegated to the excellent notes, which precede and follow almost every entry. We are fortunate that Verdi and Boito lived in the apex of the epistolary age, when letters were long and personal and mail was delivered efficiently.

Letters of Giuseppe Verdi, selected, translated, and edited by Charles Osborne. New York: Holt, Rinehart & Winston, 1971. 280 pp.

Osborne presents a good array of letters to friends, collaborators, and business partners, but the correspondence with Piave is not represented. This is a great loss, since Piave was famously thick-headed, and Verdi's nagging letters to him tell us much about the composer's ideas.

Verdi Films

THERE ARE dozens of good videotaped live performances of Verdi operas, and I highly recommend this method of appreciating Verdi. This chapter does not address those, but rather two films made out of Verdi operas and two movies about Verdi subjects. After these, we will look at some interesting uses of Verdi's music as movie soundtracks.

La Traviata (1982) One minute into this stylish film and you are certain this could only be the work of Franco Zeffirelli. The sets and costumes are gorgeous, the men and women are gorgeous, the photography is gorgeous—hell, even tuberculosis is gorgeous in this reasonably faithful film version of the opera. Violetta and Alfredo don't just move to the country, they seem to have shacked up in the Garden of Eden. Flora's ball (Act III on stage) would not disgrace the Hapsburgs. Not only does the whole movie look like it was filmed through gelled lenses, much of it looks like it was shot through a mattress.

Teresa Stratas is a spellbinding Violetta, and Plácido Domingo is much more appealing than your average Alfredo, even though neither of them look like they're in their early twenties for a moment. Cornell MacNeil is appropriately bourgeois as Giorgio Germont. Stratas begins dying in the opening scene and never stops. Zeffirelli got some well-deserved flack for tinkering a bit with the score, and added sound effects to the general detriment of the movie. *La Traviata* is highly recommended viewing for those who are not alienated by all the sumptuousness.

Otello (1986) Having achieved something of a triumph with *Traviata,* the indefatigable Zeffirelli decided to tackle the big whopper of them all, *Otello.* Part of his stated purpose was to capture the full magic of Domingo's portrayal of the role, an opportunity denied to many earlier tenors. The results are decidedly mixed.

Domingo has honed his characterization of Otello throughout a lifetime of appearing live on stage. On film, the nuances in the voice take a back seat to facial gestures (developed for live performances in the world's largest opera houses), and here he often looks like he's just scowling. Also, you never forget that he's wearing makeup. Musically, the chorus and orchestra are excellent (La Scala), but Lorin Maazel conducts quirkily and often so slowly you'd think he was popping quaaludes.

The same partiality to extraneous sound effects that was annoying in *La Traviata* is really out of control in this movie. During the opening storm scene, soldiers run around through the armories of the castle and rattle weapons while the orchestral soundtrack is muted. The film really gets offensive with its cut-and-paste job on the score. The fire chorus, the Willow Song, and the concertato are basically cut out entirely, and there are other infuriating and inexplicable cuts throughout. By way of compensation, we get some of the ballet music. Zeffirelli is probably the only person on the planet who still thinks this opera is improved by the inclusion of a ballet. One scene stands out for sheer camp value, if nothing else. When Iago relates Cassio's dream (in Act II of the opera), we cut to a flashback of Prince Urbano Barberini (an actor-model cast as Cassio) pleasuring himself in a half-asleep wet dream, mouthing Desdemona's praises along to Iago's singing.

Camille (1936) Greta Garbo and Robert Taylor play Marguerite and Armand in this adaptation of Dumas's play *La Dame aux camélias,* the source for the opera *La traviata.* This classic film has one thing going for it—Garbo's face. If possible, see it in a theater to get the full effect of the gorgeous black-and-white photography.

Musically, the less said the better. The opening credits sequence is florid Hollywood film music of the Max Steiner school, suddenly transforming into *"Ah! Fors'é lui"*—as a waltz! I guess they had to get it in there somehow. Verdi is violated at other momentous points of the film as well. Robert Taylor is even more of an uptight prig than Alfredo Germont, and that's no easy accomplishment.

Verdi (1985) This BBC/RAI coproduction was aired on public television in America and is now available on video. It is a long biographical documentary, using much local color to inform the story. In fact, it is so earnest and well-meaning it becomes a bit cloying after a while. This is not helped by the narration of Burt Lancaster, who insists on saying "Verdi" to rhyme with "birdie." Ronald Young does an admirable job with the difficult task of portraying Verdi, while the great ballerina Carla Fracci is rather delightful as Strepponi. The research is excellent, as are the location shots. If you can handle the corny tone, *Verdi* is informative and occasionally entertaining.

Verdi Soundtracks

VERDI'S ART has resonated far beyond the walls of the opera house. It implies something to people, including people who never have and never will attend an actual opera. One way to begin looking at this phenomenon is through movies, the supreme popular art of the century. First of all, Verdi stands for Italy. In Italian movies, Italy is often a contentious mass of forces in a constant state of self-creation and self-destruction. Americans and American movies have a conflicted view of Italy and its people: Italians are inheritors of a huge cultural legacy (as we are not), but their anarchic tendencies pose a threat to American ideals of order. In short, the idea is that they decorate, cook, and sing well, but they also saddled us with the Mafia. In *Donnie Brasco,* Al Pacino's title character walks down Mulberry Street in New York's Little Italy, exchanging colorful Sicilian *bon mots* with the Goodfellas while *"Va, pensiero,"* no less, plays on the radio in the background. Tsk tsk. Verdi stands for opera, as no other composer does, and the American relationship with the concept of opera is conflicted in the extreme. Opera is extravagant (emotionally and otherwise), extroverted, suspiciously foreign, and even a little queer, in every sense of the word. On an episode of the sitcom *Friends,* the likable WASPy regular Chandler goes to visit an old Italian tailor, and gets his genitals felt up during the fitting. Amusingly, *"Questa o quella"* from *Rigoletto* plays in the background. The opera house itself is a vital locus of American mythology. As we saw at the beginning of this book, it is the playground of the rich, the superficial, and the overdressed. The popular imagination clings to this myth, and our cultural iconography would be in trouble without it. The notion of Verdi, the populist rustic, as emblem of the privileged elite may be one of the great ironies of cultural history.

Through these layers of conferred meaning, however, there is a third significance of Verdi's music that emerges. The inherent emotional frankness in his music has not been entirely eclipsed by prejudices about Italians or the opera house. As we will see, Verdi's music is often the signal for a character accepting his or her true self.

Babe: Pig in the City (1998) As the mean pit bull chases our hero sheepherding pig through the city, the Anvil Chorus from *Trovatore* plays. Chaos ensues. *Trovatore* always signifies mayhem and confusion.

The Adventures of Priscilla, Queen of the Desert (1996) The defining moment of this charming film takes place in the middle of the Australian desert. While three female impersonators leave their familiar turf of Sydney and cross the Outback in a tour bus named "Priscilla," one member of the troop gets on top of the rolling bus wearing a silver-lamé gown with a train of at least a hundred feet. We hear none other than *"Sempre libera"* as he spreads his wings and lamé billows over the desert like an unhitched spinnaker. A brief but beautiful union of sight and sound, and an excellent use of Verdi's music as emblematic of a person who is alienated from society accepting their true emotional core and subsequent destiny.

In the Shadow of the Stars (1991) This very well-made and interesting documentary, which won the 1991 Oscar for Best Documentary, shows us some of the people who make up the San Francisco Opera Chorus. Verdi is everywhere, including some extended scenes of *"Patria oppressa"* from *Macbeth,* sung superbly. Beyond background music, Verdi represents more to these individuals. One baritone dreams of singing Rigoletto some day. We see him preparing *"Corteggiani, vil razza,"* and though he is talented we are left to ponder whether he has what it takes to sing this most challenging of all baritone roles. This movie gives poignant insight into some of the unseen human drama on the operatic stage.

Pretty Woman (1990) This movie was marketed as a Cinderella story, but it actually has as much in common with *Traviata,* which, in fact, plays a central role in the story. Julia Roberts is a streetwalker with the proverbial heart of gold, and Richard Gere is the spiritually challenged rich corporate raider. At first, the opera house is put to classic use in this movie. Gere flies Roberts up to San Francisco from L.A. to attend opening night of the opera. Roberts is stunning in a red gown and jewels. They sit in the first box. Roberts points to the orchestra and squeals, "Oh, look! They have a band!" The strains of the prelude to *Traviata* are heard as Gere intones, "People either love opera or hate it the first time they hear it. . . . If they hate it, they can learn to appreciate it, but it will never be a part of their soul." This *aperçu* may or may not be true, but at least it shows us that Gere has a soul after all.

Wall Street (1987) If you think Oliver Stone could have made this morality tale about the financial greed and social climbing in the 1980s without one reference to Verdi, then you haven't been paying attention. When the hot-shot wunderkind played by Charlie Sheen starts hitting the big time, he gets the penthouse on the Upper East Side and Darryl Hannah. Then the two sit down to a sumptuous candle-lit dinner, while *"Questa o quella"* from *Rigoletto* plinks in the background. There you have it. Money, status, and romance all signified by Verdi. The choice of the particular aria slyly suggests that Sheen's interest in the babe at his table might be a bit superficial.

Aria (1987) This odd movie, which enjoyed a brief vogue among the terminally hip, is a collection of eleven short films by various famous directors using operatic selections as background music and generally the only narration. Three of the films use Verdi's music, plus snippets of the prelude to Act IV of *Traviata* function as a bridge between episodes.

Manon des Sources (1986) and *Jean de Florette* (1986) These celebrated movies tell the story of a small village in Provence and a beautiful young woman (Manon—her mother was an opera singer) who is believed to have an otherworldly ability to make the springs flow. We're talking major extended metaphor here. The tale unfolds in the sort of poor but bucolic French countryside that exists only in the imaginations of the Paris Academicians who collaborated on the project. The basic idea is that actions in the past can dominate lives over several generations. What better soundtrack music to make this point than *La forza del destino*? The haunting adagio from the Prelude and the third tenor/baritone duet are used constantly throughout the film.

Tosca's Kiss (1984) This fine documentary explores life at the Casa Verdi, the retirement home for singers Verdi built and endowed in Milan, with poignant insights into the experience of those who lived for art without achieving lasting fame or riches. Verdi hovers over every inch of the place and every moment of the residents' lives, venerated as a god. When the ancient retirees gather in the music room, they warm up with an excellent group sing of *"Va, pensiero."* One retired baritone visibly recovers his youth and life's purpose as he dons his costume for Rigoletto. A soprano actually has a shrine to Verdi in her room. This film is a superb tribute to Verdi.

The Night of the Shooting Stars (1982) This beautiful movie by the Taviani brothers recounts a story of Tuscan villagers during the Second World War, as the Germans and Italian Fascists are retreating before the Allies. The Germans round up the villagers into the cathedral, as a supposed safe spot. One group refuses to trust them and heads out for the hills. In the cathedral, the tenor solo from the *Lux aeterna* of the *Requiem* is sung during holy communion—a stretch, liturgically, but effective. Soon the full score of that haunting section fills the soundtrack. But a bomb explodes in the cathedral, killing some villagers. One escapes to the hills, but cannot remember exactly what happened through his trauma. He hears the *Lux aeterna* in his head, however, and when the refugees choose assumed names, he calls himself simply *"Requiem."* We never see any actual Germans until later, when some wounded soldiers are marching home and one sings the "Evening Star" from *Tannhäuser* hauntingly and beautifully. Verdi and Wagner, at it again. There is a blood bath in a wheat field between the refugees and a band of Fascists. The hair-raising fanfare of the *Tuba mirum* blasts through the air as Italians of opposing stances kill each other. The suggestion is that the cosmic battle represented by the *Requiem* is the same as the battle for human, no less than Italian, identity.

Before the Revolution (1962) Bertolucci's early neo-realist stunner is still a favorite on campuses and in art houses, with its talky ellipses on culture, politics, and sex. The film is set in Parma and the surrounding countryside (Verdi country), a choice illustrating a struggle for the soul of Italian identity. The camera makes quirky love to the old city, including the main square with the hundreds of men standing around chatting. This creates the strange buzz of male voices that George Martin thought was seminal in Verdi's musical formation, with his emphasis on baritone voices and even cellos in his orchestra.

The hero, a handsome self-torturing Communist scion of a bourgeois family, breaks up with his pretty girlfriend in front of a church, carries on a very didactic affair with his aunt for the next two hours, and is finally reunited with his girlfriend at opening night of the Teatro Regio, which happens to be a performance of *Macbeth*. The opera scene is a full fifteen minutes, with the score of *Macbeth* all jumbled up as background music and the onstage business having no

relation to the music being played. It is surreal, positing Verdi as symbolic of an Italian status quo. The interior shots of the Regio are appropriately sumptuous. This film is a must-see for anybody wanting to know about Verdi and Italian polemics, or anybody wanting a tour of the Regio.

Senso (1954) Director Luchino Visconti hit the world after the war with his own brand of neo-realism, celebrating Marxist values and aesthetics in his masterly directing style. Later, he did a 180 and became noted for elaborate historical productions and sumptuous cinematography. The moment of change occurred with this 1954 film, starring Alida Valli and Farley Granger, of all people. *Senso* is based on a story by Camillo Boito (architect of the Casa Verdi and brother of our favorite librettist), with dubbed dialogue by Tennessee Williams and Paul Bowles. It is the tale of a patriotic Venetian noble-woman during the Risorgimento whose life is destroyed by her love for a cad officer in the occupying Austrian army. Passions rage and storm. What better way for Visconti to proclaim a new, extroverted aesthetic than to use Verdi?

We get more than a snippet. In fact, the first quarter hour of this movie takes place in La Fenice during a performance of *Trovatore*. Patriots throw red, white, and green confetti down from the boxes onto the Austrian soldiers in the orchestra, police break up the near-riot, and meanwhile a struggling tenor sings a rather good rendition of *"Di quella pira"* on the stage. It's the best depiction you'll ever see of Verdi's music as central to Italian national consciousness and the iconography of the Risorgimento. It's also a sly signal on Visconti's part. The singers on the stage are extremely, well, stagey. They use elaborate gestures reminiscent of opera parodies, and the tenor actually puts one foot on the prompter's box to declaim his big aria. Yet the audience is genuinely stirred into a revolutionary frenzy by this production, despite the apparent apoliticism of the opera. The rest of the movie is even more "operatic." It is Romantic grand opera without the singing. The director is clearly reveling in the frank emotionalism of the story. It also implies that an uninhibited approach to art is more authentically Italian than the cool, French-inspired detachment

of neorealism. If nothing else, *Senso* demonstrates how many complicated issues are at stake for Italians when they look at Verdi.

The Lost Weekend (1945) Everyone admires this film, featuring Ray Milland as a downward-spiraling alcoholic, but few people remember that *La traviata* played a key role in the character's tale of woe. When hard drinker Don Birnam, on a binge brought on by writer's block, tells his story to the sympathetic bartender, he recounts, "It all started at a matinee of *La traviata* . . ." Birnam (in a flashback) goes to the performance, starts sweating during the *"brindisi,"* hallucinates bottles of rye whiskey while the choristers lift their champagne glasses, and has to leave. Iago's drinking song in *Otello* would probably have sent him out on a crack binge.

There is another interesting tangent possibly at play in this movie. In *The Celluloid Closet,* film critic and social theorist Vito Russo brilliantly analyzes *The Lost Weekend* as an elaborately coded depiction of a man struggling with his own homosexuality, using alcoholism as the metaphor. More recently, Ethan Mordden, Wayne Koestenbaum, James Jorden, and others have written about connections between homosexuality and opera. Whether or not this has any basis in science, it is clear that mainstream Americans have long perceived such a connection, and part of selling opera to middle America has always entailed allaying fears that the medium is too "foreign" and "queer." It might also be worth noting that Birnam meets the woman who "saves" him while he's escaping from the opera in search of a drink. If the movie is using the opera as part of its homosexuality code, this would explain the seemingly random notion that "It all started at . . . *La traviata.*"

Wonder Man (1945) Danny Kaye performs one of filmdom's most famous send-ups of opera as the slapstick climax to this comedy. Being chased by the mob, Kaye runs through a dark alley, into an open door, and—wouldn't you know it!—right backstage at the (old) Metropolitan Opera. He quickly jumps into a costume and tries to blend in with the jabbering (Italian) choristers in the wings. The schtick with Kaye trying to pass himself off as a chorister is excellent,

as he demonstrates the proper production of vocal sound by pointing first to his *"diaframmo,"* or "belly," and then to his *"masco,"* or "face." Naturally, Kaye lands on stage with the soprano. The district attorney, to whom Kaye must relay important information, is sitting in the first box (the only seat in the house, if you believe movies). Kaye sings the info through the *"Miserere"* from *Trovatore* and the *"Addio!"* duet from *Rigoletto*. Of course the mobsters end up on stage and pandemonium ensues, but it's pretty rich comedy while it lasts.

A Night at the Opera (1935) The Marx Brothers trash the world of opera by basically destroying a performance of (you guessed it) *Il trovatore*. My personal favorite moment is when the mezzo is tearing up the stage singing *"Stride la vampa"* and Groucho exclaims, "Ooooh, boogie-oogie-oogie!" I'm not sure how, but somehow the Marx Brothers manage to romp without bitterness or unnecessary sarcasm. The spirit of fun triumphs. The butts of all the jokes are the pompous characters in the opera world rather than all opera people as pompous.

Glossary

adagio ("at ease") A musical tempo directive. It takes a subtle musician to sense the difference between this and plain old "slow," but it is an important distinction. Slow is "lento," and implies a sort of dragging effect. "Adagio" is more like "leisurely," and tends to be appropriate for reflective moments, rather than the outright sadness of "lento."

andante ("moving") A musical tempo directive, not quite so slow as "adagio."

aria ("air") A set piece for solo voice, or what mere earthlings would call a song.

aria di bravura A show stopper, a big florid vocal fireworks display that may or may not have anything to do with the goings-on in the drama. In Verdi's day, the trend was against such operatic "stillness" and toward a more cohesive sense of drama. Fine, except audiences, in our boundless ignorance, still fall for a great piece of singing.

aria di sorbetto An aria that is less than thrilling, providing a good opportunity (in the old days) to slip into the lobby and enjoy a chic and tasty sorbet.

arietta (Italian, "little aria") Basically, if a singer has a solo but fails to chew up the scenery and end by demanding an ovation at the footlights, it may be regarded as an *arietta*. *"J'ai la vue/Io la vidi"* from Act I of *Don Carlos* is always referred to as an *arietta,* to the great annoyance of tenors, since it's his only extended vocal solo all evening.

arioso A loose structure of song somewhere between an aria and recitative.

banda Onstage musicians.

brindisi A drinking song, as in *Macbeth* or *Traviata.* The accent is on the first syllable.

brio Spirit, fire. A musical passage may be marked *con brio,* which is simple enough to interpret, but voices are also said to have *brio* or to lack it.

cabaletta The bang-'em-up final section of a solo or ensemble scene.

cadenza In opera, a cadenza is the difficult and flashy run of notes directly before the very end of the solo. In the baroque era, singers improvised their own cadenzas. Verdi tended to write his out before dispensing with the form altogether, although there are instances where he expected improvisation. These are marked *a piacere,* or "at the singer's pleasure."

cavatina Broadly, an aria in one section without repetitions. In a standard grand scena, the cavatina is the slow part, or adagio section, followed by an interruption (usually recitative), and then a cabaletta. If the piece stands on its own and is not followed by a cabaletta, it is called a romanza.

comprimario ("with the lead [singers]") A singing role of important, but not primary, ranking. Arvino in *Lombardi,* Wurm in *Luisa Miller,* and the Monk in *Don Carlos* are all comprimario roles of great importance.

concertato An elaborate ensemble, technically called a *pezzo concertato,* that traditionally ends one of the later acts of an opera. A concertato generally begins with a vocal solo, evolves into an ensemble with three or more soloists, then is followed by a chorus with or without solo vocal lines. The layered effect of introducing the various themes one at a time creates a rich aural experience, and, most significantly, presents a musical analysis of a given situation. The concertato is one of the glories of Italian opera. The device became a bit fossilized through overuse, and Verdi was always searching for ways to reinvent the form. Verdi's most famous concertatos occur in *Ernani, La traviata,* and *Otello,* each at the end of the third act.

crescendo ("growing") A musical passage that gets progressively louder. The term can be used for a single phrase or a large hunk of music. In a very vague sense, Act III of *Luisa Miller* is a crescendo.

diminuendo A musical passage that gets progressively softer; the opposite of crescendo. "Decrescendo" is also used now, although it makes many people twitch.

fiasco An outright disaster. This word has made it from the opera houses of Italy to the living rooms of America. In Italian it literally means "flask," a flawed bottle that must be wrapped at the base in straw, such as those still found dangling from the ceilings of the tackier Italian restaurants.

forte, fortissimo Loud and louder.

fugue A form of music, brought to a pinnacle by J. S. Bach, in which a subject is stated by the first voice or part, then repeated in turn by the other voices. Verdi closed his theatrical career with a very successful fugue, the finale of *Falstaff*

furore (Italian, "sensation") A great success, a rave, as we might say. Verdi had his share of opening nights that could safely be placed in this category. The definitive *furore* of Verdi's early career was the premiere of *La battaglia di Legnano,* at which the audience was so charged with patriotism and excitement they hardly noticed the music.

grand opera Specifically, an opera of the kind presented by the Paris Opéra throughout the nineteenth century: five acts, sprawling historical theme, a big ballet in the middle, choruses, and great solo arias. *Les Vêpres siciliennes* and *Don Carlos* are indisputably grand operas. Generally, any big opera is a grand opera.

grand scena Specifically, in baroque or bel canto opera, a solo scene beginning with recitative, followed by a cavatina or slow aria, more recitative or the entrance of a messenger (who then leaves as unobtrusively as possible), and a cabaletta. This form, structured though it may appear, allows the soloist to display a full range of emotions and, one hopes, techniques. Broadly, a grand scena is any solo scene covering a wide display of emotions, or any, well, grand scene.

legato ("bound") The "binding" or smooth connecting of notes in a phrase, rather than playing them distinctly and separately, or staccato. Legato can also refer to the overall style of music production, or building a phrase (as opposed to stringing notes along). Singing Verdi requires almost an inner sense of legato, not to mention the air supply to make it happen.

leggiero Light, graceful. Many people are surprised to discover that Verdi uses this direction frequently, even, believe it or not, in *Il trovatore.*

loggionisti The experts in the *loggione,* or balcony, of Italian and other opera houses. Tradition dictates that only the most serious opera lovers will sit in the cheaper seats.

longueur (French, "length," "slowness") A long boring part. Verdi is remarkably short on *longueurs.* He himself was easily bored, and his correspondence with librettists is full of injunctions to make the action faster and more terse.

melodramma Spoken words with musical accompaniment. Verdi uses the device effectively in *Traviata,* when Violetta reads Alfredo's letter while the violin saws his "love theme" in the background.

mezza voce (Italian, "half voice") Sung without full power in the voice. In Verdi, this technique is often used for certain passages to contrast with forte passages. Some very promising tenors who can peel off the wallpaper never have major careers because of an inability to master this seemingly simple technique. Done badly, it's called "crooning," and is not complimentary.

parola scenica The "scenic word" Verdi was forever trying to coax out of his librettists.

passaggio A dreaded place in a singer's range marking the spot between upper and lower registers. A singer must reshape his or her throat and mouth (and therefore face) to produce the requisite sounds of upper and lower registers, while the *passaggio* requires a separate placement of its own. And you thought all those opera stars on TV were just mugging because they were bad actors! The *passaggio* is especially frightening to tenors, since the upper range of their voice is completely unnatural territory when sung in chest tones. For most tenors, the *passaggio* occurs between the notes E and G, with F and F-sharp being a particular minefield. However much singers may dread the *passaggio,* composers love writing music right in it, since it has an inherently emotional sound.

piano, pianissimo Quiet and quieter.

pizzicato ("plucked") An indication to string players to pluck their strings rather than bow them. When the merry wives in *Falstaff* sing *"pizzica, pizzica"* as the children harass the fat old knight, it means "pinch him."

portamento ("carrying") In vocal production, the technique of "carrying" the vocal line from one note to the next in a continuous glide. Too much portamento is called "scooping" by normal people or "Golden Age singing" by opera fans.

presto A musical tempo direction meaning "fast," or a musical passage so marked. How this became the buzzword of magicians as they pull rabbits out of hats I cannot tell you.

recitative In baroque and bel canto opera, a "talky" part between arias and set numbers, for speechlike dialogue or narration. The recitative could be accompanied by a plinking harpsichord, called "dry" or *secco,* or could be punctuated by strums from the orchestra and even a bit of melody, called *accompagnato.* Verdi and others in the nineteenth century increasingly blurred the distinction between recitative and set number (such as an aria); by the time of *Falstaff* it may be impossible to say where one ends and the other begins.

romanza A slow solo of a melancholy character, especially when it is not followed by a faster passage. *"Ah si, ben mio"* from *Il trovatore* and Elisabeth's solo in the monastery garden scene of *Don Carlos* are romanzas.

rubato ("stolen") A fluctuation in tempo within a musical phrase, wherein a little time is "stolen" from one note and given to another, and a little spontaneity is introduced. In opera, the term is used mostly for vocal solos. If no rubato is used, the singer can sound mechanical, while too much sounds vulgar.

spinto ("pushed") A voice having both lyric and dramatic qualities. In English, saying a voice is "pushed" is a criticism, but *spinto* in Italian describes a voice with some heft to it. Most of Verdi's lead roles require a voice of this type.

squillo (Italian, "ping") An elusive quality cherished in voices, especially those of tenors, that "pings" through the theater and generates excitement. This is the word used for the sounds made by ringing telephones, alarms, and ambulances in Italy. It is also a safe word to use when bemoaning the dearth of tenors today, as in "Of course he was satisfactory, but he lacks *squillo!*" Otello and Manrico are thought to require extra helpings of *squillo.*

staccato ("detached") The separating of notes in a phrase, rather than playing them smoothly connected, or legato. For voices, this means an actual cessation of air (and therefore sound) between notes. For other instruments, it means a discernible silence, however brief, between notes. Without judicious application of this technique, the score of *Falstaff* becomes a mush.

stretta The final part of an aria or ensemble, where the main theme is usually repeated and pounded out with clear rhythms and orchestral accompaniment, making sure the audience will whistle the tune for days to come. The use of a *stretta* was regarded as primitive by late nineteenth-century critics, and most composers, including Verdi, abandoned or altered the form. Thanks to its disappearance, audiences for new compositions throughout the entire twentieth century have been left wondering what it was they just heard.

tenore di caglioni (Italian, "tenor with balls") This term isn't considered any more refined in Italian than it is in English, so be careful where you drop it. It is commonly assumed that the size of the male genitals in question are directly proportionate to the size of the voice, even though science tells us otherwise. Perhaps this myth is inferred by reverse logic from the phenomenon of the castrati. In any case, it is a sort of double-edged accolade. Sure, it means the tenor has a big hefty voice, but the implication is that his endowment in the reproductive organs is compensated by a paucity of the cogitative organ.

tenorino (Italian, "little tenor") This refers invariably to the size of the voice, rather than the man himself. It is not a compliment.

terzetto A trio, or the part of a trio when all three singers are actually singing simultaneously.

tessitura The average pitch of a role. Verdi was notorious in his day for writing his vocal roles with a very high *tessitura*.

timbre (rhymes with "amber") The tone distinctive of a voice or instrument. It can refer to the color quality of the voice, and is therefore quite subjective. Renata Tebaldi and José Carreras are reputed to have "ravishing" timbres, while Plácido Domingo and Maria Callas are thought to compensate with musicianship for what they have lacked in it.

trill The rapid alternation of a note with the note immediately above it. A genuine vocal trill is very hard to accomplish, and people who learn operas from studio recordings are often disappointed in the opera house.

Acknowledgments

In my previous book, I cited my indebtedness to Frances Berger and Rich Lynn as the two most perfect Wagnerites in my life. Now I find I must thank them before all others as the two most perfect Verdians as well, which only proves a point I have long suspected. Their generosity in sharing their inexhaustible love for these subjects has made these projects possible.

In writing this book, I have relied greatly on the patience and support of friends (and their private stashes of recordings, books, videos, and scores). I have also relied on the generosity of experts (in the fields of music and theater, to be sure, but also in such diverse ancillary fields as history, religion, film, language, psychoanalysis, and Internet research). In fact, I can no longer tell for certain who are the friends and who are the experts. (Most are a combination of the two.) Therefore, in alphabetical order, I would like to thank Adam Abramowitz, Christopher Alden, David Bauer, Ramón Berger, Tom Bogdan, Ed de Bonis, Connie Coddington, Jay Corcoran, Marion Erwin, Charles Flowers, Dr. Arthur Fox, John Graziano, David Groff (whose integrity and generosity have been crucial to all my work), Anya Grundmann (NPR), Father Michael Holleran, Phil Jiménez, the incomparable James Jorden, Ken Lockwood, Craig Lucas, Jim

Lynch, Vinny Maniscalco, Dr. Larry Mass, the ever-supportive Stephen J. Miller, Mark Mobley (NPR), Rose Rescigno, Mike Roberts, Adrienne Rogers, Lou Rufalo (OONY), Lou Santacroce (NPR), Sandy Schuster-Jessen, Stuart Sender, Tom Spain, Jeff Stone, Chuck Suttoni, Jon Tavenner, Scott Wald, John Yohalem (Metropolitan Opera), Al Zuckerman (Writers House).

I recently read an article about common complaints authors have against publishers, and realized that I did not share a single one of those gripes. Therefore, a very special thanks to all at Vintage Books, especially Julie Doughty, Walter Havighurst, Susie Gilbert, and, above all, Marty Asher.

And a continuing thanks to the late Chris De Blasio, without whom all this might have been possible, but wouldn't have been half as much fun.

Index

WAGNER WITHOUT FEAR
Learning to Love—and Even Enjoy—
Opera's Most Demanding Genius
by William Berger

Do you cringe when your opera-loving friends start raving about the latest production of *Tristan*? Do you feel faint just thinking about the six-hour performance of *Parsifal* you were given tickets to? Does your mate accuse you of having a Tannhäuser complex? If you're baffled by the behavior of Wagner worshipers, if you've longed to fathom the mysteries of Wagner's ever-increasing popularity, or if you just want to better understand and enjoy the performances you're attending, you'll find this delightful book indispensable.

William Berger is the most helpful guide one could hope to find for navigating the strange and beautiful world of the most controversial artist who ever lived. He tells you all you need to know to become a true Wagnerite—from story lines to historical background; from when to visit the rest room to how to sound smart during intermission; from the Jewish legend that possibly inspired *Lohengrin* to the tragic death of the first Tristan. Funny, informative, and always a pleasure to read, *Wagner Without Fear* proves that the art of Wagner can be accessible to everyone.

Music/Opera/0-375-70054-4

VINTAGE BOOKS
Available at your local bookstore, or call toll-free to order:
1-800-793-2665 (credit cards only).

THE VINTAGE GUIDE TO
CLASSICAL MUSIC

by Jan Swafford

The most readable and comprehensive guide to enjoying over five hundred years of classical music—from Gregorian chants, Johann Sebastian Bach, and Wolfgang Amadeus Mozart to Johannes Brahms, Igor Stravinsky, John Cage, and beyond. *The Vintage Guide to Classical Music* is a lively—and opinionated—musical history and an insider's key to the personalities, epochs, and genres of the Western classical tradition.

Music/Reference/0-679-72805-8

VINTAGE BOOKS
Available at your local bookstore, or call toll-free to order:
1-800-793-2665 (credit cards only).